This book is dedicated to

JED MARK SHIVERS
DAVID BENJAMIN SHIVERS
ANNE MARIE SHIVERS

with love

Prudens quaestir dimiduim scientiae

Copyright © 1980 and 1986 by
Princeton Book Company, Publishers
All rights reserved

Library of Congress Catalog Card Number 85-063512
ISBN 916622-44-4
Printed in the United States of America

Cover Design by Design & Illustration
Typography by Delmas Typesetting

Recreational Leadership

Group Dynamics and Interpersonal Behavior

Second Edition

Jay S. Shivers
University of Connecticut

Princeton Book Company, Publishers
Princeton, New Jersey

Recreational
Leadership

Second Edition

Table of Contents

Preface

This second edition of *Recreational Leadership* was written to include the latest theoretical developments that have appeared in the relevant literature during the past five years. New experimentation in the specialized field of neuroscience has caused a great deal of rethinking about personal traits and leadership potential. These facts, among others, prompted the decision to revise, update, and explore new ideas about the leadership process.

Of particular interest is the extensive material included on the communications process and its impact on leadership. Additionally, new case reports and practical problems, together with their solutions, have been compiled and inserted at appropriate places. All of this has been included with an eye toward providing careful explanations of why people who are called leaders act the way they do.

What this book provides is a detailed explanation of the processes and techniques of leadership in relation to the field of recreational service. Although it is written fundamentally for students in colleges and universities who are preparing to enter that field, it should also be of considerable value to recreationists generally, laymen who volunteer for service with recreational departments or agencies, educators, government officials who are concerned with the professional competencies required for employment in recreational service, and administrators and supervisors in related fields including group work, social work, counseling, and psychology.

Although thousands of articles, pamphlets, theses, and books have been written about leaders and leadership, few have been oriented toward the field of recreational service and its personnel. There are only two or three books that offer adequate coverage of the subject. Many texts deal either with personnel administration, program direction (as if instructional technique were the basis for leadership), or offer only superficial and questionable observations. There are, for example, still those who question the need for background in leadership theory and want to know why social psychological concepts need to be included in such a text. It appears that a definite need still exists for an objective, critical analysis of the entire phenomenon of leadership as it concerns the field of recreational service—what it is, what it does, what are its sources, and who is involved in the process. The discussion of leadership is not limited to an agency, time, or place;

but includes many types of situations in which the direction and development of individuals, groups, and their objectives are purposefully influenced and guided.

A considerable body of information is now available on outcomes of leadership in group situations, on motivational aspects of human behavior, and on interpersonal relationships, much of which has been condensed and simplified in this volume for better understanding by students and practitioners. Because of the vast amount of literature, it has been necessary to be selective and to group similar writings, choosing from several excellent presentations the one which best summarizes them and provides additional data. Then, too, there have been a number of classical entries which have been kept because they lend color to the topic or offer the best explanation of the topic they illustrate.

Some of the basic questions this book attempts to answer are whether or not the recreationist is to lead or merely reflect the wishes of most of his constituents. Is he to develop each of his follower's talents or is he merely to organize the prevailing current opinion? Is he to be an independent thinker or is he to conform? Indeed, who is a leader? What does the leader do? On what does leadership rely? Many of the answers to these and other questions may be found in this text. Moreover, the book indicates how one may become a leader, what methods certain individuals have used to reach leadership status, and which pitfalls may await the unwary. There are no facile rules or principles that gain a leader's place, but rather a fortuitous set of circumstances coupled with an individual's personality that answers a particular need of a group of people at a particular time or place.

The author recognizes that both male and female students and practitioners will utilize the concepts described in this book. It is only for the sake of brevity and the omission of awkwardness that the text employs masculine pronouns exclusively. There was no intent to overlook or disparage females. The author is fully aware of and appreciates that the field educates and employs males and females, and the writing is, therefore, directed to both sexes equally.

Finally, it is the author's intent to explain the characteristics of the leader, to describe the situations which call him into being, and to define leadership and its essential components for practical use and study. The translation of theory, as recorded by researchers, into correct practice for those who need to know such information is the most important contribution this work can make to the field of recreational service.

Jay S. Shivers
Storrs, Connecticut

I

Leadership and the Individual

CHAPTER ONE

Leadership in Recreational Service

Every enterprise requires leadership. The field of recreational service is vitally concerned with working with people. Its paramount mission is to provide recreational opportunities to the organization's users, as well as internal and external interpersonal relationships that determine the effectiveness of the agency in delivering such services. In order to present various positive leisure activities for individuals, groups, and large masses of people in diverse settings—whether under the jurisdiction of a public authority or the control of a private body—leadership is essential.

As a calling dedicated to providing human services, the profession is primarily devoted to offering activities that will be beneficial to the recipients. All human service fields deal with people. People are in some way changed as a result of having come in contact with the services, activities, situations, or personalities the field uses in providing significant social services according to specific methods and principles.[1] The recreationist or professional practitioner performs a variety of leadership functions. The subject of this chapter is how such functions are performed in different settings for people with a wide range of abilities, interests, and needs.

THE FIELD OF RECREATIONAL SERVICE

Recreational service may be organized and promoted in every sector of society. It is certainly a function of government on every level and is an integral part of commercial interests. The field of recreational service has emerged in response to definite human needs. Its essential principle is the enhancement of human life through the provision of recreational experiences, with the goal of helping people achieve happiness, an optimistic view of life, and relief from stress. The professional obligation of recreational service personnel is to provide

---

1.   R. G. Kraus, *Recreation and Leisure in Modern Society* (Glenview, Ill.: Scott, Foresman and Company, 1984), pp. 122–123, 176.

3

stimulating activites covering all phases of interest. The range of activities should be wide enough to challenge the human mind and emphasize the educational, social, cultural, and physical development of the individual. Because the quality of internal and external interpersonal relationships determines to a large extent an organization's capacity to deliver required services, leadership is essential. As a matter of course in professional practice, the recreationist must perform a variety of leadership functions.

FACTORS INFLUENCING ORGANIZATIONAL EFFECTIVENESS

Ideally, public recreational programs start with the full cooperation and assistance of citizens in the community. Interested and informed citizens are supportive and generous with recreational agencies because they realize that such organizations make the community a more pleasant place in which to live. Additionally, these departments often return economic wealth to the community by causing land values to rise where new parks and other facilities are constructed. Where legally constituted public recreational service agencies are established, the creative services of professionally qualified workers may be secured. When such an agency coordinates the efforts of other public, private, and commercial agencies, the community benefits and the result is optimum service. From this cooperative effort, the citizens of the community may find a way to lead more effective recreational lives. In actuality, full cooperation is not always forthcoming, and a number of other factors influence the effectiveness of a recreational service agency. These factors include internal and external forces which will be discussed in the following sections.

Any number of forces at work within the community or internally within the agency can disrupt attempts of recreational leaders as they try to provide life-enhancing services. There are also failures of recreational service agencies to commit themselves to democratic processes which maintain departmental efficiency and retain able workers. Without leadership, the creativity and spontaneity of workers can be stifled, if not destroyed. Neither the maximum effectiveness of agency operations, nor the best recreational services for the community will be realized. Leadership is required to clear the way for people to realize their potential. Leadership in the field of recreational service requires professional preparation, dedication to the work, and a devotion to the ideal of democratic practice.[2]

---

2. R. E. Carlson, *Recreation and Leisure: The Changing Scene,* 3d ed. (Belmont, CA.: Wadsworth Publishing Co., 1979), p. 291.

In a world increasingly full of human organizations, success or failure rests on leadership. Never have there been so many organizations which encroach upon the daily lives of most people in the world. Whether the organization represents a multi-national corporation or a smaller enterprise, it is obvious that all organizations require leadership. They need leaders whose primary concern is the development of human relations necessary to engender loyalty, productivity, and a desire to support the organization and its goals. People, not things, determine the effectiveness of any organization and ultimately sustain its existence.

Recreational service organizations must be concerned with internal and external forces that influence operations. The human factor plays the most important role. People are involved in carrying out the duties and responsibilities of any given recreational service agency, and it is to the people who make up the constituency of the agency that the service is dedicated. Without their enthusiasm, the agency cannot provide the kind of comprehensive recreational service (program, places, direction) which professional personnel are mandated to give. Employees affect the ability of a recreational service agency to function effectively. Unless there is an atmosphere of cooperation and willingness to work toward achieving specific goals, the value of the agency will be minimal. Political and appointed office-holders also influence the agency's effectiveness. Their attitudes toward the agency may reduce or enhance its capacity to perform well.

External Forces

Two major external forces influence the recreational agency's successful performances: 1) politically powerful people whose positions, whether in government or private enterprise, give them entree into the agency's environment; and 2) the targeted population which is the agency's constituent.

People who wield power through political office or economic control have enormous voice in the affairs of any organization over which they have nominal authority. Whatever their philosophical orientation, they are in a position to assist or retard the effectiveness of the agency by creating difficulties or ameliorating problems. Whoever controls the levers of power can play the role of spoiler or enabler to the agency.

Leadership by agency personnel is necessary to gain the support of powerful individuals with legal, economic, or other interests. This may mean establishing good working relationships with politicians as soon as possible, providing information which will shed the best light on the organization and its services by demonstrating its cost-effectiveness, and portraying its performance as an effective public service to which the politician may point with pride. Private agencies must find ways to appeal to influential people through their policy making board. By using various leadership techniques, agency personnel may be able to persuade these individuals to further the functions of the organization rather than disrupt them or detract from the agency's ability to perform optimally.

Because the constituency of an agency cannot be forced to accept that agency or to participate in or otherwise support agency activities and enterprises, and because an agency cannot impose its concepts of what is enjoyable or valuable upon its constituency, a recreational service agency must depend upon the good will and voluntary interest of those whom it is attempting to serve. It should guide the public by applying sound techniques and strategies to which most people can respond.

Advocacy and greater political awareness have replaced, to a certain extent, previous public apathy. There is a growing restlessness among people to expect public agencies to meet their needs which frequently manifests itself in confrontations during direct personal interviews, in mass meetings, at public hearings, or through an agency's own fact-gathering procedures. The public is beginning to recognize its own power to control public sector organizations and most likely will continue to assert itself in the future to attain its goals. To meet this situation, public functionaries must overcome the bureaucratic tendency to live behind the anonymity of governmental structure.

The day of the domineering clerk is over. The realization that government exists for the people, not the reverse, has finally come into its own. People are starting to demand a voice in the development of plans, programs, and operations of agencies. They want more of a say in how their money will be spent, by whom, for what purposes, and then they want an accounting of the effectiveness of the expenditures.

If this is true for public sector organizations, it is no less true of the private and quasi-public sector organizations. Private corporations which offer services to people are just as vulnerable to disaffection and contempt as are public agencies. A disenchanted public applies pressures to which agencies succumb unless they are willing or able to devote considerable time and effort to using leaders effectively. Leadership is the single most important ingredient that any organization must have if it is to maintain itself and reverse a hostile environment brought about by rising discontent.

Both public and private agencies are now aware that the public is tired of incompetence, arrogance, and indifference. Many organizations, in every sector of society, must undergo an agonizing reappraisal of personnel behavior, program offering, facility development, and communication policy if they are ever to gain the support of their constituency. Leadership is the key to achieving success in these areas.

Leadership and Interaction

Man's ability to interact in a meaningful way with others is at the root of all human society. How the individual is enabled to act to create trust and confidence is the foundation of leadership. Leadership is one of the ethical methods by which others can be persuaded to lend themselves to those enterprises which have as their goal the enhancement of human life. The fundamental element of the individual's social environment is the presence and existence of other people. The human relationships which are determined by and determine the interaction process are profoundly influenced by leadership. If individuals are led, rather than dictated to, there is the greatest likelihood that the product of such interaction will result in personal satisfaction, enjoyment, and goal achievement.

It is obvious that the careful cultivation of public support requires leadership. Bureaucratic fiat and regulation of public behavior through prohibitive directives, without justification of the rules, must be eradicated. Just as citizens have begun to learn to command their employees in government, so must public agencies learn the techniques, properties, and qualities of leadership in order to function for the good of the public. An agency should employ persons who have the technical competence and skill to help people fully realize the greatest satisfaction and personal growth. To ensure that employee skill is focused primarily on this ideal and not wasted on defending the agency against attack, the organization must perform those leadership tasks which will evoke mutual trust, confidence, and support.

Internal Forces

The internal structure of any agency can be positively maintained by a democratic climate. Management-employee relationships have only recently become humanized; formerly, organizational relationships were strictly of the superior-subordinate kind. Position was all. Supervision meant transmitting orders without discussion. Relations developing out of an imposed authority rarely produce the whole-hearted support of the individual in the inferior position. Most individuals of intelligence resent directives not open to discussion or to an understanding of why certain concepts or functions must be done in certain ways.

Authority handed down without channels for communication or recommendations of alternatives will always create dissatisfaction and eventual disinterest on the part of the subordinate.[3] There are, of course, individuals in subordinate positions who enjoy an authoritarian relationship and would find themselves incapable of performing without it, but this is not the norm. Almost all organizations operate under conditions which suggest that only superior-subordinate relationships are tolerated within the structure and any questioning of the hierarchy will be met with disciplinary action.

Leadership and Democracy

Leadership permeates any organization's structure and may create a climate in which democratic interdependency can develop; it is the philosophy of the administrator which sets the tone. If the chief executive believes in democratic leadership practices, it is probable that everyone connected with the organization will benefit from such belief. When the opportunity to be a part of the decision-making process is offered, a failure to do so may be due to unwillingness or inability. Good leadership practices prevent mere lip service to a given concept.

Employee loyalty can never be won by imposition of authority. This is particularly true of recreationists as functioning professionals. Intelligent people do not want to be treated as ciphers within the impersonal outlines of an organizational chart. Today human relations are a significant factor in employer-employee interactions within organizations. When individuals feel that they have a part in effecting policy which guides the agency, or that their suggestions for activities, plans, or programs of the agency are recognized as contributory, they will be much more likely to devote greater effort toward the agency's success. When they become so involved with an organization that they begin to identify with it, they want the programs and other themes which are synonymous with the agency to be effective. In this manner, as the agency achieves its objectives, the workers in it obtain satisfaction.

The democratic validation of leadership seeks neither a paragon of virtue, nor a superhuman being, but it does require an environment in which leadership can respond to social influence. Leadership emerges through interpersonal relationships willingly entered into, without

---

3. Meme Black, "Irrationality at the Top," *Science Digest*, Vol. 92, No. 9 (September, 1984), p. 14.

any overtone of implied threat or inherent fear. But the democratic concept requires more than personal volition on the part of the followers. It opens up mutually satisfying relationships between participants in the decision-making process through the formulation of plans or policies by which the group moves toward its goal, and the opportunity to articulate opinions, make suggestions, ask questions, and obtain a hearing. The democratic process necessarily encourages opposition as well. The real paradox of leadership operates on whether or not leadership is actually present.

Some confusion exists between types of influence and leadership. Any influence is not leadership. People may be influenced by threat to personal safety, intimidation of family members, economic reprisals, loss of freedom, torture, and death. Other procedures such as manipulation or propagandizing are designed to persuade the individual to comply with some demand through deceitful practices. None of these types of influence can be construed as leadership.

Real leadership must be based on the democratic principles of providing factual information and open communication. The ability to make judgments, freely arrived at without fear of retaliation, coercion, or manipulation, affords the greatest possiblity for acting intelligently and responsibly, and exerting a positive influence. The essence of democracy is that it permits participation in the decision-making process by those who will be directly and indirectly affected by any decisions made. Democracy is concerned with people as individuals. It is not just a passive system of values, but an active process. Democratic practice ensures that when liberty is available people are capable of determining their own destinies and may freely associate with others, the more readily to achieve their common goals. Democracy here is not considered a political system.[4]

Leadership is a democratic relationship of mutual dependence and shared developmental responsibilities. Each person is encouraged to participate insofar as his abilities, intelligence, and needs permit. The leader offers whatever counseling he can. He moves to assist others as help is required. By empathizing, rapport may be established between him and his constituents. By encouraging self-discipline, he enables each person to make his own decisions. In some instances, mutual trust and respect develop the confidence of participants so that they can deputize others to represent and act for them.

Democratically operated organizations are not anarchical. People have certain duties and responsibilities to fulfull. They also have an

4. M. D. Cohen and James G. March, *Leadership and Ambiguity: The American College President* (New York: McGraw-Hill Book Company, 1974), p. 32.

opportunity to express themselves on issues which may influence officials' decisions. Democracy is viewed as a system or process which induces participation by group members and permits ready access to the decision-making process.

Democracy is more than a governmental form. Basically, it is an instrument of association and reciprocal communication. It involves responsibility for one's actions, particularly as they affect the interests of others. It requires open participation in reaching decisions so that prejudice will not affect a person's ability to perceive and perform in the most advantageous manner for himself and the greater community.[5]

Organizational Objectives and Leadership

Working for money alone will not elicit from professionals the loyalty, devotion, and assumption of responsibility necessary to do more than is merely required. The individual who is bound to the agency through identification with it will perform in ways that money can never buy. All of the detailed work which is lovingly undertaken for the good of the agency and, incidentally, for the worker's own satisfaction is due to the inspiration of morale. No organization can purchase morale. It is an intangible factor that develops with harmonious and sound peer relationships. Like the development of rapport, morale originates in a climate of personal interaction and group indentification. Organizations can hire technical proficiency, but they cannot pay for individual dedication. The agency must offer the kind of warm interpersonal relationships which emerge from an administrative structure based upon sound leadership.

It is possible to recruit well-qualified workers, only to lose them through the insufferable imposition of petty tyrannies, mind destroying conformity to stale ideas, and rigid adherence to behavioral patterns that may no longer be necessary or even worthwhile. Many will not agree with democratically run organizations because of the apparent time-consuming aspect of democratic practices in decision-making. However, employee morale will soar, each person will have a chance to contribute, and each will have made an extra effort reflected in an attitude of belonging which may not have existed previously. More importantly, lines of communication will be opened between superiors and subordinates. Suggestions can be made without the

---

5. John Dewey, *Democracy and Education* (New York: The Macmillan Company, 1966), p. 87.

threat of retaliation that so often stands between employees and employers. When workers feel that they make an important contribution to the success of the agency and are rewarded monetarily and with recognition, greater cohesiveness within the organization is likely. This willingness to remain with the agency, despite outside blandishments, may also affect worker productivity, creativity, and responsiveness to agency needs.

Organizational objectives can be reached when professionally educated, enthusiastic, reliable, and intelligent people are employed to carry out the functions for which recreational service departments are operated. But even the most aggressive of these individuals can be thwarted and eventually demoralized if there is no outlet for his talents, ideas, and abilities. Most debilitating of all is the continual negating of supportive human relationships as a result of line and staff inflexibility. When professionals are given free reign to put their ingenuity to positive use in the development of creative and satisfying programs, the foundations for better human relations are also laid. Leadership can foster rapport and encourage the kinds of personnel relationships that function and grow in an environment designed to promote association, communication, and a desire to perform at top capacity.[6]

Leadership and Interpersonal Relations

The capacity to be effective in interpersonal relations has become a paramount objective of organizational leaders. Interpersonal relations means the entire spectrum of behavior between persons acting reciprocally in situations of informing, working together, modifying attitudes, problem-solving, and persuasion. This involvement with interpersonal relations in various organizations comes at a changing point in social history.

The transitions which social agencies are experiencing have the impact of crisis about them. Their problems are typically derived from the frustrations and fears which are manifested when an individual concludes that he is just an insignificant cog in an impersonal machine. Competent employees may simply quit in resentment against oppressiveness. Of course, there is always the possibility of conforming to the demands of those in authority, but automatic conformity, regardless of degree, diminishes the person's faculty to answer as an individual. Whatever his potential may have been,

---

6.   Joseph E. Curtis, *Recreation Theory and Practice* (St. Louis: The C. V. Mosby Company, 1979), pp. 122–123.

whatever original ideas could have flourished, whatever his selflessness, all is reduced to the extent that hostility exists toward the encouragement of free and useful relationships with others.

Current interest in human interpersonal relations has not been able to overcome most bureaucratic inertia in the promotion of free and constructive associations.[7] Authoritarian administrators still exist because these individuals are either unwilling or unable to dissociate themselves from practices with which they are comfortable. Administrators' behavior and attitudes tend to reflect the system in which they operate and are, therefore, out of step with current leadership goals. Only when they learn to recognize how rigid their practices are can there be any hope for positive change.[8]

Individuals may no longer be thought of as impersonal properties of the organization. Rather, the organization should be used as a means to advance society. When this is achieved, the quality of interpersonal relations within the organization will be effective and people's needs will be served. To this end, each member must develop self-awareness, sensitivity to others and to human conditions, and skill in communication. The initiation of change calls for both empathy and personal commitment.

EXCHANGE, COOPERATION, AND ADAPTION

Integral to the interpersonal activities essential to leadership are the exchange of ideas, cooperation, and change. Fundamentally, leadership is the transmission of an idea to one or more others. It is a process of sending and receiving both verbal and nonverbal messages. Subtle emanations that accompany the word may have a meaning of their own and can either assist in the translation of ideas or frustrate the exchange of information. Similarly, nonverbal signaling, by acting, feeling, or intonation, may facilitate understanding or totally cancel any communication.

A group's communication relies on the formation of individuals into a cohesive force. The capacity of individuals to share the means of achieving objectives, submerge ego needs, and combine their efforts for some common goal is cooperation. At a time when special interests and technical expertise often frustrate coordination, broadly based contributions in order to carry out fundamental ideas are still

---

7.   F. E. Fiedler and M. M. Chemers, *Leadership and Active Deliberate Management* (Glenview, Ill.: Scott Foresman Company, 1979), p. 7.

8.   Peter J. Graham and L. R. Klar, Jr., *Planning and Delivering Leisure Services* (Dubuque, Iowa: Wm. C. Brown Company Publishers, 1979), pp. 145–146.

desirable. To accomplish tasks most effectively, combined effort through interpersonal relationships is vital. The singleness of resolve obtained through willing participation with others usually occurs when each person appreciates the worth of coordinated activity.

Associated with the processes of exchanging ideas and cooperation is adaption. Adaption is the change of subjective values, views, aims, or inclinations in those who are associated in groups, for a combined effort may require some adjustment. Each party accepts a modified attitude toward a particular individual, place, or thing. Because emotions are the pith of most psychic interrelationships, adaption will be influenced by the person's degree of concern and the degree of acceptance that person can achieve. Concentrated concern may permit marked alterations in outlook. In these circumstances, considerable knowledge is encouraged because friction is lessened and greater understanding and emotional sustenance between individuals are promoted.

All of these developments are interrelated. The exchange of ideas is blocked when potential recipients of communication refuse to accept or comprehend the message. In this way they demonstrate an unwillingness to combine complementary skills for the common good. At the same time, unless there is a basis for adaption, there is no foundation for rapport. When individuals cannot agree to remove areas of friction or to acknowledge the need for compromise, there is no basis for cooperation. In the same way, exchange can reduce misrepresentation and reveal information so that hostility declines and intellectual identification develops. The exchange of ideas can seal cooperative efforts in coordinated operations. Similarly, change can be both process and product in the stimulation of communication and unification.

The Leadership Impact

What is the effect of leadership upon the organization? Leadership actually defines individual growth and development of followers and often is the key factor in determining whether a worker will be retained by the department or decide to seek employment elsewhere. In any group or organizational situation there is a tendency for some hierarchy to be initiated. In every organization there is a constant process of appraisal by which the individual's ability—functional performance and social interaction—is gauged. Within the hierarchy, the leader is recognized as an eligible guide and initiator to the group or organizational member. Hence, the leader becomes one more link in a line of authority figures on which almost all individuals depend throughout their respective lives. Many authority figures constrain individual choices by exercising their influence through the position they hold; others narrow possible alternatives through the imposition of wealth or shrewd maneuvers. Leaders open up choices while focusing efforts on specific goals by their superior intellect, ability to meet situational exigencies, personal insight, empathy, or in consequence of group processes.

The adroit leader represents to followers a quality of consistency and consideration. His values are mirrored in ethical behavior and he projects a charisma which implants an unshakable faith in his inevitable success. More important is the followers' perception that their interest lies with the leader's interest. The leader is the personification of the group and thereby determines the direction for the organization to follow. His conduct becomes the standard to be emulated by others, and the leader's values become the values of the group. Leadership presupposes modifications of group norms as one way in which influence is exercised. How does the leader prevail as a change agent when conformity to group values or standards is one of the perceived assessments made in the selection of leaders? Is it possible that as one's status level is raised within the limits of group life, certain tolerance ranges are simultaneously opened? This might explain how leaders could re-direct a group's effort or, perhaps, its value system without losing the support of the membership. Thus new ways of thinking and behavior become accepted, despite a previous reliance upon conforming behavior, when an individual's status is raised to a point where group members expect to entertain such changes. Tolerance of innovative methods or even the acceptance of nonconforming conduct might presage the arrival of an individual as a leader. It can also be assumed that nonconformity for one member might be looked upon as conforming behavior in another. An expedient method for expressing these relationships is to look upon status from the point of view of the perceiver. How the individual perceives another may well incorporate all of the sources of input necessary to emergent standing as well as for the working qualities of such posture.

Emergent leadership requires one individual's recognition of another's behavior and personal qualities. It affords expanding assurance of one's influence. It also modifies social presumptions so as to permit deviant behavior from the group norm without costing the emerging leader either acceptance or status with those who perceive him as a member of the group. As an individual gains status within the group, he may act more autonomously insofar as the exercise of influence is concerned. Whether the individual chooses to do so or not will depend upon his own inclinations, social and emotional needs, personal perceptions, and motivations.

Relationships such as these require careful investigation because they are directly concerned with the development of leadership. Not only is there a symbiotic relationship between the concepts of influence and leadership, there are also important parts dealing with the mechanisms that produce them as well as those controlling their developments. More to the point, however, these personal and extrapersonal factors stem from interpersonal perception brought about by actual interaction as well as by specialized kinds of vicarious interplay. It also appears that time, as a sequential model of interaction and coincidental perceptual alteration, is a significant variable if any understanding of influence and leadership is to be contemplated. Therefore, the consequence of conforming behavior at one time may be in direct relation to another's anticipation of, or indulgence toward, nonconforming behavior at some other time. Attitudinal alteration can be brought about by comparative instrumentalities operating to reveal information sources in light of previous experience. This concerns facets of credibility, visibility, and comprehension. Research in this area basically reflects the idea that leadership is a relationship between an individual exercising influence and those who are influenced. This social process is most advantageously observed within the framework of group life:

> As a current focal point for studying influence effects from social interaction, leadership has ramifications to many other concerns relevant to group process, including conformity, morale, and social change. The study of leadership must accordingly contribute to knowledge about the dynamics of influence processes because, in a strict sense, leadership is neither a unique personal attribute, nor is it separable from social influence more generally.[9]

It must be remembered that the overt exercise of influence is not required for one to have leadership status or to perform the leadership role. Individuals who work behind the scenes, as powers behind the throne, may be willing to subordinate their ego needs in order to fulfill their desire to exert influence. Such individuals may have to operate by indirection, perhaps within the confines of a leader's entourage. Despite the apparent lack of leadership role fulfilled by individuals who have indirect influence, their objectives are gained through controlling others. Whether these individuals exert direct or indirect influence, they still lead if their ideas, goals, plans, or methods are acted upon. An elected leader, or one appointed to a leadership position, often relies upon another to supply needed technical information and solutions to problems, to carry out delicate missions,

9. E. P. Hollander, *Leaders, Groups, and Influence* (New York: Oxford University Press, 1964), p. 3.

or to be the confidant of the leader. This person will have influence with the leader and may be looked upon as assuming leadership functions. It does not matter that the group or collection of followers accords the central figure the position of leadership. What is significant is that the individual's indirect influence is brought to bear on the group and that it acts in ways he desires. This is real leadership. To the extent that one person has influence with another, the degree of influence is the leadership impact which follows as a consequence of motivating individuals to behave some deliberate way.[10]

The leader's successful rise to a position of status is almost always associated with the existing environment, both as group members know it from current communications and as they retain associations of persons or points of view, past and present. A change of the influence framework must inevitably reduce the opposition which these elements impose and promote. It is not so much the individual or the situation, as it seems to be, as what he reflects in terms of any current problem. Nevertheless, having attained high status through influence, what he does may not and perhaps need not satisfy the previous expectations. In preservation of his position, he is under constraint to satisfy new expectations which develop as the situation changes.

TYPES OF INFLUENCE

If leadership is really an interactional relationship involving one individual's attempt to gain influence with another, then the distinction made between types of leadership is called sharply into question. Where influence is accepted, leadership emerges. Where influence is imposed, there can be no leadership, only acquiescence to authority. Contemporary social psychology has long accepted the classical studies of leadership conducted by K. Lewin, R. Lippitt and R. White which enhance the research literature concerning the autocratic, democratic, and laissez-faire.[11] A real, as well as a semantic problem, arises when the term "styles of leadership" is used. Can any but a democratic context exist for leadership? Can anarchy contribute to leadership? Does the imposition of authority automatically prohibit leadership from occurring? These questions must be examined before any definitive explanation of leadership can be made.

---

10.   M. Kalb and B. Kalb, *Kissinger* (Boston: Little, Brown and Company, 1974), p. 98.
11.   K. Lewin, R. Lippitt, and R. White, "Patterns of Aggressive Behavior in Experimentally Created 'Social Climates,'" *Journal of Abnormal and Social Psychology, Society for the Psychological Study of Social Issues Bulletin,* X (1939), pp. 271–299.

The Lewin experiment described the effects on groups of three different environments which derived leadership styles from three different styles of influence. In the autocratic setting, the determination of and dictation of tasks was made without reference to group desires. The leader was personal in his praise and criticism, but remained aloof from the group. In the democratic setting, all policies were a matter for group consideration with leader participation. The leader was objective in praise or criticism and freely participated in group activities. Under laissez-faire, there was complete freedom of group or individual decision without leader participation. The leader served as a resource and contributed only when requested. There was no attempt on the leader's part to interfere with or take part in the activities.

The laissez-faire concept, as defined by Lewin and his associates, does not coincide with the political systems characterized by democracy and autocracy. Rather, a better term would have been anarchy. Anarchy specifically refers to a political system and therefore shares a common frame of reference with democracy and autocracy. The manner in which the term laissez-faire was utilized would have been closer to the characteristics of anarchy than to the conditions of laissez-faire. Anarchy denotes the absence of social or government control over individuals. Individuals perceive themselves as completely free of all restraints and act in ways calculated to bring satisfaction to themselves. However, instead of absolute freedom to behave in whatever way one pleases, all freedoms are restricted to the lowest common denominator, because the freedom of any individual is subject to the limitations imposed by all other individuals and there are no established behavioral guides to protect individuals in their freedom of activity. In such circumstances it is doubtful that any leadership can occur. If each person simply goes his own way, the likelihood of accomplishing any task, even that of survival, would be questionable.

When there is neither commonality nor a desire to postpone instantaneous gratification for a later, more highly satisfying experience, there can be no leadership. When individuals move in different directions, without regard for the feelings, rights, or freedom of anybody else, there is no basis for personal interaction and therefore no possibility of the exertion of influence.

Headship

Some attempt should be made to distinguish between organizational influence and that which emerges from human relations. The acceptance of influence, which is conditional upon the consent of potential followers, is leadership. Leadership only occurs under conditions of voluntary involvement; it must be distinguished from domination, or organizational authority. C. Gibb has offered the most cogent statement of leadership and domination.

The principal differences are these: 1) Domination or headship is maintained through an organized system and not by the spontaneous recognition, by fellow group members, of the individual's contribution to group goals; 2) The group goal is chosen by the head man in line with his interests and is not internally determined by the group itself; 3) In the domination or headship relationship there is little or no sense of shared feeling or joint action in the pursuit of a given goal; 4) There is in the dominance relation a wide social gap between the group members and the head, who strives to maintain social distance as an aid to his coercion of the group; 5) Most basically, these two forms of influence differ with respect to the source of the authority which is exercised. The leader's authority is spontaneously accorded him by his fellow group members, the followers. The authority of the head derives from some extra-group power which he has over the members of the group, who cannot meaningfully be called his followers. They accept his domination, on pain of punishment, rather than follow. The business executive can be an excellent example of a head exercising authority derived from his position in an organization through membership in which the workers, his subordinates, satisfy many strong needs. They obey his commands, and accept his domination because this is part of their duty as organization members, and to reject him would be to discontinue membership, with all the punishments that would involve.[12]

This does not mean that individuals who hold positions of authority, or at least give the appearance of leadership, cannot, in fact, be leaders. It is possible for leadership and headship to reside in the same person. There are many situations where the positional status of the persons occupying some superior rank within an organization does not preclude those characteristics which make them acceptable as real leaders. Despite their position, they behave in ways that are perceived by subordinates as being absolutely democratic. They offer relationships that guarantee their recognition as leaders, even if they do not hold high positions within an organization. Much of the so-called leadership of the world is of the headship variety, so that most people tend to think of leadership in terms of organizational structure and title. There is the nagging fact that either elected officialdom or appointed authority clearly implies legitimatization for those who attempt to define leadership.

---

12. C. Gibb, "Leadership," in G. Lindsey and E. Aronson, eds., *Handbook of Social Psychology*, 2d ed., Vol. 4 (New York: Addison-Wesley, 1969), p. 213.

Despite the obvious identity between leadership and position attainment, a certain amount of confusion has been noted. There remains a tendency to designate as leadership those dominance characteristics and functions which clearly belong to the concept of headship.

It is erroneous to consider as "leaders" those who have rigidly restricted, programmed functions within an organizational hierarchy. The organizational position of headship requires tightly made choices, regulated by controlling policies. Bavelas asserts that the functions of those in headship positions may be definably different from personal attributes or characteristics.[13] He suggests that on the whole such "leaders" are those who carry out certain tasks rather than share idealized personality traits. Bavelas indicates his orientation by asking not who the leader is, but what functions are to be satisfied by the person who has responsibility.

Interaction and Influence

Leadership is of considerable significance wherever individuals cluster and form groups. Although there are a number of possible definitions currently in use, leadership is most often defined as the exertion of influence with others. Whoever is conceded to be most influential in the interaction between people is the leader at that particular time. Intelligible leadership structure is much more prevalent when the group is large, commentary time is short, the objective is difficult, and the consequences are either extremely significant or a matter of complete indifference.

In all of the research catalogued in the fields of social psychology, group dynamics, and human interaction, there remains some controversy in determining who is apt to become a leader. Why is one individual recognized as a leader while others—who may be just as competent—are either overlooked or neglected? One of the possible responses to these questions has been a reliance upon specific personality factors which leaders are supposed to have. Such characteristics, if valid, would support the contention that individuals who possess them will inexorably rise to positions of leadership in any group in which they find themselves. However, studies performed to precisely define and enumerate those traits shared by leaders in varying situations have been less than conclusive. While some traits have been indicated, they are by no means wholly centered upon the leader. This is perfectly comprehensible when one appreciates the

---

13. A. Bavelas, "Leadership: Man and Function," *Administration Science Quarterly,* Vol. IV (1960), pp. 491–498.

large number of variables converging upon the leader in any situation and the demands which must be met as situations change.

Current views of leadership occurrence may be termed "interactional." This orientation takes the position that any attempt to predict the leadership role in a group situation must consider all of the variables interacting to produce the desired central figure. Thus, personality makeup of group members, group syntality, problems which the group confronts, the kinds of activities which the group must perform to achieve its goal, and the personal attributes which may promote one person's ascendency or emergence as a leader must be considered. For example, it is likely that group members will be more willing to accept influence from a leader whom they recognize as having legitimate status. The individual who is most conspicuous and who is perceived by himself and other group members as most likely to contribute to group goal achievement and group maintenance will probably assume leadership. Similarly, followers are more inclined to accept influence when the leader is perceived as having greater skill or competence than they have.[14] It is assumed, therefore, that as the situation changes, the person who is recognized as the leader in the group will also change. This conclusion is open to question.

When the condition affecting the group stabilizes, leaders tend to share common traits. Individuals who are achievement-oriented, have good interpersonal skills, have resistance to frustration, and possess empathy and good intellectual ability are much more likely than other people to have leadership potential. In other than leadership situations, there are individuals whose need to exploit dominates any sense of equity. These people are willing to disregard ethics and morals to gain influence over others. In investigations carried out to determine the propensity of individuals to employ so-called Machiavellian inclinations, it was found that people who scored high on the Mach scale were more likely to use manipulative and coldly calculated acts designed to obtain whatever ends they desired. It was also shown that manipulators did not always succeed. Only when there was insufficient information on which to base a decision, in extremely volatile or emotion rousing situations, and in close personal confrontations did Machiavellian types gain influence. But such personalities are not within the leadership context. On the contrary, it is probably more appropriate to classify such behavior with demagoguery, headship, and dictatorship.

---

14. Mack Snyder, "The Influence of Individuals on Situations: Implications for Understanding the Links between Personality and Social Behavior," *Journal of Personality*, Vol. 51, No. 3 (September, 1982), pp. 497–513.

Another contemporary approach discusses variables which influence the emergence of leadership in terms of the situation. Situationalists claim that a high incidence of leadership acceptance can be traced to extra-group leadership recognition and appointment. The cultural environment also imposes certain pressures in relationship to whoever will finally enjoy leadership. Certain group members may be perceived as having the kind of personality or technical competence which the group needs and values. The structural mold of the group may have important effects insofar as group recognition of an individual as a leader is concerned. Some individuals may emerge as leaders because they have the social and emotional make-up which supports group members. Others, who are formally hailed as leaders, are chosen because of the ultimate reward or satisfaction they can obtain for the membership.

The pattern of personal characteristics exhibited by group members prevails as far as the group's selection of leadership is concerned. Furthermore, the ability of the membership to achieve success is associated with its own capacities to perform and will therefore have some effect on leadership development.

One of the most important factors determining leadership is the process of communication. It can be illustrated that leaders dominate the communications network within the group. This does not necessarily imply that greater contributions to the communications process will ensure the emergence of leadership, but positive pronouncements which are useful to facilitate group goal achievement or to open lines of communication are directly related to the degree of influence any person will obtain, the individual's visibility within the group or organizational structure, and the extent to which original ideas, suggestions, or plans may be employed to serve the group's purpose.

Leadership does not rely upon status quo to maintain itself. Once the leader is recognized, he must continually provide the action, climate, and goal identification to sustain what the group initially perceived in him. There are any number of tactics that leaders employ to remain in the leadership position, but this is not to be confused with any manifestation of behavior commonly used to advance in corporate, bureaucratic, or organizational models where headship is the determining factor. Leaders face a paradoxical situation. They wish to remain leaders, but they realize that they must develop secondary and potentially opposing leaders while they lead. How they

---

15. R. G. Kraus and B. J. Bates, *Recreation Leadership and Supervision: Guideline for Professional Development* (Philadelphia: W.B. Saunders Company, 1975), pp. 11–16.

resolve this dilemma will be discussed at some length in Chapters 12 and 16.

Leadership is characterized by different behaviors which vary as the situation changes. In a number of studies it was determined that among the prominent demonstrations of leadership behaviors are those which are either task-oriented or supportive of socio-emotional associations. On occasion, the two behaviors are found in one person. It may, therefore, be necessary to alter leadership behavior as the situation demands. Where supportive leadership is required, the warm relational leader will emerge. Where there is anxiety, exigency, or stress, the task-oriented leader may better serve the group. It seems safe to say, at this time, that there are several behaviors which leaders may utilize as conditions change and pressures are exerted upon them to act or react in certain ways. What has worked well in previous situations may not work in current ones. In this respect, then, situations play a determining role in the emergence of leadership and how the leader will perform.

It is obvious from much of the foregoing discussion that the kind of person the leader will be is contingent upon any number of variables. It depends upon the personality of the individual who may be chosen for leadership; the group or agency in need of leadership; the situation in which the group finds itself at any particular time; the purposes or aims of the group or organization; the personal make-up of the individuals who are members of the group; the dynamics of interpersonal relations which are ongoing; how the group sees itself; the hierarchy of the group (if any); and the pressures which are brought to bear upon the group by external forces of society, its culture, or subculture of which it is a part and from which the members come. These and countless other collisions, both major and minor, will be directly reflected in the kind of leader the group will choose and the manner in which the leader will perform.

Any attempt to understand leadership theory will have to consider relationships, group structure, personality characteristics associated with leadership, emotional needs and attitudes of group members at any time, the environment in which the group exists, and those conditions requiring solutions. Leadership is input, process, and product related to all of these variables acting one upon the other. The outcome of this interchange doubtless creates a preference for a leader. Such designation cannot in any way alter membership contributions toward effective group life.

PROFESSIONAL PREPARATION

As a leader, the recreationist employs his intelligence and ingenuity to solve problems which emerge from day to day. He may do this within the recreational program or find himself ranging the community as a detached worker whose special knowledge of local groups gives him access and insight into their special requirements.[15] However and wherever he works, his effectiveness as an enabling agent is based upon an education which is systematic, directed, and appropriate for resolving the problems which the social environment develops. Intellectual application to achieve certain missions or resolve problems begins with professional preparation. But there is more to professional practice than intellectual content and discipline. Professionalism demands sound judgment, personal commitment to the field, and a standard of behavior based upon integrity, ethics, and a sincere concern for people. These are the bases for professional conduct, but they do not reflect the basis for leadership. Leadership is a complex of intellectualization, personality need, and practice. One can *learn* about the phenomenon of leadership; one must *practice* to be a leader.

Leadership can begin with the intellectual content and personal dedication found within the rigorous education of the profession, but leadership is action-oriented and requires fulfillment in doing. Knowledge without practice is futile.[16] For example, there are individuals who know about leadership, but do not lead; there are those who understand what empathy is, but who cannot empathize. There are individuals who could be problem solvers but do not try. Knowing how something should be done and actually doing it are two different things, but it *is* possible for the thinker and man of action to be contained in the same body. History is filled with action-oriented thinkers.

Theodore Roosevelt has been characterized by Henry Adams as "pure act," and his dynamic personality made him immensely attractive to the American people, but what most people did not understand was that Roosevelt was a man of great intellect. He had scored extraordinarily well while a student at Harvard College and was a student of history, the science of conservation, and biology.[17] Furthermore, he was a practical politician who could reverse his field if

---

16. Chris Argyris, *Increasing Leadership Effectiveness* (New York: John Wiley & Sons, 1976), pp. 130–134.

17. Edmund Morris, *The Rise of Theodore Roosevelt* (New York: Coward, McCann & Geohegan, Inc., 1979), pp. 91–92.

he saw that public opinion or the necessary votes were not available at
the time. He saw himself as a steward, serving the entire nation rather
than merely geographic districts or single states, and he felt that he
was responsible to all of the people. In interpreting his constitutional
powers, his orientation was liberal rather than that of strict
constructionism. He believed that as long as he acted in the public
interest, anything he did was justified as long as it was not specifically
prohibited by the Constitution or the laws.

Roosevelt was a pragmatist, not a theoretician or visionary. More
importantly, though, he was the President who made reform palatable
and respectable. For the first time in history, the federal govenment
actually prohibited some abuses by commercial interests and
subordinated some industries to the control of law. Roosevelt brought
efficiency, morality, and high-mindedness to the federal level. He
enlarged the office and used its power to benefit all of the people.

Woodrow Wilson was the first professional scholar to become
President of the United States. He graduated from Princeton and
studied law at the University of Virginia. He then took his doctor's
degree in political science at Johns Hopkins University. He joined the
Princeton faculty and his fame as a teacher grew. In 1902 he was
appointed president of Princeton. In 1910 he resigned from Princeton
to enter politics and was subsequently elected Governor of New
Jersey.[18] As President, Wilson practiced executive leadership because
he believed that the British Cabinet system of direct leadership in
Parliament was superior to the American separation of powers. He did
not attempt a constitutional amendment because he understood that
the American President has sufficient power if he wishes to use it. Of
course, this is valid only if Congress is willing to accept a President's
leadership. The unfolding of the Wilson administration through two
terms, from neutrality to participation in World War I, and the efforts
to organize and engage America in the League of Nations taxed his
strength and will. History has reserved a place of greatness for him.
However, no other President among those who are generally
conceded to be great ended his office in such defeat. During his last
years, after suffering a stroke, he was disregarded by all but a few
friends. Still, to those who remembered his consummate skills and
intellectual capability, he remained the indefatigable leader whose
work was incomplete rather than failed.

Roosevelt succeeded in many domestic and foreign affairs. He was
successful in, among other things, the creation and construction of the

---

18.   Theodore H. White, *America in Search of Itself* (New York: Harper & Row, Publishers,
1982), p. 232.

Panama Canal. Wilson succeeded in winning World War I for the allies. Both failed in obtaining supreme goals which they set for themselves. Roosevelt lost a third party bid for the presidency and Wilson could not persuade Congress to ratify the treaty which would have gained access for the United States to be a member of the League of Nations.

These two men, so different in style and use of language, were essentially moved by their understanding of the world during their respective terms of office. They acted to force change after reflecting upon the consequences. They brought their considerable intellectual powers to bear upon problems which confronted them and moved deliberately so that there would be no misunderstanding on the part of those who opposed or sided with them. They were men of intellect and action.

However, there are instances where wishful thinking overrides any action. An example of this phenomenon in the field of recreational service is illustrated in the following case history:

Mr. C:, director of X Recreational Service Department in a large New England city, continually brought idealistic plans dealing with the development of new recreational areas and facilities for inner-city neighborhoods to the Commission responsible for department policy. Although the plans were generally conceded to be excellent, Mr. C. invariably postponed any action because, as he stated, "The plan is not perfect." The Commission members became increasingly dissatisfied with their director's procrastination and requested that he act on the plan and be responsive to the needs of neighborhood residents who were, at the time, demanding the kinds of facilities envisioned in the plan. Mr. C. could never bring himself to give the go-ahead to any version of the plan. He always thought of reasons why it would fail if just one more aspect or configuration was not added to the final concept. Thus the plan was never implemented. Mr. C. was so concerned about obtaining perfection that he failed to understand a basic tenet of leadership. It is better to have a good or sound plan and act upon it vigorously than it is to have a perfect plan, theoretically operable, but never performed. That is why theory without practice is futile. There is never any test of potential.

Professional preparation can provide a background for leadership but whether the individual will become a leader depends upon how he views himself and upon other factors which tend to elicit a leadership response. Among these factors are personal satisfaction, desire for recognition, an intrinsic need to project oneself, fulfillment from entering into supportive relationships, and a sense of achievement as a problem-solver. Additionally, the times, place, potential followers, or favorable conditions could trigger a leadership response.

The necessity for a professional preparatory program to effect change in the attitudes, beliefs, and biases of students is apparent. Unless students are receptive to the behavioral objectives of the program, there will be insufficient foundation for professional practice.

The potential recreationist must be exposed to the conceptualizations of his future field and the values and ethics which support it. Without these frames of reference, the service will be less than professional and possibilities of utilizing leadership theory in practice will be nullified. The education of a future recreationist is developed in terms of knowledge about the field in all of its ramifications, the behaviors of people, problem-solving approaches, decision-making, and the aims of those to whom and for whom he has responsibility. A brief examination of professionalism may be of assistance at this point.

Public Recreational Service and Professionalism

When recreational experience is described in terms of professionalism, the meaning becomes very different from the definition of the nature of recreation. Professionalism in recreational service connotes highly specialized preparation, organization, humanitarian appeal, certification, and general acceptance by society and other professions as a recognized field.

Professional Learning Experiences

Because recreation is a part of human behavior, the recreationist must be steeped in educational functions which enable him to supply positive action in any situation. He should have basic courses in psychology and, when this is mastered, progress to advanced courses in social and educational psychology. Since the basis of all leadership is psychological understanding, the pre-professional must have this knowledge in order to perform his work most effectively.

A basic education in communication is also of prime importance. Such preparation would include course work in self-comprehension, understanding the feelings and needs of others, practical knowledge of the social group situation, public speaking, sources and types of influence within some organizational framework, and sensitivity to others or empathy. There must be some kind of integrated learning process to pull together elements of social psychology, group work, motivational theory, and communicative behavior. Such information provides the student with references as to why, where, and how effective communication can be made operational. Typically, such a course also deals with the methods by which the leader in the field of recreational service employs communication to attain, stabilize, and retain influence with others as he or she practices.

The graduate of a college- or university-level recreational service educational program should have a thorough knowledge of recreational philosophy in concert with modern educational philosophies; what it is, what it means, and a definitive frame of reference for its use. His studies should include a wide association with the liberal arts and humanities, which broaden learning and sensitivity to knowledge. There should be major studies in recreational service as it relates to other organizations of the social order.

Such course content would produce keener insight into the learning processes and develop technical and specialized skills in the transmission of ideas. At its most effective, the program would provide a logical progression of intellectual activities culminating in the practical application of theory to actual field conditions.[19]

Approaches to the Task of Professionalizing Recreational Leadership

Potential recreationists must be recruited through the usual channels of socially significant fields and provided with the necessary educational preparation for work in the field. They must be selected on the basis of outgoing personality and concern for others. The recreationist must view his role as one of enabling others to achieve. Commitment to the idea that interaction is essential to self-actualizing is at the heart of the matter. Recreationists will be concerned with facilitating group and individual achievement without motives for self-aggrandizement. Thus, it is apparent that recreational service requires persons of superior quality, tact, and preparation.

Recreational service, like education, is too important an area of public concern to be in the hands of those who mean well but who cannot perform well. Care must be taken that the field is not inundated by mediocrities. If an organization existed which could systematize field problems, ethical standards and codes, professional qualifications, research and technical studies, there is a chance that the field of recreational service would attain professional status, a goal not yet achieved although practitioners aspire to professionalism.

Several things must be acquired if the field is to become a fully qualified profession in the eyes of society and the other accepted professions:

---

19. Charles A. Bucher, Jay S. Shivers, R. P. Bucher, *Recreation for Today's Society*, 2nd ed. (Englewood Cliffs, N.J.: Prentice-Hall, Inc., 1984), pp. 304–312.

1.   There must be a powerful professional organization which will control applications into the field by the initiation of high standards for entrance and practice, and which will perform other functions to maintain the public's awareness of the field.

2.   Recreational service, as a field, needs to attain an economic and community standing of such quality that it will attract people of ability.

3.   There must be a specialized education based on Western philosophy and the social, natural, and physical sciences for better understanding of human abilities and learning.

4.   There must be a centralized governmental authority, preferably on the state level, to certify and license recreationists and to enact legislation that will help the field carry out its functions economically, effectively, efficiently, and in accord with well-conceived ethical-practice codes.

5.   Entrance to the field should be limited through a system of board examinations given by recreationists to applicants after they have graduated from accredited institutions. The matter of state reciprocity and national recognition must be worked out in great detail before this machinery can be set in motion.

6.   There will have to be established an ethical-practices code to which all practitioners must adhere.

7.   A system of valid testing will have to be constructed to appraise the ethical behavior of potential candidates for admission into the field at any time they enter upon their professional learning experience.

QUESTIONS FOR DISCUSSION

1.   Why should interpersonal relationships be a significant concern in the field of recreational service?
2.   Discuss the factors influencing recreational service organizations.
3.   How can leadership affect worker productivity?
4.   How do external forces influence recreational service effectiveness?
5.   Can leadership be anything but democratic?
6.   Discuss the statement: all influence is leadership.
7.   What is the effect of leadership upon the individual in the organization?
8.   How can professionalization assist in the development of leadership?

BIBLIOGRAPHY

Edginton, Christopher R., and Phyllis M. Ford, *Leadership in Recreation and Leisure Service Organizations* (New York: John Wiley & Sons, Inc., 1985).

Kraus, Richard G., and Barbara J. Bates, *Recreation Leadership and Supervision: Guidelines for Professional Development* (Philadelphia: W. B. Saunders Company, 1975).

Kraus, Richard A., *Recreation and Leisure in Modern Society*, 3d. ed. (Glenview, Ill.: Scott, Foresman and Company, 1984).

Niepoth, E. William, *Leisure Leadership* (Englewood Cliffs, N.J.: Prentice-Hall, Inc., 1984).

Sessoms, H. Douglas, and Jack L. Stevenson, *Leadership and Group Dynamics in Recreational Service* (Boston: Allyn & Bacon, 1983).

Sessoms, H. Douglas, *Leisure Service*, 6th ed. (Englewood Cliffs, N.J.: Prentice-Hall, Inc., 1984).

Shivers, Jay S., and Hollis F. Fait, *Special Recreational Service: Therapeutic and Adapted* (Philadelphia: Lea & Febiger, 1985).

CHAPTER TWO

Leadership Theory and Research

Leadership research continues to proliferate, and some models have been formulated which offer greater opportunities for understanding this important feature of social interaction. So far, a precise definition of the constituents of leadership have not been enunciated. The intricacies and variables that form the basis for promoting or denying an individual's leadership attempts have not been isolated. The changing conditions, interpersonal relationships, and dynamic social interaction which may evoke leadership remain imperfectly understood by behavioral scientists investigating this phenomenon. Old theories are discarded only to crop up again, with apparent support. New breakthroughs in the biological sciences may enable those who study interpersonal behavior to make more astute judgments about leadership needs, behaviors, and successful attempts. They may finally be able to explain why certain conditions foster the emergence of leadership and why an individual strives for, or is propelled to, a position of leadership.

Why is leadership such an endlessly fascinating phenomenon? Because many are called to exercise leadership, but few are actually chosen to lead. It is exhilarating to explore the selection process that results in certain persons being thrust into the full glare of leadership positions. Are these people really leaders or do they simply occupy a position of leadership?

The times cry out for leadership while nations and lesser communities or organizations founder under the burden of inept bureaucrats, professional politicians, or fanatics whose rise to power coincides either with social disintegration, collapse of law, or occurs simply by the process of elimination through longevity and seniority. Whether such persons are leaders or time-serving caretakers remains for history to decide. If they are not really leaders, to whom can people turn in times of tremendous stress and uncertainty? Where are the great captains of yesterday? Who are today's leaders? How have they achieved leadership?

THE TRAIT THEORY

Scientific redefinition of leadership stripped many of the supernatural and destiny myths from the concept of leadership. The trait theory, which holds that there are personality elements uniquely associated with leadership, failed to provide any consistent pattern that inevitably designates leaders. This does not mean that personality has no part to play in the determination and effectiveness of leadership. On the contrary, personality factors are enormously important. However, the specification of particular personality patterns that affect leadership must be refined. There are certain personality characteristics which seem necessary if leadership is a goal. Such personality patterns will not in themselves determine the selection of a leader in any group situation. The impact of what a person is and what that person can do cannot be ignored. Of supreme importance is the relationship between the individual and the potential followers.

The study of personality and the motivational forces which appear to drive individuals in their quest for leadership does not end with the simple statement that the trait theory is passé. Personality remains significant. This is particularly true in light of recent research concerning the dominance factor.[1] A new emphasis on self-confidence, among other leader attributes, seems to have sufficient power to markedly affect leadership beahavior.[2] Leaders may actually be different from other people in some key traits.

Laboratory experimentation in the field of neuroscience has revealed substances known as neurotransmitters which conduct nerve impulses across the gaps between nerve cells. These substances play a significant role in human behavior. Chemical substances which may enhance leaderlike behaviors have been found.[3] For example, known leaders have been found to have higher blood levels of the neurotransmitter serotonin than have followers. Serotonin seems to affect and stimulate a dominance trait. Humans whose blood levels of serotonin are higher may very well have a need to lead because of genetic factors rather than as a result of learned behaviors. It may be that some persons are, indeed, born to lead.

----

1. Stephan A. Small, R. Shepherd Zeldin, and Ritch C. Savin-Williams, "In Search of Personality Traits: A Multimethod Analysis of Naturally Occurring Prosocial and Dominance Behavior," *Journal of Personality*, Vol. 51, No. 1 (March, 1983), pp. 1–14.
2. Henry P. Sims, Jr. and Charles C. Manz, "Observing Leader Behavior towards Reciprocal Determinism in Leadership Theory," *Journal of Applied Psychology*, Vol. 69, No. 2 (May, 1984), pp. 222–231.
3. David Stipp, "Open Mind," *The Wall Street Journal*, Vol. CCII, No. 119 (December 19, 1983) pp. 1, 17.

CENTRALITY AND LEADERSHIP

Writing in 1957, Ross and Hendry discussed the concept of the central figure within groups. Commenting on the function of a central person, they admitted that the central figure might be incompetent, or might not be the most influential, most liked, or most helpful in directing the group toward its goal. Most groups do have a central figure who is the leader:

> This leads one to suspect that groups and organizations "need" such a central figure who is called the "leader." In a significant sense this person *is* the leader beacuse he is perceived by the members of the group to be the leader. This is not simply a matter of semantics; for the person so designated is actually given influence, authority, and status which he would not have as a "member" of the group.[4]

Why would groups desire a central figure for leadership? The variable inputs suggested by social expectations, appearance, ideas, talent, empathy, or practical payoff do not adequately answer such questions. More pertinently, if the central figure is not the most competent, influential, liked, or helpful member of the group, why is he then accorded a place of centrality which tends to reinforce his leadership position? The answer might be that there is a biological impulse which continues to operate as stimulus to behavior.

Raising a compelling figure to the focal role satisfies a perceived inadequacy. In this way an age-old desire for protection against hostile elements may be assuaged. Groups tend to recognize and accept central figures and expect those central figures to be leaders. This could be one explanation for a behavioral pattern which tends to recur whenever groups are formed.

There may well be an overwhelming desire for central figures to take on leadership roles, and subsequently for groups to attribute specific abilities to that person, to accept activities which he performs to be those of leadership, and to define leadership as those functions which are exercised by the person holding a central position. This does not imply that others within the group may not also be responsible for satisfying goals or supporting interpersonal relations. On the contrary, it recognizes that another group member may be a great facilitator, energizer, and task achiever without being recognized as the group's central figure. When all is said and done, the central figure carries each individual's perceptions of leadership for that particular group.

---

4. M. Ross and C. Hendry, *New Understandings of Leadership* (New York: Association Press, 1957), p. 34.

Under these conditions, leadership is viewed less as a series of behaviors by an individual, or range of functions, than as an integral part of group or organizational existence. It is intrinsic to group life. Central figures are leaders because they are viewed as such. Their behaviors are seen as the behavior of leaders, and they are accorded influence and deference while they serve as central figures. In nearly all groups a central role is reserved for one person. Who these figures are and how they gain recognition and retain the position is the basis for all leadership theorizing and study. Seen in this light, leadership theory has not defined or described the process or abilities which result in the designation of a leader. Yet so significantly distinguishable are leaders from followers that special roles are assigned to them within the structure of group life.

When a special place in the group is designated for one member, a complicated mass of variables begins to operate. Whether group expectations will be fulfilled by the leader depends upon a range of elements all converging simultaneously. Among these factors are anticipations of those who rely upon him, the emotions and attitudes of group members at any given time, the job to be done, the character of the organization, the current atmosphere in which the group abides, external forces for cohesion or disintegration, internal forces for subversion or disaffection, and, most specifically, the leader's own experiences, intelligence, understanding of how he should perform, and his capacity to do so. Until the group decides to follow someone else, the designated person remains the leader. The fact that any individual is so elevated implies that he has something that makes him expedient for this role. Thus the creation of the central-figure role is yet another facet of leadership not previously resolved by contemporary theories of leadership.

Regardless of where leadership resides—within an individual or within a group structure—the element of situation or problem still remains to be explained. Changing situations may force a change in leadership. The conclusion reached is that the demands of the situation predominate. This line of reasoning leads directly to the situational approach to leadership study.

THE SITUATIONAL THEORY OF LEADERSHIP

Leadership as a function of situation arises from the need of a group to perpetuate its members' initial satisfaction. It suggests that a leader is an individual who at a certain time and in certain circumstances has the particular qualities or problem-solving skills which the group requires. As the situation changes, a new leader may take over. As Gibb indicates:

Since individual personality characteristics are, by contrast, very stable, it is to be expected that group leadership, if unrestricted by the conscious hierarchical structuration of the group, will be fluid and will pass from one member to another along the line of those particular personality traits which, by virtue of the situation and its demands, become, for the time being, traits of leadership. This is why the leader in one situation is not necessarily the leader, even of the same group, in another different situation.[5]

The outcome, then, has been recognition and acceptance of the situational theory. The theory consists of three sets of variables: leader, follower, and situational characteristics. Typically, the situation is thought to be of greatest significance because it presumably contains the most variables. Fiedler is one of the researchers who has made important advances in understanding leader-member relationships and demonstrated the vital role of motivation in determining the behavior of leaders. He and his colleagues developed an evaluative instrument called the LPC (least preferred co-worker) scale whereby leadership styles and movement toward the satisfaction of group goals could be measured.[6]

The LPC scale consists of a series of semantic differential type items, in which the respondent is requested to describe, among all of those with whom he worked, the one with whom he worked the least well, i.e., the least preferred co-worker.[7] The least preferred co-worker is rated on such personality traits as pleasantness, efficiency, and cooperativeness. Since all of these trait adjectives demand an appraisal of the individual being rated, the instrument measures how positively or how negatively a person feels toward his least preferred co-worker. The person who manifests negative feelings toward the LPC says, in effect, that an individual's poor work performance is clearly associated with undesirable personality characteristics. Low LPC raters are so task-oriented that they cannot differentiate. Those who rate the LPC positively are stating that they can distinguish between work performance and personality. High LPC raters seem to be more concerned with establishing good interpersonal relations, and are less concerned with tasks. Furthermore, Fiedler states that low LPC people who are in leadership positions feel much more positively about a group and about themselves when the group has achieved its mission

5. C. Gibb, "Leadership," in G. Lindzey and E. Aronson, eds., *Handbook of Social Psychology*, 2d ed., Vol. 4 (New York: Addison-Wesley, 1969), p. 248.

6. F. E. Fiedler, *A Theory of Leadership Effectiveness* (New York: McGraw-Hill Book Company, 1967).

7. *Ibid.*, pp. 40–41.

than when it is unsuccessful. High LPC people in analogous positions do not show this difference.

Fiedler also reports that when a group is confronted with a stressful situation and its ability to reach a pre-determined goal is threatened, low LPC leaders are more likely to engage in acts of task leadership than are high LPC leaders. Thus, Fiedler interprets LPC ratings in this manner: "We visualize the high LPC individual as a person who derives his major satisfaction from successful interpersonal relationships, while the low LPC person derives his major satisfactions from task performance."[8]

Fiedler cites other data which suggest that groups confronted by stressful situations are more likely to achieve their objectives when the leader is a low LPC type. Although further research is needed to validate these findings, it would be expected that leaders in groups under deteriorating circumstances tend to be LPC negative; the high LPC leaders would have been rejected by virtue of ineffectiveness, or the group itself might have disintegrated under pressure. The success of low LPC leaders would tend to maintain group membership and, in consequence, the group might become more efficient in achieving its goals without any referral to the leader's LPC score.

Whether the task-centered leader is more effective than the person-centered leader is thought by Fiedler to be dependent upon the situation. The initial method for determining leadership effectiveness was to create a test that would evaluate the leader's style. The LPC test resulted, but it could not show that either style was superior in every leadership situation. Fiedler then developed a classification of situations with the most apparent differentiation of situations being the degree to which conditions are favorable to the leader. Fiedler states that three factors in a group situation chiefly indicate the degree of favorableness to the leader: 1) the leader's personal relationships with group members—how well the leader is liked and admired; 2) the organizational structure of the group—the specific way duties and responsibilities for each member of the group are fixed; and 3) the leader's actual power or authority—the actual payoff or access to rewards and punishments which can be meted out to the group members.

Fiedler theorizes that under conditions of high favorability, the task-centered leader would be more effective than the person-centered leader. Thus, when the leader has the support of the group, the goal is clearly identified, and the leader's power is real, the group members may approve of the leader's concentration upon the task.

---

8. *Ibid.*, p. 45.

Under conditions of low favorability, when the leader has poor relations with group members, the task is dimly perceived, and the leader has little actual power, the task-centered leader would also be more effective because it would be necessary to focus on the task in order to achieve group goals.

Whenever the situation is moderately favorable, however, the person-centered leader would be more effective than the task-centered leader because group members would require support of a personal nature to assist them in carrying out their assignments in accomplishing their goals. The person-centered leader would focus on building individual morale and good personal relations so that group members could gain motivation for task performance. Both kinds of leaders can be effective under the right conditions.

In Fiedler's classification of favorable leadership situations, is the personal relationship between leaders and followers always the most important determinant? Are there other variables, besides the three used in the model, that might influence the degree to which a specific situation is favorable to leadership? Does the leader have to function primarily as a task-oriented or person-oriented individual?

Fiedler has very carefully stated that the LPC score is an index which is more significant to the leader, but it is possible that both might be of equal concern to some leaders. In fact, attention to both people and tasks may be the most highly effective leadership style.

The Situational Reaction

Much can be said for a situational approach to leadership theory, but there is too little information currently available to include other than conditioning forces which the group encounters. Leadership is not something that can be forcefully imposed upon a so-called docile group. It is a phenomenon that derives from at least four discernible factors which must merge before any leadership is apparent.

These forces—the individual with leader potential, the follower who will be a member of the leader's group, the entire group, and the situation which provides the confrontation—must be assiduously dealt with simultaneously. Leadership is surely as much a function of a given situation and group need as it is of an individual's ability to make the effort to solve problems which frustrate group members. Research and theory concerning leadership seem to favor the situational approach. Now, however, there have surfaced basic questions which are giving scholars pause and creating a reaction which could set the stage for a round of definitive experiments. All this activity should shed additional light on the human predilection for leadership. Situationalists themselves are beginning to detect in individual leaders attributes which are of sufficient power to have a marked effect on leadership behavior.

One of the major criticisms of the situational approach is that it assumes that leaders influence their groups but are not, in turn, affected by their followers. A great deal of evidence indicates that a leader's behavior is strongly shaped by the demands, perceptions, and actions of other group members. As more understanding of this basic fact has emerged, a new and more complex approach has developed in the interactional view.

GROUP INTERACTIONAL THEORY

Any discussion of role relationship admits the fact that where there is no recognition, there can be no interaction. The interactional aspects of leadership required in the same way as do other role relationships, the sharing of attitudes and expectations by role participants. The leader and group members may identify and interpret a specific objective situation in very different ways. Obviously, the leader-follower relationship is dynamic. Situations may provide stimuli, but the constructions and attitudes of group members and their leader may change the stimuli. Therefore, the relationship between leader and followers can and does change.

In the interaction theory of leadership, there is a problematic situation, the needs of a group, and the selection of some individual who can best satisfy the emotional, intellectual, and apparent task needs of the group leader. Leadership, then, is a bi-lateral influence relationship in which followers, as recipients of influence, reciprocate by asserting a degree of influence on the leader. The leader must be willing to accept some influence by group members if the interactional relationship is to continue.[9]

The complex concept of social influence cannot be overlooked in attempting to explain how an individual's behavior is affected by others. This requires an examination of a number of psychological tests and measures, including discrepancy hypotheses, cognitive dissonance theories, theories of interpersonal perception, and assessments of social desirability, dogmatism, and conformity. These quantitative instruments all focus upon one overriding determination concerning progress toward group goals, group standards or norms regarding values, and specific traits which are intrinsically desired.

---

9. E. P. Hollander and J. W. Julian, "Contemporary Trends in the Analysis of Leadership Processes," *Psychological Bulletin,* Vol. 71 (1969), pp. 387–397.

GROUP FUNCTION THEORY

The group function theory has evolved chiefly as a result of the failure of the trait theory to portray leaders and differentiate them from non-leaders. This new theory suggests that leadership is not a possession of any one person, but properly belongs to groups. This theory sees leadership as a series of acts directly constrained by group structure.

Despite differences of opinion, group theorists tend to believe that leadership is a collection of functions concerned with goal achievement and group maintenance. Thus, these functions are defined by the internal and external properties of the group. Therefore, leadership is behavior undertaken by group members to achieve ends for which they have originally joined the group.[10] Group maintenance, goal identification, goal achievement, and membership satisfaction are viewed as integral elements.

Funtions which are necessary for group effectiveness may be performed by a member and perceived by the group, thereby earning potential leadership status for that person. A person may be permitted to have influence to the extent that the leadership task which is being performed satisfies group needs.[11] Leadership is passed from one member to another as the variables confronting the group change and the individual's skill or knowledge is competent to deal with such conditions.

In addition to these fundamental premises, the group function theory of leadership emphasizes that the traits a leader requires for the successful performance of a group will vary according to external and internal group influences.[12] Different groups, or even the same group, under differing conditions will probably look to various kinds of leaders and leadership functions. Moreover, when any group member contributes to the attainment of anticipated goals or group solidarity, a leadership role is being enacted. As observed from the group approach, the separation of formal from informal leadership is distinct and typical. When leadership is defined as a set of functions, the personal characteristics of a particular leader are not emphasized. Any behavior that moves a group closer to its goals is seen as a leadership function. This really means that all group members are

---

10.   D. Cartwright and A. Zander, eds., *Group Dynamics, Research and Theory* (Evanston, Ill.: Row, Peterson & Company, 1953), p. 538.

11.   R. B. Cattell, "New Concepts for Measuring Leadership in Terms of Group Syntality," *Human Relations*, Vol. 7 (1951), pp. 167–184.

12.   D. Kretch, R. S. Crutchfield, and E. L. Ballachey, *Individual in Society* (New York: McGraw-Hill Book Company, 1962).

potential leaders. F. Redl, using a psychoanalytic approach, introduces a central figure (the leader) and differentiates ten kinds of emotional relationships, perceived to be leadership functions, between the central figure and other group members.[13] Theoretical as well as empirical studies stress the importance of two basic types of leadership: goal achievement and group maintenance. It is obvious that many different behaviors can effectuate these two functions, and any group member can act in ways that will assist the group in attaining its goals and/or sustaining itself. It must be understood, however, that these leadership functions almost always become centralized in the custody of a select few, especially in groups that are relatively long-lived.

Consideration of others and initiating and dominating behaviors are of considerable importance in establishing leadership.[14] The nature of the group, its maturity, and its immediate situation will determine the transcendent function, its articulation, and its implementor (leader). Under adverse conditions in which divisiveness threatens the group with immediate dissolution, there is every expectation that group maintenance will characterize the behavior of its leaders. If the group has potency in the membership, then maintenance behavior will personify them as well. Of course, such stressful conditions may well produce new leaders capable of handling the crisis.

It has been observed in small informal groups that eventually members bestow a position of leadership on a task specialist or a personal relations specialist.[15] The task-oriented person moves the group toward its objective much like a general with a mission to accomplish. The manner is authoritative and typically the person is not well-liked by the membership. The personal relations specialist, usually a well-liked individual, is concerned with creating internal group harmony and reducing potential or actual conflict. The development of leadership in informal groups shows that leaders tend to modify their behavior according to the needs and interests of those who are potential followers.[16] In fact, while group leaders influence the behavior of group members, they are, in turn, influenced by and

13.   F. Redl, "Group Emotion and Leadership," *Psychiatrist*, Vol. 5 (1942), pp. 573–596.
14.   A. W. Halpin and B. J. Winer, "A Factorial Study of the Leader Behavior Descriptions," in R. M. Stogdill and A. E. Coons, eds., *Leader Behavior: Its Description and Measurement* (Columbus, Ohio: Bureau of Business Research, Ohio State University, 1957), monograph 88.
15.   R. F. Bales, "The Equilibrium Problem in Small Groups," in T. Parsons, R. F. Bales, and E. A. Shils, *Working Papers in the Theory of Action* (New York: The Free Press of Glencoe, 1953).
16.   H. H. Jennings, *Leadership and Isolation,* 2d ed. (New York: David McKay and Company, 1950).

are expected to fulfill the demands of the leadership role perceived by the group members.[17]

In informal groups there are many factors that determine whether or not an individual will engage in leadership behavior or become a leader. Even if the person is eligible to lead the group, he may have no desire to do so.[18] Other members of the group may attempt to assume leadership roles when designated leaders prove inadequate.[19] Status within the group may also stimulate leadership attempts. Those who are relatively well-placed in the group hierarchy may decide to engage in leaderlike activities whereas those who are less well-placed in group esteem probably will not engage in leaderlike behavior because they feel slighted.

There has been serious debate over whether leadership responsibility should be concentrated in the hands of one or a few persons or widely distributed among the group membership. Some have stated that centralized leadership is required in order to carry out objectives and prevent disruption. Others have opposed this view and stress that authoritarian behavior lowers morale and promotes conflict. The centralization of leadership does result in better short-term group performance on tasks but it does lower group morale.[20] White and Lippitt reinforce the point that in long-established groups there will be a consequent deterioration of group effectiveness due to lowered group morale.[21]

The question of whether leadership should be democratic or autocratic has also been raised. In the case of authoritarian personalities, all significant group functions which affect group behavior are in the leader's hands and only the leader dominates the group. The democratic leader exercises his influence by sharing responsibility and the decision-making process with other members. Individuals respond to both kinds of leadership styles. Some followers can respond only to authoritarian personalities, to previous

---

17. J. Weroff, "Development and Validation of a Projective Measure of Power Motivation," *Journal of Abnormal and Social Psychology*, Vol. 54 (1957), pp. 1–8.

18. Kenneth H. Price and Howard Garland, "Compliance with a Leader's Suggestions as a Function of Perceived Leader/Member Competence and Potential Reciprocity," *Journal of Applied Psychology*, Vol. 66, No. 3 (June, 1981), pp. 329–336.

19. R. L. Kahn and D. Katz, "Leadership Practices in Relation to Productivity and Morale," in D. Cartwright and A. Zander, eds., *Group Dynamics*, 2d ed. (New York: Harper and Row, 1960), pp. 554–570.

20. H. J. Leavitt, "Some Effects of Certain Communication Patterns on Group Peformance," *Journal of Abnormal and Social Psychology*, Vol. 46 (1951), pp. 38–50.

21. R. White and R. Lippitt, "Leader Behavior and Member Reaction in the Social Climate," in D. Cartwright and A. Zander, eds., *Group Dynamics*, 3d ed. (New York: Harper & Row, 1968), pp. 327–330.

conditioning experiences, or to their own need to be controlled. Under highly stressful conditions of personal danger or fear, individuals may be strongly attracted to authoritarian leadership.[22] Others, having been nurtured on democratic concepts and within participating structures, react favorably to democratic leadership.

The group function approach to leadership asserts that the relative effectiveness of authoritarian and democratic styles will rely upon the internal and external properties of the group. Research by F. E. Fiedler offers extensive support for this conviction.[23] Using selected measures, Fiedler identified leaders on a continuum ranging from high socio-emotional to high task involvement. For some group circumstances, the socio-emotional leader was effective; in other situations, a task leader produced more effective group action. To accommodate these findings, Fiedler provided a theoretical analysis of variance concerning group exigencies in terms of their "task-structure relations" and "position power" properties. Some group conditions included a structured task, favorable leader-member relations, and a leadership position with authority; others were extremely low in all of these aspects; and still others fell between these two poles. Thus, Fiedler demonstrated that groups which are either very high or very low in all three of these dimensions produce more effectively with a task-oriented leader than with a supportive socio-emotional leader. The latter has greater success with groups that contain moderate attributable forms. Moderate attributable form implies low position power, where the influence of the group for the member is negligible, or where the tasks and structure of the group have little significance for the follower.

Despite a reliance upon group structure, position within the group, and perception in determining leadership performance, there still remains the need to depend upon some suitable individual with technical competence and usable personal qualities for changing situations. The group function theory does not discard the individual in favor of "a group mind." It recognizes that there is a distinct need for individual performance and even individual willingness to perform. The theory emphasizes the idea that individuals are the foundation of any group and become the limiting factors on any leadership structure.

---

22.   J. T. Lanzetta, "Group Behavior under Stress," *Human Relations,* Vol. 8 (1955), pp. 29–52.

23.   F. E. Fiedler, "The Contingency Model: A Theory of Leadership Effectiveness," in H. Proshansky and B. Seidenberg, eds. *Basic Studies in Social Psychology* (New York: Holt, Rinehart and Winston, 1965), pp. 538–550.

If leadership were interpreted only as a function of the group, there could be no question of individual qualities that emerge as a result of group need. Everything would be done by group consensus. This is patently not true, because group structure also works within constraints which increase as unabated internal and external pressures force the group to change. As the group confronts conditions that may require the technical expertise and intelligence of one leader and then another leader, individual personality patterns are injected into the process. What the indvidual is, what the individual brings to the group in a particular situation, and how membership perception permits the individual to gain influence—these concepts all suggest that leadership as a function of the group does not exclude the idea of individual leadership.

Even those who are committed to a situational approach to leadership have begun to detect personal attributes in individuals which makes it difficult to deny that such leadership characteristics exist. These personality qualities are of sufficient power to have a marked effect on leadership behavior.

THE NEED TO LEAD

Another possibility emerges as a motive for leadership assumption, and that is an insatiable desire, a need to lead. There are individuals whose craving for power is so compelling that they must seek leadership roles by placing themselves in situations where it would seem favorable for a leader to emerge. These individuals are neither rebuffed by rejection nor frustrated by inhospitality to their leadership attempts. Their stimulation comes from a personality drive that can only be satisfied when leadership is attained. A hunger for power can be the major force that motivates an individual's search for a leadership role.[24] This concept has recently been supported by experiments performed in neuroscience. It has also been shown that leaders are inclined, on the whole, to score higher on measures of dominance.[25] If it can be supposed that such measures actually mirror a desire on the part of a person to be in dominant positions, then the need to lead may be evidenced.

Self-Esteem and Confidence

One of the more consistent findings in the literature dealing with leadership research is that leaders have higher self-esteem than do

---

24.   D. Cartwright and A. Zander, eds., *Group Dynamics*, 3d ed. (New York: Harper & Row, 1968), p. 311.
25.   C. Gibb, "Leadership," pp. 218–221.

nonleaders. Individuals who are motivated to lead do so because they are confident that their leadership attempts will be appreciated, that they will gain the influence they require, and that the leadership role will be accorded to them. An individual may have the ability to solve problems or accomplish tasks that are beyond the capacity of other group members and potential followers to perform. Leaders seem to be convinced of their probable effectiveness in whatever situation they find themselves. If potential leaders did not believe that their ideas were accurate appraisals of the situation to be confronted and that they would be effective in achieving a stated goal, they would be less likely to make leadership attempts.

Communication and Intelligence

Another probable factor in the relationship between self-esteem and leadership is the leader's ability to communicate confidence concerning the group's potential accomplishment. This kind of communication is particularly important in situations where group members have only a vague perception of goals or the methods for reaching such goals. Under these circumstances the group members will use the leader's confidence to determine their progress and capacity to perform tasks designed to lead to goal achievement. Leaders must never permit the group to lose confidence in them. They must, therefore, undertake whatever problems or tasks arise and confront them with such strong confidence in the ultimate success of the group that the membership is buoyed by the leaders' apparent competence in dealing with problems. High self-esteem evokes equally high self-confidence. The leader must transmit this to the group for the sake of group cohesiveness and its ability to act as a unit.

Communication plays an essential part in the determination of leadership and indicates whether or not an individual is effective in establishing verbalized associations with others. Implicit in any understanding of leadership is the idea that leaders and followers must be able to communicate with one another. Without communication there can be no leadership. More to the point, however, is the fact that more effective communication between people permits a greater likelihood of initiating leadership behavior. Better communication means that the effective transmitter is in a more advantageous position to acquire information, to signify possible alternative methods and group goal achievement, or to gain cooperation, develop coordination, and organize the group membership to accomplish tasks. Research shows that individuals who are in the best position to communicate with others in a group tend to be selected for leadership roles or are, in fact, looked upon as leaders by group members.[26]

Communication networks are important to leaders because the individual who attempts to lead requires some means for sending ideas to potential followers. Individuals who can coordinate various pieces of information fed to them due to their position within the communication network will probably be able to combine problem-relevant items for quicker and easier solution, thereby enhancing their leadership.

A more subtle element affecting leadership acceptance is the extent to which members of a group share certain commonalities. P. J. Runkel, for example, determined that commonly held ideas dramatically increase effective communication between people who share a value system.[27] Commonly held concepts among people may be an extenuating ingredient which supports the finding that the I.Q. of leaders is apt to be somewhat higher than that of other group members.[28] If there is a great discrepancy between the leader's I.Q. and that of other group members, communication might be blocked because of the leader's inability to translate his ideas into language easily understood by the potential followers. Of course, highly intelligent individuals who want to be leaders could find some way to transmit desired information to others, thereby enabling influence to occur. It does seem, however, that highly intelligent individuals would rather interact with those for whom they have an affinity than lead a group of people who are far inferior to them intellectually and with whom they share virtually no common values.

THE THEORY OF GROUP FACILITATION

One concept of leadership visualizes leaderlike behavior as facilitating group goals. As groups participate in their different activities, various members make certain contributions toward group goals. These contributions differ in kind and degree with some members rendering services of more significance or necessity, some of which ease the way to goal achievement. When any member's contributions are particularly valuable, that member is looked upon as leaderlike; and proportionately, when any member is recognized by

---

26. M. E. Shaw, "Group Structure and the Behavior of Individuals in Small Groups," *Journal of Psychology*, Vol. 38 (1954), pp. 138–149.

27. P. J. Runkel, "Cognitive Similarity in Facilitating Communication," *Sociometry*, Vol. 19 (1956), pp. 178–191.

28. C. Gibb, "Leadership," pp. 217–218.

others as a reliable generator of such contributions, that member is leaderlike. To be thus recognized is to have a role relationship to other members. If leadership is viewed as a facilitative role relationship, then it follows that it is not particular behaviors on the part of the leaderlike person that make his contributions valuable, but rather his or her relationship to others in the group.[29]

The perception of leadership promotes the idea that at least two generalized classes of behavior are present if individuals are accepted as facilitators. Many groups identify special facilitators of task achievement, and recognize those whose distinctive service is encouraging satisfaction among group members.[30] Leaderlike behavior is therefore generated by several individuals within a group. Group members whose enabling efforts are not recognized by others do not thereby cease to contribute toward group goals. Nevertheless, it is more correct to state that their activities are more leaderlike than their personal attributes. Any discussion of role relationship admits the fact that where there is no recognition, there can be no interaction. As in other role relationships, the interactional aspects of leadership require the sharing of attitudes and expectations by role participants.

The designations of task specialist and socio-emotional specialists were formulated to describe enabling performers. These facilitators are necessary for group goals which lead to task satisfaction and individual member satisfaction. To facilitate task achievement, it is necessary to plan and solve problems as well as to persevere until the desired goal is achieved. In groups which have experienced coordinated action toward a goal, there is the likelihood that one or more group members will become recognized as a reliable enabler because they are ingenious, practical, persuasive, dependable, capable of identifying problems, and skilled in planning and coordination. Those who are identified as leaders tend to maintain satisfying interpersonal relations. Although some groups exist only for the purpose of achieving specific objectives, such accomplishment may be assisted or retarded by membership interpersonal satisfactions or dissatisfactions.[31] Other groups appear to have few objectives other

---

29. T. M. Newcomb, R. H. Turner, and P. E. Converse, *Social Psychology, the Study of Human Interaction* (New York: Holt, Rinehart and Winston, Inc., 1965), pp. 474–475.

30. R. F. Bales, "Task Roles and Social Roles in Problem Solving Groups," in E. Maccomby, T. M. Newcomb, and E. L. Hartley, eds., *Readings in Social Psychology,* 3d ed. (New York: Holt, Rinehart & Winston, 1958), p. 441.

31. R. L. Kahn and D. Katz, "Leadership Practices, in Relation to Productivity and Morale," in D. Cartwright and A. Zander, eds., *Group Dynamics, Research and Theory,* 2d. ed. (New York: Harper and Row, 1960), pp. 557–558.

than the pleasure that members find in interacting with one another. Most groups do have both kinds of interest. Whatever the intent of the group's primary goal, the achievement of it can be smoothed by any member who serves as a source of satisfying intermember relationships. Leaderlike behaviors that directly correspond to such facilitation may be described as follows: highly supportive and sociable; extroverted; tension resolving; encouraging; capable of displaying equanimity; and capable of remaining impartial.

Those who become emotional leaders are confronted with a contradiction: How can they offer support and warmth equitably to all groups and simultaneously offer negative criticism to individuals? According to Fiedler, accepted leaders tend to depersonalize their relationships to group members. They become task-oriented rather than person-oriented. When task objectives are shared, the supportive behaviors can be subordinated to goal achievement, and in these circumstances discrimination in terms of who is effective and who is not becomes evident.

Whatever the leaderlike activities that serve satisfying interpersonal relationships, they will be most effective if (as in the case of goal accomplishment) they permit a group member to increase his own utility through others. Satisfying interpersonal relations, such as task completion, are the results of personal interaction within the group as a whole. How certain members behave to promote effectiveness, thereby gaining recognition and leadership status, must still be explained. What the leader is as a person, what the leader must do to gain acceptance, and how the leader employs his capacities to perpetuate influential interaction remain for consideration.

CENTRAL FIGURE THEORY

Zoological resources cannot be overlooked when examining where and why leadership occurs. Although there has been a tendency to downgrade the idea of leadership individuality in favor of group norms, situational factors, organizational structure, or social climate, most groups still recognize a central figure. In almost any culture most groups lean toward a central figure. This individual may be indigenous, appointed, or imposed upon the group. Regardless of how the position has been achieved, this individual is looked upon as the leader. Whether the imposition is formalized through a hierarchical organization, made informally as in any recreational group or achieved through a natural selection process from the need to survive, one central figure is typically designated as leader. Now why should this be? Is it, indeed, a fact? A possible explanation for the central figure phenomenon may be found in the evolutionary process.

Desmond Morris writes that the ancestral forebears of man probably lived in much the same manner as other primate species. These social animals are dominated by a single male. The entire life style of the group revolves around this one central figure. The dominant male is the most powerful and usually the largest of the animals. Consequently, every member of the group seeks to appease him or face bodily harm. The dominant male is at once the group protector and arbiter. He prevents outside forces from overcoming the group and he controls any intragroup quarrels that may threaten safety or unity. In short, the dominant male is all-powerful. He makes the decisions and reaps all benefits first. His authority is absolute and godlike:

> Turning now to our immediate ancestors, it is clear that, with the growth of the cooperative spirit so vital for successful group hunting, the application of the dominant individual's authority had to be severely limited if he was to retain the active, as opposed to passive, loyalty of the other group members. They had to want to help him instead of simply fear him. He had to become "one of them." The old-style monkey tyrant had to go, and in his place there arose a more tolerant, more cooperative naked ape leader. This step was essential for the new type of "mutual-aid" organization that was evolving, but it gave rise to a problem. The total dominance of the Number 1 member of the group having been replaced by a qualified dominance, he could no longer command unquestioning allegiance. This change in the order of things, vital as it was to the new social system, nevertheless left a gap. From our ancient background there remained a need for an all-powerful figure who could keep the group under control.... [32]

It is not surprising, then, that one aspect of leadership should focus on the concept of central-figure domination based upon a biologically transmitted heritage. If, as Morris suggests, humans are still controlled by fundamental animalistic motives accumulated from their genetic legacy, then it is entirely possible, even inevitable, that they should behave in ways that accede to impulses which are many millions of years old, rather than to those which have been acquired relatively recently over the past few thousand years. The hominoid group has always been dominated by some central figure and wherever there are groupings of social animals there is the likelihood that a central figure will emerge. This may be based on an unconscious

---

32. D. Morris, *The Naked Ape* (New York: Dell Publishing Co., Inc., 1967), p. 147. Reprinted by permission.

desire on the part of group members to submit themselves to one who has the power to provide protection and satisfaction of need, or to maintain some kind of supportive relationship which is beneficial to the accepting person. It is surely worth exploring the possibility of leaders as central figures based upon biological urges as opposed to purely social considerations.

A complete theory of leadership incorporates all of the concepts which have been discussed. Leadership, without doubt, requires some identifiable personality traits or characteristics which differentiate the leader from other group members despite the situation or group need. The group's perception of itself, its structure, and goals will also affect the choice of leader. The leader's behavior will be conditioned by membership needs, group standards, and other variables imposed from without or as part of the group structure. Finally, more than one person may perform leadership functions within one group and, to the degree that this is so, contribute to the concept of leadership as a group function.

Leadership is a dynamic form of human behavior and cannot be adequately defined by any single theory. Nor can the combination of various theories into one formalized package be justified. A continuing examination of leadership in light of new models and behavioral insights indicates several acceptable theories: leadership must account for the structuring of roles within groups; leadership is intimately connected to personality characteristics; needs of group members will play a determining factor at any given time; all of those factors are predicated upon prevailing conditions. It is very likely that leadership is generated from the coincidental confrontation of these factors. The aspects which distinguish the leader from all others, without reducing or denigrating group members' contributions to the overall effectiveness of group life, remain just beyond precise identification.

QUESTIONS FOR DISCUSSION

1. Discuss the significance of current neuroscience research on the trait theory of leadership.
2. How does the group funcation theory differ from the group facilitation theory?
3. What is leaderlike behavior?
4. What contradictions do socio-emotional leaders face?
5. Why do groups seem to have a central figure?
6. What is the LPC scale and what does it assess?
7. Explain group interactional theory.
8. How may leadership modify group norms?

9. What is the difference between democratic and autocratic leadership?
10. What is the significance of Central Figure Theory to contemporary leadership theory?

BIBLIOGRAPHY

Bass, Bernard M., *Stogdill's Handbook of Leadership* (New York: Free Press, 1981).

Berkowitz, L., ed., *Advances in Experimental Social Psychology* (New York: Academic Press, 1978).

Davis, Allison, *Leadership, Love and Aggression* (San Diego, Cal.: Harcourt Brace Jovanovich Inc., 1983).

Kellerman, Barbara, *Leadership: Multidisciplinary Perspectives* (Englewood Cliffs, N.J.: Prentice-Hall, Inc., 1984).

Koenigsberg, Samuel, *Leadership in the Eighties* (Albuerque, N.M.: Institute for Economic & Political World Strategic Studies, 1982).

Torkom, Suraydarian, *Leadership* (Agoura, Cal.: Aquarian Educational Groups, 1984).

CHAPTER THREE

Insight and Self

In every group situation or individual confrontation, people invariably spend much time thinking about what other people are really like. What goes on beneath the façade that people use to protect their egos from the supposed onslaught of a hostile environment? We want to know which latencies within the individual may influence behavior. How accurate is our knowledge of others? We realize that some people appear to be remote, aloof, or more inscrutable than others. We also recognize that we have close friends to whom we can confide our most cherished and hidden thoughts, feelings, and to whom we can expose what we call "the real me." Such close contacts are rarely found. For the most part we are content to reveal bits and pieces of ourselves to a select few, and then only after those individuals have proved worthy of trust. In our culture the subjective aspect of human relations and our understanding of the self are played down. We are also aware that these facets of human nature exert considerable influence on human behavior and, subsequently, on whatever knowledge we may expect to learn about our fellow beings.

UNDERSTANDING HUMAN NATURE

Some people, particularly those who hold positions of authority within organizations, believe that human motives are unintelligible and that individual behavior can best be analyzed and directed by externalities, that is, tangible rewards and observable reactions. Those who adopt this viewpoint diminish the power of subjective responses. They think of individuals as objects and try to determine the motivations which instigate actions. Thus, they magnify man's conformity and have little regard for individual constancy and integrity of personality in changing circumstances. These people believe that humans are automatons, susceptible to the stimulation of events and responding more or less compulsively to them. They believe in dictating personal or collective behavior. They rely upon the conditioning factors of an individual's response to basic biological stimuli or to such extra-personal impositions as customs, codes, domination, and regulations.

Conversely, there are those who conceive of people's behavior as deterministic, that is formulated chiefly through the comprehensions, analyses, and drives derived from intellect. They consider people to be in command of themselves, their faculties and, therefore, capable of selecting a course best suited to meet their exacting needs. They appreciate the consistencies in a person's conduct and regard regulation of behavior as a responsibility of individual will, personal posture, and ethics.

Probably, the truth lies between those two extreme views of man. If people only respond to externalities, there is no logical explanation for personal uniqueness and imaginative contributions to the social world. If, however, man is thought of as arbiter, there is no explanation for his gregarious nature. In order to be able to understand human nature there is the need to think of individuals in terms of environmental influences, such as the culturally specified roles that one plays, and the hidden factors of mind and personality which also supply regulatory influences on behavior. These hidden factors may well influence how the individual perceives, how he idealizes, and how he understands himself. The environmental situations which condition actions are merely one part. There are also the subjective influences of mind and, particularly important, the interpersonal relationships which everyone has. By centering on this interpersonal aspect, we may begin to understand the behavior of people and develop an insight into the leadership phenomenon.[1]

The emergence of self profoundly affects behavior. It is an intellectual mixture of subjective thoughts and a result of interpersonal interaction. Throughout life most people are concerned with their personal reputation. Specifically, most people actively seek approval from others. From our earliest years of life we attempt to gain the affection—and thereby the security—from people who play significant roles in our lives. During this process we construct some image or perception of conduct which calls forth approval and affection. This developmental model helps to form an intellectual concept of what and who we are in relation to other people; that is, what others think of us.[2] Individualization begins in early childhood when we start to distinguish ourselves from our environment. As these occurrences continue, we gain a feeling of existence apart from our surroundings, of being a discrete body—having size, shape, power,

---

1. B. B. Smith and B. A. Farrell, *Training in Small Groups* (New York: Pergamon Press, 1979), pp. 58–60.

2. D. R. Omark and others, *Dominance Relations: An Ethological View of Human Conflict and Social Interaction* (New York: Garland STPM Press, 1980), p. 322.

peculiar characteristics which readily identify us as living organisms, uniquely endowed with sense and mind. Simultaneously, we perceive an inner state of the mind which gradually becomes the seat of our emotions, ideas, options, and judgments.

An understanding of the environment and a growing awareness that other people have attitudes which relate to us emerges progressively in our development. We acquire comprehension of physical torment, mental suffering, and the impact of praise or censure. We learn modes of conduct which satisfy us. We seek out ways of behavior which provide us with rewards rather than disparagement and repudiation. We finally realize a personal and distinctive identity composed of values, convictions, objectives, and a rationale through which we are able to assess ourselves as well as others.

One of the paramount qualities of this self-concept is its consistency. Within each of us there is a kernel of identity which, from a personal point of view, gives us a characteristic and animate form. We adopt these values, ideologies, and experiences which appear relevant to our self-concept and we either repudiate or modify those which do not.[3]

When we are confronted by conditions which endanger our feeling of unity or self-esteem, we enter a state of tension attended by vague feelings of anxiety and we produce defensive postures. Such problems may arise from environmental situations; we may be threatened by another person or thing. Some anxiety may stem from inner discontent. In certain instances and under peculiar circumstances, we may believe that we are unable to control particular impulses which drive us to perform in ways leading to pain, punishment, or rejection. On the other hand, we may undergo dissonant experiences which clash with our morals, thereby filling us with mental dread.[4] The following statement is an example:

> I am at odds with certain thoughts that I have about my appraisal of certain others. I am incapable of accepting and supporting feelings as I experience them. They make me apprehensive, and if I cannot contend with them insofar as their actual nature is concerned, I will be unable to control myself. Unaware of this, I look for a scapegoat. Rather than face the torment of guilt feelings, I seek a safe object for blame. It is possible that my feelings are so intense that I simply

---

3.   C. L. Cooper and C. P. Alderfer, *Advances in Experiential Social Processes* (New York: John Wiley & Sons, 1978), p. 71.

4.   G. A. Vlett, *A Synopsis of Contemporary Psychiatry*, 5th ed. (St. Louis, Mo.: The C.B. Montez Company, 1972), pp. 71–74.

withdraw, disengaging myself from reality by fantasizing, regressing, or otherwise acting defensively.

In this way we can hide behind a barrier of our own making where we neither reveal ourselves nor allow others to appreciate our real selves. Nevertheless, there is a part of us which always knows who we are, what we are, and has a realistic appreciation of us. This contrasting behavior is self-defensive; it assists in banishing painful experiences to the subconscious while we luxuriate in and reflect relative security in the conscious state.

While the defense mechanism helps to make life satisfactory and offers a form of constancy in our relationship with others, it may also encourage a tendency toward closed-off thinking by narrowing possible choices which might produce greater insight and comprehension for our own benefit. When we hide behind a façade of our own making, we are erecting protective devices that are also barriers to self-understanding. It is unlikely that we will recognize personal deficiencies and be able to alter them. From our defensive posture we display differential behavior—adjusted to the event and reaping commendation—as we confront other individuals in the social milieu. The problem is that the two facets of ourselves have different dimensions, yet they overlap.

Actually, we are many things because of our attempts to modify our behavior as we deal with others in the various social settings we encounter. We become the expression of many subjective and objective selves. With each transference, patterns of behavior and alterations in our image are induced. At any moment these various selves provide us with those qualities that give us identity.

The Inner Self

Our subjective self is what we think we are and hope to be. It includes all the desires, hopes, and idealistic dreams that we want for ourselves. It is the self that we know best, and that we protect most of all. Some psychologists assert that the one basic need of man is to perserve this self-image, and that all behavior may be explained and even predicted in the light of the individual's desire to maintain it. The one basic human need is the urge for self-esteem. All other so-called needs or drives are in reality subservient to this one:

From birth to death, the defense of the phenomenal self is the most pressing, most crucial, if not the only task of existence. Moreover, since human beings are conscious of the future, their needs extend into the future as well, and they strive to preserve not only the self as it exists but to build it up and strengthen it against the future. We might combine these two aspects in a formal definition of the basic human need as: the preservation and enhancement of the phenomenal self.[5]

Thus, a person's interpersonal behavior may reflect his struggle to protect his inner self. It is through conformity that we tend to find security and sustain our balance. We are what we are because we are afraid to be what we would like to be. We have, therefore, come to employ defense mechanisms. The problem is that although these exercises do guard us from emotional failure, we can never really comprehend who or what we are if we cannot free ourselves from these maneuvers. At the worst, they can result in the ultimate destruction of the self. Some (although not all) of these mechanisms are important and identifiable behavior forms, such as withdrawal, sublimation, direct aggression, indirect aggression, suppression, repression, fantasy, and rationalization.

Withdrawal. Withdrawal is the immediate method by which the individual seeks to remove himself from stress or difficulty. It is probably the least painful procedure for the ego. All that is required is cessation of whatever activity is being undertaken. Of course, withdrawing from any situation where mastery is impossible is the sensible thing to do. However, simple frustration should not lead to withdrawal if there is the probability or possibility that the individual may succeed. Withdrawal leaves one with a sense of inadequacy and defeat.[6]

An example of this behavior may be seen in the failure of an elementary school-age child to perform some physical feat requiring muscular strength and coordination beyond his years. If the child lacks readiness to function in a specific act, he or she should withdraw into some other activity where physiological development is consistent with the required action, but the child should not withdraw irrevocably from all physical activity.

Sublimation. Sublimation is a directing of hostile or aggressive impulses into acceptable lines of behavior, as in the case of a musician who works out his anger by playing rather striking out at someone. Sublimation may also be a realization of socially acceptable desires by indirect means, as in the case of a childless woman who takes up teaching.[7] As Mikesell has stated:

---

5. D. Snygg and A. W. Combs, *Individual Behavior* (New York: Harper, 1949), p. 58.

6. A. F. Grasha and D. S. Kirschenbaum, *Psychology of Adjustment and Competence* (Cambridge, Mass.: Winthrop Publishers, Inc., 1980), pp. 343–356.

7. R. R. Bootzin and J. R. Acocella, *Abnormal Psychology: Current Perspectives*, 4th ed. (New York: Random House, 1984), p. 35.

The individual with a love of art need not fold his hands in abject worry when he sees that the lack of means might not enable him to educate himself in the skill of an artist. He should plan to sublimate in case of actual disappointment in art training by forming study clubs of art, becoming an art critic, or having a splendid library of art books. With an insight into sublimation, a man who sees that his wishes for a college education might not be realized could eventually plan to give vent to his ambition by becoming an expert in some particular line of thought.[8]

Direct Aggression.   Direct aggression or discharge is an outburst of hostile behavior which completely disrupts a preconceived action from reaching an objective. It is generally called "loss of temper" and may be seen in such loss of control as inability to speak or function coherently. In children, or those who are considered emotionally immature, the tantrum is a way for the individual to relieve himself of frustrating conditions. The playground is a good place for viewing direct aggression. The child who does not get his own way in game activities or who picks up his ball and quits the field when a decision goes against him, thereby spoiling the game for everyone else, shows temper and direct aggression.

Direct aggression as a method of retaliation after frustration may be seen in this example from the record of the Tenth Street Dragons, a pre-adolescent boys' club operating within a fictitious recreational center in New York City:

> Tommy was the acknowledged leader of the group. To this worker, Tommy was an indigenous leader of an autocratic type. Perhaps he came to power because of his pugnacity and physical ability. There were nine boys in the original club. Harry was an original member of the club, but he also had leadership aspirations. He was successful in alienating three members from Tommy's sphere. In any team game Harry always chose his three cohorts first. Finally he was successful in bringing two other boys into the club as members of his clique. There was continual disagreement between the two boys.
>
> During a game in which the contestants hop toward each other in an attempt to bump the opponent off balance, Tommy simply charged into Harry and knocked him sprawling. Harry wasn't able to get up for a while and, when he did, he left the center. A few days later he came to the worker to say that he was leaving the club.

---

8. W. H. Mikesell, *Mental Hygiene* (New York: Prentice-Hall, 1939), p. 328. Reprinted by permission.

Tommy's attack had embarrassed him to the extent that he was not able to face the group.

In this instance it is easy to understand Tommy's behavior. He was not able to cope with a situation where he would lose his leadership status, and he thus took the most direct steps to eliminate his opposition. His open hostility and physical attack overwhelmed and cowed his antagonist to the point of withdrawal.[9]

Indirect Aggression. Indirect aggression is a well-understood form of action. Whenever the individual may not be able to "blow off steam" from pent-up emotional stress for fear of retaliation, he must discover safe objects or persons against whom he can express his aggressiveness, although they have had nothing to do with his frustration or state of stress.[10] Thus, in the child's pecking order, it is usually someone weaker who is attacked in order that the attacker's frustration or annoyance be compensated.

It is considered a criminal offense for adults to assault anyone, regardless of wrongs, particularly of a verbal nature, which have been inflicted. At the very least, physical violence is boorish vengeance for an insult or for loss of face or property. The adult, therefore, has conceived of the indirect assault which compensates for feelings of frustration and hostility which may not be discharged directly.

Satire, sarcasm, innuendo, or aspersion, or the questioning of customs, codes, or authority are the usual forms of indirect aggression. Well-known phrases, used to describe an antagonist or indict a society, have been created because of the frustrations and tensions to which the author was subjected. Zola's courageous *"J'accuse"* condemned a bigoted France; FDR's use of an oath from *Romeo and Juliet,* "A plague on both your houses," found outlet against warring union factions; Bevin's "that dessicated calculating machine" ridiculed Hugh Gaitskill. Each of these epithets can be assumed to have been derived as compensations for its author's inability or disinclination to use direct physical force as the method to relieve his hostility.

The recreationist must be able to understand individual use of behaviors which are manifested in overt or indirect aggression. He must realize when such behaviors represent rational and irrational

9.   S. Feshback and B. Weiner, *Personality* (Lexington, Mass.: D.C. Heath and Company, 1982), pp. 478–479.
10.   E. J. Phares, *Introduction to Personality* (Columbus, Ohio: Charles E. Merrill Publishing Company, 1984), pp. 542–544.

resolution. The individual who adjusts to group living, and its attendant frustrations, with conduct disproportionate to any thwarting he has suffered, indicates this indirectedness. Indirect aggression satisfies a peculiar need in the individual who utilizes it. The recreationist, understanding why the individual acts the way he does, is better able to counsel, condone, or negate such activity.

Suppression. Suppression may be defined simply as hidden feelings. When the individual has experienced some highly emotional provocation but cannot, because of social convention, conveniently discharge or express himself, he suppresses that emotion.[11] Many individuals cannot express themselves because they are fearful of convention, painfully shy, or so completely maladjusted to their social environment that any attempt at expression may destroy their self-concept. The person who is usually the butt of all jokes, who is "put upon" by other, more aggressive individuals, but will not make any defense, suppresses emotional hostilities because he cannot do anything else.

Tension resulting from this inability to release frustration or resentment gradually builds up to a point where the individual may be unable to handle it, and some collapse may occur. At best, suppression is a method of escape from uncomfortable or untenable positions, and in its mildest form is exhibited by the overcautious person whose extreme caution arises not from lack of knowledge in the particular situation, but because of possible criticism that may accrue from replies or actions taken. The overcautious person never does things on impulse. In the main, he is steady, conservative, and perhaps successful, but he is usually rigid in terms of personality and thinking.

The recreationist recognizes that the method of suppression is one frequently utilized by people attempting to adjust to group mores and traditions. However, he attempts to encourage self-expression, particularly emotional expression, by recreational activities, as long as such expression is not belligerent and does not interfere with group interaction.

Repression. Repression is suppression in its most extreme form, with the added factor of non-awareness of the behavior. Thus, the individual denies to himself any thought or action which he actually had or did, as though it had never existed. The individual is so horrified

---

11. L. W. Doob and R. R. Sears, "Factors Determining Substitute Behavior and Overt Expression of Aggression," *Journal of Abnormal and Social Pscyhology,* Vol. 34 (1939), pp. 293-313.

by his thoughts or acts that he strives to forget their occurence by telling himself that they never happened. Repression derives from feelings of guilt or shame resulting from conflicts between ideas and ideals.[12]

The most negative aspect of repression is that the feelings of shame and stress remain within the individual and perhaps increase in time. There is no acknowledgment of the cause of tension because the individual tends to forget specific attitudes. Having repressed a fearful thought, the individual may deny that he ever had that thought, particularly if the thought represents something which he considers sinful or at fault. Since the thought is repressed, he will have to live within a frame of reference which consistently places him in contact with the fear from which he is trying to withdraw. In refusing to confirm what he fears, he continually undermines himself and exposes himself to excessive strain.

The recreationist is in no position to treat or even to diagnose repression in any individual. He will, however, begin to understand individual behavior within group structure as he notices patterns of conduct emerging from daily experience with the person. Only where there is long-term association will such suspicions be identifiable, but there is little likelihood that this will occur unless there is an overt expression from the subject.

With the exception of those recreationists who actually work in therapeutic situations, long-term association with any individual on a professional basis is extremely rare and may even be nonexistent. While knowledge of human behavior and its causes is extremely important for better communication, its application remains academic. Nevertheless, from the standpoint of mental hygiene, such knowledge is worthwhile if only to make the recreationist aware that such anomalies exist in human personality.

Fantasy. Fantasy is one outlet for suppressed feelings. The individual who finds himself inadequate in some activity in which he would like to participate makes up for his deficiencies by daydreaming about them. In his dreams he becomes the champion, hero, great scholar, or other outstanding character with all the skills and abilities which he does not in fact possess.[13]

Fantasy, or the projection of wishes, is not harmful in itself. Wishes

---

12. D. Schultz, *A History of Modern Psychology*, 3d ed. (New York: Academic Press, 1981), p. 331.
13. G. W. Fisher, *The Disorganized Personality*, 2d ed. (New York: McGraw-Hill, 1972), pp. 147–149.

may actually serve as the stimulus for later action. When fantasy draws the individual away from contact with reality to the extent that daydreaming becomes the entire focus of attention, the cycle of removal is complete. The individual who spends his time in fantasy removes himself from the immediate problem or frustration which confronts him. He also postpones the time when he must face up to the problem. In its extreme form, the individual loses contact with reality and substitutes his dreams for what is actually occurring. Unable to distinguish between what is real and what is wish, the individual travels a dark road of mental illness.

An illustration of this need to attain satisfaction may be seen in the following hypothetical situation:

Danny, a fourteen-year-old, was a member of the Greatful Dead, a street gang in X city. He was not particularly robust or bright, but his older brother had been a member of the gang, and so he had been accepted. His activities were mainly those of the follower; he went blindly with the group. He was never able to hold his own with any member of the gang in any activity. A rival gang had invaded the "turf" of the Greatful Dead, and a "rumble" or fight was scheduled. Danny was not aggressively minded and had been a fringe participator in previous clashes with other groups. When the two antagonists met, Danny held back, merely watching. After the fight, with some members on both sides hurt, some of the Greatful Dead questioned Danny about not taking part. Danny was very vague in his replies but finally came out with the story that he had been in the middle of the fight, had beaten one of the opposing gang members and had, in fact, done more than any other member to rout the opponents. He continued to expound this story, although everyone knew it to be untrue. It was assumed by this recreationist that he actually believed what he said.

From the above, it can readily be understood that the adjustment to the group situation was simply too much for Danny to handle. As conflict, tension, and thwarting increased, he became incapable of coping with his own inadequacies in the group. As a result, his break with reality came when he could no longer carry the burden of stress to which he was subjected. He saw himself as he wanted to be in real life and wove a story around the fiction of his wish. In this fantasy he gave himself the opportunity to become heroic, to gain status, to glorify himself. This dream proved so satisfying and compelling that he substituted it for the facts in the case. Although the recreationist was not present at the time of the gang fight, word reached him concerning Danny's behavior. He was successful in persuading

Danny's mother to let the boy see the school psychologist for examination. after the referral, Danny was placed in the municipal diagnostic clinic for observation and was found to have developed marked schizoid symptoms of the paranoid type.

Rationalization. Rationalization is escape from thwarting by redefining a frustrating situation in such a way that the individual's needs are satisfied without further action. It is a special form of daydreaming that is quite overt and may be verbalized to reinforce the reinterpretation.[14]

An individual frequently resorts to rationalization in order to adjust to some situation: a lowering of aspiration if goals are set too high; an instance of "sour grapes," where failure is excused on the grounds that "I really did not want it anyway." The individual who fails to achieve some object may rationalize his failure in order to conceal from himself and others the real reasons, which may be considered shameful, weak, or inferior.

This may be seen in the racial prejudice which is found everywhere. Blacks may be denied equal opportunity or service because they are considered inferior by Caucasians. The following illustration is indicative of such bigotry:

Mr. K is resentful of blacks. The basis for this bias stems from one occasion when a black worker was granted a position which K thought he should have received. Mr. K realizes that the black knew more about the work than he did and does not represent all of the blacks in the world. Nevertheless, K experienced such frustration at the denial of the job in favor of this member of a minority race that he was not able to recognize the facts. He has therefore adjusted to this emotional strain by rationalizing his complete rejection of blacks in a way that justifies his stand. He claims that all blacks are potential miscegenists, and he is thus protecting the purity of all white women from sexual attack. In this way, K defends his self-concept. First he placates his original frustration at losing a position; second, he presents what he thinks is a more acceptable argument than mere jealousy.

Each of the foregoing mechanisms used by the individual to adjust to group living situations and protect the self must be understood if the leader is to deal with them. All of these aspects of interpersonal behavior are encountered over and over again in every conceivable

---

14. R.L. Atkinson, R.C. Atkinson, and E.R. Hilgard, *Introduction to Psychology* (New York: Harcourt, Brace and Jovanovich, 1983), p. 435.

social condition. Only when these compensatory behaviors are recognized will a leader be able to guide individuals within a group to grow in self-awareness and function smoothly as a part of the group. The leader can assist individuals in achieving success, thereby reducing frustration and creating an adjustment that is mutually satisfying to the group and the individual.

On the positive side, the inner self can perform the task of maintaining the individual's real, not neurotic, identity as it interposes itself between him and the process which neatly attempts to gain conformity to mores. Where the inner self is not submerged or threatened by an individual's association with others, it appears as individuality, the manifestations of one's uniqueness in contrast to the beliefs, biases, and values which we hold in common with others. The inner self enables the individual to cope; it is the mechanism by which a person learns to adapt to and exist cooperatively with others in society as he attempts to attain the maximum development of his own personality and abilities.

The External Self

How we appear to others and how we think we appear to others are manifestations of the external self. A person is capable of painting several different self-portraits for the benefit of particular relationships with others. Indeed, people could produce a complex array of social images if they were not regulated by common values. A person's conformity to commonly held values is vital to group life if social efficiency is a valued goal. The external self recognizes the expectations others have for one's social and psychological behavior. It is the external self, for example, which allows leaders to empathize with followers and thus see themselves as others see them; this ability enables them to comprehend the impact of their actions as they are experienced by others.

The potential for variety in the presentation of the external self is always present, and deviations from the expected have an important influence on the ways in which a person relates to others. Fortunately, one's concept of how he thinks others see him and how they really see him can, and do, generally coincide. Sometimes, however, these images are so dichotomous that there is no commonality whatsoever. When our view of how others perceive us coincides with how they actually perceive, we can achieve greater communication with others. As communication increases, so the achievement of durable social goals increases. The hazard to the individual who conforms completely with social mores is that uniqueness may be lost; to the individual who conforms not at all, contact with reality may be lost.

The total self, then, is formed by these two interdependent yet dissimilar components. The degree to which an individual will be able to integrate these components and develop a personality, or self-awareness, is dependent upon relationships with other people. Only through association with others is personal growth possible.

Personality Development

Self-awareness is a product of interpersonal relationships; without the latter, selfhood could probably never develop. The educational philosopher, Philip Phenix, renders this explanation for interpersonal relationships:

> Human personality can develop only through association with other persons; there can be no personal growth in isolation. It is not merely that other human beings constitute a favorable environment, giving protection, enjoyment, and instruction. They play a more fundamental role than that. Other people are essential because the relationships the growing person has with them are actually constitutive of the self. A person is not a self-contained entity who happens to be related to other persons. The relationships enter into the very being and essence of the personality. A self is not a thing-in-itself but always and necessarily a person-in-relationship. This does not mean that when no overt interaction is occurring between persons, selfhood disappears. The constructive role of the interpersonal simply means that the self, whether alone or in company, is what it is largely by virtue of the encounters experienced with other persons. There would be no self had solitude been the only experience.[15]

The self reveals itself as we contact others and interact with those who assume some significance in our lives.

Interpersonal communication is a mutually supporting process which has as its goal an interchange of messages between two or more people so that each can understand the other at the most personal levels. Where emotions are concerned, the problem of understanding becomes the relationship itself. Attention is placed on the intricate defense mechanisms and self-concepts of those involved. Since the individual is motivated to maintain his own integrity by deep-seated internal forces, he can facilitate this effort for the other person by his own self-perception and empathy.

---

15. P. H. Phenix, *Philosophy of Education* (New York: Henry Holt and Company, 1958), pp. 193–194.

LEADERSHIP AND BEHAVIORAL CHANGE

In order to persuade others to follow, there must be some sort of voluntary desire to coordinate efforts and cooperate for mutual benefits. Cooperation, on occasion, necessitates modification in interpersonal relationships. The leader's skill enables positive change in others. He must also recognize the necessity for modifying his own attitude and behavior if he wants to become a leader. He would have to apply his knowledge and capacity to ensure change through interpersonal relations. When personal modification is involved, the individual must appreciate the desirability for transformation. His conduct should confirm his ability to redefine and recast his attitudes. Personal change results only when the individual wants to change. Learning procedures, which are intimately associated with the communication process, follow.

We understand others in terms of our own needs and outlooks which we learn from our personal experiences. People exist in conformity to what we think they are and what we have come to anticipate from them. What we believe about others colors our attitudes and affects our behavior toward them and their behavior toward us. Our competency in interpersonal relationships is directly observed by our attitudes and conduct toward others which are received or felt by them and to which they react. What are attitudes and how may they be modified through leadership? Sherif states that:

> Attitudes refer to the stands the individual upholds and cherishes about objects, issues, persons, groups, or institutions. The referents of a person's attitudes may be a "way of life"; economic, political, or religious institutions; family, school, or government. We are speaking of the individual's attitudes when we refer to his holding in high esteem his own family, his own school, his own party, his own religion, with all the emotional and affective overtones these terms imply. We refer to his attitudes when we say he holds other groups, other schools, other parties, or religions in a less favorable light or at a safe distance (as "safe" is defined by his attitudes).[16]

Of course, possessing an attitude means that the individual takes a position for or against some issue or object. Leadership brings pressure to bear by helping the learner to recognize his internal patterns of emotions and attitudes toward himself and others and, where necessary, providing remedial measures so that inadequacies

---

16.   C. W. Sherif, M. Sherif, and R. E. Nebergall, *Attitude and Attitude Change: The Social Judgment-Involvement Approach* (Philadelphia: W. B. Saunders Co., 1965), p. 4.

can be overcome. For deficiencies of knowledge, educational methods are applied. Changing a person's social behavior by strengthening his ability to encounter others is a difficult process. Frequently, modification of behavior means that the individual must divest himself of certain habitual ways of thinking as well as altering specific attitudes which he has about himself and others. Additionally, the social learner will have to utilize other experiences in which he has had more competency.[17] Recreationists often have a direct opportunity to contribute to social learning and attitude change, as illustrated by the following postulated situation:

> Nine-year-old Ljubljana, who had recently come to the United States from Yugoslavia, was having difficulty gaining acceptance among her peers at the neighborhood recreational center. When she tried to learn an American folk dance, she was confused by the rapidly spoken English directions of the instructor. The other children laughed because she made wrong turns and was unable to follow the directions.
>
> The recreationist assembled the dance class after the lesson and asked if any of the children had ever seen a traditional Slavic dance. When they said that they had not, she explained that these dances were far more complex than the simple folk dance they were trying to learn. Knowing that Ljubljana knew some Croatian dances, she asked her to demonstrate for the class. Ljubljana executed the dances gracefully and well. The rest of the children admired Ljubljana's dancing and asked her to show them how to do the steps. They soon discovered how difficult it was to learn something completely foreign to their experience, even when the instructions were given in their own language.
>
> From an admiration of her dancing there developed a new respect for their Yugoslavian playmate. Fortunately, the recreationist knew of the skill which Ljubljana had. It was relatively easy to show the other children her uniqueness without a great deal of moralizing or explanation. Particularly when working with children, the recreationist-leader's approach should be to accentuate the positive by bringing out the individual's skill, knowledge, or talent. Such things are recognized and appreciated almost immediately.

Behavioral change is founded upon intensive and prolonged interaction between the individual to be changed and the change agent. This is a process which enlists the personal concern and

---

17. A. Pines and C. Maslach, *Experiencing Social Psychology*, 2d ed. (New York: Alfred A. Knopf, 1984), pp. 55–63.

willingness of participants. As the individual becomes more ego-involved and identifies with the process, effectiveness is greatly enhanced. The person learning to alter social behavior must initiate such change. Unless modification is perceived as valid and significant, the learner will not alter his self-image.

Change originating from within necessitates a particular type of association between the leader and the individual undergoing change. Initially, the leader has to assume that the person to be changed has the ability to effect change; he then becomes the focus of all effort for any attempt at attitudinal modification.[18] The thrust for change and the ability to comprehend one's own emotions and perceptions are an internal problem and may be understood vaguely, if at all, by the person effecting change. The same may be stated about any behavioral change relationship, whether of the individual or group type. As Kemp indicates:

> Leaders can help members to recognize that some resistance is a fact of life and to distinguish between resistance which may prevent one from understanding and resistance which appears as rationalizations for disregarding insight. Members can be helped in the use of productive imagination to diminish or eliminate the underlying fear. The group will eventually perceive that basic to various forms of resistance is the fear of change. The leader hopes to develop a psychological climate in which resistance is accepted and understood and the fear of change reduced.[19]

Attitudinal change and associated behavior necessitate an assessment by the person who is changing. The probability for such assessment remains unlikely in the absence of a secure psychological environment. Only when the change agent can assure the follower of a protected situation will there be any motivation to change. This requires empathy on the part of the change agent so that the other's perception of acceptance and understanding is clear. In the absence of empathy and the sensitivity which it connotes, recalcitrance to modification hardens.

This idea of modification is based on the belief that the nature of man is rational and on a recognition of the self as a special and unique presence which moves through an uninterrupted sequence of existence. This affirms that existence is absolutely personal and only the individual has the capacity to differentiate from the continuum of his experience those components which sustain and are in accord with

---

18. C. Rogers, *On Becoming a Person* (New York: Houghton Mifflin, 1961).
19. C. G. Kemp, *Foundations of Group Counseling* (New York: McGraw-Hill, 1970), p. 190.

his self. If there are external forces encountered which appear hostile to the unity of the self, then protective devices are raised to thwart their effects, unless the individual's desire to know is so powerful that it becomes reticence and suppresses such defense mechanisms.

The desire to know is a superior instrument for modification. Nevertheless, it cannot have influence unless the individual undergoing change realizes the weaknesses in his self-structure which bar him from further personal development. He needs, therefore, to view himself realistically. The role of the change agent is to provide the kind of sustaining atmosphere which will enable the follower to reduce those defense mechanisms that can obscure an attempt to examine flaws in the self-structure. The leader acts circumspectly in effecting modification; he offers whatever assistance is necessary for the follower to alter his own perceptions and occasionally becomes the model which the follower attempts to emulate. Under these circumstances, the leader satisfies the needs of the follower for improved forms of behavior to substitute for the old.

The Process of Modification

The entire process of modification of human behavior is actually directed learning. In fact, one of the definitions of learning is that it is the modification of behavior.[20] Despite this very logical and accepted formulation of altering human behavior, there are the frequently discussed moral or ethical questions about one person changing another. Modification of behavior may be viewed as an exercise in manipulation when ulterior motives and subversive ends are detrimental to the individual being changed. Where manipulation is employed there is a general climate of deceit, that is, the individual who is changed is a victim of another person's unscrupulous motives. It cannot be denied that some types of interpersonal behavior involve one individual controlling another through manipulation.

Manipulation has no place in the leadership process or in the process of behavioral modification. Essentially, manipulation is externally produced by forces brought to bear on the individual to be commanded. Modification, as has been explained here, is an internal procedure occurring only at the will of the one who is to be changed. The sole reason for modification is to enhance the ability of the individual to deal with interpersonal relationships or to make him a more capable person. The aim is not to make him a better agent of

---

20. L. J. Cronbach, *Educational Psychology* (New York: Harcourt, Brace and Jovanovich, 1954), pp. 47–49.

society or of the group, although these results may, naturally, accompany the process of modification. Basically, all change is concerned with the individual and his needs, anything else is coincidental.

The distinction between internal and external modification is minimal, but it has immense importance for the change relationship. We recognize the importance of the universal need for personal growth and development. Therefore, we regard modification as voluntary self-improvement. Internal change requires that an enabling relationship be developed between the leader and the follower. The objective of such an association is to provide conditions in which another person, insofar as his own motivations, aims, and attitudes are concerned, takes responsibility for his actions in determining how he may better become a more effective human being. The leader is merely the catalyst in the relationship and undertakes the enabling role, not the managing one.

Modification originates from a facilitating relationship and is a direct contrast to the managed-subordinate condition in which external pressure is applied to gain acquiescence. The empathetic modification process is founded upon an association in which the leader is the instrument, not the person being changed. This type of relationship views rational persons as having the ability to assume responsibility for learning as well as intellectual capacity to discriminate and make appropriate choices. Real learning requires internal growth and development on the part of the learner as improved behavioral patterns are assimilated and adopted for use.

Instruction for Change

All interpersonal relationships occur in some group situation. In attempting to effect change within the individual the leader resorts to certain facilitating methods which can have a positive impact on the follower's attitude toward himself and others. A most significant technique is instruction through which the follower is made aware of the outlooks, values, and referents of the group, with the leader as model. In this way, greater sensitivity to the self may be initiated. Self-awareness is vital if the individual is to have an opportunity for expanding his range of experience. This invariably increases the efficiency of interpersonal relationships, uncovering the capacity for personally satisfying encounters within the social milieu. Each encounter contributes to self-understanding and unity. Even negative experiences may be accepted as a perfectly normal aspect of existence if similar experiences have previously been assimilated in the self-structure. The ability to acknowledge and appreciate the presence of positive and negative facets of our self enables us to see that others also have the same characteristics. However, it is the totality of self that is a matter of consequence.

As a corollary, if openness to experience is to be maximized, there must be a subsequent increase in data from experience which the individual is capable of recognizing as being coherent with his self-structure. As self-awareness is heightened, protective mechanisms are minimized, feelings of personal cohesiveness and consistency are augmented, and contact is made with reality. As the self-system is an outgrowth of social experience, it may be changed by social experiences that assist the individual in reassessing and scrutinizing his aptitude for adjusting to situations which appear to menace his self.

Under the domination of genetic variables, internal pressures, and environmental constraints, the self-system is constantly changing throughout the life span. In this encounter between one's self-structure, one's heredity, and one's external circumstances, conflicts are alleviated either through adapting their origins to an existing idea of self or through altering the self-system, which requires the integration of new concepts associated with similar changes in the self-structure. Above all, the process of reconciliation and accommodation should be positive and developmental. Unfortunately, some people are stultified by the inadequacies of previous experience or by contemporary social standards and values. The process of personal growth which would subscribe to the formation of a better interpersonal environment becomes frustrated by defensive behavior. On the other hand, the substructure of self-continuity may be coupled with inactivity, thereby slowing the rate of change in the self-structure to the extent that it cannot satisfy the requisites for competent behavior in specific circumstances. In these instances, the change process needs new directions or new impetus. Problems which may arise as a result of inability to change may be observed in the following instances:

> The director of X Recreational Center thought it would promote better intergroup relations if an occasion were arranged where members of minority groups could become acquainted. The recreationist suggested an intergroup dance between the teenagers at his center and those of another center. The date was set, an orchestra was employed, and invitations were sent to the youths of the other center. On the night of the dance, the teenagers of the host center arrived first and danced among themselves while waiting for the other teenagers to arrive. When the guests finally did arrive, they were ushered into the gymnasium where the dance

had already started. The guests paired off with one another and danced exclusively among themselves for the rest of the evening.

During the evening, the recreationist in charge made several attempts to stimulate some interchange between the two groups. A few of the hosts invited girls from the other center to dance, but they were rebuffed. After some refreshments were served, the visiting teenagers left the center. Instead of promoting better intergroup relations, the activity may have actually worsened them. Poor planning resulted in a hardening of attitudes.

A better procedure might have been to invite a joint committee from both centers to actively participate in planning the evening. The activity should not have begun without all parties in attendance. There should have been some kind of mixer scheduled first. Exclusionary practices could have been frustrated if diversionary activities had been planned so that intermingling would have been mandatory. Intergroup contacts are not facilitated through dances. The setting has proved to be too formidable and formal. Dance requires overt behaviors from age-group members who are typically reserved among their own friends, and more so among comparative strangers. Other activities, previously planned, such as sports contests, exhibitions, and so on, might have been a more productive lead-up to the dance.

Instructional Consequences

The entire range of instructional technique is geared to behavior modification through the promotion of critical and social skills and, sometimes, by heightening self-perception and altering personal attitudes toward the self and others.[21] Modifying behavior by augmenting an individual's knowledge about particular issues, things, and concepts is typical of all educational procedure. With the assimilation of more factual information, different behavior may be likely unless the additional information is in some way qualified by a condition of related attitudes or biases pre-existing in the self-structure. Those people with the intellect and the desire can learn almost any non-emotion-provoking skill. Where there are emotional aspects to learning, however, opinions, attitudes, or referents conditioned by the social environment act as screens, changing perceptions and inducing behavioral outcomes conformably. Normally, the individual's behavior results from an intricate mixture

---

21. R. B. Lacouisiere, *The Life Cycle of Groups: Group Development Stage Theory* (New York: Human Sciences Press, 1980), pp. 188–189.

of positive and negative attitudes based upon experience and such immediate influences as situation or position. For this reason the connection of attitudes to behavior is not easily understood.

This connection has been established in many ways by psychologists. Behavior is capable of being obseved by others, and is more plastic than attitudes. Cultural standards frequently require conformity to certain expectations whether the individual actually approves or not. Thus, to avoid embarrassment, we sometimes overlook or do not comment upon obvious inaccuracies made by one person in company, even though we may wish to correct misrepresentations. To add to the confusion, attitudes do not always take priority over behavior. They occasionally change in consequence of behavior. Attitudinal modification may also result from some experience where sudden insight is gained.

This network of associations between attitudes and behavior inevitably affects instruction. It may be seen that certain attitudes concerning the disclosure of one's feelings may hamper learning. There is no way to understand how worthwhile or authentic such feelings may be unless they are revealed and information about them is interchanged. Such exposure and exchange may best be brought about in small group situations where role-playing is employed as a learning method.[22] Jourard has indicated that self-disclosure may be the essential factor for acquiring self-knowledge. He states:

> Through my self-disclosure, I let others know my soul. They can know it, really know it, only as I make it known. In fact, I am beginning to suspect that I can't even know my own soul except as I disclose it. I suspect that I will know myself "for real" at the exact moment that I have succeeded in making it known through my disclosure to another person.[23]

Attitudes are more open to change when the individual is committed to an interest and finds himself involved in an equivocal situation. Let us say that the person has undertaken a role-playing assignment. In such a situation, the group's expectations require the revelation of the inner self, and if we determine through feedback that attitudes are inconsonant or unaccountable in relation to our self-concept, we become anxious. If the social situation is empathic and the concern is strong, defensive behaviors may be avoided as the individual attempts

22. A. Blumberg and R.T. Golembiewski, *Learning and Change in Groups* (Middlesex, England: Penguin Books, 1976), pp. 25–28.
23. S. Jourard, *The Transparent Self: Self-Disclosure and Well-being* (Princeton, N.J.: D. Van Nostrand and Company, 1964), p. 10.

to subdue the disagreement or the sense of vagueness which confound him.

The results of modifications of self which derive from different instructional methods—case method, role-playing, discussion groups, self-study, T-groups, etc.—will differ with the stage of concentration.[24] Where the focus remains on a record of experiences concerning other people rather than on the person who is learning to change, perceptual modifications may be anticipated in social conduct as participants relate to the social circumstance in the group. Cognitive alterations will also occur in the participants' comprehension of social and psychological phenomena. Group members will develop such fundamental skills as observing, analyzing social conduct, and taking pertinent action. However, until the leader introduces the group members, or individual, to an intensive regard of personal attitudes and emotions, modification of values and subsequently of personal inner behavior will not occur. Thus, cognitive alterations may take place which affect the social self, but not the subjective self.

Sustaining a reduced state of personal concern, a typical representation of the case method and role-playing techniques, is simultaneously more beneficial and less gainful in comparison to more comprehensive kinds of personal instruction. The instructional environment may be intentionally designed to handle inner values and attitudes that comprise formidable barriers to necessary personal growth and development. The result should be more effective behavior. The particular aims of instructional methods are to modify personal values, enhance interpersonal skills, and augment the effectiveness of groups in gaining their goals. Sometimes effort centers on only one of these objectives, sometimes several, and often on all at the same time. Therefore, the consequences of instruction are associated with positive modifications in cognition, communication skills, openness to experience, emotional adaption, sensitivity, and other facets of human behavior.

The Formulation of the Modification Process

Modification is a process which insists upon the development of the individual's capacity to modify himself through a unique form of association between the leader (catalyst) and the person or persons to be changed. People do have the ability to learn new ways to perceive and behave as they respond to an empathic and interpersonal

---

24. R. D. Mann, *Interpersonal Styles and Group Development* (New York: John Wiley & Sons, 1967), pp. 76–79, 163–178.

environment. Although individual personality has probably been crystalized by the age of twelve (some psychologists say it is an even earlier age), there is no need for any individual to remain trapped at some indeterminate point, always answering to situations in ingrained childhood ways. People must discover their own capacities as they interact with others. Humans tend to coordinate their efforts and act cooperatively when they perceive support and enabling behavior in others.

The fundamental assumption is that man's inclination toward positive behavior can be guided and made to predominate. When individuals are offered the opportunity, they can reach logical conclusions about themselves and, in coordination with others, participate in helpful and encouraging relationships. Among the techniques which can be employed to good effect are those which tend to reflect the learner's self-motivated approaches to acceptance, openness of communication, a supportive psychological atmosphere, and innovation. The application of these attributes to normal interpersonal relationships in group life is a necessary concomitant.

Finally, group participation in the decision-making process is a corollary to what is typically thought of as the practice of democratic principles and the utilization of interpersonal references as the basis for such practice. It is concerned with the decentralization of authority and widespread acceptance of group-based ideas, plans, and programs. It is apparent that this signifies the need among members of a group or personnel of an institution for personal attention and involvement in the expression of group or organizational aims and the various ways they are to be achieved.

While there are some who decry the operation of group participation in the decision-making process because it lengthens the time within which decisions will be reached, or promotes other problems, the evidence for such application is compelling. For the group, it means the inclusion of all members in a process designed to create ego-identification with group goals and thus perpetuate cohesion and viscidity. For organizational bodies, it permits access to expertise so that decisions can be reached intelligently. Essentially, it means commissioning those with the skill and knowledge to act on problems confronting the agency rather than relying only on those with authority of position. It encourages the idea that knowledge may be gained from all levels of institutional operation and not only from positions at the highest rank. If all personnel could be involved in the decision-making process, the sum of the human potential for innovation might be directed toward highly beneficial ends. Democratizing institutional society encourages personal involvement with the tasks to be completed and, consequently, provides the incentive for individuals to perform more effectively. Additionally, ego-identification with group goals or agency objectives makes participants eager to assure their success and accept responsibility for them. People who are in the midst of the continuous process of decision-making are more likely to be receptive to change, if only because they can more fully appreciate the necessity for change. In the process of group or agency decision-making, the vital task of the leader, whether as supporter, enabler, or facilitator, is assisting in developing cohesiveness, esprit de corps, better interpersonal relations, and the openness required to reduce the prejudice that typically accompanies defensive behavior. The outcome is greater individual, group, or institutional maturity and progress.

QUESTIONS FOR DISCUSSION

1. Contrast two opposing positions concerning human nature in terms of organizational structure.
2. What is individualization?
3. Why does internal tension develop?
4. What are defense mechanisms?
5. Why do people tend to erect protective barriers between themselves and others?
6. What is the phenomenological self and how does its protection explain human behavior?
7. How does human personality develop?
8. How does interpersonal communication operate?
9. How do personal referents influence behavior?
10. How does manipulation enter into the interpersonal behavior process?
11. What techniques can a leader utilize to assist followers' self-growth?

BIBLIOGRAPHY

Altman, Irwin and Dalmas A. Taylor, *Social Penetration: The Development of Interpersonal Relationships* (New York: Irvington Publishers, 1983).

Bittner, John R., *Each Other: An Introduction to Interpersonal Communication* (Englewood Cliffs, N.J.: Prentice-Hall, Inc., 1983).

Bormaster, Jeffrey S. and Carol L. Treat, *Building Interpersonal Relations through Talking, Listening, Communicating* (Austin, Texas: Pro-Ed, 1982).

Carr, Jaqueline B., *Communicating and Relating*, 2d ed. (Dubuque, Ia.: Wm. C. Brown Co., Publishers, 1984).

Chelune, Gordon J. and others, *Self Disclosure: Origins, Patterns, and Implications of Openness in Interpersonal Relationships* (San Francisco: Jossey-Bass, Inc., Publishers, 1979).

Cooper, Cary L. and Clayton Alderfer, *Advances in Experimental Social Processes* (Englewood Cliffs, N.J.: Prentice-Hall, Inc., 1982).

DeVito, Joseph A., *The Interpersonal Communication Book*, 3d ed. (New York: Harper & Row, Publishers, 1983).

Eisler, Richard M., and Lee W. Fredericksen, *Perfecting Social Skills: A Guide to Interpersonal Behavior, Development* (New York: Plenum Publishing Corporation, 1981).

Halloran, Jack, *Activity Guide to Applied Human Relations*, 2d ed. (Englewood Cliffs, N.J.: Prentice-Hall, Inc., 1983).

CHAPTER FOUR

Communication, Knowledge, and Leadership

Leadership is a special relationship between two or more people and intimately involves processes of empathy and communication. Whereas science is concerned with the accumulated knowledge related to the methods and behaviors of leadership, communication deals with the application of techniques. The presumption that this knowledge can be learned is a fundamental precept.

WHAT IS KNOWLEDGE?

The mere collection and isolation of facts does not constitute science. If this were true, all of the reliable knowledge outside of "pure science" would be considered inferior to scientific content. Science defined as a method, however, broadens the scope of possibility and permits the inclusion of various aspects of knowledge and theory. A scientific method which justifies the inclusion of knowledge into one of the many areas of science relies upon standardized process. Such a process usually contains basic steps and procedures which when followed lead to the validation of some concept or principle.

Beyond the method of science is a scientific attitude which is probably the most important discipline this field has imposed upon humans. Of the many interrelating parts of this attitude, the spirit of adventuring into the unknown is a primary motive. Pushing back the barriers of ignorance and investigating phenomena which have never before been conceived, much less perceived, result in a constant source of inspiration. The continual quest to widen man's horizons and find new ways to gain dominion over the world of things is the basis of this attitude. The spirit of science believes in progress and in the infinite perfectability of man. The intellectual achievements of science provide the knowledge and increase the realm of human understanding. Leadership employs scientifically developed knowledge and humanizes it through self-understanding and interpersonal relations.

Knowledge and Function

Knowledge is essential to human development and learning. Without knowledge, there is no possibility of understanding the world around us or of communicating with others.

Knowledge is the acquisition of a wide variety of facts, theories, principles, and symbols all relating to our environment and giving meaning and significance to the things which we see, hear, feel, taste, or smell. The accumulation of experience, both direct and vicarious, also provides knowledge. For example, functioning within a particular set of circumstances or under specific or general conditions provides the human organism with an immediate and direct knowledge about the situation in question. However, it is just as important to have knowledge about a place, thing, or person without having experienced personal contact. Depending upon the subject matter, the value of direct or vicarious knowledge will be judged.

Knowledge may be derived by observation, experimentation, classification, and conceptualization. Observation and experimentation are processes of gathering knowledge by direct means, while classification and conceptualization are intellectualization or theorizing processes in which the imagination may add knowledge which the senses may not perceive.

Knowledge may be considered from an objective or subjective point of view. Thus, anything which can be perceived may be qualified in terms of subject-oriented symbols or in terms of the object. The subject refers to the individual who is making the observation, examination, or classification. The medial proposition is the one more likely to be valid under most circumstances. The medial view indicates both subjective and objective comprehension of things in terms of individual perception. This takes form as a co-relational view wherein any knowledge may be explained in completely associated or coincidental ways. Anything which is known may be known only insofar as the subject is aware of it. Any object contains only those properties which are given to it by the subject and which therefore tend to define the subject according to what he understands or is aware of in the object.

Knowledge and the Senses

Knowledge emerges from the individual's sensory perceptions. It is primarily through the senses that the physical environment is interpreted to the human organism. Sense perception depends largely on the physiological excellence of the various organs or receptors, which consist of specialized cells highly sensitive to a particular stimulus but relatively insensitive to other kinds of stimuli. Thus the taste buds are stimulated by dissolved substances, the retina of the eye by light waves, and Corti's organ in the ear by sound waves. Such receptors are intimately connected to the cerebrospinal nervous system, and their stimulation summons forth body responses—the adjustment of the entire organism, or any of its parts, to the specific environmental condition which was the origin of the stimulus. To a considerable extent it is unlikely that any learning will take place without sensory perception.

Emotional imbalance, artificial stimulation, or physiological malfunction may and frequently do throw sense organs out of kilter. Under conditions of stress, the organism may perceive objects which in reality are either wholly imaginary or else distorted in some way, usually by abnormal vision, smell, or hearing. For example, pressure from a brain tumor may produce an olfactory sensation which is quite different from what is actually present. Certain forms of mental disease produce illusions and hallucinations which are very vivid and real for the sick person, but which are, nevertheless, totally imagined. Psychosomatic illnesses may be traced to emotional disturbances which, in turn, affect receptors.

It may be shown that the knowledge arising from sensory perceptions is not only formulated by the quality of the sense organs and the environment which produces the stimulus, but also by the psychological, social, and physiological condition of the individual. As this is true, it follows that knowledge gained through the senses is composed of mental as well as physical states, and what the individual perceives is closely related to the way in which he receives the stimulus at any given time.

Knowledge also emerges from reason. Reasoning, or analytical formulation of symbolic systems, serves as a guide in the perception of things. To the extent that a person is sensitive to specific objects, he is guided by his concepts of what that object is or means. It is through reasoning that sense perceptions are conditioned. The individual sees, hears, tastes, touches, or smells what he conceptualizes to be the reality of the object. An example of this can be seen when an individual is made to believe that something he is going to touch will be very hot. Even if the substance turns out to be ice, the individual will pull his hand away from the coldness, upon first contact, as though it were actually hot. Only with repeated tactile contact and verbal assurance that it is ice he is touching will the person begin to be aware of coldness rather than heat. Knowledge, therefore, is not only a product of the senses, but also of reason which makes logical and understandable all that the individual perceives in his physical world.

Knowledge and Communication

Knowledge is power. To know is to be able to do. This value is the most important. Knowledge has a social dimension because knowledge is created and arises out of social contact. Knowledge has its chief utilization within the human family. The associations and connections developed in a social environment employ knowledge to bring sense and order out of the physical and natural forces which impinge upon man. Since knowledge is basically of use to human society, there must be some common means by which it is readily transmissible. Such transmission and interpretation is expressed as the process of communication.[1]

Leadership is concerned with social issues, human relations, and the dynamics of human interaction, so it is necessary that there be accumulated a body of fact and theory concerning this phenomenon in order that the intangibles can be understood and easily learned. The underlying premise of this process is hidden within the social forces of our times. Through knowledge, the methods by which leadership may be implemented, studied, and made understandable will become a part of the educational preparation received from institutions responsible for transmitting human experience.

As leadership emerges from the myths and common misconceptions which commonly surround it and sometimes submerge it, it will fulfill its basic social function: the promulgation of ultimate aims, values, and decisions of what is trivial and poor and what is significant and worthwhile in human society. The rapidly growing body of knowledge produced by research in the natural and physical sciences, as well as in the applied social sciences, has greatly changed our ideas of human growth, nature, development, and the infinite perfectability of the human being and his society.

With knowledge has come the belief that the nature of human personality and learning can be neither confined by subservience to some artificially created ideology nor suppressed by force. Conformity, mediocrity, and isolation are not possible or congruent with the new supply of knowledge. As Thomas Jefferson stated, "Enlighten the people generally, and tyranny and the oppression of mind and body will vanish like evil spirits at the dawn of day."[2] Jefferson was vitally concerned with science, education, and human freedom. He revealed

---

1.   J. E. Baird, Jr. and S. B. Weinberg, *Communication: The Essence of Group Synergy* (Dubuque, Iowa: Wm. C. Brown Company, Publishers, 1977), pp. 8–14.
2.   Paul L. Ford, ed., *The Writings of Thomas Jefferson* (New York: G.P. Putnam's Sons, 1892–99), Vol. 6, p. 592.

this concern in a letter written to Dr. Willard from Paris in 1789, when he said, "Liberty is the great parent of science and of virtue; and a nation will be great in both in proportion as it is free."[3]

Knowledge and Leadership

Our challenge in the face of the abundant and widely distributed knowledge is directly related to our national moral and ethical tone. We have not followed the admonishments of Jefferson. Just as muscle tone is lost with disuse, so, too, is moral fiber weakened and then atrophied with misuse or no use. The moral code among "leaders" in such diverse areas of human affairs as economics, politics, and the professions, leaves much to be desired. There are unethical methods used to conduct the state, the nation, human vocations, and spiritual enlightenment. A revision of some of these methods is a vital future challenge which may be met through the knowledge of leadership and its applications.

Leadership, as knowledge indicates, is inseparable from democratic principle. There is only one type of leadership—that which has influence with people because they want to follow, not because of pressure or fear of a physical, mental, economic, political, religious, or social nature. Dictatorship, anarchy, or laissez-faire are not forms of leadership; there are no true leaders who are not democratic. There may be individuals who control the means to exact accord, but they are not true leaders in the sense of this discussion. They may have power over people through use of coercive devices, but this is not leadership. Rather, it is headship, demagoguery in extreme form, or dictatorship.

The knowledge provided by science, and the concepts provided by philosophy, psychology, and education, absolutely forbid authoritarianism. Power through fear has no place in true leadership. The headship concept must make way for a democratic institution which attains its objectives by creating a spirit of cohesiveness, high morals, and cooperation in the group and in society at large.

Only where there is knowledge can the battle for human integrity, morality, and intellectual achievement be won. It is generally understood that people of purpose may commune. With knowledge, the last hindrance to human relationships is stripped away and a community of discourse arises. This is communication. The social view of knowledge leads one to the logical conclusion that only when the truth is universally established can understanding occur.

---

3. H. A. Washington, ed., *The Writings of Thomas Jefferson* (Washington, D.C.: United States Congress, 1853-59), Vol. 3, p. 17.

Knowledge validates and sets up the standards by which truth shall be known.

THE COMMUNICATION PROCESS

The study of leadership has been partly concerned with a reappraisal of the communication process in human relations, and with a redefinition of how and why leadership occurs. The study of interrelations and systems of communication has been especially prominent.[4] One of Gibb's statements is:

> One feature of a group which affects its leadership, as well as all other aspects of its performance, is the communication system or pattern available to it. It is impossible, of course, to exaggerate the importance of communication in group behavior. Communication is the process by which one person influences another and is therefore basic to leadership. . . . And it is to be expected that restrictions upon communication can affect perceptions of leadership.[5]

The communications process is central to leadership. All knowledge relative to group and individual behavior is utilized in the process. To communicate, one must understand several areas: human feeling; possible problem solutions; analyses of data relevant to any conflicts of interest in the group; the decision-making function; and, finally, the method by which one person reacts and interacts with one or more other individuals.

Communication, Coordination, and Modification

Among the interpersonal processes vital to any understanding of the leadership phenomenon are communication, coordination, and modification. Of these, the essential function is communication. All leadership is based upon an idea which one individual attempts to transmit to others.[6] It is the process of transmission—as well as reception—of verbal and symbolic thought, the nuances generated by tone, gesture, stance, and visual impact, which dominates leadership attempts. The unspoken language of manner, emotion, and

---

4.   C. A. Inoko and J. Schopler, *Experimental Social Psychology* (New York: Academic Press, 1972), pp. 422–427.
5.   Cecil A. Gibb, "Leadership," in Gardner Lindzey and E. Aronson, eds., *The Handbook of Social Psychology*, (Reading, Mass.: Addison-Wesley Publishing Company, 1969), Vol. 4, p. 241. Reprinted by permission.
6.   L. Berkowitz, *Group Processes* (New York: Academic Press, 1978), pp. 158–160.

expression may do much to clarify intent or may completely disrupt the interchange of ideas.

Associated with and contingent upon communication is the union of individuals into a cohesive force. The ability of individuals to pool their resources, subordinate personal goals for group goals, and work together for the common good is the process of coordination. At a time when specialization and division of labor often block integration, there remains the need for widespread sharing of functions if tasks are to be accomplished in the most efficient and effective way. Underlying this need is the human process of interpersonal relationships. The unity of purpose gained through voluntary association can only be developed when each individual clearly understands the benefit to be derived from interdependent activity.

Closely related to and similarly dependent upon the processes of communication and coordination is modification. Modification is understood as the transformation of personal values, outlook, or biases in one or more individuals involved in a relationship. Achieving coordination may require the element of compromise, where each party accepts a modified attitude toward a given person, place, or object. To the extent that emotions lie at the core of most interpersonal relationships, modification will depend upon the degree of involvement and the strength of accord that can be attained. Intensive involvement may demand radical modification. In such an environment, significant learning is promoted because antagonistic reactions are reduced, thus enhancing interpersonal insight and emotional support.

Each of the three processes described above has a bearing upon the others. Directed communication is impossible when those at whom the communication is aimed will not make the effort to understand or to combine complementary abilities and information toward a common cause. Unless there is some basis for modification, there cannot be mutually determined understanding. When individuals are unable to set aside hostile points of view or compromise to achieve a desired end, there is no foundation for coordination. Simultaneously, comprehension of the process of communication can eliminate much distortion of meaning and open up avenues of information so that antagonism is minimized and empathy is maximized. Communication may do much to effect cooperative endeavors for combined action; modification can be both outcome and causative agent in the encouragement of communication and coordination.

Communication is one of the fundamental methods by which leaders function and by which they may be identified. The effectiveness of communication is of supreme importance between groups and between individuals within a group. It is the skill of sending and receiving information, the establishment of rapport between the leader and the led, and the process of identification and projection. It involves the expression of the self to others and the ability to perceive meanings, recognize behavior for what it is worth, and understand what others are trying to say.

Communication requires the talent of patient listening, watching, and interpretation. In order to have communication there must be a two-way line of exchange, transmission and reception.

The Significance of Communication

Communication is basic to human life and association. It is probably valid to state that without communication there would be no human beings as we now interpret the term. There would, most likely, have been no human communities without communication. Communities and association have developed only as wants and needs were expressed by commonly understood sounds. Without the cooperation that is necessary for human communities to become organized, interpersonal relationships could never be formed. Effective leadership is achieved when another person's cooperation in accomplishing a specific objective is obtained through the process of communication.[7]

For the moment, let us consider communication as a process and how it affects interpersonal relationships from which leadership may emerge. The process of communication cannot be readily understood until language comprehension is attained. Language is the essential form of human communication. If language were nonexistent, there could be no remembrance of the past nor conjecture about the possibilities of the future. Without language, the range of man's universe would be completely minimized. Beyond its definitive function of directing one's attention to a person, place, thing, or idea, language promotes the formation of ideas about things, their qualities and properties. Language permits abstraction, revealing a universe which is superior to personal experience.[8] If we had to depend upon personal experience for knowledge, we would be limited indeed. Abstraction allows learning about things, people, and places which we will only experience vicariously. We begin to know as we verbalize:

---

7. M. L. DeFleur and O. N. Larsen, *The Flow of Information* (New York: Harper and Brothers, 1958), p. 31.
8. N. D. Gardner, *Group Leadership* (Washington, D.C.: National Training and Development Service Press, 1974), pp. 60–61, 62–63, 69.

"Man, the talking animal, not only talks but he talks about talking."[9]

Language is necessary to the formation of interpersonal relationships and, by extension, of groups. The group's aims, standards, expectations, and attitudes are directly related to shared communication. Language is the instrument by which groups may be formed and maintained. Initially, language creates role relationships which may be viewed as status molding. How one person addresses another assists in defining relationships.[10] Second, language opens the way to group acceptability and accessibility. Unless the individual uses the terminology (jargon) of the group, which has a tendency to reassure, support, and indicate common attitudes and values, the individual seeking membership may be rejected.

Of course, there is unspoken as well as verbalized language. It is a speech of gestures, facial expressions, physical symbols, and signs. All of these constitute a quite distinct language which transmits information as effectively, if more subtly, than does speech.[11] Because the very essence of social existence is founded in the communication process, both verbal and symbolic, the art of communication assumes major proportions in the development of interpersonal relationships and the possibility of emergent leadership. A great deal can be learned about group coalescence from attention to the language and communication pathways utilized by the members. It is equally important to understand that both social reality and group viscidity can be altered by language.

Personal Involvement

If leadership is the gaining of cooperation from another, then communication is certainly the indispensable way in which it is elicited. Communication proceeds on several planes. One plane, perhaps the simplest, is the transmission of information between persons without any emotional exchange whatsoever. This may best be exemplified by a passenger asking a bus driver about advantageous stopping points closest to his destination. It may be observed as a professor provides some historical or scientific fact to a class. Such transfers of data should not evoke emotion and therefore are accepted easily in response to generalized needs for information. If there is a

9. John E. Baird, Jr. and S. B. Weinberg, *Communication the Essence Group Synergy* (Dubuque, Iowa: Wm. C. Brown Company, 1977), p. 26.

10. D. M. Schneider and G. C. Homans, "Kinship Terminology and the American Kinships System," *American Anthropologist*, Vol. 57 (1955), pp. 1194–1208.

11. Ibid.

language barrier, however, all communication stops, becomes frustrated, and may terminate in hurt feelings or reinforced stereotypes.

A second level of communication might be explained in terms of mutual dependencies, such as those which typically occur in organizational contexts. On this plane, associations between superiors and subordinates may involve relational problems concerning norms, judgments, opinions, and attitudes. These can be reduced by the expectations of each party about the behavior of the other. If status-casting differences are confirmed and accepted, and value variations and rewards are in agreement with these differences, then communication and its outcome—cooperation—can occur without too great an expenditure of effort.

The most complicated level of communication is that which involves interpersonal relations. Here strong emotional ties become significant. The consequences of an encounter may produce results ranging from complete harmony and accord to outright distrust, hostility, misunderstanding, and aggression. In the former, the self-appreciation systems and relevant values of the parties concerned are consonant and reciprocally supportive. In the latter, the inability to communicate results in a threat to these systems of one or both of the individuals involved.

In the complex of human communication, all three levels may be operating simultaneously. When this happens the course of understanding between individuals is precarious. What is said by one person to another may conceal true meaning or suppress experiences which seem threatening. Twisted meanings may occur, the explanations of which cannot be consciously perceived by the individual. What is received by the other party may or may not be consistent with reality. When this happens, there is a denial of truth or little truth to be shared.[12]

Leadership and Communication

Happily, this state of distrust or anxiety is not general and can be rectified. The act of communicating meaningfully is so necessary in carrying on the normal course of human endeavors that the process must be facilitated. Here the art of leadership comes into play. How the communication process can be improved and how self-systems and empathy are connected to communication are questions which will now be addressed.

---

12.   A. G. Athos and J. J. Gabarro, *Interpersonal Behavior: Communication and Understanding in Relationships* (Englewood Cliffs, N.J.: Prentice-Hall, Inc. 1978), pp. 50–61.

Communications Concepts

Communication begins with a source. Where a message originates and how effective its transmission will depend upon the credibility of the sender. The quality of the source is not always significant, but the credibility of information is augmented if there are compatible records from other sources. On the other hand, it is suspect if inconsistencies develop. Successful transmission is secured by easy access to communication networks.

The substance of the transmitted information also plays an important role by its effect on the receiver. Messages can be biased by reporting only one point of view, by distorting meanings through connotative word usage, or by lying. Another aspect of slanted information is the effect of anxiety-provoking messages. One study suggests that strong fear statements have less effect upon the listener than do more moderate ones.[13] Messages which reach a conclusion or press home a particular point of view seem to be more acceptable than those that place the burden of drawing conclusions upon the receiver. Repetition of content appears to be most effective with those who have had limited education or with those without great mental ability because of the opportunity to appeal to the lowest common denominator.

Directed thought is one of the more effective devices for gaining influence. This method employs existing wants, attitudes, and values instead of establishing new ones. It is easier to exploit something with which an individual already identifies than to have to build a case for an unfamiliar value. Thus, if an individual sees himself in the role of conservationist, it is relatively simple to involve that person in a cause which espouses environmental protection. This, in turn, may lead to further participation in activities dealing with mass transportation, the restriction of nuclear power plant construction, offshore oil drilling operations, use of pesticides, abolition of the federal Highway Trust Fund, or to the passage of legislation affecting the use of private property. Depending upon the person's original sense of values and degree of concern, influence may be achieved in terms of co-identification.

Bales' investigations into the implications of communication deal with informative or tension-releasing communication.[14] According to

---

13. I. F. Janis and S. Fleshbach, "Effects of Fear-Arousing Communications," *Journal of Abnormal and Social Psychology*, Vol. 48 (1953), pp. 78–92.

14. R. F. Bales, "The Equilibrium Problem in Small Groups," in T. Parsons, R. F. Bales, and E. A. Shils, eds., *Working Papers in the Theory of Action* (Glencoe, Ill.: The Free Press, 1953), pp. 111–116.

him, interpersonal communication is intimately bound up with a
homeostatic process. It appears to be composed of alternating
informational efforts which create tensions between group members
and tension-releasing communication which alleviates the stress. It is
probable that the relative balance between these facets of
communication is significant for persuasiveness. As with mechanical
systems, the behavior of a person occupied with interpersonal
communication influences and is influenced in turn by the behavior of
others. When individuals interact, communication occurs against a
mutual background of interchanged information in which reciprocal
feedback is continuous.[15]

Interpersonal Communications

Communication is related to almost every aspect of social existence.
One's attitudes and values are group oriented. An individual is usually
not receptive to communication which diverges from the norms of his
group. Messages are transmitted in the group by the group's opinion
leaders. When communication is a component of the leadership
structure, the flow is not from source to receiver, but from sender to
an intermediary (opinion leader), who then passes it on to the receiver.
Opinion leaders serve as evaluators, determining which messages will
be transmitted and analyzing the content for interpretation as they
send it along.[16]

Human communication is a reciprocal process which depends upon
the language of speech and symbol for interpretation, intensification,
and clarification. In human communication, information which is
returned to the organism so that adjustments can be made to maintain
a steady state (negative feedback) is employed to ensure continuity in
interpersonal relationships. On the other hand, positive feedback
demands modification and interrupts equilibrium with the
environment. This is true for the individual as well as for the group.
For example, there are several states of group change which have been
commented upon by Lewin and others. There is a steady state where
no change is noticeable. This is seen as a balance between positive and
negative arguments or influences. Equilibrium can be altered either by
employing pressure in the required direction, or by reducing opposing
arguments. In the first instance, the new state would be attended by
stress. In the latter case:

---

15. M. Argyle and J. Dean, "Eye-Contact, Distance, and Affiliation," *Sociometry*, Vol. 28
(1965), pp. 289–304.

16. E. Katz and P. Lazarsfeld, *Personal Influence* (Glencoe, Ill.: Free Press, 1955), p. 45.

If the resistance to change depends partly on the value which the group standard has for the individual, the resistance to change should diminish if one diminishes the strength of the value of the group standard or changes the level perceived by the individual as having social value. It is usually easier to change individuals formed into a group than to change any one of them separately.[17]

In any aspect of human communication, neither positive nor negative feedback is harmful. Each serves a specific function which is determined by the given situation. Thus, negative feedback is necessary when stability is required, and positive feedback has value when modification of behavior is needed. However, when either form of feedback operates to the exclusion of the other or persists unabated, then potential disorganization is likely and growth and development cannot take place.

Change within the individual, a group, or an organization comes from acquiring new ideas, outlooks, responses, and behaviors in relation to other people, places, things, and situations. This learning is based upon the individual's intellectual ability and interest, and the skill in overcoming barriers to learning such as healthy skepticism or a lack of self-acceptance as illustrated by defense mechanisms. To be effective, learning in interpersonal situations requires a stabilized relationship and modification on the part of the followers. In interpersonal relationships, negative feedback concerns how one's behavior affects others, while positive feedback deals with how the individual should act. The following hypothetical situation exemplifies this concept:

A group of boys at a playground requested that they be allowed to have a cookout at the barbecue pit fireplace. Several of these youngsters met with the recreationist in charge. When it came to deciding the menu, frankfurters were suggested as the main course. One youngster reminded the others that two of the other boys were Hindus and were not permitted to eat meat. Another boy stated, "Let them eat meat like everybody else! It won't hurt them."

The recreationist suggested that it would be an easy matter to provide a meatless substitute for the two Hindus. The rest of the group thought that this would be the best thing to do. The cookout was successful. The two Hindus had potato pancakes while the others ate hotdogs.

---

17. K. Lewin, "Group Decision and Social Change," in G. Swanson, T. Newcomb, and E. Hartley, eds., *Readings in Social Psychology* (New York: Henry Holt & Co., 1952), pp. 459–473.

The recreationist, as a leader, must help people to accept the diversities of custom and religion or ethnic traditions of others. In this way, the young can be assisted to become relatively receptive to differences among people. Although the recreationist's suggestion worked in this situation, it might have been better for all concerned if there had been a discussion by the entire group. This latter circumstance may have provided increased insight and an accommodation in which all might have shared.

Interpersonal communication is a mutually supporting process which has as its goal an interchange of messages between two or more people so that each can understand the other at the most personal levels. Where emotions are concerned, the problem of understanding becomes the relationship itself. Attention is placed on the intricate defense mechanisms and self-concepts of those involved. Since the individual is motivated to maintain his own integrity or unity of self by deep seated internal forces, he can facilitate this effort for the other person by his own self-perception and empathy. In this manner each can effect an openness and sense of security in the relationship which can increase the interpersonal process of communication. Newcomb and others state:

> Communication is the form of interpersonal exchange through which, figuratively speaking, persons can come into contact with each other's minds. The mechanism of communication includes the encoding, through symbols, of information; the behavioral transmission and the perceptual reception of those symbols; and their decoding. Following the exchange of a message, if the exchange has been sincere and reasonably accurate, transmitter and sender have more nearly the same information about one or more referents of the message than before. Such equalization of information is not the goal of communication; it is only a relationship between the participants, usually not recognized by them, through which the motive satisfaction to which communication is instrumental can be attained.[18]

COMMUNICATION AMONG INDIVIDUALS

Most people think of communication as the flow of verbal symbols over distance. Sometimes this idea is broadened to include the gestures or signals which are commonly understood. Communication

---

18.   T. M. Newcomb, R. H. Turner, P. E. Converse, *Social Psychology; The Study of Human Interaction* (New York: Holt, Rinehart and Winston, Inc., 1965), pp. 185–219, 219–220.

does include these forms but, in the sense of this discussion, it goes far beyond the simple aspect of transmission.

Communication concerns the relationship not only between individuals but with individuals. One must communicate with someone else in order for leadership to occur.[19] There must be awareness on the part of the recipient that an attempt is being made to reach him. Unless he "tunes in," so to speak, no communication takes place.

Awareness

We can say that awareness requires the attention of the recipient in order for him to comprehend or recognize the substance of what is transmitted to him. Such transmission may be a verbalization, gesture, stare, shrug, or sound. Even at this point, when there is conscious awareness of the transmission, communication does not take place unless there is acceptance of the message. Without acceptance, the first phase of influence with others disappears. Unless this initial process is effected, leadership cannot exist. Certain relevant factors produce a climate which may cause acceptance or rejection. They include: the thought or idea which the sender wishes to convey; the sender's personality or mannerisms; proximity of sender to the recipient; the tendency of the recipient to be biased for or against the sender; the time; the place; and, finally, the need.

Perhaps the basic necessity in the process of communication is awareness.[20] If we are not sensitive to the things around us, we cannot assign values to them, nor can we provide definitions to those things which give meaning to life. If the individual is aware of his environment, he is able to receive some sort of picture which allows him to judge what is happening around him. As long as he can understand what he is trying to do or what is happening to him, he can adjust to the changing stresses placed upon him by daily living. Sometimes an individual loses touch with reality because a lack of awareness causes situations in which he becomes so tangled that he cannot find any meaning. Such a breakdown in communication may result in the deterioration of a person, or it may cause the individual to seek ways of communication that will bring meaning to things again. The first step in opening up channels for communication is awareness and the realization of the need to do so.

Awareness provides a focus of attention on the object under

---

19. Baird and Weinberg, *Communication,* pp. 195–196.
20. Athos and Gabarro, *Interpersonal Behavior,* pp. 24–35.

consideration. In order for awareness to occur, conscious involvement with a stimulus is necessary. This means that the observer must bend his attention to the matter concerning him. Interest must be captured before attention will be given. When the attention of a person is arrested because of a particular attraction, awareness and recognition follow. In the social context, recognition generally means the granting of status and acceptance.[21]

Recognition

Awareness implies recognition. In order for one individual to be aware of another, he must recognize him as a distinct personality and accord him a certain status in the hierarchy of his social group. Recognition includes the concept of familiarity and comprehension. Thus, for an individual to be aware of something, it must be familiar to him or exhibit a pattern, behavior, shape, or form which has meaning for him. Recognition further assumes that one individual accepts another. In addition to knowing about a subject, there is a social connotation.

How many times have we observed a person on the street encountering another person who greets the former but is rebuffed by not getting a greeting in return? Most people would call this type of behavior rudeness. More than that, however, is the implication which such behavior has in terms of recognition. The individual who fails to return the salutation intentionally shows that he is not aware of the existence of the greeter. In other words, he is telling the world that he considers this person inferior and he will not deign to give his attention to so insignificant a person. Communication cannot take place between the two because there is no common bond of awareness, no recognition or status accorded, and certainly no acceptance. All of these factors must be present if there is to be an exchange of meaning.

Opportunity for Communication

The pathways open to communication between individuals are related to the frequency of interactions, the ease of maintaining the relationship, and the persons involved. Individuals have a need to express themselves. To do so, they must communicate. The medium of communication may be words, symbols (as in the visual or plastic arts), gestures, or reactions. Generally, similar interests will provide a common bond of association and thereby offer an opportunity for communication. The hobbyist, with his particular inclination for some

---

21.   R. K. Greenleaf, *Servant Leadership* (New York: Paulist Press, 1977), pp. 27–29.

subject matter or material, will go to great lengths to describe his collection. His greatest joy, however, will be in discussing the pros and cons of his hobby with others who enjoy the same interest. Common causes, ideas, or interests invariably create the need for communication.

Perhaps the greatest opportunity for communication between people comes when there is close identification with either the communicator or the idea he is attempting to transmit. Thus, communication is more likely between associates than between comparative strangers; between people who have the same religious beliefs than between non-believers; and between those who hold the same economic, political, or educational views than between those who do not.

For the leader to successfully communicate his ideas to those he wishes to follow him, he must first determine what their thoughts on particular matters are. Whether or not his ideas coincide with theirs is not important. The leader, when he knows what thoughts people hold, can adjust his views to resemble those of the group he wishes to influence. When he has gained the necessary attention to impart his views, he may slowly educate his audience to his own point of view. If it is radically different from his potential followers' orientation, he is less likely to be able to communicate and will probably not be accorded leadership status by the group.

The recreationist is afforded myriad opportunities. Since his work takes place in an extremely permissive setting, it is only logical to assume that people are already interested in the experiences provided by his agency. He is, therefore, able to make contacts with many individuals under favorable conditions. If he can communicate his ideas to others and influence their choices in the selection of activities to meet their diverse needs, he is a leader. His responsibility also includes listening for requests from people regarding which services should be offered. In order to program the activities which interest the individuals in the community, he must understand their needs.

All individuals want to talk about themselves. Each person has a need to tell others about himself, his desires, dreams, and activities. The recreational leader utilizes this knowledge of people to serve them better. By listening he is able to formulate ideas concerning personal beliefs, opinions, attitudes and background, and with this knowledge he is in a better position to understand expressed behaviors.

The leader must place himself in a position where he can readily communicate with others. It may be necessary to utilize the mass media or other audio-visual aids to capture the attention of the public. He may resort to mass meetings, speeches to whatever group will listen to him, round-table discussions, and debates with public figures where possible. He may have to become an author in order to sell his message. He may gain a following by teaching in schools and other educational institutions. He may have to become a celebrity, authority, inventor, diplomat, or entertainer in order to gain attention and have people listen to him and believe his ideas.

In recent years, with heavy television exposure, many entertainers have become powerful sources of influence in this country because of their ability to gain and hold the attention of millions of people. Whether such individuals have any knowledge of their power or even why they have this power is immaterial. Currently, the public is confronted with immoral activities in local, state, and federal governments.[22] Yet, in listening to those who would either whitewash or ridicule the entire occurrence, it seems that the public hasn't taken these activities seriously or bothered to determine the truth or falseness of the charges. Thus, people have taken two courses of action: They were shocked and then silent; or they lightly passed these matters off as part of the course of events in this society. "Everybody is doing it, everybody is a thief—if he can get away with it. Live and let live is my motto."[23] This is the all-too-prevalent attitude of those who are persuaded by listening to a few misguided, but well-placed individuals.

Opportunities for communication are unlimited. The leader takes advantage of these opportunities to press his claims and to influence others. But the leader goes beyond merely taking advantage of an opportunity. If it is not present, he manufactures it. He prepares a climate conducive for him to communicate with others. He determines what they want, why they want it, and seeks to have such inclinations identified with his goals. Thus, he adjusts himself to any situation which he finds and proceeds to gain his objectives by stressing how closely his aims resemble the wishes, needs, and opinions of the people.

Facilitating Communication

There are several basic factors which enable communication to occur. The first of these is gaining and retaining the recipient's attention. This is facilitated when the transmitted idea is identifiable

---

22.   Thomas D. Williams, "Kinsella Panel Urges Impeachment," *The Hartford Courant,* Vol. CXLVII, No. 123 (Wednesday, May 2, 1984), pp. A1, A14. Andrew H. Malcom, "Federal Jury Finds a Cook County Judge Guilty of Corruption," *The New York Times,* Vol. CXXXIII, No. 46,076 (Friday, June 16, 1984), p. A14.

23.   Arnold H. Lubasch, "Prosecutor Asserts Pisani Abused His Position to Embezzle $80,000," *The New York Times,* Vol. CXXXIII, No. 46,032 (Wednesday, May 2, 1984), p. B5.

with attitudes held by the potential recipient or is concerned with something which promises to be profitable to him. Once attention is focused upon the message, it is necessary to carry the listener along on a wave of sound, easily followed and understood. Retention will be most effective when a series of connective thoughts are given, starting with a simple premise and leading to a final objective closely related to the receiver's objective.

Ideas must be stated as precisely as possible to avoid any confusion. Unless the receiver gets the same mental picture as the conveyor wishes to establish, there is little likelihood that communication will occur. All of the facts must be available and usable by the receiver. Care should be taken to provide that information which is essential for the recipient. If the transmitter does not clearly provide all information, it is possible that vital facts which may influence the potential follower's decision may be omitted. When this happens, the premises upon which such ideas are founded may lose some of their attractiveness through illogical presentation.

The free flow of communication between individuals may be hampered or disrupted whenever there is any distance between them. Proximate distances are not only measured in linear feet but may also be considered as social, ethnic, economic, or status distances. Rarely are individuals of radically different social or economic backgrounds accepted for leadership or able to communicate with others outside their environment.

Only when the transmitter takes the time to create an atmosphere of friendly informality, or when he approaches potential receivers with the idea that he is "one of them" will he be able to break down the barriers which hinder communication. He must have the ability to develop confidence on the part of the individuals with whom he wishes to communicate, so that mutual understanding may result. With increased trust is created a climate of cooperation which yields better relations. When rapport has been established, individuals are more likely to reveal what they actually think and feel.

Empathy Development

If the leader is a person who is sensitive to the needs of his followers, he can elicit information which serves as the basis for communication. Such information is neither written nor verbal. It is, rather, the "feeling" which the leader has about individuals or the group as a whole.[24] This is generally verbalized as "getting the feel of the group,"

---

24. A. G. Athos and Gabarro, *Interpersonal Behavior*, pp. 406–408.

that is, getting to know and understand individuals and their attitudes or ideas concerning a variety of subjects.

It has often been stated, "It isn't *what* is said, but *how* something is said which gives insight into the true meaning a person places on anyone or anything." This is valid only insofar as an observer is ready and waiting for such clues about human feeling. Unless there is a sensitive person to translate the meanings of certain voice tones, gestures, facial expressions, or postures, these guideposts signifying deep-seated attitudes relating to conduct are overlooked and valueless. These sensitivities may be learned, but there is also an art to appreciating this process.

Social Veneer

Every individual has two faces. The one which he presents to the world at large may mask the emotions and inner conflicts or tensions created as a result of particularly strong feelings about occurrences in daily living:

A recreational leader was in charge of a group of boys at a private school in X community. Each afternoon they either went to the gymnasium or the nearby park to participate in a variety of recreational activities.

On a rainy spring day, cancellation of a scheduled trip to the neighborhood park was necessary. Instead, the group of seven- and eight-year-old boys, approximately twenty in number, went to the gymnasium. Once there, it was decided that a game of kick-baseball would be the feature event of the day. Teams were chosen; each side had ten boys. Positions roughly correspond to those of a softball team, except for an additional shortstop between second and first base. The worker became umpire for the game.

Tommy T, a stubby boy of eight, came to the plate with two out and two men on base. The ball was rolled up, and he kicked at it, but missed, and was called out. In the next inning, Tommy came to the plate again with two out and the bases loaded. The ball was rolled up; he took a mighty kick and again missed. In the final inning of play Tommy was once again up. A look of grim determination showed in his face. He waited for the ball and kicked it just right, and it headed on a line drive for right field. Unfortunately, Tommy was not a particularly fast runner, and by the time he reached first base the baseman had the ball and tagged him out.

This was the last straw. Tommy dissolved into tears, walked off the floor, and hid his face in his hands. The worker appointed one of the boys as umpire and walked over to Tommy, who by this time was inconsolable but trying hard to hide his feelings from the other boys. The worker took Tommy behind a partition which was conveniently placed. He gave him a handkerchief, and the boy attempted to control his tears and dry his eyes.

The worker asked what was wrong and Tommy said, "I struck out twice, and the only time I kicked the ball I was put out before reaching first. I'm no good." The worker said nothing, giving Tommy time to settle down. He then asked, "What's your favorite sport?" Tommy said it was baseball. The worker asked, "Who was the player with the most number of home runs?" "Hank Aaron," was the immediate reply. "Who was the player who had the most number of strike-outs against him in his career?" Tommy admitted that he did not know. The worker told him that Hank Aaron was credited with striking out most of all. "You see, Tommy ," he said, "in order to hit the most home runs, Hank Aaron had to miss the most times, too. A man has to try many times before he may ever get to do something right, or hit the most home runs. It really isn't so bad to miss; it's more important to keep trying. Remember, it's not how many times you miss that counts; it's the few times that you come through and connect." After the talk, Tommy said he felt better about the whole thing and wanted to try again.

What this example shows is the art of communication which was necessary in order to "get through" to the individual in question. There was no sense telling an eight-year-old about perseverance or other high-sounding but, to him, meaningless words. What was necessary was an understandable symbol with which he could identify. Once he was able to transfer the meaning of the Hank Aaron story to his own situation, he could readily see the importance of trying in the face of disaster (for him). The worker was attempting to communicate a particular idea to the boy in terms he could understand. He, therefore, had to utilize the symbols which meant something to the boy, instead of abstractions which would have meant nothing and perhaps would have served only to confuse him and not provide the support which he needed at that point. The successful recreational leader demonstrates specific behavioral patterns of empathy. The individual, for practical reasons, has learned to cover his primitive urges behind a façade of equanimity. Perhaps this is true because he has been hurt when facial expression or posture have betrayed his inner tensions and disturbed the façade he has attempted to preserve. Perhaps he has found it more expedient to assume the innocuous exterior of a blank expression for fear of exposing his true feelings about certain controversial subjects which, if known, might damage his reputation or demean his status in the eyes of some groups. All people have a second face, shown to a few intimates or exposed during moments of intense anger, frustration, or uncontrollable emotion of any kind. It reveals what the person is actually thinking or feeling at the moment. This, more than any other behavior within a socially acceptable context, presents a valid picture of character. It is the moment of truth, when all of the barriers and civilized manners are down. For that instant, when the emotions and attitudes of an individual are fully apparent, the careful observer may discover a wealth of information.

Transmission of Ideas and Feelings

Being observant, however, is not the final objective. One must know how to react to and utilize the insights which have been gained. A lifted eyebrow, a thinning of the lips, clenched jaws, thrust of neck, tightening of the facial skin, coloring of the face, or other sign is clear evidence that some strong sentiment has taken hold. Such movement may serve to reinforce what the individual is saying, but in many instances it belies what the individual is stating. If such reaction is a reinforcement, appropriate counteractions can be taken as necessary, unless there is agreement. If this is the case, then there is no need for any action except approval. If, on the other hand, the tone or expression is at variance with what is being said, the individual is obviously in conflict. Efforts to placate, soothe, or answer these unconscious reactions must be swift and sure if communication is not to be disrupted.

The attentive listener is given unmistakable clues to the feelings of the person undergoing conflict through the tone of voice, its loudness or softness, the harshness of speech, and general response to whatever the situation may be. One can sense an undercurrent of tension within other persons. They seem to exude tautness, much like the smell of fear which is recognizable to the lower animal, and have difficulty in maintaining the usual tranquility which characterizes most of us.

If the observer wants to have influence with another, and he can readily see or hear what the attitude relating to a particular subject is, he may attempt to draw the other person out a little more, appear to agree with him, or seek to show how their views coincide. This is not the time to educate or orient a person whose views are diametrically opposite. The setting for such conversion must be properly prepared. It is a fairly slow process and can occur only after some confidence has been established between the individuals.

Conversely, when the leader attempts to transmit his ideas and feelings to another individual or to groups, he must realize that there are many barriers to the creation of similar ideas or feelings. He should, therefore, create an image in the minds of those he wants to influence and make them understand what he is saying with careful use of terms. He must paint so lucid and realistic a picture that it would be difficult for another not to understand. His gestures, voice, expression, and posture must be an extension of the idea. The very atmosphere must become charged with his special electricity. He must act the role of whatever he is saying and present to all a picture of what he wants to convey. Only by completely identifying himself with the idea or feeling which he is attempting to transmit will he be entirely successful.

Communication between an Individual and a Group

One immediate challenge confronting the recreationist in any face-to-face situation in the field is the initial meeting with a new group. Wherever it occurs, that first meeting—either with a long established group or with a newly formed group—may create patterns of behavior which will always be followed thereafter, sometimes to the discouragement of the recreationist in the leader role. The problem is the recreationist's uncomfortable feeling that he may not be accepted by the group of strangers; they are strange because each arrives with preconceived and different ideas of what he wants from this group situation or gathering and because each has formed a first opinion of the worker.

Invariably, all groups treat workers or new members in approximately the same manner. All those not belonging to the established group are not accepted with open arms until they have been tested in some way. Even after the testing, the group may withhold membership status from the newcomer. The worker faces this situation with every new group to which he is assigned. The group may have to tolerate the worker, if it wants the support of the sponsoring agency which allows the use of a facility, but it does not have to accept the worker as one of its members.

Actually, the worker does not want to be accepted as a member of the group. He wants the group members to accept him as a professional, not on the same basis that they would accept a peer. This attitude should by no means be misconstrued to say that the worker feels he is superior to group members. It does mean that the worker can best provide his particular professional service if he is not considered as just another member. He is placed with the group to help it in any way he can to accomplish its aims and to aid its individual members to assume their places as responsible and effective group members. The worker does this best by working indirectly in his role as leader. He serves as a resource rather than an advocate; a guide and confidant rather than a director; depending upon the abilities, background, experience, resourcefulness, and confidence shown by members of the group.

The Testing Situation

Communication between the worker and a group still relies upon the foundation of mutual trust necessary for any transfer of ideas to occur. No group accepts or rejects without some trial period before making a decision. This is a "feeling out" time, a measuring and appraisal of intentions. A push here, a prod there, a casual remark, a meaningful glance or word, and the lines are drawn. The question being asked is: What are the limitations?

Some groups are comparatively easy to enter. These are groups of very young children, older adults, middle-aged adults, or groups without traditions. The other age groups are fairly suspicious of newcomers and especially of assigned workers. This is true because such groups are more concerned with their prerogatives, whereas the other age groups either do not care about the decision-making process or cannot participate in decision-making to any great degree.

With groups which are quite concerned about their goals and methods of attaining them and which have an initial distrust of anybody who is imposed upon them, the problem of establishing rapport and communication is the most pressing and perhaps most difficult. Once communication and understanding have been fostered, much conflict may be overcome and much distrust can be dispelled. A case in point concerns the incident of the crippled Bears:

> I was assistant superintendent for plant and maintenance operations in a large west coast department of recreational service. The division for which I was responsible had just purchased a number of all-purpose power equipment tractors called Bears. These vehicles were new to me and my division. The Bear Company representative sent to assist the division with any difficulties that might arise due to technical problems was a master mechanic named Harris.
>
> The mechanical section of the division had been segregated into two crews, one crew for motor maintenance and one for maintenance of the electric console which operated the Bears' attachments—cherry picker, backhoe, etc. A leading foreman was in charge of each crew, and the district foreman had twenty-five years of experience in the park system, most of which had been spent in natural resource development, landscaping, and grounds

maintenance. This was his first assignment to the mechanical aspect of plant maintenance and he seemed to have a "short-timer" attitude.

Five days after the Bears had been received and were operational, we began to experience abnormal mechanical difficulties. The superintendent called me into his office for an explanation. I could not give him one satisfactory reason for the failures. I called the district foreman and asked him about the crippled Bears. He replied that the Bears were unsatisfactory, and that he was having too many problems getting the crews properly trained to handle the equipment to be concerned about mechanical failures. A conference with the lead foreman and the district foreman revealed that Mr. Harris was telling the men how to do their jobs and this was causing considerable friction. The district foreman was transferring crew men around in their jobs. The men did not understand why, or even feel sure that there were sufficient reasons for these job changes.

I knew that I had to use all of Mr. Harris's technical expertise to obtain maximum performance from the Bears. But how could I settle the situation between the Bear representative and Mark, the district foreman, between Harris and the men, between Mark and the men?

The essential problem was the relationships between personnel dealing with the machines. Obviously technical knowhow was available to produce maximum machine performance. What was absent, and contributing to the difficulties experienced, was a cohesiveness and group spirit which could have stimulated cooperation instead of conflict.

Behavioral scientists who have researched the phenomenon of group dynamics and activities have come to a conclusion that should be readily apparent when dealing with collective interpersonal relations: there is a vast difference between being *in* or *out* of a group. Until an individual is accepted as a member of a group, he is an outsider and as such is neither treated in a way that will relieve tensions nor will he be accorded anything but the least civilities. It does not matter about personality, knowledge, or discipline. The person who is, for the moment, outside the group is barely provided with whatever amenities there are to be had. In this case, both the Bear representative and the district foreman are outsiders. In Harris's case, he is not even an employee of the department. His expertise as a master mechanic is overlooked. At the same time, the in-group maintenance men are asking themselves why an outsider is permitted to issue orders in the first place.

The district foreman is an outsider because he has never been associated with mechanical maintenance work. There are all kinds of psychological reasons for the crew men to reject his authority. Mark has not shown a great deal of interest in becoming a part of the in-group; what appears to be a "short-timer" attitude is attributable to his coming retirement.

The study of insiders and outsiders is most valuable. It is concerned with group cohesiveness, permeability, and cooperative effort. Conversely, it is also concerned with hostility, noncooperation, and outright rejection in some instances. Additionally, not only are Harris and Mark outsiders, but other factors also impinge upon the situation. Men do not like to be told how to perform a task which they believe they already know. If they recognize the fact that they lack technical proficiency and experience, they will typically tolerate or even welcome advice and training from someone with proved ability. Such technical know-how should be provided in a straight-forward manner, never condescendingly. More importantly, a public demonstration should not be made of the matter; no individual's mistakes should be pounced upon, nor should anyone be made to look ridiculous in the eyes of his group.

The outsider is in a precarious position to instruct insiders. He must keep in mind and display the idea that he is there to assist and nothing more. On the other hand, he has the advantage that outsiders tend to be seen as experts, and generally will be looked upon with favor. If he performs in ways that are designed to get along with everyone he comes in contact with, there is every likelihood that he will be welcomed as an insider. In this instance, the district foreman made the situation more tense by making new job assignments without indicating the reasons. Significantly, the men were not convinced that there really was a reason for job changes. A person likes to think that he can do his job as well as anybody and far better than most people. Usually, a foreman or supervisor should attempt to prepare a man for a job to which he is best suited, and then retain him in that position for as long as it is appropriate. When there is any reason to reassign a person, it should not be done abruptly and without explanation. Failure to offer logical explanations for transfers or job shifts not only hurts morale, but it occasionally causes loss of personnel who might otherwise have been retained for many productive years.

Communication is an extremely important process which should be kept operable in job situations. Not only is personal security and dignity involved, but the question of rapport—mutual respect and confidence—becomes a factor. People resent impersonal treatment. They want to be accorded equitable treatment and told about all plans for work responsibilities and new assignments. Humans, unlike animals, will not stand for herding. When peremptory shifts are inflicted on the individual he begins to lose his security. Unless the individual can rely upon some certainties, he starts to entertain doubts about job security and his own competency. If an individual is moved around without so much as a simple explanation, then self-doubt sets in. Moreover, failure of communication results in mistrust.

Realizing all of these issues, the assistant superintendent should probably contact the Bear representative to discuss problems. The lead foreman of each crew should also be called in for informal conferences. The assistant superintendent will have to explain that he understands the general unfamiliarity with the Bears, and he might indicate that in their initial use the crews did very well on their job assignments, and that he is very satisfied. But since the section has been experiencing mechanical breakdowns, what are their opinions about the reasons for these failures? After an evaluation of the views, the assistant superintendent could advise the lead foremen that steps will be taken to clarify the situation and alleviate whatever misunderstandings had arisen. However, since they are primarily responsible for the efficiency of the section, they are immediately required to see that the machines perform well. The essential purpose of the machines is to do the most effective job possible for the department, and the crewmen and all concerned have to do their best regardless of personality problems.

After the lead foremen returned to their crews, the assistant superintendent might diplomatically describe the situation as he sees it to Mr. Harris and to the district foreman. He could suggest to Harris that he remembers how it must have been when he was an apprentice and how no foreman wants to be bypassed by anybody and feels particularly sensitive when someone attempts to give orders to his subordinates directly instead of going through him. All people in supervisory positions tend to feel this way.

The assistant superintendent's approach to the district foreman should be considerate but firm. He should make Mark understand that he is aware that personnel shifts must occur from time to time, but that such shifts should be held to a minimum and that sound reasons should be given for any changes. He should emphasize that the district foreman is in a key position and he is supervising two groups. A good supervisor makes the lead foremen run their own operations to the greatest degree possible. The district foreman should concentrate his attention on overall planning, seeing that the crews are coordinating their efforts and cooperating as much as can be expected. Perhaps the district foreman does not have a "short-timer" attitude at all, but is reacting to the fact that on a new assignment, after years of experience with other kinds of responsibilities, he is an outsider to the mechanical crews. It is possible that having been given outsider treatment he is throwing his weight around to assure himself that he is still the boss. If the assistant superintendent can make the district foreman feel important because of his responsibilities, the man will probably delegate the details of operation to his lead foremen and concern himself with coordinating the entire program.

In the same way, Mr. Harris, the Bear representative, may be reminded that giving orders to crewmen is not part of his prerogative as technical advisor. The lead foremen are capable of handling all such matters, giving him the opportunity to focus on the important technical problems and providing the instructional assistance necessary to teach the men how to handle them. These methods may be the basis for finding the solution to the relational problems that crop up when outsiders are confronted with a closely knit group. Groups generally test outsiders. Either by active or passive resistance they tend to make things difficult for the individual who confronts them. Such resistance should not be taken personally because this is a common occurrence. Rather, efforts should be made to make oneself acceptable to the group as necessary in order to accomplish the determined objective.

Initial Contact

Enthusiasm for the assignment and personal confidence in one's own ability to carry out the responsibilities of the position are, of course, of great benefit to any recreationist who functions as a leader. Nevertheless, even the most enthusiastic and confident worker must be careful in transmitting his ideas to the group and interpreting their feelings and thoughts. The free flow of ideas does not occur in an atmosphere of tension or misunderstanding. A climate must be established that encourages thought and exchange of opinions and discourages the creation of ill-will and conflict.[25] The key to producing such a climate is understanding. The initial meeting may produce stony ground where nothing will grow or, through the recreationist's ability to understand himself and others, there may be a fertile field where interpersonal relations and the exchange of ideas can flower.

---

25. H. B. Trecker and A. R. Trecker, *Working with Groups, Committees & Communities* (Chicago: Association Press, 1979), pp. 43–45.

Initial contact with any group of people can be satisfying and stimulating or frustrating and negative. Since turnabout has always been considered fair play, the entire question of group acceptance of the worker hinges upon the worker's acceptance of each member of the group. To the extent that the recreationist is able to accept other people as they are, rather than as he would have them be, the first meeting may pave the way for additional responsive relations. The professional must utilize his skill in understanding the behavior of individuals within a group context: why they are there; what they are seeking; what their particular talents, abilities, and weaknesses are. He must be willing and able to accept them as they are.

The recreationist who has developed the skill of listening can demonstrate by the careful attention he pays to individuals and the group as a whole that he is clearly more concerned with the plans, ideas, and goals of those he serves than with the promotion of his own self-concepts, aims, and methods. Recognizing that the recreationist accepts them and is interested in their problems, the group is more likely to accept the worker.

Building Rapport

At the outset, the recreationist should be most concerned with his impact upon individuals within the group rather than upon programming or structuring. Personal contact and social sensitivity are required. The worker must begin to obtain information about and become acquainted with group members, but he cannot interrogate or demand answers to an extent that causes friction and distortion of motive.

The first contact between the recreationist and his group, or with any people to whom he is assigned, will pose many problems and questions. Each will want to know something about the other. The group is eager to learn whether he is there to support them or to command them, to assist them in activities which they consider necessary or to direct them in activities for some other purpose. The group is interested in the worker's personality: his permissiveness, agreeableness, sense of humor, strictness, and whatever other characteristics he possesses.[26]

The worker's natural questions will concern his relationship to the group and their response to him. He is interested in membership intelligence, group cohesiveness, esprit de corps, any indigenous

---

26. E. K. Marshall and P. O. Kurtz, *Interpersonal Helping Skills* (San Francisco: Jossey-Bass Publishers, 1982), p. 487.

leaders, backgrounds, abilities, and whether or not they will accept him. Such questions will arise automatically during the first meeting.

It is natural to experience a twinge of anxiety at these initial meetings. Such doubt is not unique to any one individual. The most successful or understanding leaders have faced and continue to face this problem every time they are in an unfamiliar situation. Gaining knowledge of certain skills, techniques, and experiences at other meetings with other groups will help to alleviate many of the uncomfortable sensations associated with these circumstances, but that hollow feeling we usually associate with fear or danger still persists. There is good cause for that feeling. No one can say with any certainty how individuals will react at any given time. The whole question of human nature involves an unknown factor, not entirely understood by anybody. Human nature can never be completely depended upon to act or react even where situations can be controlled and duplicated. The human factor is the greatest unknown with which any field of knowledge contends. Those who are brash will say that an individual possessing skill can overcome any obstacle, or even eliminate it. Such people claim that feelings of uncertainty will not appear at all when an individual is confident of his skill.

This is a mistake made by those who do not fully appreciate the wariness of a group in accepting a new individual, especially if that person has been placed in nominal charge of the group and represents some authority, usually from his agency. No matter how much skill and experience an individual may possess, he must fully realize that whenever a new group situation comes into being, there will be a certain lack of acceptance on the part of the group during the first meeting. It will, however, be up to the recreationist to dispel this lack of acceptance and this caution through his attitudes, mannerisms, patience, and acceptance in subsequent meetings with the group, as well as in the initial situation.

Interpersonal Relationships

Before satisfactory interpersonal relationships can be achieved between the leader and the group, there must be a build-up of security and mutual trust between them. For this to occur, the leader and the group must learn and become knowledgeable about each other.

It would perhaps appear that the reactions of all group members would be similar. This, however, is not a valid assumption. Regardless of the fact that the newcomer is initially viewed with suspicion, this is not always universal. Each member of the group sees what he wants to see in the newcomer or worker. Depending upon the viewers' experiences, home environments, prior associations with other workers, relationships to other members of the group, unique and particular personalities, habits and behavior patterns, and how they feel toward the agency, peers, or the worker will color and suggest wide differences of attitude within each individual of the group.

If group members have had prior experience with other recreationists, reactions to the worker will vary with the degree of identification which such relationships have upon the individual. There will be some ambivalent feelings of love and hate, attraction and repulsion, a desire for support and a rebellion against authority. Within this multivariant expression of behavior, the recreationist must take and make opportunities to provide a climate in which individuals may "come of age," that is, mature and take their places as responsible, dependable, and if possible, skillful group members. The worker does this through his knowledge of human behavior and through the technical ability which he has at his command.[27]

Cues and Clues

Throughout the entire association between the worker and the group, the recreationist continually seeks to better understand the behavior of every person with whom he comes in contact. In the process of communication, he systematically observes and interprets overt reactions to uncover more of the hidden factors of human personality and behavior.

As the interaction of personal relationships grows during the process of communication and acceptance, there is an assignment of roles given to the worker through the needs of each member. The worker then assumes the status of teacher, father, mother, sibling, enemy, rival, or companion toward those who are expressing various behaviors. As long as there is communication and association, there will continue to evolve some form of interpersonal relationship. As there is deepening trust and as more is learned about the individuals, the worker will gain full acceptance and will be able to interpret every nuance in the behavior patterns of his group.

The development of sound interpersonal relationships occurs when group members feel that the worker accepts them as individuals, with all of their human frailties and strengths, ideas and goals, functions and responsibilities.[28] Such a relationship is achieved when the worker has the necessary professional attitudes and knowledge about human beings and their needs. While skill does build confidence in the leader's

---

27.   Rene Dubos, *Celebration of Life* (New York: McGraw-Hill Book Company, 1981), p. 229.
28.   R. C. Tiller, *The Social Self* (New York: Pergamon Press Inc., 1973), pp. 40-45.

ability to organize and/or conduct a given phase of the recreational program, it should be recognized by the leader that his appearance, actions, method of presentation, speech, and mannerisms are even more important in the eyes of the group. The effect of his personality on group members can be readily seen in the reactions of the group and tests it gives him. Tests forever occur, but many times when acceptance has been given, the test is simply part of ritual rather than any "line drawing" for criticism. Then it becomes part of the group pattern of behavior.

If the leader is reserved, retiring, or unobtrusive in manner, the group may take this as a sign of weakness, coldness, aloofness, superiority, or just plain dislike. On the other hand, if the leader is highly effervescent, too frank, too forward, overly ambitious to be a part of the group, too anxious to change organizational structure or to start a program, the group may take this for aggressiveness or overt hostility. Worse, they may think that the worker is dictatorial and is attempting to reduce their status or take away the most precious possession of the group—their decision-making function. Such possibilities are not too far-fetched. The group is universally sensitive to its prerogatives and is quick to discern real or fancied attempts on the part of another to usurp the planning or command function.

Acceptance and Self-Appraisal

This attitude is more likely to be attributed to a worker who is reinforced by the authority of an agency than it is to just any newcomer. The onus of "takeover" rests with the worker until he proves himself to the group. The suspicion or outright fear which greets the professional person in many group settings is never as intense toward any other "outsider." Perhaps the group realizes that it has the common defenses of lack of acceptance or even ignominy to use against an outsider, but that the worker is an element who cannot be subverted from his course and must be lived with. However, the recreationist is armed for this with the knowledge he has acquired in the preparation for professional life. He knows that these are the typical thrusts and retreats, the give and take of group behavior. Thus, it is he who must go all of the way to meet the group's needs. There is no equitable sharing at the beginning of a professional interpersonal relationship. There is no marriage partnership here. Whatever success the worker has with his group will result from his complete readiness to accept behavior and the level at which the group members operate.[29] This does not mean that the worker condones anti-social conduct, but it makes him aware that such behavior may occur.

---

29. Athos and Gabarro, *Interpersonal Behavior*, pp. 408–409.

When the recreationist is perceptive of individual differences, when he can understand his own feelings, attitudes, and personality traits, he will be able to act accordingly and take the proper precautions to block negative conduct directed toward him by the group. If and when he comes to comprehend his own ambivalent feelings or motives and the reasons he acts the way he does, he will have won nine-tenths of the battle for acceptance by his group. The rest comes with recognition of and sympathetic understanding for the individuals around him. The greatest unknown quantity is within each of us. When we have finally come to understand our own emotions and our raison d'être, we can begin to understand those with whom we are involved. All people need to feel that they belong, that they have a place, recognition, status, or some respect accorded them because they are human beings. The leader must give this security; he cannot afford to withhold it.

Self-Confidence

Skill, which builds confidence, is an important factor in approaching a group situation. The most important factor, however, is a person's knowledge of himself and his understanding of those he works with in the recreational program. While skill and experience are necessary in establishing and maintaining confidence to work in any group setting, a moderate course of mannerism presentation is usually the best to follow. The recreationist should enter a new group activity with the idea that he will succeed, while realizing that each group and every individual in the group is oriented toward or away from him for a variety of latent reasons. He must determine the reasons and act according to what he discovers. The worker must participate with the wholehearted acceptance of others—as they are and not as he would like them to be. It requires great effort, but the true leader will expand this effort because the result will be the rewards in knowledge and satisfaction given and received.

There is no field of work more difficult than working with people. All individuals are different. It is necessary to fathom where, how, and, most important, why they differ. Each person varies in mental capacity, physical capacity, sensitivity, creativeness, taste, and many other aspects. Individuals have their own personal philosophy of life, idiosyncrasies, and talents. In any particular situation, each feels and reacts differently.

It should not be too difficult to realize that every person is unique and desires direct attention. The leader is able to provide this attention to help solve conflicts which occur in daily living.[30] If it takes just a

---

30. R. B. Lacourisiere, *The Life Cycle of Groups* (New York: Human Sciences Press, 1980), pp. 234–235.

little more patience, a little more kindness, or a little more empathy, then the leader, as the individual with the responsibility for influencing others toward certain preconceived goals, must be willing to expend that extra effort in order to succeed.

Involvement and Identification

When individual needs are not met within the social milieu of the group experience, there will be more profound personal involvement by the members. Those who find satisfaction do so because they are intricately bound up in the entire group process. A wider range of their needs is being affected, and they can find placement and fulfillment of them. If psychic interrelationship is the common denominator of the group, then individual involvement will be in direct ratio to the degree or amount of attention and reaction which his presence creates in the group.

The recreationist must be aware of the process of involvement. As a facilitator or enabler, he is the person who provides support for the unsure and attempts to obtain group acceptance for every member. In all groups there are those who are completely a part of the activity and participate to the fullest extent. This serves to meet their immediate needs, and it is probably beneficial to the group as a whole. Such a person wants the group to continue and performs in ways which help to maintain the group's existence. Personal needs for the group are met, and since this situation is important to the individual, the group context becomes more significant. There are, however, some individuals who "belong" to a group in name only. They want to receive just as much attention and take just as large a role within the group but, because of some lacking aspect of personality, they are unable to command the respect or indulgence of others, and they become isolated or fringe members. Nevertheless, they continue to come to the group even though their relationship is tenuous because, unsatisfying as such a relationship is, it is still better than having none at all.

The worker should be able to see these personalities interact and know who is on the fringe and who is centrally involved. It is the worker's place to attempt to bring peripheral members to the attention of the group, to seek to improve their status so they, too, can find the need satisfaction which prompted their original motive for membership.

It is true that individual needs are sometimes quite different from the collective needs of the entire group. Awareness of this creates a problem for the recreationist when he works with groups. During any group meeting, the primary responsibility of the worker is to perform in such a way that the aim of the group is achieved. He must keep uppermost in his mind the concern for psychic interaction of the members and the collective intentions of the group. The value of the entire experience is based upon the relationship between members and the goals of the group. Whether or not the group achieves its purpose is important, but how they reach their objectives is also significant. In order for a feeling of belonging to take form, there must be a sense of the worthiness in participation. Each member has to know that he contributes to the group goal, and that, as an individual, he has meant something by being in the situation. His involvement with others in the accomplishment of some end will add to this feeling.

In any group situation personal needs are expressed. These may take the form of "gripes," hostilities, or other negative reactions, as well as positive behaviors. There may be conflicts of interest or friction between members and the agency or between some other group or organization. Such differences are considered, perhaps solved, and sometimes eliminated, depending upon the degree of intensity of feeling about the object. When decisions are made concerning these problems, it may be that several members are not completely satisfied with what has occurred. Their particular hostility may not have been assuaged. Such dissatisfactions may lead them to change group decisions made at another session; however, as a group the members are satisfied with their relationships and know that they are moving in the directions they want to go. Satisfaction with the group and its aims and the feeling of togetherness or unity is the cement which binds the group membership to one another. This is the basis upon which group life is maintained. It is the worker's obligation to see that such a feeling exists and to foster a climate in which interpersonal relations are developed to maximize this sense of cohesiveness and involvement. The leader does this as he communicates with the membership. He is aware of each individual, understands the needs of every person, and functions in answer to the purpose of the entire group.

In effecting the interacting processes within the group situation, the leader has two ends in view. First, he has the responsibility to move the group toward a specific goal, presumably because this is the purpose for which the group was formed and is the basis for satisfying individual needs. His second obligation is to protect and support those individuals whose personal struggle for fulfillment may be self-debilitating while still forwarding the group. The worker has a function to help such individuals, but not at the expense of the entire group. The leader, aware that some of society's ills may be negated in great degree by the group process, plays a dual role. He enables individuals to adequately perform the group tasks in order that each may realize how to utilize the group process for achievement of purposeful and socially acceptable ends. Under these conditions, the good of the whole group must take precedence over the immediate desires of a few of its members.

Because the group is the means by which members are able to realize their potential value to society, the entire group must be furthered and strengthened. Group maintenance is important in order to provide services to each member. The significance of these statements is clearly seen in the idea of interdependency. The group serves individuals. As individuals are served, the group as a whole is served. This social process of involvement and interaction produces an inherent value to society. If individuals are able to fulfill their potential as citizens and productive entities because of group living, society as a whole develops and benefits.

QUESTIONS FOR DISCUSSION

1. What is knowledge? How do people assimilate information?
2. What is meant by the statement, "knowledge is power"?
3. Why are real leadership and democratic principles inseparable?
4. What does the communications process have to do with leadership?
5. What is status molding?
6. What is the function of feedback in interpersonal communication?
7. What is the sequence of events which culminates in leadership?
8. How are communicative opportunities facilitated?
9. When does the group test the leader?
10. What is the role of communication in developing groups?
11. How can rapport building lead to effective communication?

BIBLIOGRAPHY

Brown, John T., *Fundamental Perspectives on Interpersonal Communication* (Chicago: Victoria Island Press, 1984).

Dickman, John, *Human Connections: How to Make Communications Work* (Englewood Cliffs, N.J.: Prentice-Hall, Inc., 1982).

Edwards, Dan W., *Communication Skills for the Helping Profession* (Springfield, Ill.: Charles C. Thomas, Publisher, 1983).

Folger, Joseph P., and Marshall S. Poole, *Working through Conflict* (Glenview, Ill.: Scott Foresman & Co., 1983).

Howell, William S., *The Empathetic Communicator* (Belmont, Cal.: Wadsworth Publishing Co., 1981).

Stech, Ernest L., *Leadership Communication* (Chicago: Nelson-Hall, Inc., 1983).

Steward, John, *Bridges Not Walls: A Book about Interpersonal Communication*, 3d ed. (Reading, Mass.: Addison-Wesley Publishing Co., Inc., 1982).

Swetz, Paul, *The Art of Talking so that People Will Listen* (Englewood Cliffs, N.J.: Prentice-Hall, Inc., 1983).

Verderfer, Rudolph F., and Kathleen S. Verderfer, *Interact: Using Interpersonal Communication Skills* (Belmont, Cal.: Wadsworth Publishing Co., 1983).

Weaver, Richard L., *Understanding Interpersonal Communications* (Glenview, Ill.: Scott Foresman & Co., 1983).

CHAPTER FIVE

Domination, Power, and Influence

Leadership derives inevitably from certain relationships between people. The interpersonal relations typically associated with leadership are domination, power, and influence. In effect, the behavior of one person causes the behavior of another. Inherent within the leadership process is the ability to motivate or stimulate people to move toward a particular goal, that is, the idea of change and action. The results of domination, power, or influence are the same—to change another's behavior.

Any conceptualization of leadership includes human relationships which deal with dominance, influence, and power. There is a close enough association between these three terms to cause some misunderstanding. Perhaps the most common misunderstanding is the idea that persuading another to change his behavior is a component of leadership, but it is not.

DOMINATION AND SUBMISSION

Domination is control of others by the application of superior force. Domination belongs to a category of relationships which includes flattery and other kinds of manipulation, threat of loss of security (personal safety, economic capability, freedom, etc.), aggressive physical violence, imprisonment, and even the loss of life. These are some of the ways in which a person can exercise authority over another or alter the attitudes and behavior of one or more others.

When dominance is structured and generally accepted within a culture, we typically think of parental control over children or the institutionalized control of higher ranks over lower ranks within military and paramilitary organizations. Even in corporations or organizations, dominance stems from and operates within social interactions. To state that one individual is dominant suggests that there is another individual in a submissive position. Unless there is subordination, there can be no superordination.

Fromm offers a most compelling statement concerning domination and submission:

> The common element in both submission and domination is the symbiotic nature of relatedness. Both persons involved have lost their integrity and freedom; they live on each other and from each other, satisfying their craving for closeness, yet suffering from the lack of inner strength and self-reliance which would require freedom and independence, and furthermore, constantly threatened by the conscious and unconscious hostility which is bound to arise from the symbiotic relationship.[1]

In a dominating relationship, one individual has the capacity to restrict or in some way control the decision-making functions of others. Such restraint may also be the stifling of personal expression or indulgence in destructive ways. It may also be seen as enlightened despotism or paternalism.

Why do some people enter into a relationship where one person is dominant and others are submissive? The personalities of those seeking to be dominated or those who want to dominate require such a relationship to cope with their present situations.[2] An individual may view another in light of some previous experience and seek out a father surrogate or authoritarian personality in order to obtain protection or favored position. There are individuals who try to offset their low status within an organization by ingratiating themselves with, or assuming a submissive attitude toward, an individual above them in the hierarchy. This subordination of self is performed to obtain a form of security, status by association, or a feeling of safety.

Among the basic factors to be considered in any study of dominance is the need, drive, or ambition of an individual for dominance and the associated desire of another to be submissive, revealing the personality of each. There is the presupposition that individuals who "go along" will not have the personality that would ever permit active opposition to domination. Obviously, such domination can only be thought of in a social sense, rather than in the physical sense of force or its threat. Under such circumstances, submission is involuntary. Social domination, on the other hand, requires a desire to submit.[3]

---

1. E. Fromm, "Values, Psychology, and Human Existence," in D. E. Hamachek, ed., *Human Dynamics in Psychology and Education* (Boston: Allyn and Bacon, Inc., 1970), p. 666.
2. D. R. Mark and others, *Dominance Relations: An Ethological View of Human Conflict and Social Interaction* (New York: Garland STPM Press, 1980), pp. 80–82.
3. R. L. Burgess and T. L. Huston, *Social Exchange in Developing Relationships* (New York: Academic Press, 1979), pp. 262–263.

Abnormal desires for dominance have long been acknowledged. The individual who needs constant recognition has this desire. The Napoleonic complex appears to be a compensatory behavior for those who feel the need to make up for their short stature. Perhaps other perceived physical limitations may be a factor contributing to the ambition to gain mastery or command in order to counteract feelings of inferiority. An individual's abnormal need for dominance may also be the outcome of early childhood experience in which extraordinary parental domination emerges in later years as an effort to dominate others.

A normal desire for dominance does not offer such a facile explanation. Certain cultural pressures (for example, success and its perquisites are highly regarded in western society) can produce an inclination for mastery, motivating individuals to compete for rank, prestige, or power.[4] The desire to assert oneself is a learned response to environmental forces which tend to assist in the development of personality as the individual matures. Family life, peer relationships, societal demands, and personal tendencies are closely related in determining the level of each person's need for dominance.

Conversely, the need for submission, both normal and abnormal, is comprehensible when parent-child relationships are explored. Babies are born helpless and in need of physical support. Only among humans is the period of immaturity and dependency of such long duration. In fact, many societies mandate continued dependency of the young upon the adult population even after there is mental and physical capacity for self-care. It is not surprising that people become so completely habituated to submission. Just as individuals learn to become dominant, they also learn to become submissive. To the extent that submission, or in this case dependency, is enjoyable there is a corresponding attitude that being protected and cared for is extremely advantageous.[5] In normal situations, however, there will eventually be an attempt to break away from parental control and achieve personal independence. When this occurs varies with the personalities of the individuals concerned. Some seek autonomy at a relatively early age, some after reaching the age of majority, and some never leave the nest.

As the individual matures and develops, there is a consequent ambivalence—it is the conflict between the desire to submit, be

---

4. A. G. Athos and J. J. Gabarro, *Interpersonal Behavior Communication and Understanding in Relationships* (Englewood Cliffs, N.J.: Prentice-Hall, Inc. 1978), pp. 274–275.

5. A. Blumberg and R. T. Golembiewski, *Learning and Change in Groups*, (Middlesex, England: Penguin Books, 1976), pp. 213.

protected, and cared for (with all its associations of pleasant security and disagreeable restrictions) and the vaulting determination to be free (with all of its satisfactions and unattractive responsibilities). How this contradiction is resolved will probably depend on how our parents behave toward us and also the extent to which an individual wants to play submissive roles in the social groups or organizations he joins.

Social Domination and Human Development

A child with a particular hereditary endowment will mature, differentiate, and have a concept of self only to the degree that his social milieu permits. Domination is behavior that denies the social expression and hinders the inspiration of others. It thwarts human impulses to perform with enthusiasm, and it assaults the indivisability, position, and equity of another to think and act as an individual. Domination is behavior that claims for one person the capability to visualize himself as superior and another as inferior. Regardless of its justification in specific instances, it is a violation of the democratic process; a stress-creating barrier to maturation. Individuals with emotional problems have probably experienced a relationship with someone who was overly severe, intimidating, or unrelenting. How may domination be explained insofar as growth and development are concerned?

Acceptance. Perfect accord in human relations is rare. Perfect agreement would necessitate absolute understanding of other's aims and wishes as well as one's own. Because each of us has difficulty in verbalizing personal desires, it is inconceivable that others would have complete understanding of us. Even with excellent human relations, each person contributes some problem to those within his social sphere. Each person finds his own initiative somewhat reduced by the well-intentioned actions of others, but each of us takes a great deal of such inconvenience as a matter of course. We continue to have affection and appreciation for friends without holding a grudge for minor irritations. Acceptance permits those involved to reveal an inner self without the need for defensive mechanisms.[6]

Interpersonal behavior based on acceptance is likely in a relationship where individuals may become more intimate and gain better understandings of one another and still maintain their individuality. This is really an ideal relationship. For development, differentiation

---

6. R. K. Greenleaf, *Servant Leadership* (New York: Paulist Press, 1977), pp. 20-21.

can be maximized when an individual is recognized and appreciated for his uniqueness at an early age.

Avoidance.   In families where the offspring are emotionally secure, the children are able to discuss any issue whatsoever with their parents without recrimination. Unfortunately, some families have neither established the rapport nor the opportunities for such discussions. It is little wonder, then, that children learn very early to be especially cautious and discriminating both in the subject matter which they discuss and in the behavior which they disclose to their parents. When one person is required to reside in close proximity to another, and realizes the other tends to frustrate freedom to act, that person will avoid confrontation but will otherwise be himself. This form of behavior supposes that the domination is so overwhelming that it cannot be accepted, and protective countermeasures must be taken. Keeping back information from one's parents or conducting discreet conversations with one's peers are typical of such a relationship.

In the acceptance and avoidance patterns of dominating relationships, response to comparatively mild inconvenience which impinges on one's own spontaneity is not sufficient to divert energies from fundamental objectives. If it is necessary to be less than candid or to hide ideas, there is probably going to be less understanding in the relationship. Nevertheless, this kind of behavior is found in relationships where there is neither a breach nor conflict. In both of these situations adaptations may be made so that domination cannot interfere with the essential purpose of the individual.

Opposition.   When domination reaches a peak where it can no longer be avoided without a substantial change in life style, integrity, or individuality, it must be actively opposed. The relationship is then characterized by open conflict, the inception of the negative spiral in human behavior. Dominance breeds dominance (opposition), which tends to magnify the level of conflict rather than diminish it. It reduces understanding to such negligible proportions that it forces the combatants to employ deceit so that they may assault each other with more strength. People who lie to others usually do so as a form of self-protection in a contentious relationship.[7]

Some adults mistreat children and act in ways that would seem shocking by any civilized standard of behavior. Name-calling, physical abuse, sarcasm, and rejection are imposed. It is not amazing when the

---

7. Burgess and Huston, *Social Exchanges*, pp. 90–91.

subject of this abuse finally has had enough and actively begins to oppose such treatment. Then another round of abuse is begun. With resistance there is further aggression. This promotes more hostility and opposition. The only way out of this spiral is to stop the counterproductive behavior which initiated it and seek solutions to the conflict. Domination must be obliterated and greater understanding substituted.

Submissiveness. When an individual realizes that opposition to domination can only meet with personal catastrophe, he is inclined to submit. Submissive behavior reflects a much more reduced level of will than does opposition. Submission presents an outer appearance of agreement or agreeableness, which persons in authority find pleasant or actually work to attain. In so doing, they squeeze every vestige of spontaneity out of the individual and leave a passively conforming, manipulable object in place of a vital human being. Adults frequently misinterpret a child's shyness and submissiveness for agreement. What they do not comprehend is that the child fears self-expression because of recrimination or retaliation.

As the child's extemporaneous behavior and expression of personal ideas are thwarted, misunderstanding is created. Similarly, there is an increased risk that the behavior of others will miscarry and not be in accord with the child's real aims and wishes.

Submissive behavior provokes more and more misunderstanding. Conforming, retiring, anxious, and apprehensive people are liable to grow further away from others. Inmates in concentration camps were constantly pulled in opposite directions as they strove to maintain their personal integrity. When individuals are so dominated by environmental factors that opposition cannot be attempted without risking death, the individual begins to lose his sense of identity and essence.[8]

Combatting Domination

The most direct method for abolishing the malignant spiral of domination is to accept people for what they are. Both the timid and the hostile person are fearful. The difference in their responses to domination lies, to a great extent, in the degree of imposed domination and in the variance of capability. The timid individual and the hostile person are both in conflict with their surroundings. The basic difference between the two situations is that the hostile person is less fearful.

---

8. Frederick Forsyth, *The Odessa File* (New York: Bantam Books, 1974), pp. 27–55.

The method for dealing with timid, withdrawn, and conforming behavior is to augment the individual's expression of self and will. As self-expression is increased, any threat within the environment is reduced. As domination is decreased and expressiveness begins to assert itself, it is to be expected that the timid person will undergo a stage where he is irritating to others. Agreeableness is learned behavior through activity. It may be taught through indoctrination, but it is really only assimilated through interaction with others. It should be anticipated that the withdrawing individual will come to resemble the aggressive person for a while. During this period, he will develop high initiative, but will remain low in accord.

Almost antipodal behavior will be observed in the overly hostile individual. The aggressive person is high in initiative and low in agreement. Negligible accord, however, forms environmental obstruction to his high initiative, and the negative spiral comes into full play. The method for reversing the spiral in which the hostile person finds himself also requires acceptance. Accepting the individual as a person, while disapproving of antisocial conduct, tends to minimize the perceived threat. With the threat reduced, the individual no longer needs to destroy his environment. It takes time before the individual becomes aware that danger to himself has been reduced. This is part of the learning process that accrues with activity.

Accepting the individual as a person promotes socially integrative associations because it augments the individual's voluntary expression and initiates agreement that was not previously available. Socially integrative behavior is reflected by a positive cycle. When such behavior is exhibited, there is a tendency to evoke corresponding behavior in one's companions. Rapport—the development of mutual trust and cooperative effort—promotes socially integrative behavior and ends the malignant spiral. Indeed, the whole process induces harmonious interpersonal relations, reduces domination and rejects protective behavior, opening avenues to understanding both the self and others.

Hero worship is another form of submission. The idolizing of certain individuals and the search for great men to guide the destinies of nations has a long history. Among the writers who have concerned themselves with this form of submission is Thomas Carlyle, who wrote:

Find in any country the Ablest Man that exists there; raise him to the supreme place, and loyally reverence him: you have a perfect government for that country...what he tells us to do must be precisely the wisest, fittest, that we could anywhere or anyhow learn; the thing which it will always behoove us, with right loyal thankfulness, and nothing doubting, to do so.[9]

The worship of heroes and the search for an infallible person to proffer support and protection in times of stress is an adult expression of an infantile attitude toward one's parents. During periods of stress, some people become overwhelmed. They long for the time when they could run to their parents for security, and so seek a dominant person—a surrogate parent upon whom burdens may be unloaded. Reliance upon such an individual requires the same idealization with which small children sometimes picture their parents. *However it is rooted and for whatever reasons it is called upon, domination has no place within the process of leadership.*

Within social action ranging from anarchy to an entirely structured existence, groups of every kind find their position. Our position is in a world where all people must strive to become individuals. It is a world in which people either abstract or actually perceive an end-in-view. In this environment, leadership must recognize and consider the free choice of those to follow.

Persons sitting at the apex of power may dominate, command, or direct, but unless those who are led have the freedom to follow or not to follow, there is no personal leadership. Without the voluntary features of "followership" there can only be subservience. Paul Pigors crystalized this concept when he wrote that the denial of choice breeds domination which is the antithesis of leadership.[10]

Power and Social Change

The analysis of power and its emanations offer a focal point for study. The annals of power are vast and complicated as each of several disciplines consider the conditions, reasons, and structure of the existence of power. Basically, all questions concerning power stem from one idea: Certain individuals comply with what another person stimulates them to do. It is obvious that this cause and effect relationship exists, and it is also apparent that this power is not allocated evenly throughout the general population. Some individuals are more likely to be initiators of performance and others are more likely to be motivated. This division can be seen clearly along the entire array of social relationships from small primary groups to corporate bodies, and beyond to large, organized, political forces.

---

9. T. Carlyle, *On Heroes, Hero-Worship and the Heroic in History* (New York: Thomas Y. Crowell Company, 1840), pp. 259–260.

10. P. Pigors, *Leadership or Domination* (Boston: Houghton Mifflin Company, 1935), p. 20.

What is power? The English word power is taken from the Old Latin which means to be able. We also derive the word potent from the same source and give it a synonymous definition. To have the ability connotes such a broad base that the concise meaning is dimly perceived.[11] Under such circumstances, it might be better to use power in a social sense. Not from the standpoint of physics insofar as potential and kinetic energy are concerned, but rather the concept of power as it refers to human relationships.

Broadly speaking, power is either actual or potentially intended influence found within social interaction. Even within the sphere of social interaction there are nonpersonal power forms. These are the powers of cultural imperatives, moral ideas, convictions, and attitudes to which individuals conform. We can accept the often stated concept that power best reflects a causal relationship between human beings.[12]

Social power occurs when one or more individuals have an effect on the conduct, attitudes, or emotions of others. Emotional outcomes can be suggested from watching people. Power over inanimate objects is important only to the extent that it leads to social power. Accidental effects of one person on another are not included in this context. Power means intent. It is not coincidental that one person's behavior causes another to react.[13] It must be understood that interpersonal power is not only action oriented, it is the capacity to perform. Thus, social power is the ability of an individual to effect intentional modifications on the behavior of another.[14]

The concentration of great power within one person is a matter of concern because of the many differences in methods of utilization. Thus the use of power for either ethical or degrading purposes lies within the character of the individuals involved. For some, power may be a way to gain objectives. Compulsion is a factor in this type of use. Under stress this may be the only effective method if an objective is to be achieved or a goal is to be won. Very often power must be brought into play to rally the group and force those who oppose the leadership into a condition whereby they recognize a state of emergency instead of attempting to undermine the group at a crucial time. Power is sometimes necessary to compel followers to act because authority is

11.   D. Easton, The Political System (New York: Alfred A. Knopf and Company, 1953), p. 143.

12.   R. A. Dahl, "The Concept of Power," Behavioral Science, Vol. 2 (1957), pp. 201–215.

13.   R. L. Burgess and T. L. Huston, Social Exchange in Developing Relationships (New York: Academic Press, 1979), p. 40.

14.   M. E. Shaw, Group Dynamics: The Psychology of Small Group Behavior (New York: McGraw-Hill Book Company, 1976), pp. 262–263.

the only way to communicate with them or because they will not be responsive to any other form of persuasion.

Power is a hazardous instrument in the hands of an elite or given to one as an agent of many. The ego involvement of the individual with power at his disposal may prove to be the death knell of liberty. Like a moth attracted to flame, power provides a magnetic field which sometimes causes a dangerous condition in the mind of the leader. He is stimulated to act because of the power that he wields. Once he has tasted power and its concomitant thrill, he is loathe to let it go. He therefore exists from problem to problem and crisis to crisis until some overwhelming emergency gives him either supreme power or dissipates his power in a holocaust of his own making.[15] If he becomes supreme, he is a dictator, his power resting upon fear and coercion. He has overstepped the bounds of a leader. His followers work and produce, not because they want to, but because they have to. Fear is his whip. Production may continue, but at a lower rate. If he is overthrown, then his group is dissolved, and his goals are destroyed along with his group. Group chaos results, and group objectives are scattered and lost.

Typologies of Power

The literature on power brims with explanations and analyses of the variances between power and other related concepts. Some explanations of power have equated power with domination, authority, force, command, or control. Some of the examples are ambiguous, depending upon the writer's opinion of which attributes can be appended to power. Man is motivated to act by forces operating individually or simultaneously, and if he completes an activity instigated by another, we know that social power has been at work. The forces which impel behavioral changes in one person by virtue of the presence or absence of another imply a cause and effect relationship which is defined as power.[16] Power is the cause of one individual acting in a specific way because of the intentional behavior of another who wants such a reaction.

Humans are motivated by acquired general attitudes, ideas, ethics, and convictions. Behavior in interpersonal relationships is modified in consonance with them. Such extra-personal forces as religious belief,

---

15. W. L. Shirer, *20th Century Journey: The Nightmare Years 1930–1940* (Boston: Little, Brown and Company, 1984), pp. 239–251.
16. M. F. R. Kets de Vries, *Organizational Paradoxes* (London: Tavistock Publications, 1980), pp. 65–70.

political creed, and philosophical reference all have power to stimulate human behavior. Even if the individual possesses personal power which he employs to gain his objectives, he is at the same time the object of those powers to which he conforms.

Power may therefore be classified by personal attributes, those qualities of mind and body which permit the possessor to command the behavior of others in carrying out his plans.[17] A second set of powers are economic. Economic power is based upon the possession of property or other wealth and is conditioned by the social controls of custom and law. Economic power is an extra-personal power which ties man to one aspect of the world. Hierarchical power is a third type based on the social or positional status of individuals within their organizations. A fourth type of power is based upon compulsion or physical force applied to recalcitrant persons who otherwise would not alter their behavior in response to stimuli supplied by an instigator.

Nothing is innately wrong with the word "power," but it has commonly been used in contexts that have given it monstrous connotations. To many people, power conjures visions of autocracy, secret police, awakenings in the middle of the night to the thundering summons of a rifle butt, and the enslavement of millions of people by political, economic, or military means. Many think of power in terms of brute force, cunning, hatred, and injustice, with some Machiavellian character pulling the strings to which mindless puppets are attached. On the other hand, just as there is power for evil, there is also power for the right, the ethical, and the good. The power harnessed in the hydrogen bomb can be used for infinite destruction, or it can be utilized in the production of goods and services on a scale that dwarfs the imagination. The power which deals death can also heal and give life. Solzhenitsyn expressed this dichotomy when he wrote:

> Power is a poison well known for thousands of years. If only no one were ever to acquire material power over others. But to the human being who has faith in some force that holds dominion over all of us, and who is therefore conscious of his own limitations, power is not necessarily fatal. For those, however, who are unaware of any higher sphere, it is a deadly poison. For them there is no antidote.[18]

Power is not inherently evil. The attainment of power in the form of

---

17. N. D. Gardner, *Group Leadership* (Washington, D.C.: National Training and Developmental Service Press, 1974), pp. 22–23.

18. Alexsandr I. Solzhenitsyn, *The Gulag Archipelago, 1918–1956* (New York: Harper & Row, Publishers, 1973), p. 147. Reprinted by permission.

authority or influence may seemingly corrupt so that some applications of power are immoral. It is what the individual brings to the power structure that determines its use; the ethical nature of the personality will limit the betrayal of human values. Character pollution by power is not inevitable; only when a morally weak or pathologically inclined personality achieves power is it turned toward depraved ends.

To better understand the power domain, let us examine a situation which involves power sharing:

The Therapeutic Recreational Service Department of the County Hospital obtained many volunteers to help provide other than prescribed recreational activities for patients. One of the volunteers, Miss Toy, was knowledgable about music and usually played records or the guitar for patients on the wards she was assigned to visit. Mrs. Tigue, the hospital's music therapist, was upset about this practice and informed Miss Toy that she was to discontinue her musical activities because this function belonged to the music therapist. Serious differences developed between the two women over this issue, to the extent that Mrs. Tigue requested an interview with Mr. Roberts, director of Therapeutic Recreational Services. His position included the supervision of volunteers.

Mrs. Tigue was obviously upset when she arrived in Mr. Roberts' office. "Mr. Roberts, I must talk to you about this intolerable situation. Miss Toy makes me feel uncomfortable. She is so caustic and disagrees with everything I say or do. I try to determine the kinds of music that patients should be hearing, and you know as well as I that some of the psychiatric patients sometimes respond the wrong way to certain types of music. If Miss Toy is going to bring her own records to the wards and make her own selections from the departmental library, I don't think she should act as if I don't know anything about music when I suggest certain records. You know I have had years of music education and I specialized in music therapy. I really don't believe that anyone should provide music to a patient unless she knows what the effect of the music will be on that particular patient. I am familiar with all of the music which is contained in the library and I know what the musical tastes of our patients are. Besides, Miss Toy is very condescending to me. I never had any difficulty with the girl who used to volunteer before Miss Toy came."

"Mrs. Tigue, I am shocked to hear about these things concerning Miss Toy. She has always been cordial with everyone. I believe that..."

"Nevertheless, Mr. Roberts, she is not only impolite, but irresponsible as well. She uses our phonograph and record albums without a by-your-leave, and I've informed her that I do not want her using them any more. I found one of our missing albums on the orthopedic ward today."

"Miss Toy explained that to me. She sent the album back to the library with one of the candy-stripers, Trudy, and Trudy placed it on the library desk because she didn't know where it should be filed. Then one of the patients must have taken it off the desk. But after all, Mrs. Tigue, the album has been found and all is well. Miss Toy told me that she should have taken it back to the library herself and would do so the next time."

"You don't seem to understand, Mr. Roberts. I do not want her to use our records or equipment. Furthermore, I do not feel that her duties as a volunteer should include providing music. You should realize that I visit every patient in this hospital each week, and I offer all the patients whatever music they want, so long as we have it in the record library. I even work overtime. I live right here on the grounds, and the telephone operator can get in touch with me if a patient wants some music. You know that music therapy is a significant modality in patient rehabilitation."

"Now Mrs. Tigue, I realize the importance of your position and I appreciate the significance of the work you do for all of the patients in the hospital. However, my volunteers play an extremely important role in the provision of recreational opportunities for these patients. This department has direct responsibility for providing the patients with a variety of recreational activities and experiences, and music should be no exception. Miss Toy is responsible to me, and as long as I see that she is performing in a way that satisfies the needs of patients, then it is up to me to define the areas of work she will be permitted to perform. All of our volunteers are given an orientation to therapeutic modalities and receive in-service developmental training as well. Music is one of the better activities we have for developing a common ground to meet patient needs, establishing personal relationships with them, and making them happy."

"And I, on my part, Mr. Roberts, do not believe that volunteers can be music therapists. I am responsible for providing musical activities to the patients. Until this regrettable interference, I have always provided a program of musical therapy designed to meet the patients' every need, and the hospital administrator has been satisfied with my work. I have never been given a statement to the contrary. The doctors think I perform well also."

"Mrs. Tigue, I am terribly sorry that we seem to have had this difficulty. I think that we should have a meeting with the hospital administrator and see if we can clearly define our individual responsibilities. Please excuse me now, I have a meeting with the latest batch of interns. I will certainly contact you again."

The confrontation here is nonproductive; little, if any, worthwhile information has been exchanged between the two specialists. All that is apparent is that Mrs. Tigue has one point of view and Mr. Roberts has quite a different one. The original conflict between Miss Toy and Mrs. Tigue is unresolved, and a new conflict has arisen between Mrs. Tigue and Mr. Roberts. The issue of how best to meet patients' needs is lost as Mrs. Tigue and Mr. Roberts, each perceiving a threat to his own authority, jockey to gain control of the situation.

The outcome of this situation was that Mrs. Tigue resigned from the hospital. The difficulties between the two specialists were never resolved. In Mr. Robert's view, the "problem" was Mrs. Tigue's unreasonable and possessive attitude toward her area of specialization, and her resignation was a welcome "solution." Why Mr. Roberts felt so threatened by Mrs. Tigue's opinions concerning one of his subordinates is open to speculation. Clearly the two specialists had no rapport and lacked the communicative skills through which to find the real root of the problem and come up with a mutually satisfactory solution.

This example illustrates the need for interpersonal communication as a reciprocal and mutually supportive process enabling people to focus on how best to achieve well-defined and mutually agreed upon goals. When people in power are concerned primarily with maintaining that power, such communication is not possible. In this case everyone lost: Mrs. Tigue, her job; Mr. Roberts, the services of a well-trained, experienced, and dedicated music therapist; and the patients at the hospital, a well-run and integrated recreational program.

Physical Power

The nature of power may be seen in the ability of an individual to achieve goals or to produce results; it is the capacity of action. Movement of things and people is power. The usual conception of power rests with physical and emotional factors. This widely held view defines power in a negative sense. The utilization of pure physical power has both a positive and negative meaning to all. However, physical power has come to be associated with brute force. Sheer physical force has rarely accomplished anything of lasting inner value.

To influence people, a structure or form beyond force must exist for physical power to have effectiveness. The concept of legitimacy may be employed to rationalize force, as in police power or other law enforcement agencies which protect the public good against the predators of society or imprison those who would act maliciously if set free. Of course, a case can be made that incarceration—an act of forceful restraint—probably provides more opportunity for criminal learning than for rehabilitation, but that is another question. The whip and chains are not symbols of learning or rehabilitation, but rather of repression.

Human beings may be beaten into submission; they may be made into any mold or pattern under duress. Unless the threat of punishment is continually applied, few individuals willingly respond. They may be compelled to serve a cause, and they will serve, but only as long as the lash, the bayonet, or arms reinforce the demand. Human will, once it realizes any freedom, can never voluntarily assume a slavish position.

Emotional Power

Structure beyond mere brute power may readily be discerned in the second element of power, force of feeling or emotion. The close relationship of this concept to the physical factor is obvious. Both are weapons of intimidation; both are carried forward by stress of circumstances. Economic intimidation by bribery, extortion, embezzlement, or robbery is an emotion-producing influence carrying the overtones of physical force. Fear of loss of status and prestige, fear for loved ones, insecurity, hate, ignorance, and terror are all emotion-provoked; each of these is a product of the force of feeling, and each implies the shadow of some physical danger.

Influencing the security of individuals is almost always regarded in negative terms. The confiscation of property and the deprivation of health, safety, and welfare through violence, harsh disciplinary measures such as martial law, and the suspension of human rights are normally associated with power. Indeed, authority as power has widespread meaning in every phase of human existence. Control of prerogatives in one instance may lead to restriction in many cases, and the basic value structure of society can be subverted.

Moral Power. Morality may be conceived in terms of general rules, regulations, or behavior customs to which human society knowingly adheres and which are ethically significant. Moral behaviors are those which abide by socially approved conduct. Morality, therefore, is based upon ethical relationships, upon knowing what in a given culture is right and what is good. This knowledge is based upon freedom and individual decision, coordinated with criteria for evaluating possible courses of action. The worth of every decision hinges upon the understanding and analysis of the several choices presented. All available information is gathered so that each person may have the opportunity of deciding what has value in the light of social acceptance.

Morality must not be confused with conformity; it is concerned with value systems which determine free action, rather than the development of specific accepted forms of conduct. The practice of ethical activities is based upon what is good and therefore of value to the individual and to society. Hypocritical and sanctimonious efforts at morality, which sometimes disguise selfish tendencies, are not moral regardless of how good such behavior appears. Morality is vitally concerned with more than surface conduct.

Moral force is influential because it produces the most valid of possible behavior systems. The rational frame in which morality operates precludes baseness; in the long run it will consistently win over those activities for which there are no justifiable supports. Morality exercised within the human community seeks optimum coordination of human effort in the production of the good life for all. One form of recreational problem with moral overtones may be observed from the following:

A recreationist with a disability—cerebral palsy with motor ataxia—was assigned to work with two other recreationists in a local neighborhood. There was some concern as to how she would be accepted by those who utilized the neighborhood recreational facilities. The supervisory and center staff were hopeful that the transition for the new staff member would be smooth and that the community would come to accept her.

Following a discussion of neighborhood attitudes and possible prejudices, the new recreationist was asked to be as active as possible in the program. It was decided that, whenever possible, the other staff members would answer a request from a child with the statement: "I can't be with you now, but Ms. McKinney can. She is the lady over there. Just go over and ask her."

As a result of this procedure, the disabled recreationist was accepted by the children and few denigrating incidents flared. In a short time the entire neighborhood came to accept Ms. McKinney and she was a valuable member of the staff.

The idea of power is somewhat estranged from the connotation of morality. In the power ethic, the test of goodness is whether or not a thing succeeds. The good is that which brings desired results.

Unfortunately, this power ethic is one which supports immorality in the practical sense, but which may be perfectly valid in any test of truth. Dictators justify their employment of unholy means by pointing to the ends which they achieve. According to the ethic of power, such a view is acceptable. Yet any activity which is reprehensible cannot be called ethical. Murder is unethical. Killing in time of war is condoned, although the act itself is unethical, because this behavior is thought to serve an ethical end. Morality refers to the decisions which are reached on the basis of knowledge of consequences. Thus the ends, even if they are worthy and valuable to society as a whole, and not just to a select few, never justify the means which appear to be or are a violation of ethical practices.

Violence against any individual or group is unethical as such. However, in our society, violence may be supportable in certain cases. Among these are: punishment of a criminal for acts committed against society, destruction of armed might in defense of a particular system, killing during wartime, and suspension of certain civil rights as a preventive against rebellion. While these are actions which cannot be considered ethical in themselves, they may be warranted in terms of the ends which are achieved for the entire human community. Immoral means deny noble ends. Where the individual breaks the law to expose injustice or maltreatment, that person willingly accepts the possibility of punishment in hopes of gaining justice. One may not break the law with impunity and expect amnesty.

It would be outrageous even to consider ethical those actions to which dictators have generally resorted in consolidating their position. Racism, genocide, nationalism, and aggression have been used to destroy people and places. The "ends-justify-the-means" argument must be carefully weighed in the light of human dignity and service to humanity.

Those who have placed truth upon the altar of expediency also adhere to the power ethic. In the case of pragmatism, however, moral actions are taken into account and concepts are tested. The clearest statement of this idea was made by William James:

> True ideas are those that we can assimilate, validate, corroborate, and verify. False ideas are those we cannot. That is the practical difference it makes to us to have true ideas; that, therefore, is the meaning of truth, for it is all that truth is known as.[19]

---

19. W. James, *The Meaning of Truth* (New York: David McKay Company, 1909), pp. v–vi. Reprinted by permission.

Intellectual Power. The third variety of power is intellectual power, or knowledge of what must be done. Inherent in this aspect of power are technical skill, social power, and self-realization. Intellectual power has as its aim the control of natural and material things, other persons, and the self. Intellect is clearly associated with power because its use provides knowledge, and knowledge is the path to power. The content of what is known is the essence of what can be performed or obtained. Applied intellect is one method of swaying others toward the leader's desired goals. Unless it is guided by ethics, intellectual power degenerates into manipulation.

The power of technical skill may be observed in man's dominion over all other living matter. Man shapes his environment to suit his needs. This goal can be reached only when sufficient strides in technical knowledge have been made. Weather and climatic conditions are controlled by artificial means; deserts are turned into flowering and fertile farms; the sea is harnessed to produce food, clothing, metals, and power. The very earth itself is blown up, excavated, burrowed into, moved, filled, or cut—depending upon man's design. Man rides on air, he hears and sees by electricity, he is powered by atomic fission and fusion, and soon, perhaps, by solar energy. If he lacks an element, he creates it. He redistributes the molecular chain to produce new materials and chemicals for which he then finds uses. He has broken the genetic code and has researched to the very heart of life-producing DNA. He is now experimenting with weapons so horrible that their use may mean the destruction of civilization. Unfortunately, intellectual power has never stopped him from committing genocide or standing by while millions starve to death. Intellectual power is overmatched by emotional power.

Control over other persons may be explained as social power. Intellectualization is necessary in the development of language and the art of communication. By these means, the development of rational powers of persuasion may occur. Influence grows out of the impact which intellect has on specific feeling. For example, tremendous pressure is exerted upon those for whom we have affection or who have affection for us. The ability to sway behavior because of the interdependence of affection is one of the more powerful instigators to action. Also, through such personal relations, opinions and attitudes may be changed.

Power and Leadership

It requires ability to persuade others to voluntarily follow a plan of action which requires attitudinal modification or a change in behavioral patterns. An individual with power does not need this ability if he can coerce others to follow. His power may stem from what he is or what he does—he may either have means at his disposal or hold an authoritative position from which he may issue commands. A powerful person who controls group objectives can immediately reinforce his demands on the behavior of others by providing or withholding rewards or punishments. If group members are not stimulated to achieve their objectives, the control does not produce power.

Coercion occurs when individual members of a group openly, not privately, comply with the demands of another. Nevertheless, the restriction on their own free choices may produce discontent, frustration, and hostility. The weaker members of the group may simply withdraw from an untenable situation, or the membership may become so frustrated that it reacts in ways which tend to reduce efficiency and effectiveness in carrying out assignments. Another outcome is that members may counteract by forming a new group. The latter is illustrated by the following postulated situation:

> The teenage center in a changing neighborhood in X city became the focal point of ethnic rivalries. A group of Puerto Rican youngsters found themselves outnumbered by the older, established white Protestant majority. This created significant friction and resulted in fighting and severe injuries.
>
> The Puerto Ricans decided to leave the center rather than face continual harassment and possible bloody conflict. The director of the center maintained contact with these former members and when the Puerto Ricans organized a rock group, he helped them secure an audition with a recording company. A rock concert was held at the center with the Puerto Rican group as the main attraction.
>
> The group was well received and continues to appear at the center on occasion. Although the Puerto Ricans were accepted as talented performers, they were not really integrated as center members. Such status has never been accorded since their withdrawal.
>
> In retrospect, the wisdom of having the minority group withdraw in the face of threat is questionable. It is likely that other ways could have been found to permit contacts between the two groups. Initial meetings might have been much more easygoing until familiarity broke down some of the obvious biases. Withdrawal, in this situation, seems to have strengthened the alienation between the groups.

Discussion of power frequently includes the employment of sanctions. In his statement on power, Easton offers the point that a more particular, and therefore a more useful, consideration of power would incorporate the two dimensions of intention and coercion to the usual understanding of power as social causation. He writes:

> To give power any differentiated meaning we must view it as a relationship in which one person or group is able to determine the actions of another in the direction of the former's own ends. Furthermore—and this is the aspect that distinguishes power from broad influence—this person or group must be able to impose some sanctions for the failure of the influenced person to act in the desired way. Power, therefore, is present to the extent to which one person controls by sanction the decisions and actions of another.[20]

LEADERSHIP VERSUS POWER

Leadership is distinguishable from power. In the use of power, the individual with more power is capable of doing certain things. He controls whether or not other persons attain their objectives by simply determining if the other person will be permitted to achieve his aims or not. The possessor of power may also decide whether the other individual may or may not perform in a specific way. The person with power has the means to compel one behavior over another, permit achievement or deny it, or control the prerogatives of another. It must be clear, however, that in a strict sense, all leadership is a form of power because the leader enables aims or objectives to be gained and, further, provides directions for such attainment. What, then, is the difference between power and leadership? The essential factor is the reaction of a person when another attempts to influence him.[21] In the power relationship, the person with less power is restricted in his choices of behavior and performance; he literally loses his options and acts in consequence of the behavior of the more powerful person. The possessor of a lot of power can compel others with less power to participate in elected activities they ordinarily might shun, if they wish to receive his favors. Thus all decision making is extra-personal to the individual with less power.[22]

In direct contrast to this situation, leadership offers unrestricted options to the potential follower. Leadership acts are those which try

---

20. D. Easton, *Political System* (New York: Alfred A. Knopf, 1953), pp. 143–144. Reprinted by permission.
21. R.H. Hall, *Organizations: Structure and Process* (Englewood Cliffs, N.J.: Prentice-Hall, Inc., 1982), p. 161.
22. M.E. Shaw, *Group Dynamics*, pp. 270–272.

to motivate others to act in a certain way although other alternatives exist. The leadership process fosters the idea that one form of behavior or course of action is better than another. A leader may also indicate which possibilities are relevant, practical, or beneficial and which are not. The recipient of this information is in the position of accepting or rejecting the propositions. If the group members accept the ideas and act accordingly, they have been influenced; but the most important point to remember is that the decision to act or not to act lies entirely with them. There are certainly leaders with a great deal of power, but it is not through power that leadership is attempted. Power suggests imposition and limited choices: leadership implies personal choice or voluntary acceptance of suggestions both publicly and privately.

Therefore, the true leader will attempt to share power as widely as possible. He will be cautious in his use of power, and he will make every effort to disseminate power to every member of his group. By equalizing the source of power and effectively influencing others in the understanding and use of power, the leader builds up responsible persons who are capable of becoming the new leaders and handling the problems of emergency living when times, groups, and situations require them to do so. Only when power is shared by a large number of group members does this eventuality occur. An effective leader is aware of the inequality of power and actually prepares to counteract it.

Influence

If leadership is the ability to persuade people to act in certain ways or to modify their behavior or attitudes to achieve some goal, then assuredly leadership is influence.[23] Influence is defined as the capacity for one person to convince others to act in the achievement of some desired effects, *without the exercise of sanctions.* Influence has to do with one person's attractiveness to or for another and the subsequent interaction that occurs in obtaining modified behavior through convincing communication.[24] Thus, the intention of the influencer toward the one being influenced may be anticipated out of affection, respect, cooperation, or service, not because of compulsion. Influence is at work when one person voluntarily undertakes certain activities at the behest of another and adopts the activity's object as his own or modifies his behavior in order to live up to the expectations of the influencer.

---

23. *Ibid.*, p. 274.
24. Berkowitz, *Group Processes* (New York: Academic Press, 1978), p. 108.

In an interesting classification, Lasswell and Kaplan formulated a graphlike pattern in which the base and goal of influence were determined. They were able to generate 64 varieties of forms derived from the influence process. As illustrated in Table 5.1, these classifications provide any number of inferences about influence.

Influence can be used positively in a leadership situation when an individual uses it as he communicates with others in the attainment of specified aims or objectives. This social relationship is based upon acceptance of ideas which cause others to become aware of the leader, to recognize and assimilate the information he is presenting, and to move or act on the basis of this information toward some goal which has been set. Thus the leader functions in a social climate wielding the power of activating other individuals and stimulating them to perform in ways that he, or the group, has decided upon. This is, in fact, the power of influence.

Many kinds of influence exist, including economic, political, religious, military, educational, ideological, and social. However, these aspects of influence are not necessary for the true leader. The influence of leadership does not depend upon economic, political, or other types of coercion in order to achieve its objectives. The real leader does not have to depend upon physical force, bribery, propaganda, dogma, or the threat of social ostracism to reach his stated goals. The real leader wields his power with people because they want to follow him; they *want* to believe in him, what he says, what he does, how he does it, and what he symbolizes.

Influence and Power

The leader is placed in a position of extreme power through his influence with others.[25] This capacity for stimulating other people and causing them to change or move in particular directions is most important in the leader's make-up. Influence rests on acceptance and faith, while power is based on conditioning, indifference, or coercion. It entails control of actions by varied mechanisms.

An often stated claim is that influence requires the use of power. This implies that any attempt at influence would mean the imposition of power over the individual who was influenced. In the sense that this idea is being promoted, the words influence and power are not synonymous. Another specious idea is that imposed leadership, with authority granted from some institutionalized structure, must

---

25. Kurt Lewin, *Field Theory in Social Science* (New York: Harper, 1951), pp. 40–41, 176–187, 224–228.

TABLE 5.1   CLASSIFICATION OF THE FORMS OF INFLUENCE AND POWER
(Adapted from Lasswell and Kaplan, 1950, p. 87)

The Means of Influence / The Goal of Influence

	Power	*Respect*	*Rectitude*	*Affection*	*Well-Being*	*Wealth*	*Skill*	*Enlightenment*
Power	Political Power	Homage	Inculcation	Fealty	Compulsion	Polinomic Power	Directorship	Indoctrination
Respect	Councilorship	Sponsorship	Suasion	Esteem	Charisma	Credit	Guidance	Authoritativeness
Rectitude	Mentorship	Approbation	Moral Authority	Devotion	Chastisement	Ethnomic Influence	Injunction	Censorship
Affection	Personal Influence	Regard	Moral Influence	Love	Guardianship	Benefaction	Zeal	Edification
Well-Being	Violence	Terror	Discipline	Rape	Brute Force	Brigandage	Forced Labor	Inquisition
Wealth	Ecopolitical Power	Standing	Simony	Venality	Subsistence Power	Economic Influence	Employment	Advertising
Skill	Expertness	Admiration	Casuistry	Ingratiation	Prowess	Productivity	Management	Intelligence
Enlightenment	Advisory Influence	Fame	Wisdom	Sympathy	Regimen	Economic Foresight	Instruction	Education

Note: Reprinted from H. D. Lasswell and A. Kaplan, *Power and Society,* by permission of the Yale University Press.

operate within the framework of power. There are a number of elements which should be remembered when considering these assertions. Primarily, power may contain two opposing forces—agreement or influence potential, and rejection or resistance potential. Second, the rejection of influence in the presence of an attempt at influence does not mean that the influencer is without power.[26] It may simply be that the influential person has not employed all of the potential persuasion at his disposal. Inhibition in the application of actual power in imposed organizational groupings is an essential precondition for coordinated and smooth relationships. If the individual in a headship situation constantly exercises the authority of his position, he will simply erode his effectiveness in any protracted association and will develop resistance to his intended objectives or changes. Additionally, the loss of group morale and concomitant cohesiveness is likely. The unrestrained use of power in imposed organizational structures does not often occur, but there is an increased probability that mutually beneficial negotiations will grow to compensate for resistance.

Appointed Leadership and Power

A further qualification is that power may be applied incrementally. It is not an all-or-nothing proposition. Even within the most rigidly conceived structures, effective leadership and the use of power are not considered synonymous. Actually, imposed leaders must take into account the structure of the emergent group which furnishes support for the individual and offers power in the shape of a reciprocal resistance potential to the autocratic employment of power. Power to evade unrestrained demands lies with the group and this necessitates recognition of this pressure/resistance as a significant reaction. Under extreme circumstances, where power emanates from physical force and predicts the result, power is not the means of successful leadership of and by itself.

The vital idea is that attempts at influence by the imposed leader are appraised by the group in terms of the potential for generally accepted group benefits. The continuity of leadership, especially of an imposed leader, requires careful attention to the interpersonal relationships which are affected by the use of power.

Leadership operates in bureaucratic structures, institutional forms, prescribed procedures, and hierarchical expectations. It also operates spontaneously when people interact, join activities, and express

---

26.   J.M. Burns, *Leadership* (New York: Harper and Row, 1978), p. 12.

opinions. The central focus for the leader is the informal or natural organization of human ethics and types of behavior which are not included under codes of conduct, but originate extemporaneously as people interact while they accomplish routine tasks. These are the daily confrontations and stress-producing situations which group members cope with in their efforts to interpret and transform problems into goal identification and purposeful action. Striving to reach a goal supports the dynamic interchange necessary to the social structure and animates interpersonal relationships. It is here that leadership is most effectively practiced. It is here that the leader, through his influence, rather than through domination or power, can use his ability to shape and modifiy the course of human behavior and guide it to beneficial ends.

Influence and Interpersonal Behavior

The word influence suggests many effects that an individual or a group can have on another individual or group. This effect develops only from some sort of interacting relationship, and depends on the manner in which one person's behavior causes another's behavior. Influence really means that the psyche of others is intentionally reached in such a way that the individual so affected wishes to modify his behavior or change his attitudes in conformity with that of the effector.

Among the interrelational processes that are involved with influence are emulation and compliance. Emulation is any behavior which resembles another person's behavior to which it is a response. Individuals imitate or emulate others for several reasons. No one imitates unceasingly. One imitates some individuals more than others, some behaviors more than others, and some actions more than others in response to specific situations. Imitation is not a generalized tendency. It is similar to other kinds of responses that are made in relation to other people to the extent that it satisfies certain motives or reflects particular attitudes in varying circumstances.[27]

Imitation resembles all other behavioral expressions because it incorporates the basic psychological processes of motivation, perception, and learning. The act of imitation excites interpersonal perception which recognizes that the behavior being imitated tends to satisfy some desire on the part of the imitator. Imitative behavior is

---

27. A. Bandura, "Influence of Models' Reinforcement Contingencies on the Acquisition of Imitative Responses," *Journal of Personality and Social Psychology*, Vol. 1. (1965), pp. 589–595.

most probable under those social conditions where some skill or characteristic behavior is wanted. As for interpersonal relationships, an individual is likely to emulate another when he perceives qualities of superiority which are admired as well as attitudes that reflect enough similarity to his own to make the model a repository of confidence.

Compliance is an interpersonal response which depends upon the perceived requests of somebody else through direct communication. It is no overestimation to assert that routine compliance is the fabric from which most, if not all, social existence is produced. It is difficult to conceive of a society in which the common courtesies are excluded. These social compliances exert influence on and elicit response from the daily interactions which permit people to tolerate the ebb and flow of human events.

The socio-psychological aspects of emulation and compliance are universally familiar. Of particular interest are current understandings which interacting persons hold in common: anticipation that one of them will offer and the other will be the recipient of assistance or security. Such perceptions are typical of established role relationships and deal with the internalization of standards.

Also significant are associations of interpersonal attraction. In this kind of relationship influence is likely to be accepted from an individual to whom one is especially drawn. It might be stated that this attraction almost causes the one who is pulled to relinquish some control over himself. In such a relationship, some power is inherent in influence. For corresponding reasons, influence which is likely to be accepted will probably be offered by someone who is drawn to the recipient of the influence. This reciprocal process enables those who need help to accept help thereby making for a satisfactory interpersonal combination.

Influencing others is often made easier by the perceptions and attitudes of those who will be influenced if they identify in some way with the potential giver of influence. When individuals identify with someone else they may be more susceptible to influence by the respected person. It must be noted, however, that not all inordinate tendencies to be swayed by another's influence derive from ego-involvement; one may, for instance, enthusiastically accept another's influence without any desire for emulation.

The circumstances in which influence occurs are:

1. Intrinsic fascination in the behavior indicated or suggested by the person with influence.

2. Amount of captivation by the would-be influencer's perceived qualities, skill, and reliability, as well as one's own desire to gain favor.

3. Necessities imposed by the interpersonal relations between the influencer and the one influenced within an existing hierarchical structure.

If one of these aspects exists to any great extent, acceptance of influence is highly probable despite either the absence or presence of other conditions. If all are present, there can be no question that influence will be accepted. The converse is equally true.

Influence and Mutual Reinforcement

All interpersonal relationships are, in effect, participation in the exchange of influence. Let us consider those situations in which two or more individuals influence one another identically. One situation immediately brought to mind is the effect that crowd stimulation has upon the individual. No matter how it is instigated, the behavior of the crowd may cause a change of behavior on the part of the individual, who in turn adds his behavior in response. Each behavior elicits additional behavior.

Within the group situation, the kind as well as the degree of behavior exhibited by group members is frequently influenced by their interaction with one another. When the norms of any group affect membership behavior, there is a mutualized influence operating. The effects on the nature or the type of conduct expressed can be ascribed to group reinforcement. Mutual reinforcement reflects interpersonal processes wherein group standards are developed, agreed upon, internalized, and strengthened among individuals who are members of the group.

Such interaction includes communication and interpersonal experience subject to several conditioning forces. There is the immediate relationship of mutually reinforced influence involving two or more individuals in which there is an exchange of communicative capability by all parties concerned. Each participant acknowledges the other as a possible communicator and is stimulated to transmit information about some commonly held idea or activity. Even the act of originating communication opens the potential for the initiator to enter the sphere of influence of another's reaction. If, moreover, the first party is unqualifiedly attracted to the second, he is susceptible to the latter's influence within the bounds of his attraction. Attraction signifies that one finds laudable traits in the individual toward whom one feels drawn, and close relations with such a person become extremely satisfying. If the attractive person's assistance is in some way needed, he is in a position to exert all the more influence on the requestor, either by granting or witholding the required aid. A relationship of mutually reinforced influence is established to the degree that two or more persons have such perceptions of one another.

Another variation affecting the quality of behavior is consensual communication. If two or more persons are conscious of the fact that they will be fraternizing in some context—as team members, club members, group members—each will experience some hesitancy or doubt if signs of mutually accepted meanings are nonexistent. The more such individuals are thrown together and the greater the necessity for them to work together, the more vital is an acknowledgment of reciprocal agreement on conditions pertinent to their united efforts. Consensus is a prerequisite of their affiliation, and the determination that they can agree on commonly held ideas or interests is very satisfying. Therefore, each will be attentive to any manifestations that express some associated understandings. When members conform to their conscious awareness of accord by feedback information, revealing their perception and confirmation of agreement, consensus is accompanied by reciprocity. The process of forming shared attitudes and perspectives is generally coupled with much testing and accident, but sooner or later, through the practice of attitudinal modification and of simple revelation of mutual consensus, some level of communal group-related attitudes results through prolonged contact.

Commonly held attitudes tend to become internalized. This happens in communication dealing with experimentation and reaffirmation: group members show each other, through their respective actions, not merely what they believe to be appropriate behavior, but also what they expect normal behavior for group members to be. Any behavior which typifies the membership becomes normalized over time, accepted as standard, and is displayed in any number of ways. Thus, habitual dress, mannerisms, activities, meeting places, reading matter, etc., come to be reinforced and accepted by group members, while other behavioral expressions are discouraged, disparaged, or otherwise disapproved. In this way, subtle and not-so-subtle information about group behavioral standards are expressed. Everyone who accedes to the norms, particularly if it is done in a positive, predictable manner without subsequent depreciation, is thereby strengthening them. Similarly, each implied admonition at some deviation from the norms also works to sustain them.

Such group reinforcement essentially relies upon an interpersonal response of reciprocal and self-reinforcement. Each individual member of the group finds it satisfying to receive the approbation of other members so his norm-accommodating behavior will probably be strengthened, either by the approval of others or, if he has assimilated the norms, by living up to his own expectations. This sets a standard for other members who see it. While it is not unknown for some group members to conform to group norms in a superficial manner, group viability requires, in very fundamental ways, concurrent self-support and reciprocal support. Without such simultaneous reinforcement of self and others, group norms could never be established and there would be negligible group stability. The entire concept of reciprocal and self-reinforcement is essential to prolonged group life. The net effect of such standardizing results in mutual influence.

QUESTIONS FOR DISCUSSION

1. Differentiate domination, power, and influence.
2. Domination requires submission. Why do people enter into such relationships?
3. What is the ambivalence of submission and autonomy?
4. What defenses can an individual use to offset dominance?
5. What is the malignant spiral?
6. What is potential power?
7. Why should absolute power corrupt absolutely?
8. What are the descriptive components of power?
9. How is leadership different from power? How is leadership similar to power?
10. In what ways are leadership and influence synonymous; in what ways dissimilar?
11. How are influence and power alike?
12. How does influence affect interpersonal behavior among followers?
13. What is mutual reinforcement?

BIBLIOGRAPHY

Bruce-Gardyne, Jock, and Nigel Lawson. *The Power Game: An Examination of Decision-Making in Government* (Hamden, Conn.: Shoe Shine Press, Inc., 1976).

Clegg, Stewart, *Power, Rule and Domination: A Critical and Empirical Understanding of Power in Sociological Theory and Organizational Life* (Boston, Mass.: Routledge & Keegan Paul, Ltd., 1975).

Galbraith, John K., *The Anatomy of Power* (Boston, Mass.: Houghton Mifflin Co., 1983).

Giddens, A., and P. Held, *Class, Conflict and Power* (New York: State Mutual Book & Periodical Service, Ltd., 1982).

Golding, David, and others, *Power, Control, and Bureaucracy* (New York: State Mutual Book and Periodical Service, 1978).

Goodin, Robert E., *Manipulatory Politics* (New Haven, Conn.: Yale University Press, 1980).

Howard, Donald W., ed., *Power: Its Nature, Its Use and Its Limits* (Cambridge, Mass.: Schenkman Publishing Co., Inc., 1982).

Pfaltzgraff, Robert L., and Yri Ra-anan, eds., *The Projection of Power: Perspectives, Perceptions, and Problems* (Hamden, Conn.: Shoe String Press, Inc., 1982).

Van Fleet, James K., *Twenty-five Steps to Power and Mastery over People* (Englewood Cliffs, N.J.: Prentice-Hall, Inc., 1970).

Welsh, Williams A., *Leaders and Elites* (New York: Holt, Rinehart & Winston, Inc., 1979).

Wong, Dennis H., *Power: Its Forms, Bases, and Uses* (New York: Harper & Row, Publishers, Inc., 1979).

II

Leadership and the Group

CHAPTER SIX

The Leader and Leadership Components

Leadership is ability, process, and product. It is an ability in that the potential leader must have the physical and intellectual power to perform those functions which attract others to him. It is a process in that interpersonal relationships are developed and certain behavioral changes are brought about. Further, it depends upon the communications process through which ideas are transmitted, accepted, and acted upon. It is a product in the sense that the outcomes of these processes combine to effect influence with others and can result in satisfying group or individual goals.

THE MAKINGS OF A LEADER

The swelling undertone of many voices continues unabated until a brief announcement is circulated through the meeting place. There is an expectant hush as fifty thousand lungs convulsively ingest air. The stadium's atmosphere is charged with a current of electric tension; then the air is rent asunder as wave upon wave of cheers ring out to acclaim the tall distinguished figure walking to the speaker's stand. The band plays a flourish; powerful spotlights pick out the individual who, with purposeful strides, is ascending to the place of honor. The crowd is going wild. A tumult of sound reverberates over the assembly. The recipient of this homage is excellently tailored; he has a fine family background; he has been educated at one of the great seats of learning; he is independently wealthy, a pillar of his church, and a man of integrity and proved patriotism with a spotless record of public service. His speaking voice is powerful, his enunciation clear; his thoughts and ideas are intelligible to all. At every pause there is wild applause.

To the people listening to him he represents several things. He is a benevolent father—kind, patient, understanding, compassionate. He is a judge—ethical, high principled, wise, knowing the values of human behavior and travail. He is a ruler—controlling the activities of everyone, commanding, authoritative, directing, powerful when obedience to orders and efficient action are necessary. He is a public servant. An expert in the technical details of getting things performed and administering the complex plans and designs of operating the economic, political, and military structure of government, he makes life easier and more bearable for those who create the products of democratic society. He is a planner. A coordinator of men and materials for the purpose of attaining some predetermined objective, he organizes, interprets, explains, and enlightens those who will carry out the functions of production. He is a delegate of the people, speaking for them and representing them in public affairs. He negotiates, conciliates, arbitrates, and mediates for them. He mirrors the concerns and requirements of the people. He inspires, persuades, urges, and communicates his desires through stimulating personal contact. He is prophetic, idealistic, and imbued with the enthusiasm of his calling which infects and impels his followers to rush on to an objective. His image is magnified and projected into a glow of human enterprise which attempts to identify itself with him. He has personal qualities that are worthy of emulation. His thinking processes are so powerful and logical that he awes others by his critical analysis and brilliance of thought. He understands people: what makes them think the way they do; what their wants, desires, needs, and interests are. He knows the insidiousness of the human personality. He is aware of human weaknesses, foibles, strengths, purity, and morality. He symbolizes what is the ideal in all. He represents people's goals, their fears, burdens, guilt, and innocence. He is electrifying. His presence and views stimulate others to higher proficiency, morale, and principle. His spirit, enthusiasm, drive, and dynamism create a similar condition in his followers, and they arise to the occasion. He is the educator, preacher, scientist, policeman, nurse, administrator, lawyer, coach, congressman, banker, philosopher, editor, neighbor, politician, laborer, or personality who fills the bill at any particular place or time. He is the composite picture of the leader.

Let us look again at another audience and meeting place. Again we have a gathering of tens of thousands; again we have an expectant hush before a tumultuous wave of sound shatters the air. Again we listen to the tumult of hurrahs and victory screams as fanatical fans drive themselves to frenzy. Hysteria is loose. He has arrived. He is small, poorly dressed, unkempt. No one knows where he came from or who his family is. His has no formal education; he is a self-taught and self-made individual. His gutturally accented voice is hard to hear and difficult to understand, yet he hypnotizes the mass of people with what he has to say. He is acclaimed over and over again. He is the deliverer; he will make everything right again. He has great vision; he will protect and defend; he offers salvation, land, money, food, equality, independence, or a new idea. He deals with kings and presidents, industrialists and corporations, yet he is a man of the people. He lives in the city but has been a farmer all of his life. He stumps the rural sections but is city-bred. His nails are cracked, though he dines on spotless linen. He is accused of malingering, malpractice, corruption, tyranny, and evil, but those who follow him love him. He has been in jail for crimes against the state, but this act only enhances him in the eyes of his followers who venerate him. He is undisciplined, immoral, vicious, snobbish, paranoiac. An egomaniac with antisocial tendencies, he is alternately aloof, cold, friendly, kind, courteous, plain, simple, smiling, good, energetic, decisive, a man of action, passive, wise, foolish. A fine conversationalist, he is a good listener, progressive, reactionary, democratic, dictatorial, admired as well as abhorred. He speaks for us all; yet his views represent few of us. His complex thought patterns and visions are not well understood, though he communicates his ideas very well. His commands create fear, but people obey because they want to. He is the leader.

This jumble of adjectives presents a complete dichotomy that is also a composite of a leader. These two illustrations have their true life counterparts. The reader merely has to look at recent history to find individuals who fit these descriptions. Divergent as these two characterizations are in background, traits, personality, education, and benefits, they have one thing in common: they are leaders—to their followers.

Then what is a leader? What is the nature of leadership? Ask these questions of a randomly selected population sample and the conflicting answers will fill ten volumes:

The leader is one who facilitates action.
The leader is the strongest, smartest, or most popular.
The leader has the most power, money, or social status.
The leader is the boss; he tells everybody what to do.
Leadership is the ability to get people to do what is desired of them, regardless of how they originally feel about the action.
Leadership is authority or control over a group of people.
The leader can never afford to vacillate; he must never show weakness or concern, or else his group will step all over him.
The leader is always right, or good, or certain of his destination.
Leadership is a product of the situation.
Leadership is personality factors plus a sensitive feeling for the needs and desires of others.
The leader is the most influential person.

Several essential problems need clarification to disentangle them from unfounded rumor and stubborn misconception.[1] The first is the problem of what leadership should be, and this involves a question of ethics in human conduct.

Leadership is a learned ability through which other people become aware of the person attempting to lead, recognize the information or idea which he is trying to present, and move or act on the basis of the idea toward some predetermined end. The leader must be capable of getting other people to recognize this, to understand what he is attempting to communicate or trying to do, and to follow his advice. Further, he must provide his followers with reasons for accepting his ideas for planned or immediate action. A leader, consequently, may be defined as one who has unusual influence with others.[2]

The term "leadership act" is used to designate a pattern of interpersonal behavior in which one person attempts to influence another and the other person accepts this influence. Such a definition of leadership has several implications. The first is that whether an act is one of leadership or not depends in part on the degree to which others accept it. Leadership is not defined here as a quality inherent in a person, nor in an "act," pure and simple. Leadership exists in the relationship between two people. Note furthermore that in terms of this definition the person engaging in the act of leadership must have an intention to influence. That is, he intended to communicate to others, and hoped that they would accept his ideas.[3]

Leadership is based upon influence, and influence is derived from understanding the needs of others. Influence further rests on three distinct premises: recognition, comprehension, and action toward some expressed goal. When an individual can influence others in a direction which he wants them to take, he is a leader. Thus, the leader activates other individuals, stimulating them to perform in ways which he has previously decided upon.

To be most influential, the leader has certain criteria to live up to.[4] He must be capable of getting other people to give him their attention

---

1. M. W. McCall Jr., and M. M. Lombardo, *Leadership: Where Else Can We Go?* (Durham, N.C.: Duke University Press, 1978), pp. 14–30.

2. A. S. McFarland, *Power and Leadership in Pluralist Systems* (Palo Alto, Cal.: Stanford University Press, 1969), p. 154.

3. E. Stotland and L. K. Canon, *Social Psychology: A Cognitive Approach* (Philadelphia: W.B. Saunders Company, 1972), p. 530.

4. E. Hollander and J. Julian, "Studies in Leader Legitimacy, Influence, and Innovation," in L. Berkowitz, ed., *Advances in Experimental Social Psychology*, Vol. 5 (New York: Academic Press, 1970), pp. 33–69.

and recognition. This is the first step in implementing his ideas and impressing them on prospective followers. Interest must be aroused, but once stimulated, most people grasp and react to ideas which are presented to them. They make intense efforts to learn facts appealing to their self-interest, especially when concentration on a particular goal is to their advantage.

Enthusiasm and a genuine feeling for the idea which he is espousing is probably the best method by which the potential leader can sell himself and his ideas. When the individual actually believes in his project, when he sees it as an ideal to be reached, when he experiences and captures the excitement that such a vision has for him and passes it on to those who may follow, then he is well on his way to establishing influence with others.

The transmission of the electric quality of enthusiasm is quite important, for it results in attention and recognition. Attracting attention to oneself in order to gain a following requires a presentation appealing to the appetites of those desired as followers.

Recognition Seeking

The leader appeals to people by utilizing his knowledge of what they want, fear, hate, or love. He reaches them on a level which they can understand and appreciate. He plays upon their sympathies, pride, intelligence, emotion, or bias. He implies, suggests, persuades, reiterates, inspires, and infuses vitality into those whose attention he gains. He preaches about a glittering goal which will usually arouse curiosity. He stimulates the listener with questions which demand an answer. He holds out to the enraptured a panacea for their ills, troubles, or ego. This all-powerful idea and the individual who pushes it are the focal point of vast interest.[5]

Among the techniques which the would-be leader might apply as he seeks recognition are those of: 1) implication; 2) logical persuasion; 3) prophetic inspiration; and 4) repetition. No universal principle can be laid down as to when and how these can be practiced wisely. The leader probably will use one, several, or all of these methods to secure attention. A leader chooses those which are most effective in a given situation.

Implication is often used to strengthen or renew confidence in the leader. For example, the hint of popular support, whether valid or not, does more to enhance the leader's idea or movement than any

---

5. W. L. Shirer, *20th Century Journey: The Nightmare Years, 1930–1940* (Boston: Little, Brown and Company, 1984), pp. 123–131.

exhortation may. It is a subtle form of flattery for those who listen. It really means: "Why not get in on the ground floor? You are important to this plan. Besides, everybody is doing (or joining). Get in step." The leader implies that in some way he symbolizes the values of his supporters. Those who listen to him identify themselves with him. They relate to him for some reason and feel that a readily apparent connection exists between themselves and the leader. Illustrative of this is a situation in which many recreationists on the program level find themselves. They are placed into groups for which they have little, if any, affinity and are expected to "lead." If they fail in this endeavor, especially with an adult or teenage group, their lack of success is attributed to a deficiency of experience, skill, or personality. When an individual has nothing in common with others of a group, he finds it almost impossible, or at best very difficult, to achieve a place of importance with the group.

Those workers in the field of recreational service who have been prepared by education, experience, and a specific orientation would undoubtedly be unhappy serving under a superintendent who had not been similarly prepared or not worked within the various program frameworks of a recreational agency. The superintendent could be a capable individual and have a fine understanding of recreational principles but, because he has had no professional preparation and no practical experience, his workers would always feel that he knew neither the problems nor the difficulties they encounter.

If the group feels that the person who has been placed in the leader's position is too radical in his approach, that is, handling things differently from accepted mores or methods, the members of the group will feel that he cannot properly represent them. They may feel that he does not comprehend the problems they face, and that they cannot communicate with him. Their perception of him thwarts his attempts at influence. Thus the leader must suggest, hint, or imply— directly or indirectly—that he is "one of them." By symbolic or actual association, the aspiring leader must convince his would-be followers that he can represent them because he can be identified with their needs, emotions, and goals.

Logical Persuasion

Logical persuasion is a technique used by the leaders to present an idea in such a manner that its refutation seems to be overt bigotry. The technique requires the compilation and transmission of information with such precision that an audience indisputably favors the leader's cause. This means that the truth must be known and stated without coloration. But before the leader can persuade with irrefutable logic, he must explore all the eventualities or available alternative courses of action in order to anticipate their consequences. This involves the collection and examination of detailed information relating to the problem. He must then analyze pertinent data as it specifically relates to the problem at hand; he must refine the material for ease and thoroughness of presentation. He must study the probable objections to his idea and determine possible courses of action in overcoming such objections. Armed with this knowledge, he is ready to provide a rational frame of reference for the issues.[6]

A typical case illustrates this concept:

A low-income housing development, staffed by the public recreational service department, had a predominantly black population. When a survey indicated that many residents were interested in crafts, a class was scheduled. All who expressed an interest were invited. The first meeting was attended by fifteen blacks and eight whites. After the meeting, the recreationist, who was black, was asked if there were any white instructors on the staff. He received the impression that the white women would not return if the staff were all black.

The recreationist here was alert to the numerical majority of one racial group. He realized that this might lead minority group members to withdraw. He knew that he had to give the white minority a sense of security.

The recreationist managed to recruit a white volunteer to assist with the group. At subsequent meetings the white proportion of participants increased and the entire group enjoyed the crafts course. White children also came to the recreational center and participated in a variety of activities. Adults returned for other activities and soon a successfully integrated program existed.

The recreationist knew that it would be desirable to move slowly and gain the group's confidence. He determined that the first activity had to be successful. By adroit tactics he gained acceptance, overcame resistance, and was able to persuade formerly reticent individuals to be more forthcoming.

Logical persuasion is a direct appeal to listeners through public speech, debate, literature dissemination, and publicity through the communications media. Information based on fact and logic and imparted in a stimulating manner is a most valuable technique for persuading an audience and obtaining lasting influence. Simply

---

6. R. K. Greenleaf, *Servant Leadership* (New York: Paulist Press, 1977), pp. 29–35.

haranguing a group of people with sensational, irrational, and bigoted slogans may, for a short time, appeal to the emotionally immature or slow-thinking person, but ideas based on ignorance and prejudice cannot survive long without requiring overt aggressive acts to sustain them. Thus, the typical demagogue will invariably appeal to the ignorant and fearful with emotion-clouding sentiments having no basis in rationality or logic. This message—"Don't confuse me with the facts; I've already made up my mind"—causes momentary excitement which dies out when any attempt at clear thinking is made. Unfortunately, people geared to emotionality almost always fail to discriminate between feeling and thinking. Nevertheless, leaders and particularly recreationists cannot resort to demagoguery. It is neither an ethical practice nor leadership; it is manipulation.[7]

Logical persuasion is a powerful factor in obtaining influence with people, for within it lie the nuggets of truth. Those within hearing must, if they are at all intelligent, give their undivided attention to valid argument. The leader needs agreement on commonly accepted aims; through the process of logical persuasion he may achieve this end. The demagogue almost always lies as he makes his emotion-laden pitch. As usual, people finally realize the truth, sometimes before the demagogue obtains power. In any case, even avid supporters become tired of being lied to and eventually break away and withdraw their support.

There are many occasions when logical persuasion can be used to gain an objective. In order to elicit an appropriate response, the leader must define and be thoroughly acquainted with the problem. He must gather topical evidence and present it with clarity, directness, and sincerity. He must anticipate the probable objections to his aims and be conversant with other possible lines of action. He must stop any opposition before it has a chance to gain momentum and sway opinion away from his goal. Finally, he must take some kind of action to further his aims and reach his goal. His common sense and social sensitivity will unquestionably affect any influence he may gain.

Prophetic inspiration has an historical acceptability. Throughout the course of written history there are many instances where individuals have arisen and influenced others by their transcendental utterances. They have been called prophets, judges, saints, heretics, sages, fools, and fanatics. Yet, each in his turn has had his share of believers and followers. Biblical literature is full of prophetic warnings. The books of Genesis, Exodus, Judges, Prophets, and Kings

---

7. Ellen Hume, "Storm Center," *The Wall Street Journal*, Vol. CCIII, No. 82 (Thursday, April 26, 1984), pp. 1, 19.

are replete with inspiring statements by those who were leaders in their day. For example, there are the stories of Jacob and his vision, Samuel, Saul, David, Gideon and his army, Moses and the years in the desert, and Nathan, Isaiah, Nehemiah, and Jeremiah in the Old Testament and others in the New Testament. Joan of Arc was led by prophetic inspiration, and so were Savonarola, Mohammed, and other particularly gifted individuals who, from time to time, have been able to read the signs of the times by understanding what people want and why they behave the way they do.

Prophetic inspiration can be utilized when an individual understands cause and effect relationships. Attention and influence have been gained this way by crusaders or reformers, social engineers, people wishing to remake the social structure and establish equalitarianism, individuals reacting to social evil by courageously taking a stand against it, even at the expense of a martyr's demise. Prophecy, after all, is simply projection of things to come on the basis of what is now known. No one can actually foresee the future, but intelligent individuals can analyze current events, determine specific social, political, economic, military, or ideological trends, and prognosticate upon that knowledge. The doctor's diagnosis is merely of what ails the patient; his prognosis rests upon several variables such as the individual's constitution, the availability of drugs or new surgical techniques, nursing care, diet, and other factors. This is very nearly true of those who utter statements about future events. The energy crisis of 1974 was forecast ten years earlier. Predictors of future events concerning natural resources, ecological degradation, overpopulation, and other social problems are using current data to warn of things to come.

There must have been many informed people who correctly surmised the outcome of Germany's Nazification in 1933. We know that Winston Churchill was one of those who foresaw the coming conflict, but he was in no position to do anything about his prediction.[8] Many diagnosed the Japanese expansionist policy and patiently predicted the United States' eventual involvement with that power. Many people today are crying in the wilderness of public unconcern about the degeneracy of social and political mores. There are those who are vitally concerned with this country's apparent headlong rush downhill into mediocrity and unprincipled conduct.[9] There are those

---

8. Martin Gilbert, *Winston Churchill: Wilderness Years* (Boston: Houghton Mifflin Company, 1982), pp. 77–143.
9. *The New York Times*, "FAA Ethics Inquiry Asked," Vol. CXXXIII, No. 46034 (Friday, May 4, 1984), p. A19.

of enormous talent and intellect who warn of the inroads of organized crime, lack of morality, lack of intellectual freedom, lack of privacy, ideological restraint, and the mounting pressures of foolish and wasteful living. Spaceship Earth seems to be on a collision course with disaster, according to some well-informed people.[10] Naturally, society has labeled such individuals as Cassandras or Jeremiahs. They too have their followers, although their voices and influence are not yet powerful enough to make headway against public apathy or willingness to accept wasteful government, corporate collusion, political chicanery, individual cheating, or criminality.

Prophetic inspiration may also be thought of as ideas with a sense of urgency about them. Such concepts, when presented to listeners, have an impelling force which motivates immediate action, either of rejection or acceptance. When the idea is too radical for the thought and behavioral patterns of the listeners, they reject it. When it reaches them because of some affecting reason, it is accepted without reservation and with the stipulation that future action will stem from this agreement.

An example of this can be seen in the following quotation: "In Basle I founded the Jewish State. If I said that today, it would be greeted with laughter, but in fifty years from now the truth of this assertion will be understood and universally acknowledged." Thus spoke Theodore Herzl in the year 1897. Just fifty years later, in 1947, another statement, made in a place of aluminum and glass, 3,500 miles and a lifetime away from Herzl's world, was pronounced at the United Nations: "An independent Jewish State in Palestine shall be established by October 1, 1948."[11]

Of course, mere prophecy does not stir a fellowship; it is an individual's all-powerful idea delivered in a dramatic manner that fires the imagination and compels men's hearts, or their romantic inclinations, to action on some question. In the above case the idea was Zionism. This inspiring dream captivated the minds of many persons, inspired them to fulfill the prophecy of Herzl, and satisfied a dream which had taken close to two thousand years to realize. Naturally the cause was helped along a great deal by the terror and genocide of the Nazi regime, but the dream remained and was finally realized.

That is the function of the leader—to captivate, inspire, and create the desire to move toward some goal. In order for this to be

---

10. *The New York Times*, "Breaking the Wilderness Logjam," Vol. CXXXIII, No. 46034 (Friday, May 4, 1984), p. A30.
11. B. Halpern, *The Idea of the Jewish State* (Cambridge, Mass.: Harvard University Press, 1960), pp. 15–17, 23.

accomplished, the individual who wants to lead must have something with which people can identify themselves: a symbol upon which they can fix their eyes, or an idea upon which to base all of their hopes and aspirations.

Unfortunately, prophetic inspiration does not lend itself readily for use in the field of recreational service. Recreationists have little chance to bring this type of technique into play. Theirs is the day-to-day task of working with, guiding, instructing, supervising, or directing people in activities of a recreational nature. The ideas they have are of local interest or are even further restricted to a particular neighborhood or single facility.

Any idea, no matter how inconsequential to large groups or communities of people, may have significance for one or two individuals or, perhaps, to a few dozen. When such an idea gains the attention of those who listen, and when the individual presenting the idea sways opinion in some predetermined direction to attain an objective, whether important or not, he has performed an act of leadership.[12]

Any idea takes a varying amount of time to reach the attention of potential followers. It may evoke immediate response or some interval may intervene. During the course of this interval, the original contributor may have vanished from the scene. However, as long as the idea still circulates, the influence of the originator may be considered operable and functioning. The idea is a seed; once it is nourished it will eventually fulfill its potential and flourish.

Repetition

Repetition is a technique a leader can use to impress a specific concept upon an audience. The validity and reliability of this technique is evidenced by its long and continuing existence. Among the various groups that frequently use repetition are educators, political officials, the clergy, the military, businessmen, labor unionists, and, most assuredly, advertisers.

Educators have long used the repetition of facts to make students relate various pieces of knowledge. Children first begin to learn their language and the social order from constant familiarization with the same idea before they are able to either communicate intelligibly or recognize those about them. The old-fashioned method of using flash cards to teach children their arithmetic progressions and multiplica-

---

12.   M. W. McCall, Jr. and M. M. Lombardo, *Leadership*, pp. 91–98.

tion tables is another attempt at focusing attention upon a single idea or symbol.

Likewise, athletes are trained by drilling them in fundamental physical movements and in patterns of movements. Thus, the initiation of action on the part of an opposing player calls for a counter-movement on the part of the defender, with all such moves drilled into the team members through continuous duplication of activity. This same process can also be seen in military drill, where constant practice assures near-perfect execution of complex marching formations or the handling of various manual weapons. Musicians are trained in this manner also, playing one number over and over until their fingers react automatically on the instrument, almost without conscious thought.

Educational psychologists have been aware of the close association of drill with so-called learning or rote memorization. One such theory of learning dealing with this concept is connectionism, an outgrowth of William James's biological approach to psychology. James, in his classic essay on habit, states:

> Habit is thus the enormous flywheel of society, its most precious conservative agent. It alone is what keeps all of us within the bounds of ordinance, and saves the children of fortune from the envious uprisings of the poor. . . . It is well for the world that in most of us, by the age of thirty, the character has set like plaster, and will never soften again. . . . The great thing, then, in all education, is to make our nervous system our ally instead of our enemy. It is to fund and capitalize our acquisitions, and live at ease upon the interest of the fund. For this we must make automatic and habitual, as early as possible, as many useful actions as we can. . . . Never suffer an exception till the new habit is securely rooted in your life. . . . Continuity of training is the great means of making the nervous system act infallibly. . . . Keep the faculty of effort alive in you by a little gratuitous exercise every day.[13]

Here we can see how drill and incessant practice was thought to determine the acquisition of habits and particular ideas. The attention of the individual was so completely taken up in establishing the patterns that automatic response was the result. Indeed, practice has always been an important phase of the learning process.

Perhaps the most blatant use of repetition has been in connection with the "big lie" technique based on a statement in Hitler's *Mein Kampf*, and used with such telling effect by Joseph Goebbels. The cliché

---

13. William James, *Psychology* (New York: Holt, 1890), I, pp. 121–126. Reprinted by permission.

that came out of Goebbels' Propaganda Ministry was: "Tell a big enough lie, often enough, and soon everybody will believe it." Of course, this is a most cynical view of the human character. Yet, this tool is used every day by large advertising firms and companies who wish to reap profits from the gullibility and ignorance of many people. Public office seekers and holders are not above utilizing this technique as well.

Propaganda campaigns, also called advertising, are routinely operated in this country by those who are aware that repetition of a single idea, over a period of time, will focus attention upon it and make it familiar in the average household. When this happens, it is only a matter of time before a buying habit becomes set. The buyer looking for a particular food or manufactured item will turn to a product whose name he has seen or heard before, rather than to a completely unknown brand. In some cases, he may disregard differences in quality, quantity, or price. This is the influence which repetition can have.

A most eloquent illustration of this factor was the election of an individual to the State Legislature of California in recent years. His advertising (public relations) firm requested that the candidate make no personal appearances or speeches. They would simply advertise his name and picture. The man was elected. This was a pitiful expression of public apathy. Of even greater concern are the ethics of the advertising firm and the candidate for public office. Such activities demonstrate a contempt for the electorate, and—perhaps rightly so—develop a cynical attitude toward packaging, selling, and buying of candidates. This is one of the outcomes of negative propaganda. Familiarity may breed contempt under certain circumstances, but it also indicates the equality of political candidates and is a direct reflection on the attitude and intelligence of the people who vote for them.

The propaganda instruments used to elect candidates to public office are mild in comparison to what happens to dissidents in other parts of the world. One need look no further than the headlines of today's paper to realize this. Thought control by censorship and a captured press, ideological dogma pushed to the point of fanaticism, distorted principles, subjugation and brutalization of annexed people, the reiteration of lies, phrases taken out of context, and the compounding of fears are the means by which subversive ends are achieved.[14] The harassment of the Sakharovs and their subsequent degradation by the Soviet press is a case in point.[15]

---

14.   Anthony Lewis, "A Bankrupt Policy," *The New York Times* (May 24, 1984), p. A27.
15.   *The Wall Street Journal*, "Focus on Pettiness," May 25, 1984, p. 28.

Yet, repetition need not be thought of as a completely negative instrument for subverting the minds of men. The positive aspects of continuous exercise and practice are just as clear. The presentation of a new concept or idea to listeners should be made precisely. The idea must then be explained in some detail, the teller adding color and emphasis as he proceeds. After the exposition has been completed, the idea should be restated in slightly different language. The idea must be coherent to have a possibility of acceptance by those who hear it.

A rule of thumb to follow when presenting a new idea to a group is to tell what is going to be said, say it, and then explain what has just been said. This method gives the individual a chance to assimilate the information and focuses his attention upon a given point, which is the purpose of repetition. Once attention has been captured, recognition follows. This procedure is the first step in attaining influence with people.

Comprehension

Before anyone will follow, he must understand what it is he is following. The idea presented to would-be followers must be intelligible to them.[16] They have to be able to appreciate the message, either on an emotional or intellectual level, before they will take any action.[17] By emotional or intellectual basis, we mean the type of idea which is being presented. If the influencer's style and aim have an appeal only to those who are easily swayed by inflammatory remarks directed toward their basic fears and insecurities, the identification with such ideas will ensure comprehension. There does not have to be a rational thought behind this stimulus. People who allow themselves to be influenced by emotional claptrap such as ultranationalism, fear bred of ignorance, intolerance, supernaturalism, and other "isms" need no intellectualization upon which to anchor their motives. For them, it is emotionalism which spurs their action. All else fades to insignificance in the face of an appeal to basic human nature. An emotional approach completely clouds the true purpose of the message. The consequences are usually hurtful to those who follow the road of immorality, injustice, or bigotry. Comprehension, in this case, merely means that the words or symbols utilized are identifiable with preconceived notions and may therefore be adopted without undue attention given to thought processes. "Rum, Romanism, and

---

16.   Nigel Hamilton, *Master of the Battlefield* (New York: McGraw-Hill Company, 1983), pp. 47–50, 79–83.
17.   Eldon K. Marshall, P. D. Kurtz, and others, *Interpersonal Helping Skills* (San Francisco: Jossey-Bass Publishers, 1982), pp. 317–323.

Rebellion" is a good example of how this style of inflammation can produce the desired results. Today, this is exemplified in such slogans as "The Great Satan," "America is standing tall again," "Pro-life," "Alternate life style," or "Secular humanism."

Here the appeal is made directly to a mass of people whose knowledge of what these ideas convey is so hazy and vague as to lend itself readily to distortions. Fear or desire for profit play a large part in influencing people through emotionalism. A man who covets his neighbor's property is more likely to believe something despicable, although perhaps untrue, about his neighbor if he can see a way to gain the property in question by so believing. Adolf Hitler's infamous career as head of the Nazi government is a classic example of the adverse effect of gaining audience comprehension through appeal to the emotions. An individual who envies another's success is more likely to belittle the latter and is willing to believe any foul thing about him, if by so doing he gains financially or politically, or increases his status.

Americans did this to Japanese-Americans in 1941 when they deprived the Nisi of their rights and put them into concentration camps.[18] The same covetousness now goads the Palestine Liberation Organization and many Arab states in the Mideast. Someone must always pay the piper for the hate mongers who have power aspirations, but unfortunately this is usually the downtrodden minority. The payment is exacted by resorting to, and playing upon, the emotions of the ignorant and morally blind. Emotional behavior is of short duration. It must be periodically restimulated if the desired response is to be elicited. Without the continual harping upon emotional issues, the response to such affairs soon loses impetus.

Intellectual comprehension is another matter entirely. Ideas, even if unfamiliar or radical, may win followers if they are logically consistent and have something to recommend them to those who will listen. They must be based upon rational concepts and principles apparent to anyone with the intelligence to master them. The appeal to intellect must stand up under the suspicion and tests of opposing elements. No person willingly throws over traditional views and accepts unconventional ideas until he has been able to carefully evaluate them and their attendant consequences. A critical analysis of the new before acceptance will markedly affect the intensity and duration of the idea once it has been accepted. Witness the following case:

---

18. "American Scene: Tule Lake 30 Years Later," *Time*, Vol. 103, No. 23 (June 10, 1974), p. 31.

In a community where several low-income housing projects were situated on the outskirts of a middle-income Jewish neighborhood, there was little contact among the teenagers living inside and outside the housing project. Both groups attended the same high school. Mutual distrust and continued isolation threatened to develop into serious confrontations.

The low-income project and the Jewish community were each served by a community center. A joint staff meeting was arranged between the recreationists of each center. Out of this conference grew plans to form a teenage council which would serve as a meeting ground for all of the teenagers concerned. The primary function of the teenage council was to find ways for contact to be made between the various minorities represented and to develop recreational activities for potential participants.

After the council was organized, it sponsored a block party. Limited contact produced further efforts along the same lines and other successful recreational activities were programmed. From initial enjoyment grew better relationships and intergroup cooperation between formerly isolated groups.

When an individual finally decides in favor of something by a process of reflection, introspection, and reasoned inquiry, the notion is more likely to remain with him indefinitely. He will probably be highly stimulated to follow with action any thought that required intellectual exercise. The process of ratiocination urges participation. When insight is gained into the fundamental principles which originated the concept, there will be more readiness to support it.

This is the most important part of comprehension. It allows the receiver to understand not merely what is going on or being said, but why it is so. When, at last, communication is achieved, the results are mutual satisfaction, acceptance, and agreement upon common objectives. This, of course, is a main component of influence.

Intellectual comprehension as a component of influence is illustrated in this situation taken from the report of a supervisor in the field of recreational service:

As a recreational personnel supervisor in a large municipal department of recreational service for X city, I learned that neighborhood participation at a particular facility within my jurisdiction had deteriorated to the point of nonexistence. My problem was to rebuild interest in the activities and program conducted at the facility, utilizing the workers then available.

My first step was to determine the exact nature of the recreational experiences being offered at the agency in relation to the expressed desires of neighborhood constituents. Armed with this knowledge, I held a series of individual conferences with the facility's personnel in order to learn what they understood their responsibilities to be to the community, the agency, and the program.

The results of the conferences indicated that almost all of the workers were at a loss to explain the obvious deficiency of the program, that personal difficulties between workers were an impediment to the program, and that several new workers felt completely discouraged because no in-service preparation was available to them. All of these factors pointed toward a lack of direction, enthusiasm, and cooperation on the job.

I initiated a weekly group supervisory conference designed to facilitate the free flow of ideas, appointed two of the older and more experienced workers to aid the newer employees in becoming oriented and educated on the job, and began a systematic overhaul of the recreational presentation at the center. Within three weeks the effect of the new administration was being clearly demonstrated.

I introduced a professional bookshelf into the agency. I discussed, at the weekly worker-group conferences, the basic concepts for which the agency was created. I spoke about the part that each worker played in the provision of recreational services to the people of the community. I told my people about professional ethics, conduct, and that each of them had the responsibility of representing the agency to the public. I pointed out the fact that their personal reputation was enhanced or destroyed as the public identified them with a successful or poorly operated facility. The presentation of valid reasons for the present personnel program and the necessity for each worker to feel that he was actively contributing to the betterment of the entire department and, consequently, to the field as a whole apparently turned the tide.

Later, individual workers took more interest in their appearance and manner, in giving information or in instructing particular activities. Activities were better planned and scheduled. The means for communicating ideas were facilitated, and workable ideas were used and commended. Every worker seemed to respond to this appeal for dedication to the job in the service of the community, and increased participation at the facility resulted.

Directed Action

The last component of influence, but perhaps the most important, is directed action. Whatever techniques the potential leader has used to capture the attention of his audience and make them comprehend his ideas, only if the audience then acts on these ideas can leadership be said to have occurred. The chain of influence is complete only when individuals are so convinced and inspired by what they have heard that they take direct action toward a goal.

Getting others to act is no small task. The potential leader must be able to judge when the climate is right for action and assume the responsibility for inducing such action. He does this when he accepts or undertakes a specific task which he feels will result in the attainment of a given program he has in mind. Implied in his acceptance of this responsibility is risk of failure and attendant deterioration of any influence which he may have had up to the crucial point of initiating the action.

Two of the responsibilities in guiding others to a specific goal are: such an achievement must be made valuable for those who follow; no matter what the end in view or the reason for its selection and advocation, the leader must still observe moral and ethical boundaries for the benefit of his followers and the social order in which they exist. If he neglects either one of these responsibilities, he will run into difficulty. If he overlooks the welfare of his followers, they will overrule him and his dictates, and thus his influence will be nullified. If he oversteps the lines of good taste, judgment, or morality, the society in which he resides will obstruct and probably destroy or disperse his power. Further, he will do damage to his followers by leading them into trouble. In any case, his value to the group and to himself will be lost.

Basically, goal-striving or task-accomplishment plays an important part in the preservation and spirit of membership within a group. Any activity which speeds action toward a particular objective and lends itself to the continued maintenance and solidarity of the group in question serves to strengthen the influence of the leader.

The fact that the group will react to consolidate any gains it has achieved, especially when threatened by some type of conflict or pressure, means that movement toward a valued end will be more highly motivated and easier to bring about in emergency or stress conditions. One of the methods by which the leader may bring concerted action to his objective is to create situations which will cause action. The leader is obliged, therefore, to produce an atmosphere which is favorable to his aims.[19]

Situations and Leadership

Problems call for behavior which will effectively alleviate painful or apparently insoluble circumstances. The individual who successfully

---

19. F. E. Fiedler, *A Theory of Leadership Effectiveness* (New York: McGraw-Hill Book Company, 1967), pp. 181–196.

discovers the solutions for emergencies or obstructions which block goal realization enhances his influence with the group. Invariably, leadership functions most frequently in groups which are confronted with uncomfortable or anxiety-provoking situations.[20]

The movement of people toward a specific goal requires several types of behavior. One of them is planning for activity, which is a basic function of leadership. A carefully worked-out scheme, analyzed for possible errors and systematically viewed for other possibilities, is the initial step. The margin for mistake must be minimal. Where feasible, all details should be given thorough consideration before any direct action is contemplated. Thus, through the collection of highly relevant information and the sifting of fact and evidence from distortion and half-truth, a composite picture of the immediate situation is drawn. Selecting the one best route which will be least detrimental to the group or which will place the group in the most defensible position and proximity to the goal, is necessary prior to calling for action.

Initiating action is the second phase in achieving predetermined goals. Perhaps the most valid method the leader can use to arouse action on a specific subject is to have his followers participate in goal selection and the decision-making process. Goals cannot simply be pushed onto unsuspecting people. A group will not work for objectives in which it had no choice or with which it does not identify. As participating members in a group enterprise, individuals are more likely to take action. When individuals feel that they have been made a part of the group effort and that their presence contributes directly to the success of the project at hand, they will be motivated to act in order to gain satisfaction. All goals must have a personal appeal for group members, so that they may ego-identify with them and thereby seek to achieve them.[21]

Gaining Involvement

In the field of recreational service, the objectives of the recreational agency define the type of program to be presented to and for the public. Programs cannot be planned merely for the sake of having them. They must be organized to meet the needs of the neighborhoods or other local groups in the community which the agency serves.

The program cannot be arbitrary. It must be planned, developed,

---

20. C. Gibb, "The Principles and Traits of Leadership," *Journal of Abnormal and Social Psychology,* Vol. 42 (1947), pp. 267–284.

21. P. R. Penland and S. F. Fine, *Group Dynamics and Individual Development* (New York: Marcel Dekker, Inc., 1974), pp. 21–22.

and operated out of the needs of the people who will be involved. Activating a drive for the provision of a neighborhood playground within the area in which the playground will be situated is not a difficult task. Because the adults realize the benefit that their children will derive with such a facility in terms of safety, supervision, healthful recreational experiences, and personal satisfaction, they can readily identify with the need for the facility. Once the identification has been established, action follows.

The difficult phase of any goal activation is the establishment of personal benefit or ego-involvement with it. To convince another person to contribute time, money, or effort to a project which will be of no use to him is almost impossible. To promote a program, the object is to help the person see some connection between the goal and himself. This may be established by appealing to community pride, personal philanthropy or altruism, ego-building and involvement, patriotism, or an appreciation of aesthetic, cultural, or historic factors. In any case, a motivating point must be made which will induce the potential follower to participate actively in the attainment of goals which have been set.

The entire function of directed action hinges upon motivational elements in human behavior. Goal motivation has to do with threats to the individual, to his ego concept, or to his basic needs. Goals have meaning for the individual in terms of intrinsic value and symbolic value. Thus, the goal may not only represent economic gain or aesthetic, cultural, social, educational, or physical enhancement, it may also represent mastery, prestige, affection, reputation, or the manifestations of psychophysical needs. When the goal can be related to one or more of these factors, and when the potential followers can be persuaded that unless they act at a given signal or upon a particular plan, the goal or whatever they value will be lost, action will usually follow. The aspect of threat or conflict is adequate to motivate action. Where the goal is important to the individual and he realizes it may be lost by lack of action, the desired participation is usually initiated.[22]

In some instances the leader may attempt to motivate action on the part of his listeners by making use of primitive drives. He may rely on the need for food, the desire to avoid pain, or the drive for self-preservation to inflame his forces to act in a prescribed manner. Also, he may utilize a reward incentive to produce the desired results. Mohammed, founder of the Islamic faith, used the method of reward in the *hereafter* as an inspirational objective for his followers. So

---

22.   R. Hamblin, "Leadership and Crisis," *Sociometry*, Vol. 21 (1958), pp. 322–335.

powerful was this motive that Islamic generals were able to command fanatic fighting forces made up of individuals who thought that the most glorious thing that could happen to them would be to fall in battle fighting for the faith, thereby earning delights ever after in paradise. The Ayattolla Ruhollah Khomeini continues this line of support for his war with Iraq to this very day.

Usually, the leader makes indirect use of the biophysical motives, although these powerful drives are always latent and cannot be ignored by the leader. The psychological, social, and intellectual motives are the ones to which the leader pays particular heed. The leader is in a position to appeal directly to the individual's need for social acceptance, for manipulation and creation of ideas, for self-expression and self-esteem.

A leader may also use the current interests or experiences of his group members. The leader need only relate his ideas to these existing interests, and action upon those ideas will follow. For instance, knowing of the interest of citizens in the provision of community recreational service, he can expect to gain support from them for the organization of a public recreational service department. Immediate interests are usually practicable for initiating action. Once the action is underway, momentum will impel further action.

Appeals to psychological, social, and intellectual needs are also very successful in stimulating action. Ego-involvement may be the most important of the intellectual motives for action. In this case, the goal is presented in such a manner that its attainment will enhance the individual's self-concept, personal worth, and ability. The ego becomes a part of the goal whenever the individual feels that a part of him is identifiable with or attached to the consequences of goal attainment. The leader must use extreme care in applying ego-involvement as a spur to action, and be able to distinguish between those objectives which are meaningful to his followers and toward which they will strive, and those which have little or no meaning to them.

An interesting example of how the leader may utilize ego-involvement as motivation is examined in the following excerpt from the central files of an executive in the field of recreational service:

The community in which I had recently been employed had had a series of bond-issue defeats. The community was quite wealthy, with the average income of its citizens hovering around the six-figure mark. The inability to raise funds to pass any bond issues for community recreational facilities had finally forced my predecessor to resign.

This was my second year in the community, and I found that unless an increase in capital expenditures was made, almost half of the program using the physical facilities and spaces would have to be either abandoned or drastically curtailed. As superintendent of public recreational services, my legal board empowered me with the authority to seek capital funds for the construction, development, and expansion of physical facilities relating to park and recreational services. My only problem was how to gain a favorable consideration and action for this promotion from the citizens of the community. This is what I did:

With the help of my limited staff, I drew up a financial plan consistent with what was needed for the present needs of the community as well as for future growth of population, metropolitan trends, and area annexation. We brought together all of the information that was available, detailing such items as the economic base of the community, land-use patterns, age, sex, occupational status, and the educational experiences of the citizens. I called upon other community agencies, such as the school system, police and fire departments, and health services. I had access to the City Clerk's office for such information on land appraisal and value, subdivisional lines, zoning regulations, and all of those pertinent items that might prove useful in implementing a master plan for the evaluation and development of recreational facilities, capital equipment, and land acquisition. Although I was not prepared to call for bond-issue elections until a year from that time, I was going to schedule all events and leave nothing to chance.

Once the basic information was collected and analyzed, I felt reasonably secure and attempted to put the second phase of our timetable into operation. This involved the presentation of our procedures to interested members of the community.

I lined up speaking engagements with most of the social, civic, professional, and service organizations in the community. I felt that these groups might be our best bet for arousing support for this endeavor, since most community-minded people generally belong to these clubs. My presentation to the people in these groups covered several points. First, there had to be a logical explanation for the expenditures that we were considering. Second, the reasons for having recreational service had to be enumerated. Third, I wanted to involve personally as many of these people as I could in the campaign which was to come.

I utilized the data including charts, maps, and mockups of the proposed developments which had already been collected by my staff. To this I added information concerning population increments, metropolitan trends, and economic productivity which would support our proposals. I spoke about recreational needs that people have, about the growing leisure in the community, about the services that a public and recreational agency provides for all age groups. I told them about human growth and development and the educational, cultural, social, and aesthetic values to be found in recreational experiences.

Then I pointed out the economic gain that could accrue to the value of land from being adjacent to or across from community and recreational parks or other facilities. I further spoke about the benefits that convenient and well-supervised playgrounds would have for the children of the community. Since the facilities were planned so that no child would have to cross a major traffic artery or go more than one-quarter mile to reach a playground, the safety of participants was taken into consideration. Playing on dangerous streets would be avoided. Parents would be able to take their children to nearby and very accessible locations, planned for their comfort and enjoyment.

Finally, I explained that the proposed development would enhance the community setting, beautifying blighted areas and providing green spaces and recreational places which would be preserved for the health, education, and welfare of the citizens of the community for as long as they wanted them.

With this phase out of the way, I received commitments from several members of each group who pledged their support and assistance. My next objective was to form committees which would function as the campaign machine to sell the bond issue to the entire community.

With participation from the local P.T.A., denominational groups, business and professional clubs, and civic and service organizations, I was able to organize the five committees needed to administer the campaign. There was a planning committee, which met to discuss and formulate a better understanding of the community's recreational needs, so that a detailed budget could be made for financing the recreational plan. This group worked as a steering committee, which coordinated all the efforts of participating groups working on the campaign. A budget committee was responsible for estimating the total cost of the campaign and raising the funds necessary for carrying it out. We had a public relations committee, responsible for disseminating information to the public. A neighborhood person-to-person committee was formed. Its duty was to knock on the door of every registered voter within the community and solicit a yes vote on election day. Finally, a transportation committee was mobilized to see that every voter who needed it had transportation to and from the polls.

Every organization in the community supported the issue. With our detailed plan of coordinated action and each individual's participation, a record number of voters turned out on election day. As a result, over $1,872,496 was voted by more than a three-to-one majority.

What had turned the trick? Simply the utilization of people in a planned effort to attain a specific objective. The desired end was already determined, but the people of the community had to be stimulated to achieve this end. Once the citizens listened and were persuaded by the logic of the idea, it was a matter of providing identifying symbols which would bind them to the tasks and serve as the motivating power in gaining this goal. The attractiveness of the original concept, the clear analytic presentation, and the ego-involvement with this project by those who became interested carried the plan to a successful conclusion.

While several techniques were used in achieving the desired goal, it was not until the personal factor was brought in that people responded to the task. Although logical exhortation, repetition, and some emotional appeal was tried, the point that actually impelled action was ego-involvement. Individuals believed that their contribution was more important than anything else. The whole matter became one of reputation, integrity, and personal identification with the success of the bond issue. Reinforcement came with the assignments and the progress made each day the campaign operated. Rivalry between civic organizations was forgotten as each group worked to meet the indicated need. Everybody performed to some extent. Achievement of the predetermined goal was accomplished. Leadership was exhibited. Action was the result.

QUESTIONS FOR DISCUSSION

1. What is a leader?
2. How do leaders develop?
3. Define leadership.
4. How does influence result in leadership?
5. What are the components of the leadership process?
6. How does the leader gain potential participant involvement in group activities?
7. How may ego-involvement enhance activity?

BIBLIOGRAPHY

Lamb, Karl A., *The Guardians of Leadership Values and the American Tradition* (New York: W.W. Norton & Co., Inc., 1983).

Larson, Charles U., *Persuasion: Perception and Responsibility* (Belmont, Cal.: Wadsworth Publishing Co., 1983).

Lassez, William, and Marshall Sashkin, eds., 3d ed. *Leadership and Social Change* (San Diego, Cal.: University Associates, 1983).

Lindgren, Henry C., *Leadership, Authority, and Powersharing* (Melbourne, Fla.: Robert E. Krieger Publishing Co., Inc., 1982).

O'Donnell, Victoria, and June Kable, *Persuasion: An Interactive Dependency Approach* (New York: Random House, Inc., 1982).

Reed, Harold W., *The Dynamics of Leadership* (Danville, Ill.: Interstate, 1982).

Vanderlaan, Roger E., *Persuasion* (Santa Barbara, Cal.: El Camino Publishers, 1983).

CHAPTER SEVEN

Leadership Foundations

Basically, leadership is created in the interrelational factors of three distinct forces. The first of these is a problematic or crisis situation which would cause group dissolution by internal or external stress. Second, the membership of the group needs some guiding hand if it is to achieve goal satisfaction. An intrinsic part of this need is for a unifying or cohesive element around which the group can rally and on which its individual members can lean for support. The attracting figure may also help group locomotion toward specific objectives, either by formulation or decision-making. Finally, a personality must be located who can react to demanding situations and group needs effectively without assuming a dictatorial approach. These are the three distinct but essential aspects of leadership.

In the simplest circumstance—when a group begins a discussion to reach a decision of some kind, for example—a leader seems to be required. Actually, it is very difficult for a group to act or verbalize except through a designated member. If everybody speaks, acts, or plans simultaneously there will just be general confusion with each person going his own way. For the group to act cohesively, it is vital that individual members speak for it. Ordering of discussion is obviously necessary to a group. Such an arrangement can only be effected through the action of an individual. One person must articulate the necessity for order, the techniques to be employed to reach goals, the acceptance of the means for achievement, and the decision to act.[1] An individual must speak for the group and offer simple but essential methods. Even at this basic level, the need for a leader is real and recognized by most groups. When the group requires greater diversity of activity and, therefore, more cooperation and coordination, the fundamental need for a leader is heightened.

---

1. R. H. Hall, *Organizations: Structure and Process* (Englewood Cliffs, N.J.: Prentice-Hall, Inc., 1982), pp. 176–177.

THE EMERGENCE OF LEADERSHIP

The leader seems to emerge in one of several ways. The first way is mutual agreement among the members of a group who become aware that an individual serves the group more effectively than others.[2] Such accord and acceptance may be completely predictive or mere estimation, or it may come in consequence of various members' experiences. The agreement by group members may be obvious or subtle. The group member who first suggests some plan of action that is consonant with other members for achieving satisfaction of needs may collect a following for varying lengths of time. The group member who is known to possess a skill, knowledge, or other means of solving a problem confronting the group may be called upon and expected to perform the leadership role.

Another reason that leaders arise is that the person who desires some end may not be able to achieve it without the assistance of others. If he can direct the activities of others by influencing them to participate, his objectives will be met and simultaneously he will have performed an act of leadership. Groups may be sought out by individuals who seek to lead.[3] The individual who finds a group in need of leadership may also discover that unless he is perceived as one who can provide need satisfaction or problem solutions which can reduce costs and augment rewards to potential followers, there will be no followers. Thus, leadership is a symbiotic relationship between the leader and his followers.[4] Both require the other in order to fulfill their needs. Of course, there are other sources of leadership. This chapter is devoted to the ways in which the leader develops.

PROBLEM SOLVING AND LEADERSHIP

The leader steps into a situation that requires attention and enables others to act with or toward some purpose. The recreationist is supposed to be a leader. In fact, this is the work title by which most program or entry-level workers are identified.

Leadership is an explicit understanding and interaction between the person placed in the position of leadership and those of the group or other individuals who are his followers. The leader must also attempt

2. H. H. Blumberg and others, *Small Groups and Social Interaction* (New York: John Wiley & Sons, 1983), pp. 457–459.

3. N. D. Gardner, *Group Leadership* (Washington, D.C.: National Training and Development Service Press, 1974), pp. 26–27.

4. E. P. Hollander and R. G. Hunt, eds., *Current Perspectives in Social Psychology*, 3d ed., (New York: Oxford University Press, 1971), p. 500.

to reconcile whatever differences in opinion there may be. When there is a divergence of opinion, a test of leadership develops.

Leadership is often a product of crisis. Crises, however, need not always be thought of in terms of great peril, revolution, or any other catastrophic event. They may be little-known incidents which have no particular significance to anyone outside the situation. They may occur over school grades, team tryouts, dramatic endeavors, or attempts at creativity. They may occur in the church, in the home, in the community center, or on the playground. They may come in the guise of time, money, effort, or personality. The person who solves critical problems is a leader.

The Appointed Leader

The recreationist functioning as a resource or technical advisor is appointed to his position. Whether or not he is a leader, in the true meaning of the word, or merely performs in a "headship" capacity remains to be seen. A true leader is one who has such influence with others as well as the ability to motivate them toward a particular goal. The recreationist may very well function in this way. However, it is not usually from selection by the group that the recreationist derives his influence, but rather from the auspices of the agency for which he works.[5]

The appointed leader generally has some professional requirement to fulfill, perhaps as a technician, teacher, administrator, or performer. Whatever his role, his assignment comes from some source outside the group with which he will be working. Thus, the appointed leader brings with him an aura of control and authority vested in him by the agency. He must function despite the possible handicap of being placed with a group that does not want him. With appointment come obligations. He must perform within the framework of agency policies; he must attempt to influence a group with whom he works; he has no choice in the selection of his group members, but must provide them with professional service despite any negative personal feeling toward them.

The obverse is that the appointment carries with it the prestige of the agency and its sanction. Group members are more likely to look upon this leader as an individual with the special talents, skills, or techniques to help them function.[6] His word may stop conflict; he may

---

5. B. B. Smith and B. A. Farrell, *Training in Small Groups: A Study of Five Methods* (Oxford: Pergamon Press, 1979), p. 44.

6. L. Berkowitz, *Group Processes* (New York: Academic Press, 1978), pp. 126–132.

be looked upon as the mediator when argument flares. He may become the security or supporting figure to self-effacing members. He may, of course, simply become an object of intense dislike. The latter is a possible outcome when the appointed leader has usurped prerogative. Generally, however, an ambivalent reaction is the one which the appointed leader must face.

The leader, no matter how he tries, cannot always be good, kind, gentle, and permissive. There are times when his understanding of the need of the group as a whole obligates him to act in ways which may deprive one or more members from having things "his own way." Surely some hostile feeling will result from such conflicts. However, the same individual who expresses hostility at one moment may well change as the condition of the group changes. This is a part of the dynamics of group life.

The recreationist will perform his functions within the community in relation to certain cues or influences which are a part of the social and physical environment. The worker will be duly impressed by what he hears, sees, and experiences in terms of his responsibility to behave in a professional manner. From his observation of the individuals with whom he works and the community in which he serves, the recreationist begins to formulate ideas as how best to work in the situation in which he finds himself. The following factors are those which influence the worker as he attempts to fulfill his professional obligations:

1.   The community fabric involves socio-economic-political considerations, ethnic factors, and religious aspects. The life of the community, with its tradition, mores, cultural standards, and social institutions, does much to limit or extend the recreational leader's possible service. Such intangibles as class, race, education, and the like may allow or prevent certain individuals from entering a particular group. Coming from the "wrong side of the tracks," so to speak, may effectively bar persons from acceptance in organizations or cause caste lines to develop which necessitate the organization of certain agencies within one section of the community and not in others. All of these interacting forces play a part in influencing the role of the appointed leader in any recreational agency setting. How the community sees itself will unquestionably have direct bearing upon how the leader will be able to conduct himself or provide the services which he knows are necessary. An unsympathetic or nonsupportive community may cause undue hardship and create conflict situations for him. In such instances, he must create a favorable atmosphere through the use of logical persuasion, education, negotiation, and all

other means at his disposal in attempting to enlighten the community so that what he is doing will receive adequate public support and acceptance. When the community is receptive to his work, his opportunity for professional service is unlimited.

2.   The agency's policies and activities concern such diverse facets as rules and regulations of operation, function or responsibilities, and scope. Depending upon the type of agency—school, club, public recreational department, welfare department, church, or private organization—the recreationist will perform within its frame of reference. If the agency feels that it should operate in a group-work capacity or offer a wide variety of activities which are open to all or a few, it will radically affect the leader's role. Whatever reasons there are for the creation of the agency and how this objective is interpreted by the administrative body of the agency will constitute a point of reference for the recreationist's performance within any group to which he has been appointed.

3.   The agency's facilities will have a marked effect upon the work of the recreationist. The type, number, and adequacy of agency facilities will also attract or repel specific individuals. This reaction may be a limiting or inclusive factor in terms of the leader's effectiveness.

4.   The kind of group with which the recreationist is placed will, in large measure, influence his role as a leader. Whether or not he will lead in a direct manner, work through others within the group, play a resource role or an observing role, or function as an arbitrator will depend upon the interests, needs, abilities, and limitations of the individuals within the group. The amount of help which the group will accept from the leader, as opposed to what it actually needs, and the skill and efficiency of the recreationist himself will certainly restrict or extend the range of leadership functions and responsibilities. If the recreationist is a true leader and understands his position in relation to that of individuals in the group, his confidence, talent, and competence will be "on the line," and will be continually tested.[7]

All of these conditions may well create the boundaries and special circumstances beyond which the appointed leader may not go. His appointment is based upon specific professional qualities. He must function to the extent of his professional knowledge and skill, limited

---

7. H. B. Trecker and A. R. Trecker, *Working with Groups, Committees, & Communities* (Chicago: Association Press, 1979), pp. 65–70.

only by the immediate policy of the agency, the support of the community, the makeup of the group to which he is appointed, and his concept of service within the recreational field.

Crisis situations critically illustrate the leadership adequacy of the recreationist in the group setting. The appointed leader moves into a crisis with complete awareness of why such a condition exists and what must be done to control or remove it. He looks upon conflicts as a challenge to his knowledge and technical skill. Such experiences also permit the expression of genuine feelings of affection or dislike. Crises give members a chance to solve a great variety of questions which confront any association of people.[8]

The crisis is welcomed as a condition which clearly indicates the range or limitation of members in handling pressures. The reactions of group members to any strained situation provide additional insight into individual and collective needs. The observed behavior is evaluated in reference to group structure or other norms which are available. From these views of individual and group behavior the worker may draw certain conclusions about participating individuals and thereby may place himself in a position where his technical knowledge or understanding of those individuals would be useful to them. By enabling these people to meet extraordinary situations which may have been beyond their experience or ability to handle, the worker affords them opportunity to help themselves and thus grow mentally and socially.

Realizing that conflict is simply a question of points of view, experience, or knowledge about particular values, the leader is better able to give support and encouragement where needed. His obligation is to sustain his group members and help them to achieve desirable patterns of behavior in dealing with unaccustomed emergencies or predicaments.

The Elected Leader

The elected leader may not be a leader at all; he may be brought to the position of leadership through popularity, accident, design, or tradition. Such an individual could very well be a real leader, his popularity reflecting his ability to influence others, but this is not necessarily true. Our society is quite aware of popularity polls and how they may place into office or position an individual who is neither qualified nor, in fact, a leader. Fortunately for recreational programs, the recreationist is seldom, if ever, elected to his position.

---

8.   C. Gibb, "The Principles and Traits of Leadership," *Journal of Abnormal and Social Psychology*, 42 (1947), pp. 267–284.

Some elections are really popularity contests based upon so-called values which have little or nothing to do with leadership. For example, a candidate for public office might proclaim the fact that he belongs to a certain religious denomination, is married, has children, loves dogs, is a veteran, and is a member of a number of service clubs or fraternities. Few of these facts have any bearing on his qualification to hold office. They are simply a means of creating a popular image of the candidate, running on a "common man" approach rather than on his demonstrated qualifications to hold the office.

Election by popularity can be achieved if the candidate can force himself to shake as many hands and kiss as many babies as possible, or say the things which people want to hear, even if he does not believe them himself. Typical of this situation is the following example:

The Recreationist Majors Club at X College was about to elect officers to administer and operate the club for the academic year. A senior student campaigned vigorously for the president's office. She made many promises. She indicated that, if elected, she would design a calendar of activities, hold interesting meetings on topical subjects, make sure that the monthly newspaper was produced, and see to the general management of the club. These promises included a certain amount of recruitment for new club members. She was vivacious, intelligent, made friends easily, and was considered excellent material for the presidency. As a leader, she was a complete failure. She not only failed to live up to her campaign pledges, she completely ignored the club in favor of other less arduous assignments. What resulted was a deterioration of the club program, demoralization of the membership, and the realization on its part that it had "been taken."

The members had elected someone who was popular instead of making sure that they had a person who could perform adequately in a leadership position. The individual's motive for running for this office was one of self-aggrandizement. She wanted her academic extra-curricular record to show that she had held high office in the student organization of her major field. Her popular appeal elected her to the leader's position, but she was far from able to lead in that situation.

Popularity is, after all, a matter of taste. Friendliness and the common touch may appeal to many people, but they are not a guarantee that the elected office holder will be a leader. Fortunately, they are sometimes coupled with leadership ability, in which case the judgment of the electorate will have been justified.

Elected leadership through accident rather than plan is a common occurrence. We have all known cases in which an individual just happened to be present at a time when an incumbency opened and, in desperation to fill the position, the "powers" took him because he was the only person upon whom all factions could agree, or because he compromised enough to be acceptable, or simply because he was a "good old Joe."

As Haiman has noted:

> Any observer who has watched the emergence of leadership in a fair sampling of social situations would be a remarkable analyst indeed if he claimed to see important explainable forces at work in every case. Let us frankly face the fact that on a multitude of occasions, leadership falls into the laps of those who simply happen to be in the right place at the right time. They do not necessarily have any special characteristics or native endowments, they are not created by an urgent situation, there is no tradition at work—they simply happen, willy-nilly, to get in the way when the roles of leadership are assigned. There is good reason to believe that some of our less eminent American presidents came to office in this way. It also happens frequently among young children in classroom elections, where Sally happens to be elected because someone nominates her first. It sometimes happens in adult committee meetings, where someone casually says, "Well, Jack, why don't you act as chairman?" and ipso facto, Jack has the job.[9]

The accidents of outliving competition, seniority-based jobs, or birth may contribute to the combination of happy incidents which propel an average person into an elected position of leadership. Civil service incumbencies, a one-party system of politics, union activities, military positions, and family-operated enterprises are all part of this insidious system which tends to promote the incompetent over the qualified. Invariably, also, death opens the way for position in the accidental race of leadership. The dullest, most mediocre, least inspiring of individuals may rise to a position of leadership simply by staying alive longer than his co-workers. Such individuals may eventually receive general or flag rank in the military through seniority. The same is true of some civil service workers who are elevated to top positions, not because of what they know or their obvious qualification for the job but because they have been on the job longer than has anyone else.

In the houses of the Congress of the United States, the most highly qualified man or woman does not necessarily become chairman of an

---

9. F. S. Haiman, *Group Leadership and Democratic Action* (New York: Houghton Mifflin, 1951), pp. 16–17. Reprinted by permission.

important committee; the choice is the individual who has been in Congress longer than his fellow representatives or senators.

The seniority system may be an excellent protective device against corruption, but it is also the best way of promoting unqualified persons to leadership and discouraging the qualified. If no one else is available, the electorate must place into office those who cannot, by any stretch of the imagination, be considered leaders.

The accident of birth is another contributing factor in the promotion of mediocrities. Family firms, in order to maintain control of the corporate enterprise, rely upon dynastic principles in order to retain the prerogatives of management. Thus, the unqualified son of the chairman of the board may very well be elected to an executive position and then assume the mantle of leadership. Perhaps he is merely the figurehead, with the shadowy form of an administrative assistant to give him informed substance but, to the world at large, he represents leadership for that firm or industry.

How often have we seen an aspiring political figure who is a brilliant speechmaker fall flat on his face when it comes to extemporaneous talks? The truth is that some politicians have a stable full of political ghost writers who do the thinking for him. Such individuals make fools of the unenlightened or naive public who elect them to office.

This same lack of inspiration plagues the labor-management field. For some reason, some unions' rank and file seem to delight in electing to stewardship the most ignorant or least competent worker among them. In fact, the past ten years of union history is clouded by the gangsters, dictators, and underworld figures who, having pushed themselves into unionism, have been elected to leadership posts.

The Emergent Leader

Situations determine the rise of the natural or spontaneous leader. A combination of emergencies and the lack of a determining influence to shape a course of action may arouse latent leadership. Leadership potential is always present within a group. Whatever triggers this leadership performance lies within the needs of the group, within any crisis which threatens its continuation, and within the individual personality involved.

The indigenous leader, one to whom most or all of the group members gravitate for direction and affection, has the central role of the interrelational process in the group. Direction and affection are the two motivational forces which stimulate followership. Direction includes not only guidance and goal-setting, it very likely contains such force features as physical strength and economic, social, or status factors. For instance, leadership in children's groups is usually associated with the most physically capable, biggest, and consequently strongest group member. He is in a position to implement his goals by coercion or by means of the members' belief in his strength and skill. He is worthy of emulation and has influence with them.

In children's groups, leadership is sometimes seen as the "pecking order," or the position or status within the group. The expression is taken from the barnyard, where the more aggressive fowls get the grain and the passive or cowardly chickens, relegated to the end of the line, receive only the leftover crumbs. We see this type of behavior in "bullies," who by their strength and aggressiveness gain their ends at the expense of others.

Status through fear is not leadership but a form of dictatorship. Nevertheless, the indigenous leader may be highly authoritarian and obtain his position through the imposition of an impressive physical, economic, or social strength. Such an individual would neither be elected nor appointed but would emerge in a leadership position because of his forceful personality or through his use of power.

Coercion does not necessarily characterize the indigenous leader. Affection and its associated components may also merit admiration and influence others. If the group chooses to entrust its structure to one individual, then it believes in him and wants to follow his advice. His personality, just as forceful as that of an authoritarian, is of a different stripe. He wields his influence with others because he has demonstrated that his ideas are either the best or that they are most acceptable to the common interest of the group as a whole.

Emergent leadership is determined, in many instances, by the situation which confronts the group at any given time. The moment of crisis elevates an individual into the role of leader. Specific knowledge which can be applied when a situation demands such technical proficiency is generally called upon only in an emergency. When accidents occur on the highway, usually the individual who knows how to give first aid assumes the leadership role. Many people upon viewing an accident either stop to look—and do nothing—or continue on their way. This attitude is understandable, for some physicians have even stated that they would rather ignore a traffic or other roadside accident and not stop to help the victims because they might later be involved in damage suits.

The leader is one who, because of his training and specialized knowledge plus that extra personality factor, takes charge and orders whatever is necessary to alleviate the situation. He may say, "You, get to a telephone and call an ambulance and doctor. You, get to the nearest house and get blankets. You, help me with this tourniquet. You, keep those people from getting too close." It may be the policeman, teacher, medical practitioner, or some other individual who assumes the leader status for a time. When the problem has been solved, the individual may no longer be accorded the status of leader, and his following quickly dissolves with the unsnarled traffic.

The emergent leader's role is created from the need of a group of individuals who cannot function properly until they receive impetus from a stimulating source. It may be an aggressive or forceful personality or the possession of a kind of knowledge which can determine the outcome of the situation, although the two are not mutually exclusive. It may be the stimulus of an individual who has dynamic ideas or whose geniality and personal warmth make him the focus of attention wherever he is.[10]

The group itself will determine the longevity of the leadership which it creates. Depending upon the situation and the individuals involved, the emergence of a leader may be of a protracted or limited length of time. If the leader is a member of a group, his status will probably be long-lived, especially if he can function adequately to solve problems which the group faces. If, on the other hand, the emergent leader is a product of an aggregate or collection of individuals who have been brought into close proximity only because of a particular situation or condition, he is likely to lose his leadership status very quickly. In fact, as soon as the crisis which brought him into being has passed, his services will be of no value.

When the leadership role has been sanctioned through the ownership of some technique no longer needed, the status is revoked or is dissipated. Even where knowledge and magnificent personal qualities are apparent, the solved problem or alleviated crisis may cause the rejection and ultimate decline of the former leader. The emergent leader thrives on stress situations. He may even create them in order to hold his position. Without the emergency to summon him forth, the individual who would be leader may never achieve his desires or have influence with others.

One has only to look at recent past events to prove the validity of the foregoing statement. Adolph Hitler might never have achieved his ends if a crisis of his own making had not precipitated him to the position of power and dominance which he craved. Naturally, his own personality, his knowledge of human emotionalism, and his peculiar abilities aided and enabled him to carve out his niche. His goal was to

---

10. Orly Ben-Yoav, Edwin P. Hollander, and Peter J. Carneval, "Leader Legitimacy, Leader-Follower Interaction, and Followers' Ratings of the Leader," *Journal of Social Psychology*, Vol. 121 (October, 1983), pp. 111–115.

create an environment in which he could consolidate and then extend his holdings. This he did by first producing scapegoats on which to blame his failures and then going to war for various pretexts. His life, after he was accorded "Fuhrer" status, was one crisis after another.[11]

One of the great statesmen and leaders of all time was Winston Churchill. Made Prime Minister of Great Britain in its "darkest hour," after the Hitlerite forces had already been unleashed upon a weak and ineffectual Europe, he was the inspiration from whom free men everywhere took hope. His leadership, courage, and tenacity buoyed up a country which was poised in 1942 to receive the invading forces of the greatest war machine ever invented. He was the author of victory as surely as if he had directed the allied armies against the Axis. What happened to this great leader as soon as the war was won? He was relegated to the back benches, while the head of another party was elected Prime Minister. As soon as the emergency was over, the leader was replaced.[12]

Charles de Gaulle epitomized this theory. He had long considered himself "a man of destiny," and perhaps he was. His was the voice which rallied the French people after Marshal Petain capitulated in 1940. It was he who headed the Free-French government in exile and who guided and created the Free-French armed force. It was he who became provisional President of the Third French Republic in 1945. However, he was out-maneuvered by politicians in his own country and had to retire. Not until the most terrible upheaval in French political life occurred was he brought back as "man of the hour" to help save his country.

We have described three leaders, emerging in crisis situations, thriving upon emergencies, and needing such conditions to further their status and enable them to reach their goals. In each case a threatening or anxious period of time was the situation which thrust them into positions of leadership. It is very probable, however, that these men would have risen to positions of leadership even if there had not been specific situations which called upon their prowess. Their own forceful, vivid, and power-needing personalities would have carried them up in any circumstances.

Yet, there have been many times of distress when leaders were needed and none appeared. Conversely, some great personalities have never risen to leadership rank because of the lack of a mechanism or

11. M. F. R. Kets de Vries, *Organizational Paradoxes: Clinical Approaches to Management* (London: Tavistock Publications, 1980), pp. 81–85.

12. Pamela C. Harriman, "Churchill and Reagan," *The New York Times* (April 29, 1984), p. E21.

cue to trigger them. From these factors, it may not be wrong to hypothesize that leaders are created from a combination of interrelated sources, including the times or situation, the special need of a group, and the dominant personality of the individual involved.

But what of the recreationist in the emergent-leader picture? Surely it must be obvious that the professional is not an indigenous leader, except perhaps among his peers. Why then has this section been included? Basically, because within groups with whom the recreationist works, there usually are natural leaders. If the recreationist wants any influence with members of these groups, he must find it indirectly through the central person of that group.

In general, natural leadership is generated through personal relations. The indigenous leader has developed because members in the group need him. They look to him as the driving force or uniting figure. He is the individual to whom they can go when seeking advice, information, or support. It is to him that members spontaneously turn, hoping that he can instill the common bond of morale or direction, if there is a lack of cohesiveness or congeniality.[13]

Two examples of the indigenous leader's strength within the group are illustrated as follows:

A state correctional school for girls in one of the midwestern states employed a program director. During the summer, one of the recreational activities was a campfire program which included all of the girls in the school. Some of the girls indicated by their actions that they were dissatisfied with the activity and did not want to take part in it. However, since this was an all-school program, they had to be at the campfire and could not remain behind in their dormitories. One group in particular was vociferous in its protests against this activity and would neither cooperate nor give any valid reason why it should.

The program director, realizing that they would receive little or no value from an activity they disliked so intensely, called the group together and attempted to determine a reason for their adverse reactions. There was no reason given. The recreationist knew each of the girls and was quite aware of the girl who controlled the group.

The indigenous leader was an individual whose main attribute was that she was bigger and stronger than the other girls in her dormitory. However, she had a very pleasant personality, was a model student, and cooperated with the school authorities in every

13. E. K. Marshall and P. D. Kurtz, *Interpersonal Helping Skills* (San Francisco: Jossey-Bass Publishers, 1982), pp. 317–323.

way. She had been placed in the institution because she had borne a child out of wedlock. Having been adjudged delinquent by the courts, she was sentenced to the state correctional school until she came of age.

Her size, together with a warm and friendly nature, naturally pushed her into a leadership position. The girls all liked her, and she was the confidante of them all. The director asked her what she felt was causing the difficulty. She replied that there was nothing vicious behind the girls' lack of response; it was simply that they felt the activity was for younger children and that they were too "sophisticated" to participate. Upon learning this, the director recalled the group and was able to demonstrate successfully that the campfire activities may include singing, dramatics, pageants, picnics, and game or sport activities, depending upon what the participants wanted and how accomplished or adept they were in learning skills. With the knowledge he gained from conferring with the natural group leader and by working through her to direct the group into the activity, the program went off with slight interference.

The Leader as Facilitator. Here, one can see the problem that a recreationist faces when working with a formed group. Invariably, he must determine who the central person is and attempt to guide the group indirectly. He must prevent conflict between himself and the indigenous leader if he expects any positive help in influencing the group.

Although the professional can discern an indigenous leader or leaders within a group, his functions are quite different from those of a direct leader. Regardless of the situation, the recreationist must always be a guide. However, when working with indigenous leaders, the professional has an even more sensitive role to play. He must be a facilitator, one who helps or enables members of the group to achieve satisfying experiences.[14]

As a facilitator, the recreationist is available to give technical advice or assistance to the group when it lacks experience. He aids in the development of group cohesiveness, individual self-realization, membership awareness, and comprehension of personal ability or limitation. He may further enable the group to perceive any internally divisive forces or those which hinder the group from attaining complete accomplishment. He usually aids the group to formulate its

---

14.   T. M. Newcomb, R. H. Turner, and P. E. Converse, *Social Psychology: The Study of Human Interaction* (New York: Holt, Rinehart and Winston, Inc., 1965), pp. 473–486.

structure and the indigenous leaders to understand their obligations and to function in a way that will further group goals.[15]

Situational Forces.   Another illustration of the professional's role in coordinating the influence of the indigenous leader with that of his own may be seen from the following case:

> The executives of a southern region decided to form a group which would represent the professional recreational agencies. They organized an association. The first president elected was one of the older superintendents who had developed the original recreational department in the region. He was authoritarian in his methods. Individual members of the group may have had cause to dislike him, but they collectively deferred to him. Everything which he suggested was executed, and his word on any matter was the final decision.
>
> He was succeeded in the presidency by his closest cohorts. As the years went by, other recreationists joined the association, and newer members were elected to the presidency and enjoyed official status. However, the original president still ruled the roost. His aggressive behavior, personal opinions, and knowledge made him the acknowledged leader. He was successful in forming, within the association, a small hard-core clique which invariably voted the way he wanted questions to be decided. Thus, he controlled the direction which the organization took, although theoretically the president was elected to direct the group. In any matter, his ideas were solicited in order to gain acceptance.
>
> One member of this group found it necessary to request funds for a scholarship. The president of the organization was opposed, as were some of the more influential members. Simply by going through the natural leader of the group, after showing why the scholarship was beneficial both to the association as well as the recipient, this member was able to obtain an affirmative reaction to the request. However, instead of bringing the question up for vote, the member asked the indigenous leader to raise the point. With no conflict whatsoever, a unanimous approval was gained.

In this situation, there was no problem in identifying the central figure of the group. Only by aligning this individual with the course the member wanted was there any chance of achieving it. Without the

---

15.   P. Hersez and K. Blanchard, *Management of Organizational Behavior: Utilizing Human Resources* (Englewood Cliffs, N.J.: Prentice-Hall, Inc., 1982), pp. 234–263.

approval of the indigenous leader, there would have been only a slim possibility. Once he was committed to the member's ideas, success was assured. In order to get the group to agree on an idea and then act to realize it, it was mandatory that the indigenous leader be persuaded to lend his support. It was no gamble to call a vote after he requested that the money be donated.

It should be obvious that almost any action may be accomplished through indirect leadership when the figure to whom the group defers is utilized. Guiding such a person may be performed on the basis of logic, personal gain, dedication to a cause, or appeal to the ego. This latter technique may be used when the natural leader considers himself an elder statesman or enjoys playing a father role.

Appeal to the ego must be carefully considered. Such an approach places the user at a distinct disadvantage. It requests some sort of favor, and the petitioner must be ready to donate something of value in return. This can lead to complications, unless the professional really understands the individual with whom he is dealing. Arbitrariness on the part of the indigenous leader can completely wreck any chance for guidance of the group.

When the recreationist is working with an individual who views himself as a father figure, this individual must be shown that adherence to the professional's viewpoint will be most satisfying to the group and to its central person. Perhaps the most valuable strategy is to wait patiently for the indigenous leader to expose his feelings toward the idea which the professional has in mind. Once the natural leader expresses himself, it is easy to shape a course which may appear to coordinate with his, but which in reality may be completely different.

Such a technique has been used often. It simply consists of repeating what the individual has stated, making an affirmative reply, and then adding another idea. Such a process may sound like this: "I feel that our group should concentrate its efforts on the production of a community field day." "Your idea for a community field day is excellent, but don't you think that a little theater group might serve a better purpose at this time? A community field-day program would be much more beneficial to the participants if it were held later."

Stated in a way that praises the original contributor's idea, there is more likelihood that the new thought will be accepted. In general, such a response will be received with good will. The indigenous leader's reception of this type of reply will be one of reciprocity: either he is placed in a position of acquiescence or else he appears to be unnecessarily harsh or, at the very least, ungenerous.

From the foregoing statements it may be seen that leadership is produced directly from the situation. Nevertheless, leaders receive their sanction to operate from the group which creates them. The leader must have followers in order to exercise influence. To the extent that non-leaders allow a particular individual to guide, direct, or otherwise persuade them toward a specific goal, they provide that person with authority.[16]

Leadership is a conditioning process which affects followers in their continuation of sanctions of power upon a single individual as a leader. When a person has demonstrated his ability to overcome a seemingly impossible problem by decision and influenced action, he achieves some notoriety and becomes the focus of attention. Future expectation of the same sort is entrusted to him. The cliché "success breeds success" is not to be taken lightly when individuals are influenced by another's apparently miraculous talent to alleviate difficult conflicts.

The situational leader will survive in the leader role as long as the unexpected is expected. Those who have followed will follow again. As long as a suspicion remains that the chosen individual may be able to surmount hazards or seemingly critical situations, he will retain leadership. Thus, the leader's influence over his followers grows with each successful achievement. They are conditioned to accept an individual as a leader in direct ratio to the number of critical situations which he solves. Knickerbocker has succinctly explained this process:

> The leader may "emerge" as a means to the achievement of objectives desired by the group. He may be selected, elected, or spontaneously accepted by the group because he possesses or controls means (skill, knowledge, money, association, property, etc.) which the group desires to utilize to attain their objectives.... However, there will be no relationship with the group—no followers—except in terms of the leader's control of means for the satisfaction of the needs of the followers.[17]

Leadership and Success. Unless the leader attains the goals which he and the group tend to accept as their own, his influence with the group will wane. If he is to retain the position of leader, his activities must be recognized as those which contribute toward or enable the accomplishment of desired ends. The durability of the indigenous leader lies with his continued success. The recreationist must

16. I. Knickerbocker, "Leadership: A Conception and Some Implications," *Journal of Social Issues*, Vol. 4, No. 3 (1948), p. 33. Reprinted by permission.

17. M. E. Shaw, *Group Dynamics: The Psychology of Small Group Behavior* (New York: McGraw-Hill Book Company, 1976), p. 282.

recognize what is by that fact a dictum of the group: there are many leaders within any group.

Each environmental episode may call forth another member of the group to assume the place of leadership. The exigencies of the situation, the knowledge which is needed at that particular time, the unique talent or personality which is required for the peculiar crisis— all of these factors exert inextricable relational pressures which determine who will be the leader.

Where the group is conditioned to follow one individual, it will do so under an institutionalized or structured pattern of behavior. As soon as the leader disproves the followers' belief in him, his sanction to lead is withdrawn and another person is elevated to the "purple." In other instances, there is no developmental pattern; for each new situation new leaders arise to influence the direction which the group will take. Thus, the recreationist cannot always depend upon the same individual in any one group to have the same degree of influence upon others. He must therefore continually observe the shifting patterns of relationships within the group in order that he may correctly work through the current central personality. Should he misjudge who holds influence with the group, his plans may not only be thwarted, but his rapport with members may be damaged. One necessity in any group situation is knowledge of changing attitudes or shifts in alignment. The sociographic image must be kept constantly in focus.

Where applied knowledge places an individual in the leadership position, it is of relatively short duration. Those who follow because one person is endowed with a special knowledge denied the rest will follow only until the problem requiring this technical learning has been dealt with. Knowing that there is little likelihood of a resurgence of the problem, the group blithely dismisses the leader of the moment.

The achievement of success makes little difference to the leader's incumbency. Where knowledge is the only answer to difficulty, however, individuals are less prone to place their faith in the expert with whom such knowledge resides unless qualifying factors are also present such as potent personality and approachability to followers' needs. People crave the dynamic rather than the studied technique. Decisive movement which stimulates seems to be the foundation upon which leadership rests and survives.

Again, one sees the utilization of a leader by a group. Use the individual for whatever ends he may help to achieve, then, once the goal is reached, spurn or cast him aside. Loss of status is one of the hazards of leadership. It appears to be the reward and fate of those who aspire to leadership. Perhaps, in the long run, it does not matter to the individual who has attained the role of leader. For him the leader position is inherently satisfying and self-contained. It may be that the individual finds complete fulfillment from his sojourn with power. Surely he must be aware and recognize his ultimate destination, unless an unbounding optimism blinds him to the realities of life and the fickleness of human nature. Perhaps this very optimism and self-confidence carries him along, buoying him up after his term, but it could be that his personality and understanding of human behavior sustain him as a leader until he is ready to voluntarily relinquish the role.

The Charismatic Leader

A leadership role may be created from the need to respond to a superhuman source of strength. Such charismatic leadership may stem from a vague idea or an overpowering concept with overtones of spiritual guidance. It can be personalized in a man or made metaphysical in a thought.[18]

Charisma is a mystical power which raises the owner to godlike status, if not actual divinity. It is the power to perform miracles which the ordinary man lacks the ability to do. Generally, charismatic leadership develops from a verbalization or frequently repeated idea which is purported to have been originated by one individual. Regardless of the idea itself, which is usually a powerfully worded or deeply meaningful message, its continual repetition may place the mantle of leadership upon the shoulders of the originator, or upon someone who can utilize the idea to his advantage.[19]

This mode of leadership is not born of an individual who influences others, but of some striking message or philosophy. The concept is invariably directed at a particular group, but as time passes, it receives a much wider dissemination until it becomes the underlying foundation or rationale of whole populations. Such influence is of the longest duration. Continuity of this form of thinking contains power for the protagonists of the idea long after the inventor has passed from the scene. In fact, when an idea becomes the focal point around which a unique scheme of life is born, the originator may be deified by the followers. This process is exemplified by the originators of some of the world's great religions, whose exponents have raised the creative thinker to a state of godhood. Similarly, political thinkers have been accorded charisma.

---

18. I. Schiffer, *Charisma: A Psychoanalytic Look at Mass Society* (Toronto: University of Toronto Press, 1973), pp. 1–6.
19. Ibid: pp. 34–36.

Broadly investigating the political ideas of those who seek governmental domination by their party or faction will indicate that such ideas are taken as religious doctrine by those who adhere to the party line. In effect, the political idea is substituted for the religious or spiritual idea.

The course of world history and civilization has been swayed by charismatic leadership ever since man could record the daily occurrences of life. Even pre-literate societies refer to charisma in defining leadership within the tribe, clan, or state. The divine right of kings concept is a direct heritage of this theory. One need look no further than the Bible for confirmation. The patriarchs from Abraham on were supposed to have been touched by the hand of God. Their dealings with crises were influenced by having had God's counsel.

In the Book of Exodus we can read about the leadership of Moses. His actions were governed, according to scripture, almost entirely upon receipt of God's word. The final testimonial to his relationship with God—or revelation, to the purist—is his receiving from God the Ten Commandments upon which the Judaeo-Christian ethic is founded. Throughout the Old and New Testaments are repeated references to individual revelations of God. This culminates in the story of Jesus, upon whose life and ministry is founded the Christian Church with its many schisms, denominations, orthodoxies, and heresies.

In the political world the mantle of leadership has been placed upon such figures as Alexander the Great, Gaius Julius Caesar, Augustus, the emperors of Rome, various statesmen, dictators, demagogues, and saviors. Political history is replete with the names of Napoleon, Gandhi, Marx, Lenin, Hitler, Lincoln, and others who were and are thought by many of their followers to have been touched by the hand of God.

The quality which adoring followers invest in an individual whom they venerate to the point of supra-normality is charisma. Charisma, or the supernatural power of omnipotence, is granted an idolized person by those who are strongly influenced by him. Such an individual's personal magnetism has the effect of hypnotic suggestion upon those who believe. Absolute faith plays no little part in creating an atmosphere which is conducive to belief.[20]

The charismatic leader is one who either makes pronouncements with the fanatical conviction of infallibility, or one who creates the impression of indispensability through the decision-making process.

---

20.   James MacGregor Burns, *Leadership* (New York: Harper & Row, Publishers, 1978), pp. 241–246.

The success of the mystic is dependent upon the particular need of the would-be follower. Basically, such a need is found in man's insecurity. When a relatively weak or insecure person finds a protective or supporting figure, he leans heavily upon that support. He romanticizes such a figure and idealizes him to the extent that he is ready to grant him the powers of divinity, if that individual will just point the way toward salvation. Salvation comes in many guises. It may be in terms of life after death, economic or political security, a way to ascribe all weaknesses to someone else, a place in the spectrum of society, money, independence, or something called world domination. Any of these may be the panacea upon which the individual is willing to raise another to the position of leadership.

Whether the leader justifies the faith of his following makes little difference after the position has been attained. Even where charisma is simply mass hysteria or a figment of the would-be follower's imagination, the legend is at work. Thus, infallibility, the "sure hand of God," or incredible wisdom is attached to the person forever after.

One aspect of charisma may be observed among children's groups where a counselor, coach, or beloved teacher is the recipient of an adoration almost bordering on love. Idolization of an attractive person is frequently experienced in recreational service settings: camps, schools, hospitals, playgrounds, and centers. In some adult groups, overreliance on a recreationist who has a magnetic personality and recognized technical skill occurs. This is particularly true when adult members desire to participate, but abdicate responsibility for making difficult choices. The group membership may view the recreationist as charismatic especially if he is a problem-solver or his advice and guidance usually result in success.

The Charismatic Father Surrogate. Faith in some paternalistic figure is the solution which man has always utilized to gain comfort and security from the stress of life. Most people have a simple philosophy, which they construe as "live and let live." This is a policy of allowing anything to occur, just so long as it does not jeopardize the personal freedom of the individual. Ironically, this policy of isolation is one that abets tyranny and connives to make human freedom impossible at any time. The strain of having to enter another's dominion in order to determine whether one's personal liberty is being denied flies in the face of what most people consider their basis for living. This is a strain which many cannot face, and thus they deputize another to do it for them.

The characteristic of avoiding or vacillating over decisions, which many do because it is easier and does not entail the sacrifice of friends or good will, paves the way for a charismatic leader to arise. The escape from reality, postponement of decisions, and entrance to the world of irresponsibility bear just one consequence—the relinquishment of power into the hands of a leader.[21] Kretch and Crutchfield have indicated this point quite well:

> The leader serves as a perfect focus for the positive emotional feelings of the individual; he is the ideal object for identification, for transference, for feelings of submissiveness. Psychoanalytic theorists have stressed this exceedingly significant feature of the relationship of the leader to his followers, and there seems no doubt of the major role that it plays in accounting for the tremendous powers of certain leaders in special group circumstances. Roosevelt and Hitler undoubtedly served as compelling father figures for many of their followers.[22]

As long as individuals are willing to grant responsibility to one who is looked upon as infallible, the flight from reality and personal security is irrevocable. The follower rarely or never questions the leader's judgment, for to do so would bring about a general questioning of the entire structure of faith which the follower has built. Aside from creating doubts as to the dogma for which the leader stands, it tends to weaken the follower's system of values and casts aspersions of heresy upon him. The character of one who would elevate another to divine status resists any questioning. But, beyond this factor lies an even more insidious reason: it would cause the individual to question his personal rationale for believing and undermine his abiding faith. It could mean that the individual would have to break away from his complete identification with the leader. It might even mean that the follower would have to deny the premises which have sustained him, make his own decisions, and take responsibility, not only for his actions, but for others as well. Those who need the support of an all-powerful figure could never bring themselves to act in ways which might require responsible activity.[23]

Surely recreationists are neither charismatic leaders, nor are they likely to be working with those who are considered to have charisma. However, human nature, being what it is, deliberately finds the path of least resistance in its attempt to reduce conflict. One of the methods which the human community utilizes is the placement of authority so that it does not have to think or act. Such authority is construed as charismatic leadership.

---

21. S. Hook, *The Hero In History* (New York: John Day, 1943), p. 14ff.

22. D. Kretch and R. S. Crutchfield, *Theory and Problems of Social Psychology* (New York: McGraw-Hill, 1948), p. 421. Reprinted by permission.

23. J. V. Downton, Jr., *Rebel Leadership: Commitment and Charisma in the Revolutionary Process* (New York: The Free Press, 1973), pp. 209–237.

QUESTIONS FOR DISCUSSION

1. How does leadership emerge?
2. What are the sources of leadership?
3. What are the functions of leadership?
4. What triggering mechanisms may produce leaders?
5. Why is leadership a conditioning process?
6. What is leadership by indirection?
7. What is the ambiguity of leadership?
8. What is charisma?
9. How does the charismatic leader differ from the hero?

BIBLIOGRAPHY

Bathory, P. D., ed., *Leadership in America: Consensus, Corruption, and Charisma* (New York: Longman, 1978).

Geis, F. R. Christie, and others, *Studies in Machiavellianism* (New York: Academic Press, 1970).

Leas, Speed B., *Leadership and Conflict* (Nashville, Tenn.: Abingdon Press, 1982).

Loye, D., *The Leadership Passion* (San Francisco: Jossey-Bass, 1977).

CHAPTER EIGHT

Leadership and Group Dynamics

Generalizations defining the source of leadership must be understood by anybody with aspirations of maintaining influence with people. No one possesses competence to meet all crises, and no person can be all things to all people. Thus, different problems may require different individuals for leadership.

In discussing the phenomenon of leadership, there has been some attempt to define the technique, knowledge, and situations which prepare the way for its emergence. There has been some indication of who or what the leader is, and must be. To explain the nature of leadership, certain interrelational aspects have been explored to try to demonstrate how particular processes of interdependent behavior and learning responses can influence a group, a problematic situation, or forms of persuasion.

In specific areas or situations, specialized knowledge or skill is called upon. This does not mean that skill or knowledge are the sole basis for leadership, but it does imply that individuals who are best fitted to perform particular jobs because of special or technical abilities may be sanctioned as leaders. The leader is called upon because he has the desired ability and the personality necessary to project that ability in situations of crisis.[1] As Hertler has written:

> A befuddled and fearsome mass in time of crisis is nearly always ready, nay anxious, to give over control to anybody who gives evidence of ability to wield it efficiently. This situation, in turn, both demands and provides the opportunity for a leader or a cohesive minority group which offers a ready made formula of social procedure and which promises a dynamic attack upon the problems.[2]

---

1. R. L. Hamblin, "Leadership and Crisis," *Sociometry*, Vol. 21 (1958), pp. 322–335.
2. J. O. Hertler, "Crisis and Dictatorship," *American Sociological Review*, Vol. 5 (1940), pp. 157–169.

"These are the times that try men's souls."[3] The circumstances faced by the fledgling American government at the nadir of its fortunes are reflected in today's situation around the world. There is a need for leadership at a time when the world's population is undergoing a test of survival. We need calm, capable, and forceful persons to take charge and reduce the anxieties which threaten everybody. We need charismatic problem solvers who will abide by democratic principles and humanistic tactics and not impose their will by dictatorial practices.

The recreationist is usually appointed to a professional position on the basis of demonstrated ability, specific knowledge, and dynamic qualities that indicate some talent in organizing or administering broad programs of activities in the recreational setting. Such an individual must then prove his real ability to lead as he encounters his peers and works with people in the community. The recreationist must be capable of guiding and directing participants in such a way that they derive the utmost benefit and satisfaction from their recreational experiences. In this way the recreationist may gain influence with others through their voluntary availability to him. Because the recreationist works almost always in a group situation, this chapter will focus on the nature and characteristics of groups.

BASIC ASSUMPTIONS ABOUT GROUPS

The combination of leader and followers creates the entity known as a group. People seem to have an affinity for all kinds of groups. It appears that the group is the structure through which most individuals feel they can best achieve their goals. The fundamental feature of such an aggregation of people is that they have *chosen* to join together.[4] No extra-personal pressure has required any individual to become a member of such a group. Conversely, persons who are institutionalized are not considered a group, although they may voluntarily affiliate themselves with groups which they either form or join within such institutions. Initially, an individual forms, affiliates with, or remains a member of a group because he realizes that he can gain his objectives more easily by being a part of the group than he can by remaining outside it. Among the benefits accruing to group involvement are a diminution of personal costs, a magnification of effort toward personal goals impossible to achieve alone, and a

---

3. Thomas Paine, *Crisis.*
4. P. N. Middlebrook, *Social Psychology and Modern Life* (New York: Alfred A. Knopf, Inc., 1974), pp. 477–483.

reduction in the friction or painful experiences that may follow solitary action. Among the objectives are security, affection, enjoyment, status, political power, and social influence.[5]

Qualities of Groups

First, groups are self-evident and pervasive. Although groups need not endure forever or even retain the qualities that they reveal at any given time in any given social system, they nevertheless exist wherever a collection of people live in proximity. Even the most confirmed individualists form groups which are characterized by a life style, speech, dress, music, habits, heroes, and slogans which are as regimented and routine as are conforming patterns of any division of society. Second, groups marshal potent stimulants that create effects of transcending significance to individuals. A person's self-perception is highly influenced and reinforced by the groups with which he identifies, such as family, peers, religious organizations, and professional associations. This also affects the manner in which others respond to him. Affiliation with a particular group may be the climax of a long-anticipated desire or the most disappointing and troublesome ordeal; serious distress and personal humiliation often accompany either rejection by or compulsory affiliation with a group. Third, groups may occasion both positive and negative outcomes. Just as the individuals who comprise a group's membership may sometimes err or make poor judgments, so a group can make mistakes. Fourth, the dynamics of group living promote the possibility that highly beneficial effects for both the membership and society can be intentionally devised through enlightened leadership.

The Nature of the Group

Any explanation of leadership inevitably leads to aspects of the group situation. In the field of recreational service, we must of necessity speak of social groups and the leadership of such groups. Among the questions which must be answered are: What is a group? What are group dynamics? How is the field of recreational service influenced by groups? What is the social group leadership process? When and if these questions can be explained, a better understanding of leadership as it relates to recreational service will have been promoted.

---

5. L. S. Wrightsman, *Social Psychology in the Seventies* (Monterey, Cal.: Brooks/Cole Publishing Company, Inc., 1972), pp. 400–401.

Just as there are many explanations and definitions of leadership, so too are there many concepts of group. The better professional literature concerned with human relations, group dynamics, and the leadership phenomenon lists several definitions which seek to show clearly the nature and rationale of the group.[6] An overview of the collected efforts of those connected with any phase of the group process would contain some of the following ideas:

The group is a small assemblage of people, having an intimate knowledge of one another, with some central interest which serves as a uniting bond.

There must be a minimum degree of structure and purpose so that some social control may be effected.

The membership thinks of itself as a group. Each person within the collection shares the idea of a unified image.

The group is made up of individuals who are working cooperatively toward a common central purpose. From the centrality of purpose a mutual inter-understanding develops and each personality becomes part of a relational whole.

The group is a collection of people who can meet their needs directly and indirectly through the structure of a particular set of individuals.

The group is defined as two or more individuals who, through distinct face-to-face contact, have a personal knowledge of each other and, therefore, are in some sort of psychic relationship to one another.

The "we" feeling is the generic element of the group. It characterizes the group as individuals who are conscious of one another's relationship to each other. It is more than a simple collection of individuals because each member has affected every other member in a specific way. This relation results in behavioral patterns that may be termed as traits of the group.

From these illustrations it can be seen that certain basic elements appear repeatedly, indicating several ways by which groups may be defined. The minimum of *two* members is an obvious necessity, but the group may theoretically have an unlimited number of people who may be counted as members. Individuals within the group consider themselves as group members. Each person has the idea that he is a part of a unified body contributing a tangible substance to the total image by his presence or absence. There must be some form of

---

6. R. B. Lacourisiere, *The Life Cycle of Groups* (New York: Human Sciences Press, 1980), pp. 58–60.

personal interaction taking place whereby every member of the group undergoes some behavior change as a result of the interaction. Individual needs are met through the group. Finally, there must be some common bond, interest, or goal which draws individuals into a condition of interdependence by which such aims are attained.[7]

Krech and Crutchfield have defined the term group in the following manner:

> A group does not merely mean individuals characterized by some similar property. Thus, for example, a collection of Republicans or farmers or Negroes or blind men is not a group. These collections may be called classes of people. The term group, on the other hand, refers to two or more people who bear an explicit *psychological relationship to one another*. This means that for each member of the group the other members must exist in some more or less immediate psychological way so that their behavior and their characteristics influence him.[8]

From this definition the rationale of these writers is readily apparent. They hold to the interdependent aspect as the basis for group existence. Without the precise relationship between and among group members, which affects behavior in specific ways, there is no group.

In a 1951 article for *Human Relations*, Cattell states: "The definition which seems most essential is that a group is a collection of organisms in which the existence of all (in their given relationships) is necessary to the satisfaction of certain individual needs in each.[9] This definition places emphasis upon the structure of the association as providing the means whereby inividual needs are satisfied. Only through membership can particular satisfactions be achieved; any other device would end in frustration or lack of fulfillment.

Smith, on the other hand, stresses projected image as the basis for a definition of a group. He maintains that a group is "a unit consisting of a plural number of organisms (agents) who have collective perception of their unity and who have the ability to act, or are acting, in a unitary manner toward the environment."[10] Thus, the basis for group

---

7. John C. Turner and Howard Giles, *Intergroup Behavior* (Chicago: The University of Chicago Press, 1961), pp. 3–7.
8. D. Kretch and R. S. Crutchfield, *Theory and Problems of Social Psychology* (New York: McGraw-Hill, 1948), p. 18. Reprinted by permission.
9. Raymond B. Cattell, "New Concepts for Measuring Leadership, in Terms of Group Syntality," *Human Relations*, Vol. 4 (1951), p. 169. Reprinted by permission of Tavistock Publications, Ltd.
10. M. Smith, "Social Situation, Social Behavior, Social Group," *Psychological Review*, Vol. 52 (1945), p. 225. Reprinted by permission.

existence depends upon how individuals view themselves in terms of a collective entity and who reacts to unique conditions as a cohesive and coordinated body.

Freudian theory holds that the group is a product of unconscious unitary object identification. Thus, two or more individuals constitute a group if they have the same concept in their super-ego, the same object as an instrument by which inner conflicts are resolved, or both, and have, therefore, reacted to and identified themselves with each other.

Redl is the most prominent of those who follow this line of thought. His group concept stems from object identification of two or more people. Individuals are formed into groups when they have in common another individual whom they love, hate, or fear. As a consequence of these mutual bonds toward the object, relational ties among such persons are created.[11]

Most definitions of "group" contain certain restrictions. Others are so broad that every cluster of people is classified as a group. Typical of the latter is Brodbeck's definition:

> A group is an aggregate of individuals standing in certain descriptive (i.e., observable) relations to each other. The kinds of relations exemplified will, of course, depend upon, or determine, the kind of group, whether it be a family, an audience, a committee, a labor union, or a crowd.[12]

If groups were defined in this way, any coincidental gathering of people could conceivably be identified as a group. A group is two or more people in close physical proximity. The concept of observable relations does not obviate the need to distinguish further. Under this umbrella description, individuals collected at a corner waiting for a bus could be classified as a group. Even casual strangers walking along a crowded street might be defined as constituting a group. The habitual city-dweller learns to counteract crowded streets by making minute or gross corrections in his forward progress as he travels toward a specific destination. He is therefore behaving in response to the influence of crowd pressure and may be observed doing this.

Other equally weak and transitory relationships which, supposedly, may be thought of as interacting behaviors, are the coincidental meetings of people at theaters, stadia, or other gathering places. Each

11.   Fritz Redl, "Group Emotion and Leadership," *Psychiatry*, Vol. 5, No. 4 (November 1942), pp. 573–596.

12.   M. Brodbeck, "Methodological Individualism: Definition and Reduction," *Philosophy of Science*, Vol. 25 (1958), pp. 1–22.

person may be there with the express idea of being entertained, learning something, or attempting to get some idea across to another party. Essentially, the fact that many people are gathered together in one place at a certain time is pure chance. While it may be valid to say that specific reactions to being in one place with many people around produces observable behavior, the interaction is so negligible and fleeting that it would be stretching this point to include these aggregations in the definition of "group."

What Is a Group?

Just as there are many explanations and definitions of leadership, so too are there many concepts of "group." In this text, we are necessarily concerned with social groups, and we define such a group as follows:

A group is made up of two or more individuals whose reactions and behavior patterns are modified because of some interpersonal relationship developed over time and created during the pursuit of some common interest, utilizing this entity to achieve satisfaction of needs.

In this concept, the group is characterized as a relational organization meeting members' needs through interaction in pursuit of a goal. Most important is the fact that behavioral changes occur because of this interaction. Each person within the organizational structure affects every other person in such a way that attitudes and behavior patterns are modified. Every person involved in a group situation is significant to the life of the group. Every member is part of a unitary image and, as such, is dependent upon the group for satisfaction much as the group is dependent upon every member for existence.[13] The presence or absence of any one member is duly noticed and will influence the behavior of others accordingly. Also essential to this concept of group is a common interest or goal orientation. Finally, the members of such a group can be identified by the following characteristics:

1. They exhibit psychic interpersonal behavior.
2. They look upon themselves as belonging to the group.
3. They are identified by others as group members.
4. They have internalized certain standards involving matters of shared interest.

13. J. Luft, *Group Processes: An Introduction to Group Dynamics*, 3d ed. (Palo Alto, Cal.: Mayfield Publishing Company, 1984), p. 2.

5. They enter into a system of intermeshing roles.
6. They ego-identify with one another.
7. They are provided satisfying experiences by the group.
8. They participate in mutually beneficial activities.
9. They possess a generic view of their cohesiveness.
10. They tend to behave in a coordinated manner toward their environment.

Groups are the instruments by which individuals obtain self-realization and expression, thereby attaining satisfaction of personal as well as interpersonal needs. Individual and aggregate behavioral patterns may be modified through group relations. Society as a whole is made up of a large variety of groups directing social forces and sustaining social codes and mores. Through the media of group structure, the social order transmits its traditions, heritage, standards, and judgments. Leadership is derived through the group. Those who follow become parts of a group. Those who lead create conditions for groups to be formed.

If we begin with these assumptions, then we must agree with the idea that groups produce powerful forces on people and that these incentives may be debilitating to individuals, disintegrating to the group, and destructive to society in general. However, there is just as great a likelihood that cooperative effort will produce highly beneficial consequences for the individuals involved and society at large. Moreover, there are methods which can be deliberately employed to organize groups and practices which will facilitate the legitimate and socially acceptable purposes for which the group was established, thereby contributing to the well-being of the individual member and enhancing the social system.

GROUPS AND INTERACTION

The social unit recognized as a group is well known to everybody. If any randomly selected individual were to be asked to identify the groups in which he holds affiliation, he could rattle off not less than half a dozen, depending upon his education, occupation, interests, recreational pursuits, social, economic, and cultural status. The list might include such organizations as business, professional, or social clubs, special interest clubs, school classes attended, church affiliation, ethnic, political, and other sociocultural entities. He might mention his family and friends with whom he spends his time. Questioning any individual along this line would probably develop a stream of referents of the term group as currently utilized in everyday experience.

The appearance of such units is widespread throughout the social matrix. They constitute connections that are as diverse and unique as the individuals who form their membership. It is also obvious that the classification of groups is far from a simple matter, for groups demonstrate a striking difference of qualities. They vary in the number of people who compose their membership (size), longevity, aims, efforts, level of formalization (institutionalization), structure, significance to their members, and in many other presentations. Group dynamics considers the reciprocity between the qualities of groups, how specific qualities originate and vary, and how they produce responses in group peformance, internal relations, and the life experiences of members.

The Individual and the Group

Any discussion about one person and a specific group gives rise to the obvious relationships which are possible between them. The individual may either choose to affiliate or not. He may rely upon the group to supply those ideas or things which he holds to be of value. He may consider the idea of affiliation pleasing or disturbing, and the group, on the other hand, may enlist or refuse him entrance. His membership may either be forced upon him or he may willfully enter into it; or his disinclination to join may be voluntary. Of course, there is always the chance that lack of affiliation is involuntary as a consequence of group rejection. People invariably belong to several different groups at the same time, and these associations are typically complementary. The group may become the stabilizing focus for the individual's realization of certain beliefs, attitudes, or opinions. It is through the group that the individual comes to define his own behavior and values. He learns to appraise himself, the responses to his behavior, and his outlook on life and other people. These and other interpersonal relationships founded upon the group can affect both the individual and the group in very serious ways.

Group dynamics refers basically to the manner in which a particular group functions. Among the variables to consider are group cohesiveness, individual characteristics which are affected by group structure and which in turn affect group structure, interaction between individuals within the group, interaction between an individual and the group as a whole, and interactions between the group and the environment. The positions members hold within the group—titled offices or status or formal assignment of responsibilities for goal attainment—are also factors. The degree to which members depend on a recognized leader, their individual ambivalence, and shared ideas or feelings all play a part in group dynamics.

The Relationship between the Individual and the Group. The facets of individual behavior which affect group structure are those which make individuals unique in their own right. Every person sees himself in a different light; every man acts and reacts differently to the same stimulus. The patterns of conduct which individuals manifest clearly indicate the nature of the man and the group of which he feels himself a part. Every person views himself in terms of the impression that he makes upon others. He conceives of himself in terms of what others think of him or how he would like others to think of him. The way the individual behaves will be a reflection of his attempt to protect his reputation or self-image.

Degree of Individual Involvement. Anyone who is a member of a group will be influenced in some way by the fact of intimate association.[14] The effects of membership on the individual will be directly proportional to the degree of intensity displayed by the group's various characteristics. For example, the caliber of group cohesiveness affects membership response to group achievement or failure. The more intense the characteristic in question, the more likely the members are to be ego-involved in the affairs of the group and to find satisfaction in group goal attainment. Each time such a goal is attained, a member's identification with the group is reinforced.[15] Those groups which appear to be formed spontaneously by individuals who come together to seek satisfaction of needs without any other organizational pressure have a high level of interdependence among their members and are relatively long-lived.

Membership in a group is not always an all-absorbing interest; groups vary considerably in their impact on members' lives. The importance that an individual assigns his membership in a group contributes significantly to the importance other members assign their membership, to the performance of the group, and to its power which is represented by the kind of needs which the group satisfies or has the potential for satisfying. It is further reflected in the behavioral adjustment which would be required on the part of the member if the group were not available or if it should dissolve. The more significant group membership is to each individual in terms of beliefs, attitudes, and chief values, the more powerful the group.

---

14.   Turner and Giles, *Intergroup Behavior*, pp. 59–64.
15.   A. Zander, E. Stotland, and D. Wolfe, "Unity of Group, Identification with Group, and Self-Esteem of Members," *Journal of Personality*, Vol. 28 (1960), pp. 463–478.

Group Dependence. Having adopted membership, an individual frequently relies upon the group for many of the things that give him satisfaction. He may look to the group for social intercourse, security, affection, enjoyment, information, self-expression, self-confidence, and self-actualization. Under these circumstances, the group becomes the central repository of certain values or instrument through which an individual gains the status, mastery, or the contentment which he relies upon to make life worthwhile. Group dependence, then, is a measure of how securely an individual can rely upon the group for support and assistance in carrying out the activities which he would otherwise be unable to perform.

Group Cohesiveness. Group cohesiveness concerns a group's attractiveness for its members.[16] Most theorists agree that group cohesiveness reflects the degree to which group members want to remain in the group. Cohesiveness contributes to group strength and vigor; it augments the meaning of membership for those who have chosen to affiliate with the group. In effect, then, cohesiveness is the capacity to hold the membership, to muster its efforts in support of group aims, and to develop reaffirmation of group norms.[17]

Among the factors that initially attract individuals to a group and cause them to remain members are friendship, homogeneity, status, leadership, and activities. Anticipation of the conviviality and agreeableness to be found within the company of the group members is a strong motive for joining and does much to ensure an absence of complaints about others and of arbitrary behavior designed to dissolve shared experiences. When an individual is highly attracted to a group, there will be increased cohesiveness and concomitant control by the group on the behavior of the member.[18]

If members of a group share common attitudes, values, age, gender, ethnic, social and economic status, level of education, interests, and background, the group is likely to be highly cohesive; interaction among members will reinforce these shared qualities and thus promote group strength.[19]

---

16. H. Bonner, *Group Dynamics: Principles and Applications* (New York: The Ronald Press, 1959), p. 66.

17. Turner and Giles, *Intergroup Behavior*, pp. 88–91.

18. A. J. Lott and B. E. Lott, "Group Cohesiveness and Interpersonal Attraction: A Review of Relationships with Antecedents and Consequent Variables," *Psychological Bulletin*, Vol. 64 (1965), pp. 259–309.

19. E. Barscheid and E. H. Walster, *Interpersonal Attraction* (Reading, Mass.: Addison-Wesley, 1969).

Some people may attempt to affiliate with groups because of the perceived status that they associate with the group. The perceived status may be the economic strength, social importance, power within society, or political influence which the group may possess. Whatever reasons motivate affiliation with certain groups, some people appear to express a preference for those groups which display or are said to be recognized as high-status collections. Status here refers to the capacity of the group to perform in ways that enhance the likelihood of achieving goals. It may also mean association with a group that lends an aura of mastery to the affiliate. Some individuals need to feel that they belong to a group which exercises power in the community or is recognized as having influential sources at its disposal. Adherence to groups of this type may be observed in the customs and codes of those who maintain the appearance of the preferred group. A so-called "in" group may require behavior that is different from the usual behavior of the individual who desperately wants to join. Nevertheless, the desire is so great that the individual will engage in those behaviors to gain him either accessibility to or an invitation to join the group. Thereafter he must be willing to adopt the activities, values, and expected modes of behavior if he is going to continue his affiliation.

A classic story, probably apocryphal, concerns a young recruit newly assigned to a paratrooper jump class. When being inspected by the commanding general one day, the men were asked in turn whether they liked being paratroopers. Each man answered affirmatively. When the general approached the new recruit and asked his question, he was told that the recruit did not really like to jump out of airplanes. The general was nonplussed and continued his questioning. He informed the recruit that being a paratrooper was absolutely voluntary and that if he did not like to parachute he should withdraw from the troop. The recruit replied that while he personally did not like to jump, he liked being around those who did.

Here we see the individual who is willing to put aside fears, negative attitudes about heights and falling, and drastically change his behavior to conform to a group which requires an individual to have an entirely new set of values. Where the individual feels that the status of a group is worthy enough, he will undergo the most arduous personal sacrifice to gain acceptance and admission to the group. Here, the cost to the individual is not sufficient to overwhelm the rewards that such association entails for him. The perceived status of the "in" group was such that the individual in question willingly underwent severe behavioral modifications so that he could "belong." While this is an extreme example of what people are content to put up with, it is neither unusual nor infrequently observed that people voluntarily undertake severe personal hardships just so they can associate with a group whose status they value. "Social climbers" and others who want to be thought of as having membership in highly regarded groups are examples of individuals who are motivated by status seeking.

A group's attraction to potential members is influenced to no small degree by the type of leadership prevalent within its structure.[20] When there is an effort to invest the membership with power and responsibility in formulating plans and executing activities designed to reach goals, then individuals are likely to be more drawn to a group of this kind. Of course, there are individuals with an autocratic nature who require the dominance of one person if they are to perform effectively and gain satisfaction from the relationship. However, it is safe to say, for the most part, that a democratic form of organization that promotes membership participation in the decision-making process seems to produce greater attraction to the group than does one in which the leadership is centralized and decision-making is restricted. It may not be stated categorically that a clear and open relationship between democratic participation and affection among group members exists. Probably, a more meaningful variable in effecting satisfaction with the group and one another is the degree to which group membership role anticipations are satisfied.

To the extent that affiliation with a group actually involves a person in specific activities, his appraisal of these experiences should influence his adherence to the group. In fact, the attractiveness of some groups, particularly recreationally oriented ones, is primarily dependent upon the kinds of activities which are used to draw individuals into affiliation and subsequently retain them as members. Organizations which do not participate in activities which are inherently satisfying to their members will not keep them for long. Satisfaction with one's activities is frequently of paramount importance in maintaining the individual's interest, affiliation, and attraction for the group. If the activities are uninteresting, insignificant, boring, or unrelated to the objectives which the individual has set for himself, there is every indication that the individual will withdraw from affiliation.

One of the consequences of group life is that members are increasingly asked to assume pertinent responsibilities which can sustain group momentum toward some goal. When the individual is

---

20. E. K. Marshall and P. D. Kurtz, *Interpersonal Helping Skills* (San Francisco: Jossey-Bass Publishers, 1982), pp. 317–318.

requested to assume responsibilities which are either unsatisfying or beyond his capabilities, the attractiveness of the group is subsequently reduced for the person. If a group has standards of performance which its membership cannot fulfill, there will be consequent withdrawal by those who feel embarrassed or extremely anxious when placed in such situations. Conversely, members who accept responsibility for activities and have the ability to carry out assignments and thereby gain recognition and satisfaction from them augment their incentive for staying with the group. Every activity which reinforces their membership strengthens the bonds of attraction and reaffirms an intent to maintain membership. Satisfaction through activity also assists cohesiveness because it motivates members to further coalesce by inducing their fellow members to remain within the group.[21] When an individual enjoys the association of group membership and gains satisfaction through the group, that person will exert whatever influence he has on others to see that the group is sustained. This produces cohesion, maintains the group, and provides need satisfaction to the individual who promotes it.

Choice

It is possible that a person may become a member of a group to which he has no desire to belong. Involuntary association may be produced because external power impinges upon the individual's will and forces him into a situation over which he has no control. Military service, unless the individual volunteers, is really involuntary servitude forced on the individual by law. Under certain circumstances the individual is inducted into some military organization without any right of appeal. It is wartime and the person must serve or be punished by incarceration. In both instances the individual is compelled to associate with others against his will. Within such associations groups may form because of the extreme cases of interdependency which develop. Particularly is this true of combat troops. The life of any one person may be absolutely dependent upon his "buddies." Their ability to support him in tenuous situations may very well be a life-or-death matter. In such circumstances extreme mutual dependency can develop and this leads to the formation of groups.

Prison inmates are typically highly interdependent, and close and prolonged association tends to develop groups even though the initial preference was lacking.

---

21. P. R. Penland and S. F. Fine, *Group Dynamics and Individual Development* (New York: Marcel Dekker, Inc., 1974), pp. 50–54.

In other cases, an individual may be assigned to a specific group on the basis of some particularly observable physical property such as color, sex, or disability.

These examples illustrate various conditions producing involuntary membership. An individual may also be coerced into remaining a group member for several reasons: others consider him a member or fear that his withdrawal might constitute a threat to them. No other possibilities exist for him: he will incur heavy penalties if he withdraws (membership in a criminal organization is an obvious example of the latter).[22] A person who remains a member of a group for any of these reasons is likely to suffer from personal anxiety and depression and thus contribute negatively to group effectiveness. On the other hand, compulsory association does not always result in disaffection and alienation. A collection of individuals who are forced to join the same organization may develop extreme pride, confidence, loyalty, and affection toward the group and, particularly where close interaction is required for survival, friendships of lifelong duration may develop. The key to successful cohesion in such circumstances is brilliant leadership.

Multiple Affiliations. Many individuals belong to a number of different groups. Usually the values and goals of these groups will be complementary, but occasionally they are directly opposed. People tend to avoid joining competing groups because of the obvious disadvantages in conforming to opposed sets of standards. The possibility of intrapersonal conflict and personal anxiety is not normally attractive. However, a person may have special reason for joining such opposed groups. A counselor, for example, may seek out a T-group in order to learn more about sensitivity toward others so that he can improve his ability to relate to those he counsels. The same counselor may simultaneously belong to other organizations where individuality is less important than adherence to social codes. Although the counselor may find that these groups make contradictory demands, he nevertheless has the motivation to fulfill his membership responsibilities in each case.

Multiple affiliations may have various consequences for the individual and for the different groups to which he belongs. They may cause conflicts of interest, disaffection, and frustrated group action. On the other hand, they may stimulate new activities and creative experiences that enforce group loyalty and open new lines of

---

22. M. Puzo, *The Godfather* (Greenwich, Conn.: Fawcett Publications, Inc., 1970).

communication among members. Multiple affiliations may also augment a group's contacts, disclosing new alternatives for achieving group objectives. In this way the group is enabled to perform more efficiently and offer more satisfaction to its membership. A beneficial outcome of relations between groups is quite dependent upon the number of members the groups have in common. Where typically opposed groups have common members, these members will be motivated toward reconciling conflicts so that polarization will not occur.

Group Reference. In order to understand how people establish, tolerate, and modify beliefs, particularly those beliefs basic to an individual's self-concept, it is particularly useful to study the individual vis-à-vis his group associations. Whenever an individual identifies himself with a group, a reference relationship grows; the concept of group reference is thus significant in explaining the manner in which the individual develops an idea of his relative position in his immediate social order. The group serves as a point of departure in creating value judgments and it is also a balancing force to the outside social influences which affect an individual's perception, understanding, and role expectations.[23] Another facet of group relations is the degree to which the individual's behavior conforms to the norms for which the group stands.[24] The costs or rewards experienced by the individual are the result of the group's appraisal of his behavior consistent with the group's control.

All individuals owe allegiance to one group or another. The entire environment of human society is formed through groups. Thus to understand individuals fully, the groups which are formed by individuals must also be understood. The self-concept is important in maintaining an individual's drive for being. Since most human experience is the result of group living and because the individual's reputation is based upon what group members think of him, understanding of the individual will occur only in comparison with others. The measurement of persons is performed in relation to others.

Of the numerous groups familiar to any person, only a select few normally become reference groups, and the circumstances defining the choice of reference groups are still dimly perceived and vaguely understood. There is some indication, however, that an individual will

23. J. Virk, Y. P. Aggarwal, and R. N. Bhan, "Similarity versus Complimentarity in Clique Formation," *Journal of Social Psychology,* Vol. 120 (June, 1983), pp. 27–34.
24. M. E. Shaw, *Group Dynamics: The Psychology of Small Group Behavior* (New York: McGraw-Hill Book Company, 1976), pp. 200–251.

probably use a specific group as his standard for making behavioral judgments if the membership more nearly approximates his own attitudes and norms. The greater the individual's attraction for a group, the greater the likelihood that the group will become a focus for reference. Under such conditions he will be motivated to desire membership within the group and thereby use it as a positive reference.

QUESTIONS FOR DISCUSSION

1. What is group dynamics?
2. Why do people join groups?
3. How do group values concerning behavior develop?
4. What is a group?
5. What essential elements must exist for group formation?
6. Why is cohesion fundamental to group maintenance?
7. How does leadership affect group membership?
8. Why do group members renounce group affiliation?
9. Can enforced group affiliation support sustained involvement? Why?

BIBLIOGRAPHY

Forsyth, Donelson R., *An Introduction to Group Dynamics* (Monterey, Cal.: Brooks/Cole Publishing Co., 1982).

Johnson, David W., and Frank P. Johnson, *Joining Together: Group Theory and Group Skills,* 2d ed. (Englewood Cliffs, N.J.: Prentice-Hall, Inc., 1982).

Lawson, Leslie G., and others, *Lead On! The Complete Handbook for Group Leaders* (San Ramin, Cal.: Impact Publications, Inc., 1982).

Martin, Robert A., *Skills and Strategies Handbook for Working with People* (Englewood Cliffs, N.J.: Prentice-Hall, Inc., 1983).

McGrath, Joseph E., *Groups, Interaction and Performance* (Englewood Cliffs, N.J.: Prentice-Hall, Inc., 1984).

Meister, Albert, *Participation, Associations, Development and Change* (New Brunswick, N.J.: Transaction Books, 1983).

Middleman, Ruth, ed., *Activities and Action in Groupwork* (New York: Haworth Press, Inc., 1983).

Mills, Theodore M., *The Sociology of Small Groups,* 2d ed. (Englewood Cliffs, N.J.: Prentice-Hall, Inc., 1984).

Ridgeway, Cecilia L., *Dynamics of Small Groups,* (New York: St. Martin's Press, Inc., 1983).

Robinson, Russel D., *An Introduction to Dynamics of Group Leadership* (Milwaukee, Wis.: Bible Study Press, 1982).

Williamson, David, *Group Power: How to Develop, Lead, and Help Groups Achieve Goals* (Englewood Cliffs, N.J.: Prentice-Hall, Inc., 1982).

CHAPTER NINE

The Group Process

Any group in society was established at some determinate period, and its composition was conditioned by a set of peculiar circumstances coincidentally interacting.

Why are groups created? What happens when a particular cluster of individuals becomes a group? Why are they drawn together so that interpersonal behavior and other common traits are a direct outcome? In view of the great variety of groups, the answers to these questions are perplexing and enigmatic. The reasons for the formation of a group may be explained in terms of: 1) achieving some purpose; 2) through mutual agreement; and 3) spontaneously. Hinton and Reitz offer the following explanation:

> Groups are formed in two ways—spontaneously or deliberately. It is interesting to note that spontaneously formed groups exhibit a number of characteristics distinctly different from those exhibited by deliberately formed groups. For example, the former are most frequently social, while the latter constitute the majority of our formal organizations. Deliberately formed groups also usually exhibit more structure and a more autocratic style of leadership than do spontaneous groups.[1]

Just as individuals may be characterized by specific personality traits, groups are also characterized by particular patterns which may be generalized, so that groups can be categorized and typed. There are three types of groups: the primal, the mutually consensual, and the deliberately organized.

THE PRIMAL GROUP

The primal group arises spontaneously from the matrix of natural society. It is the group having the longest duration—the lifetime of the member. Membership is involuntary. In structure, it is a highly

---

1. B. L. Hinton and H. J. Reitz, *Groups and Organization: Integrated Readings in the Analysis of Social Behavior* (Belmont, Cal.: Wadsworth Publishing Company, Inc., 1971), p. 32.

formalized hierarchy with distinct functions for each member. If a particular primal group has been in existence for some time, it will have established traditions. Members are very much aware of each other even though they may be separated by time and distance. The presence or absence of each member affects all other members. This group may have one or more interests. Group members may assume heterogeneous characteristics derived from social, religious, political, educational, neighborhood, and vocational differences, but the group itself is homogeneous. Even when there is severe internal discord, group members generally present a united front toward all outsiders. Members of the group may actively dislike other members, or they may harbor feelings of great affection. In every case, members are born or adopted into this group, for it is the family, which forms the basic group of any society. No other group has the characteristics of the family, because the family combines the characteristics of all other groups. Yet without the family, clan, or tribe, there could be no society.

The family needs none of the outward characteristics of other types of groups. It survives through blood or legal ties which transcend any other interest, aim, need, or satisfaction. It stands in relation to society much as the single cell does to the living organism; it is the basic building block upon which society grows, develops, and matures.

All other groups are modifications of the family. The essential difference between the family, or primal group, and other types of groups lies in the formation or origin. All other groups are formed, formally or informally, on the basis of some central interest, need, or external pressure.[2]

Most people have social needs which can only be satisfied when they associate with others and maintain interpersonal relations.[3] Some groups arise when several people determine that their needs can be met through the interacting process which supplies them with reciprocated satisfaction.[4]

The recreationist works within the context and policy outlines of his agency. He performs in ways which are designed to further the objectives for which the agency was created. When he works with a group sponsored by his agency, he functions in ways which will help

2. H. B. Trecker and A. R. Trecker, *Working with Groups, Committees & Communities* (Chicago: Association Press, 1979), pp. 16–17, 60–62.
3. T. M. Newcomb, *The Acquaintance Process* (New York: Holt, Rinehart and Winston, 1961), p. 96.
4. P. R. Penland and S. Fine, *Group Dynamics and Individual Development* (New York: Marcel Deckker, Inc., 1974), pp. 34–41.

the group to achieve its purposes and at the same time influence the group in accordance with agency objectives. Thus his responsibility is twofold: to the group itself and to the sponsoring agency.

The professional recreational worker aids groups in achieving their stated aims. He also helps individual members of the group to develop into more effective individuals through social interaction processes, as well as through the countless educational and cultural opportunities open to them through recreational experiences.

The recreationist, when functioning in a formal group setting, does not participate within the group as do indigenous members. This is an imposed position. The worker is placed with the group in order to influence it toward objectives which the sponsoring agency conceives. The group is formed, planned, organized, or allowed to operate within the agency so that the professional may assume some form of direction and channel group actions toward the ideas which have been formulated by the agency. But the professional also has an obligation to group members. His responsibility is helping group members to achieve personal satisfaction in group living. He does this through a knowledge of program activities, an understanding of the dynamics of interacting processes which take place among members, and the relationship of these two factors.

Group members may be as active or passive within the group structure as their needs dictate. Thus the recreationist is somewhat limited. His duty is to enable group members to function as well as their individual capacities will allow. Unobtrusively he guides the group in the achievement of its stated goals.[5] His attitude must always be objective and impersonal. This is not to say that he cannot have affection for his group members. It simply means that the service which the professional offers to the group, upon its request, must be impartial and emotionally unencumbered. Should the worker overstep the bounds of professional service and enter into group activities as a participating member, he will lose the opportunity to bring his knowledge and skill to bear in a disinterested manner and thereby will not meet the needs of the participants.

The recreationist's relationship with group members, to whom he offers professional service, requires the enjoyable atmosphere of informality. This is necessary because he has no way to force attendance or adherence to regulations other than gaining the confidence of group members and having them define modes of conduct which they must follow. This is group planning at its best.

---

5. Trecker and Trecker, *Working with Groups*, pp. 68–69.

Fixing the standards of behavior and setting up personal codes of conduct to be respected add to the attractiveness of the group setting.

Constant differences are caused by shifting patterns of interaction between group members, variations in the environment outside of the group structure, variety of activities planned, and the very weather itself. Within the group each member affects every other member by his presence or absence, his activity or passivity. The extent of this effect and influence will make up the complex content of group interpersonal relations. This is the material with which the recreationist works. Through his applied skill and understanding, all members of the group will be beneficially affected, the group's purpose will be achieved, and the agency will be served.

THE GROUP ESTABLISHED BY MUTUAL CONSENT

Many groups arise with no objective other than the pleasure anticipated from interpersonal contact. Groups such as gangs, social clubs, friendship clusters, hobby enthusiasts, and subgroups or cliques within larger groups are typically formed in this manner. The group develops voluntarily since the group's membership is based upon a process of reciprocal agreement—each person wants to be affiliated in the expressed relationship and each is accepted by the others who constitute the group. Informality is the main characteristic, with changing parameters and few defined aims or responsibilities, except that of deriving satisfaction from membership participation. In time, such groups may take on a more formal veneer as internal structure develops, tasks are assigned, and purposes are determined.[6]

Establishing a specific group by mutual consent requires that the personalities concerned have sufficient acquaintance with one another to stimulate interpersonal relations. Largely through physical proximity, enough contact is made so that familiarization can lead to acquaintance. However, acquaintance alone is not sufficient to promote the formation of a group. The establishment of a group from a particular cluster of acquaintances is probable only under certain conditions. Individuals tend to be attracted to one another if they hold common values, beliefs, or attitudes. The attraction that develops among these people will be strengthened if all place an especially high value on these commonly held attitudes or beliefs.

---

6. M. E. Shaw, *Group Dynamics: The Psychology of Small Group Behavior* (New York: McGraw-Hill Book Company, 1976), pp. 82–97.

CUSTOMS AND CODES

Customs and codes will continue to play an important part in the formation of groups and in indicating the actions or behavior patterns of those who make up the group. Each individual is the product of a different group environment and, therefore, brings to a group a background of vastly different views, judgments, attitudes, customs, and codes which govern his behavior and by which he is able to assign values to temporal and spiritual things.

Customs have to do with the usual methods by which activities or conduct are performed. They are the *how* of behavior. Customs are the established patterns by which questions are resolved, values assigned, behavior instigated, and judgments made. Customs are the traditions by which the heritage of the group is conserved against the deterioration of time and the inroads of social pressures or changing standards.

Codes, on the other hand, are the rules by which behavior is guided. They are the *why* of conduct. Codes are based upon long experience and are the systematized rules or norms which confine and define behavioral patterns in the day-to-day struggle for existence. They are the commonly accepted inhibitor of non-conformist actions and do much toward exerting pressure on individuals for conforming behaviors.[7]

THE DELIBERATELY ORGANIZED GROUP

Every group applies some pressure, either directly or indirectly, consciously or without awareness, in terms of the customs and codes by which it abides. Little children feel this impact as soon as they are old enough to form friendships or are placed in contact with groups of other children. They find peer acceptance or rejection on the basis of conformity to certain activities, codes, or customs. Children learn to adjust and align themselves within the standards of the group to which they want to belong. This adjustment or conformity to an "in" group goes on all through life, in every facet of society and in all relationships between two or more people where there is individual recognition and interaction.[8]

Informal groups are characterized by a lack of ritual, tradition, established offices, or adherence to a particular creed. In addition, they

---

7. Penland and Fine, *Group Dynamics*, p. 57.
8. P. Hersey and K. Blanchard, *Management of Organizational Behavior Utilizing Human Resources* (Englewood Cliffs, N.J.: Prentice-Hall, Inc., 1972), pp. 109–111.

are relatively short-lived, exhibit vulnerability to outside pressure, and depend upon the stability of their membership for continued existence (that is, once the group has solidified, new members are not sought and only rarely admitted).

The deliberately organized group is formed because the satisfaction of needs or interests can be derived only through concerted action. Such a group's development may be predetermined by a social agency using group experience to influence individuals toward a change in behavior, toward achievement of a particular goal, or toward unanimity of thought and conformity of action. Some characteristics of the deliberately organized group are: 1) it is brought into being by auspices seeking to further predetermined aims; 2) it has a predetermined ideology; 3) members are recruited; 4) its internal structure is hierarchical; and 5) through assigned responsibilities and intergroup relations, members develop a unitary image as the group matures.

The essential condition for the formation of a deliberately organized group is the belief by one or more persons that a collection of individuals can achieve some objective effectively where solo efforts might fail. A premeditated group arises when those who constitute the group finally come to see that they cannot accomplish their aims by themselves. Or it may be brought about by some external organization which intentionally brings a collection of people together for the purpose of organizing a group through which these individuals may be controlled, counseled, or led.

The chosen objectives are varied, but may be brought into perspective in terms of generalized categories:

1. *Task groups.*   The purpose of establishing a task group is to accomplish some objective through the marshaling of personal resources and the coordination of skills, knowledge and energy. A climbing club is a typical example of a task group. Each individual within the collection has the physical and personal resources necessary to enable the entire group to make an ascent.

2. *Inquiry groups.*   The purpose of an inquiry group is to undertake responsibility for finding solutions to problems besetting the organizing agency. Through coordinated group effort, problems can be examined thoroughly and effective solutions reached more quickly than when individuals pursue their own lines of investigation independently.

3. *Social-action groups.*   The need to affect the distribution of public services or to espouse causes that directly concern people's health, safety, or welfare prompts affiliation in social-action groups.

They exist to stimulate change and to ameliorate social conditions for the benefit of affiliates and the people whose views they advocate. Individuals acting alone can barely dent the bureaucratic structure of corporate or governmental enterprise; through group action, a collection of people can significantly influence the power structure.

4. *Client-centered groups.* Client-centered groups are formed by those agencies directly concerned with the provision of services to people. Individuals may approach a recreational service department, for example, and request help in enjoying their leisure through educational, social, physical, or cultural experiences. In response, the department may initiate clubs devoted to satisfying particular recreational needs.

When assigned to a formal group setting, the recreationist must be aware not only of the needs of the entire group but also of individual members. He must be perceptive of each individual at every moment, so that he can absorb what he sees and hears, gain insight and interpret the behaviors which have been exhibited, and perform in ways which will be helpful to all individuals and, therefore, the entire group. He should know when to take direction, when to ask a pertinent question, when to give aid, and when to wait until his help is requested. He supports the quiet one, limits the aggressive or hostile individual, instructs in some skill, and exerts his influence on all persons connected with the group. His ear must be keen to detect the tone and inflection which belie the words used by a person to express ambivalent feelings. He must accept people for what they are and render his professional advice and service in satisfying recreational needs so that socially acceptable goals will be attained. He must be able to channel asocial conduct into outlets which will help rather than demoralize the individual.

Not only do deliberately organized groups vary in their objectives, they also display differences in organizational structure, lifetime and durability of association, traditions, rules, regulations, and established offices. But wherever a formal group exists, there also will be a ritualistic order, a definite division of function, adherence to a specific concept or idea, and stability of conduct or the expectation thereof. Some examples of formal groups are schools, churches, political parties, military agencies, fraternal orders, civic, service, or business organizations, professional associations, labor unions, and primary interest groups such as the National Association for the Advancement of Colored People or the American Legion. Other formal groups are those organized by recreational agencies, including teams, clubs, youth councils, and committees.

Whether the recreationist works with one person or many, he should perform in ways beneficial to the clients. His responsibility is to utilize whatever facilities are available through his agency to maximize service to individuals so that they may achieve in recreationally satisfying ways.

All individuals owe allegiance to one group or another. The entire environment of human society is formed through groups. Why any individual chooses a particular reference group is open to speculation; nevertheless, the influence the chosen group exerts on the individual is highly significant.

ROLE OF THE LEADER

The leader has many roles to play, whether he works with individuals, groups, or in unstructured situations.[9] Some people look upon him as a father figure. In order to win his approval, the individual adopts his mannerisms, physical stance, way of talking, and, in many cases, his personal standards. Such people identify with the leader's way of thinking, his value system, and his method of action. In this way they are better able to gain communication and satisfy needs. In accepting this person and casting him in the role of father, the individual may be motivated by fear, love, or a desire to be like the leader.

The leader may be placed in the role of enabler, teacher, or coordinator. Here the motivating factor is the leader's ability to impart, organize, and support methods by which ambivalent feelings of hate, love, guilt, or conflict are minimized or erased.[10] The leader's acceptance of the group members as they are without attempting to judge them manifests itself by group integration around the leader. Group cohesion may be brought about by the leader's ability to pursue those ends which strengthen group purpose and which facilitate socially approved actions.

Guidance and Coordination

In considering the particular contribution which the leader makes toward creating and maintaining the group, it must be readily noted that his functions require skills which may be acquired, as well as factors concerned with his personality. Guidance of group activities toward desirable goals, coordination of interpersonal relations, and

---

9. Thomas L. Morrison, "Member Reactions to a Group Leader in Varying Leadership Roles," *Journal of Social Psychology*, Vol. 122 (1984), pp. 49–53.
10. Penland and Fine, *Group Dynamics*, pp. 72–74.

elimination of conflicts, tension, and deteriorating forces so that group structure is conserved are three of the most significant measures of leader ability. The establishment of an esprit de corps so that group members will set aside personal animosities in order to resist pressures which might destroy the group, the elimination of self-aggrandizement by individual members at the expense of the group as a whole, and the increased group effort toward a common cause—these are the products of guidance and coordination.

The adequacy of the leader may be measured very well by the group's ability to act in unison to produce some desired effect or reach some preconceived objective. By facilitating action, reducing areas of conflict, and quietly channeling behaviors into avenues which will help maintain the group as an operating unit, the leader contributes his most vital performance.

Group Morale

Closely associated with group unity is group spirit or happiness. Most people will remain with a group, even when they are not achieving specific aims, if they receive pleasure from being in the company of the other members. Good interpersonal relations invariably satisfy the gregarious appetite. As long as sociability, fun, and friendliness are part of the atmosphere, good group morale will be the outcome. If unpleasant relationships develop after the group has been organized—friction in the form of personality clashes, cliques, lack of common experiences or education—the group may be destroyed.

Morale is the unspoken knowledge that one is part of a group as a whole. It is knowing that one is liked and others are likeable. When people feel comfortable in the presence of others, they tend to exhibit behaviors which will place them in contact with those for whom they have an affinity. Even at the risk of putting up with difficulties or inconveniences, they will attempt to take their place within the group of their choice.

But convivialty alone does not tell the entire story of group morale. The leader has an important role to play in the production of a climate free from internal strife and conducive to interpersonal harmony. The leader helps his group members feel that they are part of a greater entity. He attempts to instill in them the pride of belonging. The ego-identification which can come from being "in" with the group makes each person feel that he or she is not alone. Support and encouragement from the leader and the assistance he gives each individual in assuming responsibilities as a participant result in personal gratification. In such a climate, the individual is more willing to work and serve, and in thus maintaining his relationship with the group, he heightens group morale. Morale is also influenced by the amount of freedom of self-expression that the individual feels. More individual freedom for self-determination results in greater self-sufficiency and higher morale. The ability to promote group morale is a measure of leadership competence. In turn, the presence of an environment where enjoyable relations may flourish contributes to leader effectiveness.

Stimulating Achievement and Productivity

Productivity ranges from getting out a prescribed number of nuts and bolts in a factory to coordinating the opening night of the community theatre's newest play. It may refer to a material product or to the satisfaction in a job well done, a festival accomplished without a hitch, an out-patient trip successfully concluded, or any of the numerous goal achievements.

One of the functions of the leader is to stimulate people in such a way that they are highly motivated toward the production of something worthwhile or the achievement of a stated objective.[11] In many instances where group members or followers lack the skill, experience, maturity, knowledge, enthusiasm, or mental contact to perform in an adequate manner to reach a stated goal, it is up to the leader to take the initiative and move the group. The leader must act to make up for the inadequacies of the followers. Perhaps such factors as personal lack of knowledge or skills are not contributing causes of failure to achieve. What then is the cause?

Some groups are affected by a poor understanding of what they are seeking or where they are going and so get nowhere. Goals lack definition or description; this the leader must provide. Not only can such action mitigate disintegrating forces, it will allow a buildup of morale and a feeling of unified effort. The activity or behavior of the leader may be illustrated in terms of the functions which he must perform in order to elicit some aspect of productivity from the group. He must, where necessary, clearly enunciate the program with which the group identifies. He makes clear the objectives which group members have signified as being most desirable for them. He may focus the attention of the membership on some value he wants to gain, one which provides a base of agreement to which others may readily accede. Yet, simple agreement or even identical goal orientation will not attain achievement unless these goals are incentives for action.

---

11.   Ibid., pp. 53–55.

Research in the field of human relations and leadership indicates that adequate leadership is concerned with the clarification of the goals or the reaffirmation of the objectives for which individuals become members of a group.[12] The ability to plan ahead indicates a recognition of goals. Stogdill states: "A leader then is a person who becomes differentiated from other members in terms of the influence he exerts upon the goal-setting and goal-achieving activities of the organization."[13] Gibb's research gives credence to the idea that goal facilitation is a function of leadership.[14] Carter and his co-workers grouped forty NROTC junior students in an effort to distinguish leaders from non-leaders. They found that the behavior by which a leader may be known is connected with understanding the situation in which he is placed and taking whatever action is necessary.[15] This illustrates the concept that the leader functions as an analyzer, acting in ways which ensure group goals. Cartwright and Zander have concluded:

> If one person does devote unusually great effort toward this end, or if he is especially effective in aiding the group, it would generally be agreed that he is performing functions of leadership regardless of his office in the group.[16]

The end to which these researchers speak is goal achievement. They have further maintained that if a group remains at status quo—neither progressing toward its goal nor achieving any of its potential, going and getting nowhere—no leadership functions are being performed.

While the recreationist does function within the group setting as a professional person imposed upon the group in order to affect it in a specific way, he may still be a leader in terms of the nature of the situation in which he is placed. If he works with small groups, this function may be seen more readily because of the interaction of personalities and the outcome of such reactions. When the

---

12. J. V. Downtown, Jr., *Rebel Leadership Commitment and Charisma in the Revolutionary Process* (New York: Free Press, 1973), pp. 26–29.

13. R. M. Stogdill, "Leadership, Membership and Organization," *Psychological Bulletin*, Vol. 47 (1950), pp. 1–14.

14. C. Gibb, "The Principles and Traits of Leadership," *Journal of Abnormal and Social Psychology*, Vol. 42 (1947), pp. 267–284.

15. L. Carter, W. Haythorn, B. Shriver, and J. Lanzetta, "The Behavior of Leaders and Other Group Members," *Journal of Abnormal and Social Psychology*, Vol. 46 (1950), pp. 589–595.

16. D. Cartwright and A. Zander, *Group Dynamics Research and Theory*, 3d ed. (New York: Harper and Row, 1968), p. 308.

recreationist works, as is more nearly true, with large masses of people whose association is haphazard and whose common interest may be only the activity of the moment, he performs in quite different ways. Nevertheless, the professional must still exert influence and, as such, must exhibit and perform the functions of the leader.

Leadership is seen here not in terms of personality, but from the standpoint of clarifying, analyzing, or defining goals for followers or potential followers. The leader initiates structure, communicates with the audience or group, attempts a new approach to the problem at hand, criticizes inadequacy, and counters with suggestions which will enable some positive action to occur. He moves toward his goal, coordinates activities so that duplication of effort and waste are avoided, promotes production of the achievement of objectives, and stimulates decisions for the attainment of those things which the group feels it needs for personal satisfaction.[17]

LEADERSHIP TECHNIQUES WITH GROUPS

The group has been considered as a medium by which certain people may attain personal and social satisfaction. To the extent that these people accept group goals and function within the group structure to achieve those goals, a high degree of performance will be effected. The leader's role is to interpret objectives in such a way as to stimulate or motivate membership behavior toward their achievement. Beyond this he must play upon the need of the individual to belong to the particular group which he leads. The more the individual identifies with the group and its aims and objectives, the more responsibility will be generated to see that goals are striven toward.[18]

One of the methods used by leaders to define aims for followers is the initiation of projects which develop group awareness of collective responsibility and orientation toward a goal. The leader may use his unique skill as a facilitator to bring the group a little closer to the attainment of an end and to increase productivity. This may be seen in the following excerpt taken from the records of the Danforth Community Center, a recreational facility operated by the Town of M in New York:

> The Teenage Council was meeting to formulate plans for a local high school group event. Each spring it had been customary for the

17. N. D. Gardner, *Group Leadership* (Washington, D.C.: National Training and Development Service Press, 1974), pp. 91–116.

18. E. K. Marshall and P. D. Kurtz, *Interpersonal Helping Skills* (San Francisco: Jossey-Bass Publishing, 1982), pp. 317–323.

senior class to put on a May dance and festival which would earn enough money for the senior formal, the last dance before graduation.

The chairman of the council had some difficulty calling the meeting to order, but when he had gained everybody's attention, he did not know where to begin. He was not sure who was going to be on the steering committee, where the May dance was to be held, whether it was going to be held, how the money was to be collected, or where the donated awards were to come from. On top of that, everybody had his own ideas as to how the dance should be run. The council bogged down from an oversupply of talk and an undersupply of directed action.

The recreationist, acting as resource person for the group, did not take any action at this point. He waited until he was asked for his opinion. When everybody had finished having his say, the group still had not come to any decisions. No one was sure where responsibility lay. After the first flurry of talk, the suggestions rapidly dwindled and the council members sat looking at one another.

Finally, the chairman turned to the recreationist and asked for a suggestion. The recreationist pointed out that there had been several ideas advanced which were quite good. He recapitulated some of them. Then he asked that the chairman remind the group of the purpose of the May dance and why the festival was being promoted. Once this had been done, the recreationist explained how the ideas already given could be utilized to meet the stated objectives. Without actually telling the group how to solve their problem, he had the secretary write down the various needs which had to be taken care of before the dance could be given. Then he waited while committees were formed to be responsible for tasks concerning arrangements, decorations, invitations, cleanup, solicitation for donated door-prizes, money collection, etc. When all this was completed, the group was able to work out the details of the festival which would follow the dance. Thus, as soon as the real objectives of the meeting were made clear, group action followed.

The above is an illustration of the leadership technique used in clarifying issues in the group so that some progress toward particular goals may occur.

The next example is that of an individual who, for personal reasons, attempted to block goals so that action could not take place. The incident occurred at a midwestern minimum security detention institution for girls adjudged delinquent. The school is set up in ten separate dormitories; the administration building serves as school facility, auditorium, and recreational center:

The recreationist was asked to organize a recreational activity which might interest all of the girls and take into consideration the wide variety of talent and skill which was represented in each dormitory. The idea for a "Skit Night" was developed. Each dormitory, at is own request, would have the recreationist as a resource person for four days and put on some sort of show or skit on Friday evening for the entire school.

The first three skits were quite successful. All the girls worked hard to make their demonstrations a success, and they enjoyed the preparations as much as the performance. Some unofficial competition developed between dormitories, which reflected the group spirit which the girls felt for their particular dormitory. The fourth week, however, a group which had requested permission to stage a skit suddenly decided that it could not perform, although the request had been voluntary. Since it was too late in the week to notify another group to participate, the recreationist called the dormitory girls together and attempted to discover the hindrance.

The girls were reluctant to talk, but one, Miss Y, asked questions about what could be put into the show. Several other girls also started asking questions, and ideas were soon generated. It was apparent that Miss Y had some pet project which she wished to inject into the skit. It turned out to be a "black-bottom" dance, and, by the way she described it, it was highly erotic, if not completely indecorous. The girls were finally able to table Miss Y's dance and to settle on a pantomime to a piece of popular music.

Miss Y's aggressive and hostile attitude became more distinct as the planning sessions went on. She attempted to block every idea which was put forward and predicted dire results, including embarrassment and loss of face for the other girls. Her remarks made this clear, and she again proposed her dance.

The recreationist asked whether Miss Y would like to take the lead role in the pantomime. She accepted and the production proceeded more quickly. One day before the show was scheduled, Miss Y announced that she was dropping out. Fortunately, one of the other girls had rehearsed as understudy and was able to perform with great success.

Behavior of this type is an attention-getting device. Miss Y exhibited hostile behavior to the recreationist and threats of physical retaliation against those who did not support her proposals. Some covert homosexuality was part of her behavior. It was only when the recreationist was present that the group was able to achieve any kind of movement toward the production of the show. Her presence lent support to the girls. She acted as a buffer between them and Miss Y, whose attitude clearly showed a need for the affection which she desired but could not get from the girls. To her way of thinking, attention-getting behavior was a way of seeking affection. The recreationist suspected that there were underlying reasons for the behavior and suggested referral to the resident psychologist for clinical examination and appraisal. The group's efforts were rewarded, and the satisfaction which the members received from being able to reach their goal was worthwhile. At least one serious emotional problem was discovered and helped.

A third illustration deals with the achievement of goals through the ownership of specific skills or knowledge which others in the group do not possess:

> The supervisor in charge of program personnel assigned the production of the annual "Little Olympics" to several playground workers. This event was a combination track, field, and novelty activity which had been run with varying degrees of success in past years. The special event never failed to draw fewer than 500 boys and girls from throughout the city as participants. When a week had passed without any action on promotion of the event, the supervisor began to investigate. To her consternation, she discovered that not one of the playground personnel had ever performed in a field day; they could not effectively coordinate the activities which were to make up the program.
>
> With so little time left before the event, the supervisor organized and set up all the activities which were to occur, including the opening and closing ceremonies, and the judging, timing, and scoring systems of the events.
>
> With this example as a guide, the subordinate workers were marshaled into the program and were able to give close support after details of their functions and responsibilities were mapped out. The event was successful when measured by the number of participants who enjoyed the activities and the fact that it went off on schedule with a minimum amount of confusion, and with each worker carrying out his or her assignment.

From the above examples it is clear that a leader is one who can perform in ways which will alleviate bottlenecks. He has the necessary skill to handle problematic situations efficiently and effectively under pressure.[19] Followers can see that he is ready, willing, and able to pitch

---

19. H. H. Blumberg and others, *Small Groups and Social Interaction*, Vol. 23 (New York: John Wiley & Sons, 1983), p. 493.

in and work in order to produce the results expected from a professional. His performance supports others and aids them in emulating his efforts, thus improving their skill as group participants. As they gain confidence in their own strength, they will gain the respect of others while carrying out the obligations group membership thrusts upon them. The indigenous leader has to make decisions in order to lead; the professional leader decides only when group members cannot decide for themselves.

The recreationist's functions range from a peak of complete authority, in situations where group members are out of touch with reality, to extreme laissez faire, where the members are creative, productive, actively participating, able to determine their own best interests, and able to attain the goals they have devised. The recreationist may serve in several capacities:

1. *Director.* The leader, as director, assumes complete control of all decisions when group members are not able to act for themselves. This may be seen in mental hospitals, in children's groups where the development of group members is limited, or with retarded individuals.

2. *Supervisor.* The supervisory role is taken when group members can make decisions but, because of some behavioral lapses, immaturity, or atypical social norms, their judgments are poor. This may be seen in penal institutions, with some children's groups, or in some hospital situations.

3. *Agent Provocateur.* The recreational leader may have to provoke members of a group when they are apathetic. He stimulates members and inspires ideas. He is the sparkplug that ignites the thought processes of members so that they want to act. This form of leadership is observed in some young adult and children's groups.

4. *Teacher or coach.* The teacher directs group members when they want to perform but have neither the skill nor experience to draw upon. Here the recreationist demonstrates, illustrates, and teaches the skills necessary for member performance.

5. *Resource person.* When a technical situation comes up which the group is unable to handle, the leader becomes the resource person who provides the necessary information. In this case, the group members have the needed skills, knowledge, and experience to sustain them. The recreationist stays out of the decision-making process, except when asked to participate.

In the foregoing situations, it may be that the recreationist's functions vary within any group, or his role may remain stable throughout his association with the group. Whatever the situation, his decision to act or to abstain from acting will bolster the development of individuals within the group through their relationships as members of the group.Thelen has stated:

> All groups have some sort of leadership,whether they know it or not. The amount of leadership is roughly proportional to the rate of change of agreements or group culture. "Good" leadership is indicated when the decisions and actions of a group become more in line with reality, and when there is minimum effort devoted to achieving this adaption.[20]

Although Thelen is oriented toward the point of view which assumes leadership to be entirely an intra-group function, it is quite logical to say that without decision-making, no group could achieve its goals, nor even differentiate goals. Decision-making as a leadership function tends to help the group gravitate toward reasonable choices. The group will retain an individual in a position of leadership only so long as his judgments prove correct.

The individual, as a group member, must adjust his preconceived attitudes, values, and standards to those to which the group adheres. It is in this area that conflicts arise. Adjustment to group customs and codes produces much tension and thwarting. When this occurs, the individual may practice certain forms of behavior which tend to eliminate him from the painful or trying conditions to which he is subjected. The leader must be in a position to observe and have the knowledge to understand the clues which group members reveal through their behaviors.

With leadership, conflicts of the more emotional type can be resolved for the good of each person and of the group as a whole. Prolonged association with professional persons placed to modify group attitudes or influence members toward objectives which will help them to develop emotionally, socially, culturally, and educationally through the interaction of group life and recreational pursuits may prove helpful to the individual in reducing stress and achieving success. This is the objective toward which the recreationist strives. Such a task is the concern of the dedicated leader in the field of recreational service.

---

20. H. A. Thelan, *Dynamics of Groups at Work* (Chicago: University of Chicago Press, 1954), p. 298. Reprinted by permission.

QUESTIONS FOR DISCUSSION

1. Why are groups established?
2. What types of groups are there?
3. What is the difference between a primal group and a group established by mutual consent?
4. Why are customs and codes significant in group life?
5. How may leadership effectiveness be measured?
6. How does group morale affect cohesion?

BIBLIOGRAPHY

Blumbert, Hubert H., *Small Groups and Social Interaction* (New York: John Wiley & Sons, Inc., 1983).

Brandstatter, H., J. H. Davis, and G. Stocker-Kreichgauer, eds., *Group Decision Processes* (London: Academic Press, 1983).

Hare, Paul A., *Social Interaction and Creativity in Small Groups* (Beverly Hills, Cal.: Sage Publications, 1981).

Papell, Catherine P., and Beulah Rothman, eds., *Co-Leadership in Social Work with Groups* (New York: Columbia University Press, 1981).

Paulus, P. B., ed., *The Psychology of Group Influence* (Hillsdale, N.J.: Lawrence Erlbaum Associates, Inc., 1980).

Smith, Peter B., *Group Processes and Personal Change* (New York: Harper & Row, Publishers, 1980).

III

Leaders In Organizations

CHAPTER TEN

Characteristics of Recreational Service Leaders

Despite the fact that researchers have argued for many years against the concept of "leadership traits," it now seems that this rush to judgment may have been premature in its condemnation. It appears that there are some personal characteristics associated with leader behavior and effectiveness, and these qualities operate regardless of the situation. Although the situational requirement for certain behaviors is significant, the person involved can neither be forgotten nor underestimated. The personality is not merely a mirror of the social environment, but rather brings a unique collection of attributes to each circumstance and it is these characteristics which influence his behavior.

Researchers in personality theory and leadership are beginning to suggest that certain traits must be present for leadership to emerge and that other considerations must also be taken into account. F. E. Fiedler maintains that the leader's effectiveness in the group depends upon the group's makeup and the situation, incorporating interpersonal perceptions of both leader and followers.[1] He is convinced that the inclination of group members to be influenced by the leader is indeed conditioned by leader attributes, but that the nature and orientation of this influence is dependent on the group relations and task structure. Thus traits characteristic of leaders must be studied in their relationship to followers' perceptions of these traits.

Group members hold certain expectations regarding both the leader's performance and the personality traits they recognize as pertinent to the task at hand. Their expectations are therefore subject to change. A personality examination of any randomly selected group would probably reveal that nearly all individuals have acceptable traits for leadership. It would therefore seem that, instead of hard and fast

---

1. F. E. Fiedler, *A Theory of Leadership Effectiveness* (New York: McGraw-Hill Book Company, 1967), pp. 29–32.

leadership positions, there should be an assortment of leadership responsibilities as situations change. Whoever is capable of assuming the leader's role at a given time should be able to persuade the group to follow him.

THE IDENTIFICATION OF POTENTIAL LEADERS

What is the possibility of correctly estimating the potential leadership of an individual? What clues might enable a vocational counselor to detect leadership abilities? As yet we have no firm answers to these questions, although the problem of predicting leadership ability remains a subject of continuing research.

In the specific case of identifying potential recreationists, we offer the hypothesis that the individual who interacts easily with his peer group is more likely to be chosen by them as a leader than one who attempts to dominate them. In the recreational situation, which is highly permissive as far as participants within activities are concerned, the recreationist who can meet the emotional needs of people will more than likely earn their confidence and will have influence with them. Thus the individual who is concerned primarily with the needs of potential followers as opposed to meeting the demands imposed by a hierarchical organization is more apt to be accepted as a leader. In order for a recreationist appointed to a headship position to demonstrate true leadership, he must be as concerned with his followers as he is with his superiors. A recreationist, like any other leader, desires to lead but is also aware that his authority is limited to the agency situation; he is therefore unlikely to exhibit a compulsion for mastery and more likely to view his role as a responsibility to those dependent upon him. He will thus have minimal apprehension about his own status, be highly oriented toward the performance of his function, and be very adaptable to the requirements of whatever situation he encounters.

Of the many characteristics associated with leaders, only two are inherent and absolutely essential for a potential leader. First, the individual must have the desire to become a leader. This is a psychological necessity, but it does not follow that one who has the need will also achieve the aim. The individual's need to lead serves as the initial impetus which drives him toward a participation in group problems which may eventuate in leadership. How can we determine whether a person has the desire to lead? The most valid approach seems to lie in observation. The identification of the future leader may very well be made easier through observation of the individual in relation to his attempts at leadership. It must be kept in mind that even successful attempts at leadership do not necessarily indicate the presence of the drive. A potential leader's drive is so strong that neither failure nor success can stop it. If a person continually seeks new situations and opportunities to lead and succeeds in attaining leadership, it can be safely concluded that he has the basic drive necessary for leadership.

The second inherent quality the potential leader must possess is intelligence. The observations and empirical analyses of many researchers indicate that intelligence plays a vital role in the attainment of leadership. Indeed, at one time it was thought that high intelligence was the only requirement for leadership. But while recent research still shows a positive correlation between intelligence and ability to lead, many now support the thesis that a successful leader will be more intelligent than his followers, but not excessively so. In the words of Hollingworth: "...the leader is likely to be more intelligent, but not too much more intelligent, than the average of the group led."[2]

One aspect of intelligence to be sought in a potential leader is the ability to verbalize. A number of significant studies have determined that verbal skill is a necessity for a leader. Terman, in his early work on leadership, reported a positive relationship between verbal aptitude and leadership.[3] Bass and others have consistently found that verbal aptitude or the ability to take an active verbal part in an initially leaderless discussion group constituted some attempt at leadership.[4] There have been many studies concerning an individual's amount of verbal participation in a group and the effect that such participation has upon other group members in influencing their subsequent behaviors.

Another aspect of intelligence to be sought in potential leaders is the ability to empathize with others, or the possession of social intelligence. While no conclusive study shows absolute correlation between the ability to empathize and success as a leader, in the educated opinion of many experts this aspect of intelligence certainly rates a place. The best known study is by Gibb, who theorized that acceptance by others is due to a more accurate perception of others.[5]

2. L. S. Hollingsworth, *Gifted Children* (New York: The Macmillan Company, 1926), p. 131.
3. L. M. Terman, "A Preliminary Study of the Psychology and Pedagogy of Leadership," *Pedagogical Seminar,* II (1904), pp. 413–451.
4. B. M. Bass and others, "Situational and Personality Factors in Leadership among Sorority Women," *Psychological Monographs,* Vol. 67, No. 366 (1953), p. 10.
5. C. A. Gibb, "An Interactional View of the Emergence of Leadership," *American Psychologist,* Vol. 9 (1954), p. 502.

Thus a person seeking to discover leadership potential will look for intelligence, bearing in mind the many aspects of intelligence. He will look for the social intelligence that will enable the would-be leader to understand group members, and also for the verbal intelligence that will open the door to communication with potential followers.

The ability to verbalize well is a traditional indication of overall intelligence. In addition, the ability to "think on one's feet," and the assurance to come up with ideas on the instant and express them well, are a form of verbal intelligence particularly marked in leaders. Since the leader is generally conceded to be a more highly energized and consistent participator than other members of a group, it is logical to assume that an individual who displays these characteristixs may be a potential leader.

Measures of the various aspects of intelligence may be obtained from standardized intelligence tests. However, such a procedure can be costly and time-consuming. And even if the tests were to give completely reliable results, they would not determine whether the individual has the requisite drive to lead. Therefore, the best method for initially identifying leaders for the field of public recreational service is by direct observation. If the individual's attempts at leadership have often met with success and if he continues to seek opportunities to lead, it can be assumed that he has both the drive and the intelligence that characterize a potential leader.

The Intelligence Factor in Leadership

Intelligence is the power to know, an inherited capacity upon which environmental factors exert pressure. Unless an individual has the ability to understand and the capacity to perform, he cannot be a leader. Intelligence is, in fact, the key to leadership. As Fiedler indicates:

> It should, of course, not be surprising that the leader's intelligence affects his behavior. Intelligence may be seen as a resource which enables the individual to understand and structure tasks, which enables him to deal more effectively with his environment and thus remove the threat and anxiety which might be experienced by the relatively less well endowed person.[6]

Intellectual power, or the ability to apply learned experiences to the solution of immediate problems, is the capacity of the individual to

---

6. F. E. Fiedler, "Personality and Situational Determinants of Leader Behavior," in E. A. Fleishman and J. G. Hunt, eds., *Current Developments in the Study of Leadership* (Carbondale, Ill.; Southern Illinois University Press, 1973), p. 52.

behave effectively within his environment, to think in abstract or symbolic terms, and to function in such a way as to make the greatest use of his capacities. Through intellect and imagination the individual can shape the future. Not only can he conceive ideas; he can also formulate effective means for realizing them.

Let us examine three aspects of intelligence that underlie all interpersonal contact: social intelligence, moral intelligence, and communicative intelligence. These are the "open sesame" to leadership and thus of vital importance to every recreationist aspiring to a position of leadership.

Social Intelligence. Social intelligence may be defined as sensitivity to others. It is the ability to understand and manage others and to act knowledgeably in human relations. Both sympathy and empathy are essential aspects of social intelligence. Empathy is a process by which the individual can completely identify with the object of his immediate experience because of a past event under similar or identical circumstances.[7] Empathy should not be confused with sympathy. Sympathy is concern for another person's trouble; that is, the one who sympathizes wishes that the misfortune had never occurred. The empathizer feels with the individual because he has actually experienced the sensation or is so sensitive to the needs of people that he can place himself vicariously in someone else's shoes. Empathy is a two-way street: the individual who identifies with another and responds to expressed needs also receives identification from those with whom he empathizes.[8] Because of his capacity for both empathy and sympathy, the leader is able to satisfy, to a great extent, even the most pressing needs of his followers. They in turn recognize that the leader is aware of their needs and can help them to accomplish their aims. In general, the leader's sensitivity to others is perceived by the recipients, and they respond with recognition of his ability.

Cattel and Stice have stated, with a high degree of certainty, that the empathetic tendency, or what they call "adventurous cyclothymia," is one of the more significant factors in distinguishing leaders from non-leaders.[10] Bell and Hall succeeded in showing that the leader would

---

7. R. F. Bales, *Personality and Interpersonal Behavior* (New York: Holt, Rinehart & Winston, 1970), pp. 24–25.

8. E. Stolland, S. E. Sherman, and K. G. Shaver, *Empathy and Birth Order* (Lincoln, Neb.: University of Nebraska Press, 1971).

9. C. A. Gibb, "Leadership," in Gardner Lindzey and E. Aronson, eds., *The Handbook of Social Psychology* (Reading, Mass.: Addison-Wesley Publishing Company, 1969), Vol. 4, pp. 225–226.

10. R. B. Cattell and G. F. Stice, *The Psychodynamics of Small Groups* (Champaign-Urbana, Ill.: Human Relations Branch, Office of Naval Research, University of Illinois, 1953).

have to be perceptive of group members' needs.[11] Greer, Galanter, and Nordlie, in an experiment with army infantry rifle squads, illustrated the relationship of empathy and leadership. They concluded that the ability to understand, or accurately determine, the needs of another would result in problem-solving for the individual. They further stated:

> Research indicates that such problem-solvers are often chosen as leaders; the more a leader is perceived as a problem-solver, the more the followers appear to be motivated to help the leader. A person possessing greater accuracy in social perceptions can act with more certainty and confidence in the consequences of his interpersonal behavior. He is in a position not only to achieve with more certainty the goals of others, but also the social goals that he has for himself.[12]

Illustrative of this concept is the following, taken from the record of a public recreational agency:

> Walter, a member of the steering committee of the Youth Center, was given the responsibility for making an address to members of the Youth Center. He took the assignment in the committee meeting where he was gregarious and outspoken. When the moment for presenting the address was close, however, he withdrew his support and asked to be relieved of the assignment. He stated that he could not bring himself to speak in front of all those strangers and requested the recreationist assume the responsibility for making the talk. The recreationist realized that Walter's withdrawl was a direct result of "stage-fright." He was insecure in the face of many individuals, and it appeared that he was not prepared to deal with such a situation. The recreationist made him understand that nearly everybody, when faced with a large group of strangers, freezes or exhibits nervousness to the extent that he cannot perform. The recreationist cited several cases of famous actors and actresses whose fear of people had more than once caused them to faint or become nauseated before going on the stage. He pointed out the fact that the steering committee was depending upon Walter and that the responsibility for this job was Walter's. The recreationist showed Walter how to gain the attention of the crowd and how to gesticulate in order to emphasize points; he then

---

11.   G. B. Bell and H. E. Hall, Jr., "The Relationship between Leadership and Empathy," *Journal of Abnormal and Social Psychology*, Vol. 49, No. 1 (Jan. 1954).

12.   F. L. Greer, E. H. Galanter, and P. G. Nordlie, "Interpersonal Knowledge and Individual and Group Effectiveness," *Journal of Abnormal and Social Psychology*, Vol. 49, No. 3 (July 1954), pp. 411–414.

reassured him by saying that he would be available should the situation require him. Although Walter faltered at first, he was able to secure the group's attention. He held their interest and ended on a rising note of confidence which earned him the plaudits of the assembly.

In this instance, the quality of sensitivity toward the need of another enabled the recreationist to share his confidence and help Walter to achieve success. The ability to perceive or sense the needs of others and to satisfy those needs with a behavior pattern designed to alleviate whatever condition is out of balance, marks the true leader.

Moral Intelligence. Moral intelligence may be defined as the ability to discern what is right or true, regardless of contrary social pressure or mass opinion. It is, perhaps, the one aspect of intelligence which can be taught and learned. Moral intelligence is, in fact, "good character."

Morality is developed during the formative years. Respect for truth and belief in the value of performing for the good of the greatest number of people rather than for the good of the individual are sound principles on which to develop character. The earlier these principles are acquired, the greater the individual's opportunity for developing moral intelligence.

Simply to verbalize a convenient set of moral standards is no substitute for ingrained moral values. As long as decisions arise which entail alternative courses of action, the ability to discern the intrinsic value of each course will be vital in the decision-making process which is leadership. The morally intelligent person is quick to cut through pretense and to evaluate ideas, ideals, and patterns of conduct in the light of principle.

Communicative Intelligence. Communicative intelligence is the ability to interpret symbols and other abstractions and formulate them into logical concepts, and then transmit these concepts in terms which are easily assimilated and understood. Communicative intelligence enables the individual to reach others and, in turn, to be reached by others. It is this aspect of intelligence that allows a leader to persuade, to influence, and to establish good will. It is also the best way to instill his own goals in his followers. The latter requires skill because the leader must influence followers to accept his ideas as if they were their own. One approach which has been used by recreational personnel illustrates how leaders can instill goals in followers without dictating to them:

1.   A supervisor of athletic personnel, in a short discussion on physical fitness, says, "With fellows of your age, enthusiasm for the

game, and intelligence, it is unnecessary for me even to mention improper health habits, such as smoking, drinking, or staying out late. You are all aware, I am sure, of the harm such activities can do to your athletic fitness and personal health."

2. A group worker says, "This is one of the best groups with which I have worked; you really apply yourselves in meeting the goals which you have set."

3. A superintendent of recreational service says to one of his general supervisors, "You have the initiative and knowledge to produce a high quality and quantity of work for the betterment of this department and the community."

4. A camp counselor says, "This unit is the neatest in the entire camp."

This method of suggesting an idea in such a way that listeners interpret it as their own is just one example of using communicative intelligence. Other approaches will be more appropriate in other situations and at other times. Communicative intelligence involves a well-developed sense of timing with regard to social situations; that is, the individual must have the ability to do or say the right thing at the right time.

Character Traits

Current research now indicates that certain traits may, indeed, be inborn and can be a selection mechanism to determine leaders. Certain traits crop up in almost every investigation relating to the leadership phenomenon.[13] Courage, sincerity, stability, and other such qualities are generally admirable and looked to in times of stress. Such characteristics often manifest themselves in surprising situations and under trying conditions and result in achievement or influence. These character traits seem to be important and warrant some further explanation, particularly as they function in combination with intelligence.[14]

Loyalty is the quality of constancy, illustrated by the act of remaining faithful to an individual, group, or cause. It involves steadfastness in the face of adversity and the upholding of principles against all odds. Loyalty is normally associated with strictly ethical concepts, but individuals may show just as much loyalty to a cause which is immoral

---

13. C. R. Edginton and C. A. Griffith, *The Recreation and Leisure Service Delivery System* (Philadelphia: Saunders College Publishing, 1983), p. 69.

14. E. Ghiselli, "The Validity of Management Traits Related to Occupational Level," *Journal of Personnel Psychology*, Vol. 16 (1963), pp. 109–113.

or destructive. Thus the trait of loyalty must be tempered with intelligence.

Integrity is the quality of honor which leads an individual to seek truth and justice in any given situation. Integrity embodies a moral obligation to adhere to ethical principles of conduct. It implies honesty and consistency in thought, word, and deed. Integrity must be guided by intelligence if a person is to adhere to principles as he ponders choices and makes decisions.

Discretion is the quality of caution. It involves discernment and application of good judgment or tact to interpersonal situations. Where conflict is possible, careful appraisal and analysis are needed to alleviate tension or mediate pressure. Discretion is indispensable in those who would guide and teach others. Discretion also implies the quality of keeping someone else's confidence and can be misused as a powerful weapon by unscrupulous persons seeking gain through threatening to reveal information given them in confidence. Discretion, when used in combination with intelligence, enables a leader to help people solve their personal problems and thus influence them toward socially acceptable and ethically correct behavior.

Reliability is the quality of stability and dependability, a measure of individual competence. Reliability, more than any other quality, reflects the level of the individual's achivement in any job. The reliable person who undertakes an assignment can be counted on to achieve it, through methods characterized by balance and proportion. Emotional balance is another characteristic of the reliable person. Sometimes reliability is ascribed pejoratively, indicating that a person is "in a rut," or never varies his habitual patterns of behavior. But when found in combination with intelligence, reliability is a positive quality that attracts followers.

Responsibility is the quality of moral obligation. It implies steadfastness of purpose and faithfulness in the discharge of some duty, function, or trust. The knowledge that a responsible person is handling a problem provides those who have entrusted it to him with a sense of security. Sometimes responsibility has the negative connotation of answerability; it implies guilt. This sense of the term is particularly pertinent where the obligation involved is not of the person's own choosing but is, rather, assigned to him arbitrarily by some authority. Thus, his motivation for fulfilling it is not based on personal ethics but on fear of possible consequences. Fear impedes intelligence. The quality of responsibility is most likely to influence others and produce beneficial results when it is accepted on the basis of free choice.

Tolerance is the quality of understanding. It grows from respect for individual dignity and implies an intellectual rather than an emotional response to situations. It provides the individual with the power to endure the great variety of human failings. It is a disposition toward fair play and the exclusion of bigotry and prejudice. The ability to understand sympathetically the feelings of other people or to empathize with others is derived from prior experience and a great regard for human nature. The tolerant person accepts each individual as he is rather than stereotyping him. Sometimes a person who appears tolerant is merely refusing to face the responsibility of having an opinion. True tolerance is guided by intelligence.

Talent is the quality of creative potential or skill. It implies a native ability for some specific pursuit. A talent may be put to both good and evil use. For example, the talents of machinists, scientists, and administrators were used by Hitler for the subjugation of other nations, whereas Western democracies have attempted to use the same talents to subdue tyranny for the good of society. When talent is guided by intelligence it can make significant and worthwhile contributions to people's lives.

Sociability is the quality of getting along well with others and enjoying their company. It involves adapting to social situations in which various types of personalities come together. By demonstrating concern for things which are of greatest significance to co-workers or friends, the sociable individual can gain insight into their needs. If he is of leadership caliber, he may also be able to help them translate such needs into satisfying outlets. Helen Hall Jennings has discussed this quality in relation to leadership: "They [leaders] apparently earn the choice status of most wanted participants because they act in behalf of others with a sensitivity of response which does not characterize the average individual in a community."[15]

A leader's sociability requires more than hail-fellow-well-met exuberance. Identification with the needs of others and an understanding of how such needs can be satisfied may be accomplished only through the application of intelligence to the quality of sociability.

Perseverance is the quality of persistence. It entails continuing to do something in spite of difficulties or pursuing a course of action until a stated objective is reached. Tenacity and courage are often requisite attributes. Perseverance can also be interpreted unfavorably to mean stubbornness or annoying obstinacy. It is apparent that the quality of perseverance must be guided by intelligence if positive aims are to be achieved.

---

15. H. H. Jennings, "Leadership—A Dynamic Redefinition," *Journal of Educational Sociology*, Vol. 17 (March 1944), p. 431.

Initiative is the quality of confident aggressiveness. It is the combination of sureness and self-activation. A person who has the ability to discern advantageous conditions and act upon them, motivated by the will to succeed, has initiative. The person with initiative does not depend on "lucky breaks." He is driven by a sense of urgency that allows him to work hard to overcome obstacles; because this urgency is a form of anxiety, the person with initiative needs intelligence to moderate his drive and maintain mental balance.

Personal Attributes

Although personal attributes, like character traits, may not actually differentiate the leader from a non-leader, there are certain personal attributes a recreationist must strive for in order to advance his professional career.

Appearance. The recreationist may have no control over his facial structure, but he can do something about his clothes and the way he wears them. Appearance can be an asset for those who work with people. First impressions are difficult to overcome; if the recreationist is particularly careless about his appearance, people may regard it as a personal insult, inferring that he has so little respect for their opinion that he cannot be bothered to even present an agreeable appearance. On the other hand, if group members receive a positive first impression, he will more quickly and easily win their confidence and thus be more effective in fulfilling his professional obligations. The recreationist can only help his own cause by being suitably dressed for the occasion, whatever it may be. His taste in clothes should be moderate, not ostentatious. His physical cleanliness must be above reproach. A handsome face, a distinguished mien, or impeccable taste in clothes may have no actual effect on others in terms of leadership, but they are all assets that can help create a favorable attitude toward the person fortunate enough to possess them. But an individual need not have such exceptional attributes in order to present a pleasing appearance; personal neatness and good taste are quite enough.

Speaking Ability. Speaking ability is important to a recreationist who aspires to leadership. It is essentially through his ability to verbalize that he captures and fires the imagination of others. Merely to express oneself well in writing is not enough. The leader needs speaking ability in order to transmit his ideas effectively to his followers. Public addresses or simple conversations can be meaningful and stimulating both in content and expression; they can be simple parrotings of someone else's good ideas which lose their force through poor delivery; at worst, they can be banal in both content and expression. All the skills of public speaking are invaluable tools for the leader, especially the ability to project personal warmth and sincerity through the use of tone and gesture. Although speaking ability is a great advantage to the potential leader, it is not an absolute necessity—if he must, he can have someone else deliver his ideas. Nevertheless, recreationists are frequently sought as public speakers. It behooves the recreationist to cultivate whatever speaking talent he has.

Educational Preparation.   Leaders who are uneducated are relatively rare in any field today. The vast increase in knowledge of all kinds prevents the educationally unprepared from actively participating in leadership situations where technical knowledge is important. Educational preparation does not produce leadership per se, but it can give the individual specialized knowlege and help him gain the insight he needs if he aspires to leadership.

Mental and Physical Health.   The recreationist must have good mental health. Responsibility for the emotional, and often physical, lives of many people is entrusted to recreationists. Only individuals with sound mental health can assume such responsibility. Mental stability is a primary requisite for employment in recreational service, and is certainly a leadership quality. It promotes confidence among followers who need to feel that they can rely upon the leader's words and actions, and it ensures against mercurial shifts in temperament or in goals as the leader guides his group toward objectives.

Good physical fitness and stamina are also basic requirements for the recreationist. In a few situations, certain physical disabilities are not detrimental to the performance of functions, but in many cases physical capacity in the fullest sense is necessary for the effective production of work and the handling of responsibilities required of the recreationist.

A recreationist works with people in a wide variety of capacities. He may be required to work in athletic programs, to give speeches, to direct plays and group singing, to enter into community building projects, or to conduct surveys within the community. Whatever his responsibilities, he must have the vitality and the resources which will enable him to complete the task effectively. Optimum physical and mental health are extremely important for recreationists working in any leadership capacity.

QUESTIONS FOR DISCUSSION

1. Are certain personality characteristics necessary for the recreationist to have, and if so, what are they?
2. How may potential leaders be identified?
3. Is intelligence vital to leadership? If so, how much and why?
4. What is empathy?
5. What is "adventurous cyclothemia"?

BIBLIOGRAPHY

Bucher, Charles A., Jay S. Shivers, and R. D. Bucher, *Recreation for Today's Society*, 2nd ed. (Englewood Cliffs, N.J.: Prentice-Hall, Inc., 1984).

Edginton, Christopher R., and Phyllis M. Ford, *Leadership in Recreation and Leisure Service Organizations* (New York: John Wiley & Sons, 1985).

Ferris, Thomas N., and John P. Marchak, *Recreation Leader* (Syosset, N.Y.: National Learning Corp., 1977).

Hunt, James and others, *Leaders and Managers: International Perspectives on Managerial Behavior and Leadership Research* (Elmsford, N.Y.: Pergamon Press, Inc., 1984).

Kraus, Richard G., *Recreation Leadership Today* (Glenview, Ill.: Scott, Foresman and Company, 1985).

McCall, Morgan W., *Leadership & the Professional* (Greensboro, N.C.: Center for Creative Leadership, 1981).

St. Clair, Barry, *Leadership* (Wheaton, Ill.: Victor Books, 1984).

Selznick, Phillip, *Leadership in Administration: A Sociological Interpretation* (Berkeley, Cal.: Univ. of California Press, 1983).

Stoppe, Richard L., *Leadership Communication* (Birmingham, Ala.: Pathway Press, 1982).

Williams, Denny, *Leadership Lifestyle* (Kansas City, Mo.: Beacon Hill Press of Kansas City, 1983).

CHAPTER ELEVEN

Leadership at the Functional Level

Recreational leadership may be divided into three levels on the basis of specific activities performed by the recreationist: functional, supervisory, and managerial. This chapter deals with the functional—or program, operational, or basic—level of leadership in the field of recreational service.

WHO IS THE RECREATIONIST? WHAT DOES HE DO?

Ideally, the professional recreational worker, or recreationist, is a person who has earned a degree in recreational service education from an accredited institution. In addition, he may be certified, licensed, or professionally registered in the field. (A few states have such procedures, registration being the most common, but quite innocuous, practice.) This preparation has equipped him with a professional philosophy and a broad overview of the relationship between the field and other areas of applied social science, as well as a system of personal and professional ethics and conduct.

The recreationist's primary obligation is to serve the recreational needs of the community in which he works and to be ready at all times to deal with both individuals and groups. His ability to perform such services is based on a thorough knowledge of individual needs, abilities, and experience. He leads people, at their own pace, toward satisfying recreational experiences which may take many forms. In addition to guidance, the recreationist may be called upon to provide the needed facilities or setting where people can find recreational activity for themselves.

WHAT ACTIVITIES CONSTITUTE A RECREATIONAL PROGRAM?

Among the activities termed recreational are those that have proven, on the basis of experience and evaluation, to have beneficial effect upon the participants. The basis of any recreational program should include such activities: sports and games, arts and crafts, music, dramatics, dance, verbal intercourse, and interest groups.

Some activities are best suited to a particular group. By comparing activities which have worked well in similar settings, the recreationist is able to construct a value scale and suggest those activities he feels will have a wholly beneficial effect upon individual group members. This is not to imply that the recreationist cannot be inventive or that he should conform to established programs. Rather, his first duty is to see that basic recreational opportunities for all are made available. Then he must face the task of stimulating his membership towards these activities.

The recreationist who sets out to offer new and atypical recreational experiences must first understand the composition of his group and the needs and interests of the individuals who form it. Only then can he exercise his creative ability and ingenuity. Rather than the overreliance on physical activities programming, the most widespread pattern, the recreationist at the functional level has the responsibility, as well as the opportunity, to bring the many other areas of experience to the attention of group members. He must persuade those with whom he works that satisfaction may be derived in an infinite number of ways, some of which may move out of the center and into the community at large for resources. All people, young or old, should be provided with opportunities for understanding that leisure activities of a recreational nature can be anything that is socially acceptable. The recreationist is faced with the fundamental problem of leading people to discover that their opportunities are not limited. Once a group is freed from false constraints, it can participate in developing the recreational program most suitable for itself, a program worthwhile, spontaneous, self-actualizing, and leading to significant consequences in the lives of the participants.

It is in this area of programming that the recreationist expresses true leadership. It must be borne in mind, however, that evolution of interests and appreciation is a prolonged process. The recreationist must, with patience, overcome preconceptions, misconceptions, and limited background. He must strive to increase awareness of potential, inquiry into specific activities, and exposure to idea-provoking experiences. He must suggest projects designed to lead to subsequent investigation and exploration. In these ways he reveals to his group the wealth of possible recreational activities.

GENERAL LEADERSHIP GUIDELINES FOR THE RECREATIONIST

The professional recreational worker objectively views individuals who make up his agency's constituency, yet he shows by his behavior and methods of approach that he has recognized and understood their problems. Arousing interest, then, becomes a matter of understanding the individual and knowing his background so that new and unfamiliar activities can be related to prior experience. People's interest can also be stimulated through personal affection; an individual may be motivated because of an emotional attachment to the leader.

With these facts in mind, let us detail some of the responsibilities the recreationist undertakes in providing individuals and groups with satisfying recreational experiences:

1. Realizing that all people are unique in their interests, needs, and abilities.

2. Granting every individual a share of human dignity and respect for his own self-esteem.

3. Believing in the right of individuals to guide their own destinies and to belong to any social agency in which they feel a part.

4. Being aware that each individual brings a variety of thoughts and ideas into the social milieu and that such contributions, though they may be widely divergent from the established patterns, may have merit in their own right and are, therefore, worthy of time and consideration.

5. Achieving empathy with others.

6. Accepting others as they are without attempting to moralize to them, unless the standard of behavior is so low as to warrant an uplifting moral force; and not adapting or identifying oneself with substandard behavior.

7. Accepting the wide range of behaviors, from affection to hate.

8. Using his knowledge of human behavior to understand the various patterns which are exhibited, even though such patterns may appear meaningless to the casual observer.

9. Realizing that all behavior is useful and important as an indicator of human needs although it may not always be socially acceptable.

10. Performing within the spectrum of leadership—from strong or direct roles to resource person, depending on the situation.

11. Directing those who need guidance without prejudging them.

12. Limiting group or individual behavior when necessary and being permissive with those who require help in making decisions or performing.

13. Enabling group members to reach decisions without dictating to them.

14. Clarifying problems and indicating possible courses of action.

15. Realizing that his professional position places him over a group and may therefore create hostility rather than the acceptance accorded an indigenous member.

16. Understanding the recreational needs and interests of those the agency serves.

17. Providing active leadership to participants in the program.

18. Representing the agency for which he works by understanding its policies, philosophy, purpose, and functions.

19. Coordinating, through scheduling and supervision, the use of recreational structures, facilities, and space.

20. Referring agency constituents to other agencies in default of specific facilities or aid.

21. Guiding volunteers toward optimum service in their specialization.

22. Keeping abreast of current techniques and practices by in-service education and attendance at clinics, workshops, conferences, institutes, and schools where theory and practical learning experiences are available.

23. Maintaining professional integrity toward clients, the agency, the community, and oneself.

The Functional Level

Recreationists on the functional level, working directly with their constituents, are typically concerned with carrying out a schedule of various activities which provide recreational experiences for both participants and spectators. Such work will generally take the form of organizing, promoting, or directing group games, sports, and aesthetic activities, or providing services related to maintaining good public relations, such as answering questions posed by individuals who come to the recreational agency or any of its facilities. Instructing individuals in various skills is also an aspect of leadership at the functional level: guiding, coaching, assisting, or enabling those who participate within the agency-operated programs to achieve a certain measure of satisfaction and, perhaps, competence in an activity of their choice. Usually, these duties are performed within the confines of a recreational center, park, playground, or other specialized facility that provides recreational opportunities. Responsibilities may range from assisting in the direction of a seasonal operation on the playground to assuming complete responsibility for a center.

The following incident is typical of leadership at the functional level:

Elmer H was a twelve-year-old with the physical structure of a mature male. He stood six feet tall and weighed one hundred eighty pounds. He was of average intelligence, but his physical appearance belied his emotional level, which was normal for a boy of twelve. His manipulative abilities had not yet caught up to his muscles, and thus he was somewhat of a tanglefoot. Unfortunately, his large size and early maturity made him the butt of jokes and left him out of many games because he could fracture someone's arm or leg without half trying. His peers would not play with him because of his physique, and he could not compete with the older boys whose size he matched because their activities were too advanced or required a speed and agility which he did not have. He was, therefore, an isolated youngster.

The agency placed him in several activities, but in the end, the various instructors asked that he be kept out of their shops or workrooms because "he is always messing things up or breaking tools." This worker found Elmer trudging up the stairs from the basement crafts room one afternoon. He was going to leave the center and never come back, because he had been asked to leave the crafts room after damaging a particularly fine piece of leather by running a knife too far along a seam. "I didn't mean to cut it up, the knife slipped, and now I don't have anything to do."

The worker asked Elmer to come to his office, and together they discussed the reasons for Elmer's dissatisfaction with the center. When asked what he thought about not coming to the center anymore, Elmer replied with the time-honored formula of one whose feelings have been deeply hurt by saying, "I don't care." Although he made a good attempt to mask his feelings, there was no question of how he really felt by tears which he kept blinking back. Finally he said, "I just wanted to make something for my mother; it's her birthday." The worker took the boy down to the crafts room. The boy decided that he wanted to make a cyprus-knee lamp for his mother's birthday.

The next two weeks were filled with boiling, peeling, cutting, sanding, boring, and then smoothing, adding shellac, and finally putting in the wire for the socket attachment. At last the lamp was completed, a little rough in spots, a little off-color in others, but it had received the tender care and attention that a work of love would get. Attached to the lamp was a note, hand-printed, "To Mom from Elmer."

A week later Elmer's mother came to see the worker. She thanked him for the time and effort which he had taken with her son. She said, "He's like a changed boy, happier than he's ever been." She also said that it was the finest present she could have wanted, never suspecting that Elmer could actually make anything. Elmer still had his troubles, but for that one time, he had achieved where before there was always failure. His success gave him new heart to try again instead of just walking out.

This incident illustrates the concept of communication. It would have been so very simple to dismiss Elmer and his problems by merely listening to what he said rather than how he said it. He offered many clues to his loneliness and unacceptance. He utilized the classic reply of the person who has been hurt or pushed around by others, who wants to be liked but just does not seem to have the knack for accomplishment. By saying "I don't care," he put on a mask to hide his deep hurt, although he was not mature enough to totally conceal his emotions. By looking at the slump of his shoulders, his defeatist attitude, the manner of his speech, and his facial expression, the worker was able to discern a great deal more than was readily apparent by speaking to the boy. Once he had won Elmer's confidence and had found out that material gains were not important, the worker was able to lead Elmer to a successful project.

The worker was able to communicate with Elmer because he was aware of and seeking clues to the boy's behavior. Where others had placed more importance upon material gains, the worker was vitally concerned with the boy and his needs. Discerning the desire of the boy, the worker transmitted ideas, so that this child was finally able to achieve in ways which were satisfying to him. In this instance, the worker had influence with the individual and was able to channel his energy and lead him to the fulfillment of his desires.

Initially, the recreationist performs simple activities, often working in a leadership capacity with groups of young children or assisting a more experienced leader directing other types of groups. Usually the beginning recreationist works under supervision until he is thoroughly acquainted with the operating techniques of the agency. Most agencies offer specific guidelines of methods and procedures to be followed, and a beginning worker is subject to periodic observation and appraisal as he learns on the job. His performance is evaluated and must meet agency-established standards.

The variety of duties performed by a beginning recreationist at the functional level may be seen from the following list of typical activities:

1. Assists in issuing and collecting supplies, materials, and equipment necessary for specific activities within the recreational program, particularly playground and arts and crafts materials.

2. Helps to organize various activities, for example, games, groups, dramatics, singing, dancing, athletics, arts, crafts, and nature-oriented activities.

3. Gives instructions, guidance, or coaching in several activities, which may include explaining the rules of playing certain games or techniques useful in various athletic endeavors.

4. Assists in establishing league play, tournaments, or other competitive activities.

5. Sees that necessary precautions are observed to ensure the health, safety, and welfare of participants and spectators.

6. Provides preliminary first aid in the event of minor injury to participants.

7. Performs routine inspections of equipment in order to maintain optimum efficiency and safety to users.

8. Performs minor custodial functions of a routine nature.

As a functional recreationist gains on-the-job experience, he is assigned more difficult and complex responsibilities. He may perform skilled and technical tasks requiring direction of a great many recreational activities at a designated facility. He may be responsible for the planning, coordination, and direction of activities in a specific program area, or he may assist in directing and coordinating the entire spectrum of activities offered by the center. Usually, he is under supervision of an immediate superior, generally an area supervisor. He, in turn, may supervise the activities of a subordinate recreationist or volunteer workers.

Characteristic of the duties which a more experienced recreationist performs at the functional level are the following:

1. Helps to administer the recreational program at a center or directs a recreational program at an assigned facility.

2. Performs such public relations work as is necessary to stimulate and maintain the interest of potential and actual participants in the recreational activities of the facility in which he works.

3. Organizes, guides, conducts, and directs many recreational activities, including competitive and non-competitive sports, games, contests, hobbies, special interest groups, youth groups, children's groups, and older adult groups.

4. Keeps custody of and issues supplies, materials, and equipment necessary for conducting a variety of activities, or supervises a subordinate in the performance of this function.

5. Examines equipment and recommends needed repairs or replacements.

6. Keeps records and reports on the operation of the facility.

7. Assists in formulating recommendations or makes recommendations concerning the place his facility has in the overall community recreational system.

8. Helps analyze citizen interest in and support of the recreational service system.

Large agencies often have a third step at the functional level (in smaller agencies, a recreationist may move directly to the supervisory level.) This third step requires definite managerial ability on the part of the recreationist, as distinct from positions which require particular skills or technical proficiencies. Such a recreationist may direct a multitude of recreational activities at a large playground or center or assist in the direction of a regional recreational center. He is responsible for initiating ideas, planning, coordinating, and providing some supervision to subordinate employees as well as to the activities. He works with all age groups. His unique position allows him some latitude in exploring new programming experiences and broadening the scope of agency-sponsored activities. Most of his work is performed on his own initiative.

Some examples of service performed by such a recreationist are the following:

1.   Initiates, plans, organizes, and coordinates a great variety of recreational activities in a center or on a playground.

2.   Analyzes the recreational needs of people living in the neighborhood or using his facility and formulates immediate and future recreational programs on the basis of his findings.

3.   Provides recreational services for community organizations.

4.   Provides, upon request, individual guidance as well as group guidance on civic, social, or recreational matters within the area served by his facility.

5.   Supervises issuing and collecting of recreational supplies, materials, and equipment.

6.   Sees to the maintenance and proper use of such items.

7.   Supervises subordinate professionals and volunteers to ensure proper performance of their assigned tasks.

8.   Organizes in-service educational activities.

9.   Assists in development studies of the facility and neighborhood which it serves.

10.   Attends staff conferences, clinics, professional meetings, and other educational workshops or institutes required for his professional growth and development.

Specialists

Specialists are agency employees who have excellent technical proficiency in activity areas such as have been mentioned. Such workers may be recreationists, but usually they are part-time employees hired because of some talent or skill integral to the agency program. Often specialists hold full-time jobs or have professional careers outside the recreational service field. Specialists are assigned the responsibility for developing a comprehensive program in their particular area of specialization. Part of their job may be to offer instruction in their particular skill to recreationists within the agency so that the agency can broaden the scope of its program and reach more members of the community. Specialists may be employed expressly to influence entire groups residing in a target neighborhood or community which the agency serves.

The Detached-Worker Specialist

An especially useful person is the detached-worker specialist, who is assigned the responsibility of contacting and working with hard-to-reach groups within the community. In metropolitan communities, for example, such a worker may be hired because he has a particular ethic, racial, or neighborhood identity that uniquely enables him to communicate with and influence members' behavior.

As an example of how such a worker might qualify for the job of working with a street gang, we offer the following. He should have expert knowledge about the area, people, mores, traditions, ethnicity, jargon, and habits of those who are part of the neighborhood. He should be young enough to join a neighborhood street gang, but old enough to display the maturity that will enable him to become one of the central figures around whom a gang might gather for information or ideas. One approach to gaining entrance might be to infiltrate the infrastructure of the gang by residing in the neighborhood and casually seeking out gang leaders and their cohorts. Such an assignment could be dangerous for a recreationist, unless he also happened to be comfortable with and capable of making and retaining close association with the particular group.

The detached worker, as the term implies, is not assigned to a center or other recreational facility. He roves the streets and is employed by the department in neighborhoods or communities requiring his particular skills. He has no permanent base or office, but reports to a department official from the central office of the agency, to the general supervisor of the district in whose jurisdiction he works, or to the executive in charge of special services for the department. When an agency program calls for a significant attempt to modify behavior of antisocial groups or to provide a modicum of information for people who are ordinarily outside the communications network used for providing information about recreational activities and opportunities, the detached worker is employed.

The above descriptions of recreationists and specialists at work at the functional level of leadership within recreational agencies are typical of day-to-day operations in the field. Terminology differs from department to department and from municipality to municipality, but in the main, the functions, duties, and responsibilities described are those which normally occupy personnel working at this level.

Our discussion so far has been concerned primarily with recreationists working within public or community deparments of recreational service. In recent years, however, a new area of specialization has arisen to meet the needs of those citizens who are confined to medical institutions for emergency, chronic, long-term, or custodial care and treatment. The ill, home-bound, or disabled person requires as many or more recreational opportunities than do unafflicted members of the community, but they cannot come to a center for help. Hence, therapeutic and adapted recreational service is a rapidly growing area of specialization. With greater integration into the community of persons who are atypical, public recreational service departments will be employing more therapeutic recreationists to work out adapted recreational activities to meet the limitations imposed by disability or illness.

THE NEED FOR RECREATIONISTS AT THE PROGRAM LEVEL

A recreational service department's most direct contact with its constituent public is at the program level. It is here above all that full-time professionals are needed to fulfill the year-round recreational responsibility of the agency. Yet, many departments consistently employ seasonal workers, part-time specialists, or fill-in assistants to operate their full-fledged programs.

The excuses, sometimes legitimate, for this lapse are lack of money, the pressures of tradition, and political coercion. In many communities, the recreational service department is expected to provide jobs for a portion of the community population or summer work for the youngsters. The immediate outcome of such a practice—overreliance on nonprofessionally prepared and special-skill employees—is poor leadership and poor programming. The long-range effect will be the loss of respect, understanding, and financial support of the community.

A recreational service department can be no better than its professional staff. The recreational leader requires educational preparation, but this must be a springboard from which to learn and grow. That is the foundation of a dynamic recreational program. Recreationists should be well-rounded, take an active part in community affairs, and have private recreational interests that can contribute to their identity as interesting, socially sensitive, and responsive personalities. The study of human development, motivation, and group dynamics, the reading of professional literature and attendance at professional meetings contributes more specifically to the recreationist's professional competence.

Paradoxically, the recreationist at the program level, where true leadership is most vital, is the lowest paid, least respected, and most expendable employee. Perhaps departments will finally realize that program level personnel should be professional in every respect and possess those personality and intellectual strengths which enable them to provide the highest quality service to their clients.

QUESTIONS FOR DISCUSSION

1. What is a recreationist?
2. What are some general guidelines for leadership in recreational service?
3. Where do recreationists at the functional level operate?
4. What are some of the typical responsibilities carried on by the functional level recreationist?
5. What is a specialist?
6. Discuss the implication of the recreationist on the "cutting edge."

BIBLIOGRAPHY

Adair, John, *Effective Leadership: A Self-Development Manual* (Brookfield, Vt.: Gower Pub. Co., 1983).

Bittel, Lester, *Leadership: The Key to Management Success* (New York: Franklin Watts, Inc., 1984).

Clarke, Jean I., *Who, Me Lead a Group?* (Minneapolis, Minn.: Winston Press, 1983).

Cribben, James J., *Leadership Strategies for Organizational Effectiveness* (New York: American Management Association, 1982).

Fallon, William K., ed., *Leadership on the Job: A Guide to Good Supervision* (New York: American Management Association, 1982).

Lawson, Leslie G., et al., *Lead On! The Complete Handbook for Group Leaders* (San Luis Obispo, Cal.: Impact Publishers, Inc., 1982).

Newman, Aubrey S., *Follow Me: The Human Element in Leadership* (Novato, Cal.: Presidio Press, 1981).

O'Connell, Brian, *Effective Leadership in Voluntary Organizations* (New York: Walker & Co., 1981).

Williamson, David, *Group Power: How to Develop, Lead, and Help Groups Achieve Goals* (Englewood Cliffs, N.J.: Prentice-Hall, Inc., 1982).

CHAPTER TWELVE

Leadership at the Supervisory Level

It is now believed by most psychologists and sociologists that leadership is an interpersonal process through which an individual gets others to perform in accordance with his direction. The essence of leadership, then, consists in stimulating and influencing others to become followers. However, the best leaders also try to develop the innate capacities of their followers so that they may also achieve their fullest potential. In so doing, the leader causes secondary leaders to emerge. This is a rational behavior and not the emotional consequence of a simple desire to wield power.

THE CONCEPT OF SUPERVISION

Leaders have come to realize that only a democratic climate can produce the necessary involvement which professionals require to support the give and take of group life. Moreover, without this vital interaction there would only be mute acquiescence. Headship rather than leadership would be the logical outcome. Of course, authoritarian personalities probably would prefer the presumed clear-cut chain of command and translation of orders into performance, but it is questionable whether recreationists will be able to work effectively in such an environment.

Supervision in any field is an attempt to improve worker competencies to optimum levels. The supervisor in any organization holds the unique position of mediator between those who manage it and those who carry out its functions at the program level. He translates administrative policy into action and serves as the channel through which employee suggestions and grievances become known to management. Among the supervisor's many responsibilities is facilitating the production of those services for which the organization is established. In the field of recreational service, this means obtaining the cooperation of all subordinate workers and enhancing their work performance in every way to ensure the finest recreational activities for the agency's constituency.

The leader is the visionary who correctly analyzes the opportunities which develop in the social environment, given the limitations of whatever external forces impinge upon the group. The leader then guides the group toward the potential that he has foreseen. He promotes the development of goals that are congruent with the needs of the group and its membership. When he is successful in that task, cooperation and action are generated.

THE NATURE OF SUPERVISION

The supervisory process is inextricably bound to all the concepts and functions which define the leadership process. Too often, supervision is taken to mean simply the overseeing of subordinate workers or the imparting of technical knowledge to obtain more competent performance on the part of subordinates. Supervision, as we define it in the context of recreational leadership, includes responsibility for participant satisfaction, employee competence in activity direction and instruction and in program organization and development, and growth in individual and group work performance. It includes a commitment to seek new and more effective methods for providing recreational services to an ever greater number of people. Supervision, then, may be defined in terms of the objectives for which it is used, the aims which give meaning to the methods applied, and as a positive force for the development of interpersonal relations designed to free the talents and intellect of all those who come within its purview.[1]

If we consider supervision a leadership process, it is clearly not the exclusive property of recreationists employed at the supervisory level. As a process through which expert technique is applied to provide the best possible arrangement of facilities and experiences for public benefit, supervision may occur at any leadership level. The program worker supervises the recreational activities of participants and, on occasion, co-workers, just as executives or administrators exercise supervision in carrying out their many responsibilities. Indeed, self-supervision is an attribute of successful recreationists whatever their position within the organization.

The person who is responsible for the supervision of functional personnel involved in the activities program of a recreational service agency should have a purposeful and wide knowledge of the field. He

---

1.   Avis L. Johnson, Fred Luthans, Harry W. Hennessey, "The Role of Locus of Control in Leader Influence Behavior," *Personnel Psychology*, Vol. 37, No. 1 (Spring, 1984), pp. 61–75.

must be generally open to suggestions, but he should possess special education in the many methods and techniques available in activity presentation. He should be aware that not all workers can utilize the same procedures with the same degree of success. There is, after all, more to being a recreationist than the mere use of standardized methods. The supervisor must be impartial and exhibit integrity at all times. Nothing ruins morale faster than showing favoritism toward some while ignoring the efforts of others. He must recognize superior methodology. He must continually encourage personnel to perform to their fullest capabilities and to modify their methods where necessary. One requirement is that the supervisor's experiences be broader in content and scope and his educational preparation be richer than those whom he supervises.

Supervisors must be responsible for the achievement of the recreational program in the system. Historically, this responsibility devolved upon the functional recreationist, and failure to achieve was placed upon the worker's inability to perform. This concept should be corrected. In most cases, *as the supervisor is, so is the program.* This inference can support a foundation for evaluating the effectiveness of supervision in recreational service. The competent supervisor is a creative person. He originates criteria for the agency and stimulates close cooperation among all individuals and groups who work with him.

The supervisor as a leader has the responsibility of adapting whatever group or organization he works with to the realities of external pressures. Leadership is more than just the inspiration of followers to contribute to the achievement of specific objectives. It also considers external factors. Group or organizational enhancement, maturation, and goal achievement are not solely internal problems; they have significant external properties as well.

The supervisory leader remains alert to the direction in which the group is moving, and if a change in direction is required, owing to movements in the larger environment, he explains why modifications must be made. In this way the group is reassured that it will be consulted if deviations from expectations are made. The leader has the responsibility for keeping lines of communication open and monitoring the process by which the group's goals are redefined.

It should not be assumed that the leader is free to change goals, modify the task, or even make basic policy decisions on his own. He must conform to both internal and external forces—particularly the opinions of power figures—in much of what he does. He is the one who appropriately interprets the pressures or conditions and undertakes a program that will be successful within their restrictions.

Every supervisory leader has personal opinions or biases that are opposed to the direction in which he is attempting to move the group. However, he is realistic enough to concede that the pursuit of his own convictions may alienate his followers and cause a serious loss of efficiency in dealing with outside groups or other organizations.

A leader always recognizes that the maintenance of his leadership role depends upon the support of his followers. He attempts to shape and direct group opinion but he usually finds that external or internal pressures cause him to downplay his personal preferences for what he believes to be the greatest good for the greatest number. The supervisor avoids the stalemate of all-or-nothing situations; again, the risk is based upon conditions. He must adroitly interpret the desires of cliques and secondary leaders and the pressures of external pulls. He has to find a path of action that melds those conditions and is seen as a success or an achievement for the group. That is the way the leader sustains his influence. He is engaged in a tightrope walk. All of the forces at play may try to destabilize him but by carefully balancing these forces, the leader is capable of creating enormous personal influence in obtaining the support of the majority within the group.

Supervisory Power

The power of the leader is derived from various sources. In the hierarchical organization of the recreational service department, power has usually been accompanied by the authority associated with position. The power of a supervisor is typically felt to be a function of the authority he has to direct subordinates and whatever sanctions he can bring to bear. If supervision were only a function of headship this might be sufficient to gain compliance and even productivity but the outcome would be reluctantly obtained and be short-lived. There would also be a question of personnel morale.

Supervision, as a process of leadership, does not rely merely on the capacity to satisfy someone else's needs through rewards and penalties. In fact, this may be a detriment to the establishment of rapport—good human relations—between supervisor and subordinate because of the underlying threat contained in powerful positions. Most subordinate workers view their supervisors as threatening because of their power to increase or decrease salary, assign desirable or unattractive tasks, or cause the promotion or termination of a subordinate. The supervisor, therefore, controls important sources of need satisfaction, creating conditions that lead to conformity of behavior by individuals subject to his authority.

The supervisor must fight desperately to overcome the anxiety which is naturally produced by his legitimate authority. To do this he must raise the level of democratization to a high degree. This may be performed while creating a climate of professionalization. This means that the supervisor must be considered a scrupulously fair person, treating all subordinates equitably. It requires the creation of an environment where all subordinates may raise questions, make suggestions, offer criticisms without fear of retaliation if they oppose the supervisor's plans. The supervisor must remain objective and behave in a consistent manner. This enables subordinates to depend upon the supervisor's word. Above all, the promotion of mutual trust and confidence depends on the perception, on the part of subordinates, that the supervisor is reliable. Reliability must not be construed in any negative sense; it has to do with principle, character, and honesty.

The following incident may serve to illustrate this idea:

Staff conferences were called every week at the central office of X recreational service department in a medium-sized midwestern community. One of the reasons for the staff conference was the promotion of new ideas for the overall recreational program. Each worker brought with him a project which had been found to operate well in his neighborhood center and which could be utilized by other personnel in the agency. This conference technique had worked well for a long time; now it appeared as though a breakdown had occurred. The workers complained that the weekly meeting was simply a waste of time. Morale was low, and agency activities had degenerated to "the same old things." As area supervisor, it was my responsibility to determine why this deterioration had begun in a formerly high-producing region.

I sat in on one of the meetings, and it soon became apparent why morale was so low and why new ideas were not forthcoming. Shortly before this demoralizing trend had started, the original group supervisor had been transferred to another position, and a new group supervisor had replaced him. Unfortunately, the new supervisor, who had a number of years' experience, was not particularly openminded when it came to accepting new ideas. As a result, his subordinates stopped offering suggestions because they found that they were never utilized, or because invariably they personally received criticism for giving the idea in the first place. What had been stimulating was now a rather boring and routine meeting. Along with this routinized aspect there developed a type of conformity to the supervisor's suggestions or implied orders. No one bothered to argue or remonstrate with any of the supervisor's ideas, although some were questionable, and there was a rather passive acceptance of what he said. This pattern was reinforced by others in the group who "fell in line" as each preceding worker patronized these opinions. When privately questioned over a period of days, each of the workers expressed disillusionment with the staff conference method, indicating that they disagreed with much of what the supervisor suggested, but felt that they had to "go along" in order to retain their positions.

The pressure to conform may represent self-preservation when an individual is confronted with an uncomfortable decision. In any conference situation within an organization where a supervisor is present, subordinates may be reluctant to voice their true opinions unless rapport is established. Unless the supervisor can assume the leadership role and establish easy communication, spontaneity will be restrained and progress will be impeded. Rapport permits relaxing of tension so that professionals sincerely dedicated to the solution of problems which affect the agency and its personnel can feel free to contribute suggestions without fear of ridicule or reprisal. Face-saving and job-saving pressures make for conformity. If the hierarchy is filled with people merely filling headship positions and not truly functioning as leaders, each worker will fall into agreement with the one above him, constantly increasing the pressure for conformity.

Types of Supervision

Supervision can be classified into four distinct types: critical, custodial, instructional, and creative. With the possible exception of critical supervision, each type can be employed successfully, depending upon the situation and the personality of the supervisor.

Critical.   The danger in using criticism as a supervisory technique is the fine line between constructive and destructive criticism. Destructive criticism rarely obtains more effective work, but contributes to the breakdown of personnel morale, undermines employee loyalty to the agency, and may finally be the major factor causing good employees to leave the agency. Fault-finding is never difficult, particularly if the fault-finder feels no obligation to suggest ways to remedy the fault. And even when the criticism offered is constructive, the way in which it is offered may arouse such hostility as to render it useless. It is a rare supervisor who can use the technique of criticism successfully.

Custodial (Prescriptive).   The philosophy behind custodial or prescriptive supervision is "an ounce of prevention is worth a pound of cure." In other words it is better to see that a worker avoids difficulty in the first place than to let him get into an inextricable position. Thus a supervisor anticipates difficulties of which the worker may not be aware. These may be the nature of the assignment, facts about the local environment, citizenry, and customs, or any of a number of circumstances with which the supervisor is already familiar. Although this type of supervision is self-explanatory, one point should be made clear: as the supervisor assists and guides subordinates in avoiding difficulties, he must be careful not to usurp completely their functions and take on their responsibilities. A worker learns through experience, especially problem-solving experience. The supervisor must direct his effort to seeing that workers understand where and why problems may arise so that they are better able to confront and handle a given situation. To be helpful, the supervisor need not have direct personal experience of all the difficulties which may confront a recreationist. His business is to consult, analyze, explain, and offer a rational plan of action which the worker might take to resolve whatever problem he faces. One difficulty inherent in the prescriptive technique is that unless the supervisor is skillful in its use, workers may receive the impression that the supervisor is so lacking in confidence about their ability to handle responsibility that he tries to second-guess them or anticipates problems where none exist. This creates an atmosphere of mistrust and impedes the functioning of the system.

Instructional. Instructional supervision is akin to teaching. The supervisor who uses this technique is cognizant of weaknesses, and aids workers to recognize and understand the reasons for such failing. At the same time, he demonstrates in a constructive manner how they may be remedied. This technique involves establishing an atmosphere of cooperation in which logical advice can be both freely offered and freely taken. One who uses it successfully usually has had a considerable amount of education and experience which enables him to expose subordinates to entirely new areas of knowledge. The emphasis is on suggestion rather than command.

Creative. Creative supervision focuses on increasing the worker's effectiveness and productivity. The supervisor acts as a resource person, giving advice and assistance where needed, but encouraging the worker in his own ideas, fostering a spirit of cooperation, and stimulating self-evaluation. The purpose of creative supervision is to instill within the worker a desire to discover or produce an idea which may be utilized for more effective and enjoyable recreational service. Creative supervision flourishes where the atmosphere is conducive to innovation.

The Supervisory Level within the Agency

In the field of recreational service, the supervisory level can be thought of as the heart of the organization, whereas the program and administrative levels may be described as the extremities and the head, respectively. Supervisors perform the vital work without which the agency cannot begin to operate effectively. A competent supervisor pumps the life blood of expertise and encouragement from management to the program level and back again. He executes decisions made by administrative personnel, interprets agency philosophy, policy, practices, and scope to subordinates in functional positions, and acts as the spokesman and buffer between the program worker and the administration. One of the supervisor's functions is to bring to program personnel a better understanding of administrative practice. The supervisor allies himself with neither the administrative nor the program level workers, but serves as counselor to both. It is the function of the supervisor to offer such expert technical assistance to the administrator and to the program level workers that success in the various spheres of work assigned to them is more likely to be reached.[2]

A supervisor in the field of recreational service performs the following functions:

1. Exercises leadership and is quick to ascertain leadership ability in others and to stimulate this capacity whenever it is discovered.

2. Studies and works to improve the activities presented in the recreational program as well as the materials, supplies, and equipment, the leadership methods used, and the group process developed as a result of agency initiation.

3. Interprets recreational and agency objectives to workers within the agency as well as to the community at large. Internally, this may be considered as the guidance and instruction of recreational personnel and volunteers. Externally, it is part of the public relations function designed to explain the purpose and operation of the agency.

4. Evaluates each worker's ability and inclination for learning new methods of activity presentation and for accepting work suggestions or advice.

5. Assists workers in their professional development,

---

2. W. H. Burton and L. J. Bruechner, *Supervision: A Social Process*, 3d ed. (New York: Appleton-Century-Crofts, 1955), p. 11.

encouraging them to develop objectivity toward their work and the problems which may confront them, instructing them in professional objectives, and stimulating their dedication to the field.

6. Seeks to provide the best possible in-service education for workers so that they may improve their personal work habits. This may be done through attending individual or staff conferences, constructing situations in which workers can observe better prepared recreationists in action, maintaining a professional library, or requiring attendance at clinics, workshops, conferences, or other learning situations.

7. Observes workers on the job and conducts personal interviews of personnel for the purpose of aiding in the improvement of worker technique and recommending desirable changes in the program. This function is carried out through the analysis of records and reports as well as inspection and examination of the leadership methods in use by workers.

8. Seeks to improve competence at the supervisory level through education and evaluation of the technical proficiency of supervision with recommendations for necessary modifications. This aspect of supervision is urgently required if the supervisor is to be current in his knowledge and techniques. Self-supervision is thus implied, as well as consistent objective appraisal of supervisory tasks and methods.

Effective supervision must take into account changing conditions within the community or agency as well as the basic aims and policies of the department or system. Methods and techniques used will vary according to situation; the effective supervisor must have an exceptional ability to evaluate situations and adapt techniques to suit them.

The Supervisor's Authority

Given the hierarchical organization exhibited by most recreational service agencies, the role of supervisor carries with it a built-in confusion about what constitutes the supervisor's authority. In order to lead most effectively, a supervisor must adhere to democratic principles and procedures. But some, interpreting democracy to mean the absence of authority, are unwilling to use democratic procedures for fear of losing their ability to direct subordinates and obtain their cooperation. This dilemma, while common, is a false one.

Authority has a significant and definite place in the supervisory process. Indeed, a basic tenet of democracy is recognition of the need for some kind of authority in those who are responsible for a group.

This authority should be understood to be synonymous with official appointment and the execution of specific duties and responsibilities. For any joint enterprise there is always a need for authority, whether it is legal in nature or based upon knowledge or expertise, assigned by some institution, or given official designation. Whatever the source, authority is a genuine component of democratic cooperation.

Perhaps the most fundamental question a supervisor faces is how to determine the proper measure of authority he should exercise in any situation. No matter how competent a leader the supervisor may be, at some time he will have to deal with subordinates who either cannot function within a democratic framework or who exploit the democratic situation for their personal benefit. Usually, organizations have a set of disciplinary actions to which the supervisor can resort in order to bring recalcitrant employees into line, for example, demotion, suspension, or even discharge. Thus, the temptation to use the authority of his position to obtain cooperation from subordinates through threat may be very strong. Yet threats have no place in the leadership process. Rather, the effective supervisor will find ways to make disciplinary action unnecessary, choosing from an array of creative techniques and routine instructional procedures as befits the particular case.

A newly appointed supervisor will find the problem of exercising authority particularly delicate. By virtue of his position in the organization, the supervisor has the power not only to discipline subordinates but even to deny them economic security. Thus, any supervisor, particularly an unknown, offers a potential threat to workers' livelihood. As long as workers feel threatened, they will not be able to perform effectively. The work atmosphere will be characterized by anxiety, mistrust, and conformity.

A supervisor's first task is to dispel subordinates' anxiety and establish rapport with them. When subordinates realize that the supervisor plays no favorites, has high expectations of work performance, respects his fellow professionals, and sees to it that they have a chance to participate in the decision-making processes which shape agency operation, they will reciprocate in kind. The trust and confidence that ensure cooperation have to be earned by the supervisor; he cannot demand these qualities from subordinates simply by virtue of his position within the organization. Once rapport is established, disciplinary problems and petty rule infringements— tardiness, slovenly appearance, poor preparation, or discourtesy— tend to disappear. Naturally, such an environment cannot be created overnight. It requires patience, understanding, insight, and an appreciation for the other person's point of view.

The personal relations between the leader and the members of his group are very likely the most meaningful for leadership. As Fiedler states:

We have here gone on the assumption that the leader-member relationship is likely to be most decisive in determining the favorableness of the situation for the leader. A leader who is liked, accepted, and trusted by his members will find it easy to make his influence felt. In fact, position power, under these conditions, may be somewhat redundant. The leader who is trusted and accepted does not need much position power to influence his group.[3]

When a leader has a group whose members like and respect him, the problems which confront him are vastly different from those of a leader who is not liked by his group members. For instance, a leader who has the confidence of his group can take the support of the membership for granted; while a distrusted leader must necessarily fear lack of support and even open rebellion on the part of his membership.

The following incident, the case of the unmoving maintenance man, precisely underscores this point:

Some sections in the parks division building of the Municipal Recreational Service Department were to be moved to another wing. The assistant superintendent of parks, whose office was being moved, requested a one-man working party to assist in moving his files to the new office. I asked one of the men in my maintenance crew to help out, and considering the matter closed, went about my business as maintenance foreman which took me to one of the outlying parks of the district.

On my return to the office, I received a telephone call from the assistant superintendent asking about somebody to help move his files. I replied that I had asked one of my crew to assist and had thought that everything had been taken care of. I called in Jack, the maintenance man, and asked why he had not moved the files. He told me that he didn't feel that I had ordered him to do anything and that after talking it over with his buddies on the crew, he felt that the assignment was not a part of his job description. He also felt that the job provided personal assistance to the assistant superintendent; and since he did not get along well with the assistant superintendent

3. F. E. Fiedler, *A Theory of Leadership Effectiveness* (New York: McGraw-Hill Book Company, 1967), p. 143.

and because it was a personal request, he did not feel that he had to make the effort to help.

How should I handle this insubordination? What should I do about the other men in the work crew who advised him not to assist on the job?

Let's look at the problem and determine what the real issues are. Is this a question of insubordination? Should the foreman become involved with punishing an alleged offender and his friends, or are there other problems that must be dealt with? Any problem must be clearly identified before it can be solved. The central issue here is not one of insubordination, but of rapport or interpersonal relations. To resolve a problem, all of the facts must be mobilized. Investigation of possible solutions and their concomitant effects must be performed. Finally, a decision is made on a particular alternative and action is taken.

In a great many instances, a number of problems arise which tend to obscure a view of the central issue which is crucial in any solution. So many accompanying minor problems abound that some of them may be erroneously considered as the major problem. Frequently, a situation appears more complex than it actually is, particularly when an attempt is made to solve several problems simultaneously. Too much energy is tied up chasing ephemeral matters, or the individual is self-deceived into believing that he has found the correct solution to the central issue when in fact it has just been camouflaged by the shifting stresses of the situation.

How can any matter be correctly approached? The question should be asked whether the solution to a specific problem will cause all other problems to disappear, or, at least, be more amenable to later efforts at solution. What is the chief problem in the case of the unmoving maintenance man? Here are a number of matters that can be stated: The office files must be moved and they were not. A maintenance crew man was asked to assist in moving the files and he did not do so. Other members of the crew supported Jack in his attitude. What attitude? That he had been given a request and not a direct order. That he was asked to perform an assignment that was not part of his job description. That he did not like the assistant superintendent.

Is any of these the major problem? If any one of these issues is solved, will the entire situation be resolved? Does the initial question of the foreman, "What action shall I take against Jack?" provide the key to the basic problem? Once the problems are put into proper perspective it is fairly easy to determine what the major factor is. There is more than one individual whom Jack and the other members of the work crew do not like, namely the foreman. You have five maintenance men working under your direction. The assistant superintendent of the division asks your assistance in having his office file moved. If the men admired or liked you, would there even be a debate about whether the files should be moved, or even whether the other individual in question is liked? The question of job description would not even arise. Another question might be: How did I express the request? Could it have been construed as an order? Would I want it taken in that way? What is my relationship with Jack? How good are communications?

When rapport is established cooperation is automatic. Where interpersonal relationships break down there is a lack of communication and cooperation is infrequent. The entire question focuses on the central issue of interpersonal relations. All of the other matters are incidental to this. If everyone had been on good terms, the entire affair would have been dealt with easily and quickly. Everything hinges on this fundamental point.

Admonishment, or worse punishment, for insubordination will not accomplish what is necessary—getting the files moved. The elementary solution to the problem is to call the maintenance man into the office, tell him that the files must be moved no matter how he feels personally about the assistant superintendent, and that any other discussion can wait. If necessary, a direct order to perform the assignment should be made. At the same time tell him that there is obviously something wrong in his attitude and that you would like to discuss it with him after the files are moved. As soon as possible thereafter, Jack and the other members of the maintenance crew should have the opportunity to explain what is annoying them. In this manner, the immediate concern is taken care of. Simultaneously, the central issue which underlies all the others has been identified and steps are being taken to bring it out into the open for resolution. This is a case of poor or inadequate interpersonal relationships which have tended to poison the atmosphere of a working group. The foreman must recognize his own responsibilities and probable defense mechanisms if he is to act with equity and understanding. He must be aware of his own shortcomings and not try to find a scapegoat among his subordinates. Only the acknowledgment of deteriorated relations and the search for the reasons for such deterioration can lead to a reasonable solution for all concerned.

Of course there will be occasions when, despite a supervisor's every effort, an employee will continue to infringe upon the established policies or rules of the agency, displaying conduct that is detrimental to the service or that causes friction among other employees. In such cases, the supervisor has no choice but to exercise disciplinary authority. Although the supervisor's relationship with subordinates is characterized by consideration and personal warmth, this does not mean that he should be a pushover. The rapport established between him and his subordinates does not make him less objective. It probably increases his objectivity as it increases his insight into both the immediate and the long-term needs of those who work for him and makes his perception of their strengths and weaknesses keener. Because the supervisor's first obligation is to the agency and to the working group as a whole, he must take whatever steps are necessary to eliminate disruption, regardless of his personal feelings. A supervisor is not devoid of emotion, but he cannot allow it to cloud his judgment. When a supervisor notices minor infractions, he can discuss them privately with the employee. Often, if he can ascertain the reason for the behavior, he can help the employee to correct it without having to take disciplinary action. But no infraction can be tolerated for very long because other employees will become dissatisfied, feeling that the supervisor is showing favoritism.

In the case of the unwashed puppeteer the supervisor's role as counselor is self-evident. However, there is also a disciplinary element involved:

I was the district recreational supervisor in a municipal agency in the Midwest. The majority of my personnel were outstanding recreationists and did their work with dedication, enthusiasm, and effectiveness. One of my specialists, a puppeteer, went around to all of the playgrounds in my district and put on shows. He also instructed the construction of puppets during some craft activities which were performed periodically. After a short period on the job, I received information indirectly that the puppeteer was extremely sloppy in appearance. He had permitted his hair and beard to grow, the clothing that he wore was always soiled, and he smelled bad. The puppeteer was an individual of above average intelligence and had talent. I know that he performed creditably because I also learned that his shows were well attended and making puppets seemed popular with the children.

I could not remove the puppeteer without obtaining permission from the assistant superintendent for recreational service. If I did receive such permission, I would probably not get a replacement, even though my staff needs required two more playground workers. I was afraid that if I made a wrong approach, the puppeteer would become insulted and not do the kind of job which was expected of him. What immediate action might I take to gain a modification in appearance and odor? How can I approach him without insulting him? What if any action I initiate results in no improvement? What can I do?

Any response to hearsay evidence must be investigated to determine the truth or falsity of the claim. In this instance it would be necessary to learn whether or not the indirectly obtained information was correct. Upon finding that the situation was accurately described, further action was undertaken. First, it would be wise to see if this unwashed conduct was continuing. An individual can, in today's currently permissive styles, grow a beard and permit his hair to grow without much comment from anybody. However, if his personal hygiene is offensive to others with whom he comes in contact, then this is not only a reflection on that individual, but also upon the agency for which he works. Public recreational service departments have enough difficulties maintaining and attracting public support without giving additional reasons to those who constantly harass or want to deny tax support to the department. Long hair and clothing idiosyncrasies are now taken for granted, although there are some communities which will not tolerate these styles among their employees. However, an individual's careless dress habits and poor personal cleanliness are outward manifestations of more deep-seated problems. It is true that an individual can have a button pop off his shirt, spatter paint or ink on himself in the course of work, or have to get himself dirty as he goes about the business of setting up displays. It may not always be easy to maintain a neat appearance on the job. When the individual sustains a sloppy appearance for weeks, it becomes another question. The puppeteer was not slovenly when he was initially appointed to the position. Since he was neat in appearance before, what happened that he would precipitously let himself go? Is there trouble at home? Is he drinking too much? Is he becoming neurotic? The supervisor will have to find out.

With these preliminary aspects identified, let us address the supervisor's three questions. The first question involves the idea of not offending the puppeteer while seeking a change of behavior. The puppeteer should comprehend his responsibilities. He is obliged to dress appropriately for his line of work and be neat and clean. He is obligated to do the best job that he can insofar as puppetry and crafts are concerned. He gets paid for this occupation. If he does not like his job he can always resign or, perhaps, request a transfer to another phase of the work. Nevertheless, the supervisor is concerned about how the puppeteer will react if confronted with the fact that he is not living up to his obligations.

Human nature being what it is, an individual who is performing well will probably be discouraged if admonished. In most situations tact is required. Moreover, human relations indicate how best to correct a weakness in others without destroying their egos. But in this instance the emphasis should be directed to the feelings of the puppeteer and not upon the effect of his work. What, in fact, is the best approach? It is necessary to think of the puppeteer as a person. What is the best way to inform a person that he is slovenly while not unnecessarily hurting his feelings? Considering that the individual is above average intelligence, has talent, and seems industrious, it might be advantageous to all concerned to simply say: "Your appearance leaves something to be desired. Do something about it immediately please." Whatever approach is used, it should be accompanied by a fitting compliment based on the factual knowledge of the puppeteer's work up to that time. "Mr. X, you have really been doing an outstanding job on the playgrounds and your puppet shows are extremely popular. Nevertheless, I have to remind you about your appearance. We're all guilty at times, particularly when we've been involved in some sweaty production, but that does not mean that we should let our personal cleanliness get out of hand. I am sure that you will want to improve your bathing habits and dress with greater care. After all, you're our first line and the public judges the department by the personnel it sees carrying out recreational service functions."

Any approach similar to this should be effective. What then about the second question? Suppose the action results in no change of behavior. Then, in all likelihood, the problem is greater than it appears. If an individual has been performing well and then suddenly begins to deteriorate, something serious must have occurred. The supervisor should investigate carefully. Real trouble may be in the offing both for the puppeteer and others with whom he comes in contact. Some personal problems may be developing, perhaps alcoholism or drug taking. The supervisor must not allow the matter to get out of hand. He should talk to the puppeteer at great length, if necessary, and find out what he is doing when he is not on the job. This is not to be construed as spying. People do not begin to neglect their appearance or permit themselves to deteriorate without some deep-seated reason. It is possible that any number of crises could have hit the puppeteer to produce these undesirable changes.

The establishment of rapport between the supervisor and the specialist might induce the puppeteer to ask the supervisor for counsel. But if the puppeteer is unable to bring himself to that point of contact, the relationship with the supervisor should enable the latter to offer support to the specialist so that he may unburden himself. If the puppeteer does not change his behavior, the department will be better off if he is replaced. Working on a face-to-face basis with the public is not the place for an individual who is unable to take care of himself. He is not a desirable sort to have representing the department, particularly as much of his work is with children. Either disciplinary action will have to be taken to straighten him out or, if psychological problems are the cause, it may be that referral to an agency which can deal with such problems is the best solution. To be really effective, interpersonal relations must be founded on the recognition of the individual as a human being with psychological and social problems. With the establishment of rapport and lines of communication available and open, individuals may have a better chance of resolving situations before they reach a point where excesses force other alternatives to be taken.

The final diagnosis of the puppeteer was that his initial personality disintegration was brought on by substance abuse. Subsequently, he was referred to the appropriate municipal agency for treatment. The puppeteer never returned to the recreational supervisor's department.

The Role of Counseling in Supervision

Individual counseling is an effective technique for assisting subordinates to improve their performance and for providing them with an accurate appraisal of their status in the organization. It also offers both the supervisor and the subordinate a chance to develop a personal relationship, and thus build rapport. Such a one-to-one relationship is most effective in clearing up misunderstandings and eliminating confusion.

Often a supervisor in the counseling situation is able to detect unsuspected qualities or latent talents which may be potentially valuable to the agency's program and to the worker's professional career. With encouragement, the individual may be able to develop these abilities for both his own and the agency's benefit. Counseling is also a way to get at the root of negative behavior on the part of the subordinate without embarrassing him in front of his peers.

The counseling procedure promotes personal growth reciprocally. The worker matures as he begins to perceive his strengths and weaknesses and is able to profit by such insight. The supervisor widens his experience in personal relations and is able to use the counseling technique with increased self-confidence.

The relationship between the extent of supervision and its effects upon employee attitudes and productivity is well researched. Broader spans of control and few levels of authority seem to result in a more effective organizational structure and produce greater numbers of highly competent employees, with coincidentally, heightened morale and output. Conversely, where workers are under close supervision, there is a drop in morale and productivity. (Close supervision is defined here as the absence of delegation of authority, an excessive control of what workers do on the job and how they do it.) In a study conducted by Day and others, it was shown that close supervision adversely affects worker desire and capacity to perform.[4] Thus a supervisor's goal is to delegate to each individual the maximum authority he is able to use wisely. As the subordinate proves himself able to handle the authority and concomitant responsibility, the supervisor diplomatically withdraws until the subordinate is autonomous. In this way the supervisor makes a significant contribution not only to the agency but also to the entire field of recreational service by increasing the number of competent recreationists.

Sometimes co-workers are unable to work together in a harmonious manner. They may be too competitive, need close supervision, or simply lack the maturity and judgment necessary to get along and get the job done. The following case is illustrative and indicates the measures a supervisor must take.

You are a supervisor of recreational services in X center. Assigned to your jurisdiction are two program workers. They work in the same center. The first worker comes to you and tells you that his fellow worker is not doing a satisfactory job. The second worker comes to you and tells you that the first worker is not doing his job. They both tell the same story about each other. What do you do?

On the surface this appears to be nothing more than a personality conflict between two workers. However, there are questions which immediately come to mind in this case. How well are each of workers known to the supervisor? Can the supervisor rely upon mere allegation by each of the workers? How shall the supervisor proceed in determining the validity of these claims and counter claims? Since we can assume nothing, it is necessary to find out how long each employee has been working at the center and how well each is known to the supervisor. Even if one or both are known to the

---

4. R. C. Day and R. L. Hamblin, "Some Effects of Close and Punitive Styles of Supervision," *American Journal of Sociology*, Vol. 69, No. 5 (March 1964), pp. 499–510.

supervisor, nothing can be taken for granted. The supervisor will still have to investigate the conditions of work prior to making any decision that will affect the workers. The old American Indian maxim about walking in a man's moccasins for a week before judging him is sound advice.

During the initial interview, as each worker came in to prefer charges against the other, the supervisor should have ascertained the specifics of the situation by asking how the worker knows that the other is not performing in a satisfactory manner. What particular activities have been incompetently engaged in, on what dates? How is it that the worker was in a position to observe the details? What was the worker's assignment for that period? How long has the other worker been observed to perform unsatisfactorily? Was there only one instance of each performance or has this been a sustained series of ineffectual performances? From the responses obtained, the supervisor is in a better position to determine his procedures. Even if each worker is capable of detailing his allegations, the supervisor must obtain corroborating evidence before crystallizing some substantive action. Why, for example, should any workers at the same level be in position to observe the work efforts of others at their rank for any period of time? How is it that each was not involved in the operation of some activity or in dealing with a group or individual participants? Recreational centers are notoriously short of manpower and no one can afford to stand idly by. There is always work to be done, whether with individuals, groups, in activities, doing public relations work, or planning for future recreational programs. Then, of course, there is always the insidious question of supervisory negligence. How is it that the supervisor was not aware of friction between the two workers? The supervisor had better be scrupulously fair in attempting to discover the real nature of this case.

The supervisor will have to defer any judgment until he can validate the allegations presented. He must, therefore, observe both workers on the job. Of course, this is a continuing function of the supervisor. How else is he to appraise worker competence and evaluate performance over a given period of time? Supervisory observation may occur during routine inspection of the facility, as spot checks to determine whether or not assignments are being carried out, during routine staff meetings, and during informal or chance meetings of workers as each goes about the business of assisting in the operation of the recreational center.

If, in the supervisor's view, he finds that neither of the workers is performing in an unsatisfactory manner, he must discover the latent meanings of these charges. Under such circumstances the explanation is that hostility exists between the workers for any number of reasons. Just as there is the expectation of loyalty to one's superiors, there is also the concomitant need for loyalty to one's subordinates. It is the supervisor's function to enable these workers to overcome whatever friction there is between them so that the two may get on with their professional obligations and not take the time to invent or create situations that can only lead to demoralization and loss of confidence all around. More important, the establishment of good interpersonal relations will have a dual effect on the workers. They will cooperate with one another, perhaps complementing one another's skills and this in turn may provide better recreational services to the public. The immediate concern of the supervisor is to maintain a highly efficient and effective recreational center. He can only do this if his subordinates are capable of carrying out their responsibilities in a competent manner. Therefore, the supervisor will have to ascertain what is causing conflict. If the supervisor has established good rapport with his subordinates there is little likelihood that they will withhold information from him. If, on the other hand, there is either no rapport or if distrust exists, then little will be accomplished when the supervisor attempts to elicit information from the workers.

From the situation, however, there must have been some rapport established between workers and the supervisor, or else they would not have approached the supervisor in the first place. Surely, they must have had some confidence in the supervisor's ability to sort out any difficulties and enough trust to feel that he would be equitable in his dealings with them. If the supervisor did not enjoy this confidence, no approach would have been made to him, and the employees might simply have sabotaged the efforts of one another until one or the other quit. The supervisor has an opening wedge because there is an indication of rapport. Since he can talk to each of the workers, he must now find out how friction started. This should be done in individual conferences. It is a mistake to call two or more antagonists together and attempt to make settlement. Hostile individuals should be conferred with separately until the facts in the case can be fixed. Then there is a basis for accord. When the nature of the real or fancied slight has been uncovered, it is possible to reach agreement with each. Perhaps there were misunderstandings about functions and duties, perhaps one misunderstood tone, intent, or words utilized by the other to convey an idea. Whatever the source of irritation or friction, even in terms of personality dislikes, there is a solution amenable to all concerned.

If the supervisor determines, during his investigation, that one of the original allegations is valid, he is then in a position to act for the good of the department and all individuals involved. It may be that one of the workers is not able to function in his current setting, but can perform related tasks if given the opportunity elsewhere. The supervisor should carefully study the needs of the individual and those of the agency before coming to any conclusion. In any event, overhasty conclusions can only result in poor decisions. If the supervisor finds that the worker is simply incompetent, then the recommendation should be for discharge. If, however, the worker has the ability to learn, it might be better for him to be afforded the opportunity to augment his knowledge and skills through in-service staff developmental programs, outside readings, attendance at conferences, or formal schooling if it is available to him. In this way, a potentially good worker may be retained for the good of the worker and the department.

When irreconcilable differences between the two workers have reached a point where there is no possibility of settlement, then another solution must be found. In this instance, if both workers are competent to perform their functions, it might be best to place them in other centers or facilities which the agency operates. It may be possible to simply change their hours of work so that neither of them would ever have to meet or work together. The incongruity of having to deal with professional people in this way is apparent at once. However, there are instances where personality factors or other differences are so great that individuals cannot be permitted proximity. When such differences produce outright hostility, the negative effects may involve more than just the two original parties. Other workers may take sides and even participants in the program can be tainted with the bad feelings that ensue over these conflicts. Change of hours, separation to other facilities within the agency, or discharge with prejudice may have to be instituted if the problem is to be resolved. In the latter instance, the situation may become terribly complex because the agency cannot absorb the workers elsewhere. It could be that one or the other would have to be discharged for cause, and such a step could be potentially embarrassing for the department. If the agency were so small that no other facilities were available for placement and discharge was one of two alternatives to be offered, a matter-of-fact explanation to the individuals might be effective in quelling the disagreement—at least on the surface so that the center would operate efficiently. Such a solution would serve as a stop-gap measure until a more realistic solution could be worked out. Disciplinary action should be based upon an intelligent, equitable, and scrupulous study of all the factors relating to the situation. Taken into consideration should be the personalities of the involved individuals, nature of the offense, possible effects on departmental performance, and other pertinent factors concerning the agency and its mandatory responsibility to the public it serves. Generally, timing is of considerable importance. Whenever possible, lines of communication should be opened and made available to those who may seek advice for grievances. Preventive action is invariably better than punitive action and frequently the careful collection of facts will indicate probable solutions which would have otherwise been obscured by emotional contention.

In this case, a fancied slight, based on verbal abuse, triggered the hostility between the two parties. Open discussion between the two workers led to the resolution of the problem.

DEMOCRACY AND SUPERVISION

Supervision is most effective when it fulfills the program demands of the organization while equally satisfying the needs of the workers. Both facets of organizational life—agency demands and employee needs—are quite consistent and complementary.

As a supervisor channels his efforts toward maintaining employee morale and establishing the rapport that fosters an atmosphere of democratic cooperation, he does so not only with the goal of increasing employees' technical competence but also of stimulating their desire to remain with the agency. The more competent recreationists an agency has, the better able it will be to offer the highest quality service to the community. Therefore, the supervisor best fulfills his obligations to both the agency and his subordinates when he encourages employees to participate in agency policy-forming as well as in program execution. Only when workers feel they are integral and valued members of an organization will they remain loyal to it. The supervisor's role is central to a democratic environment and to a relationship between employee and agency that is mutually supportive and satisfying. To this end, there are a number of guidelines a supervisor may follow:

1. All decision-making functions should grow out of group needs that are directly related to organizational problems, programming, clientele satisfaction, or working conditions.

2. The physical environment should be conducive to maximum group productivity. For example, conferences should be held in a

room that is adequate in size, well lighted and ventilated, furnished comfortably, and without distractions. People should be able to see and hear one another without straining.

3.   Responsibility for task completion should be shared equally among group members and assigned on the basis of individual interests, capacity to perform and experience.

4.   At planning sessions, sufficient time should be allotted to ensure that current problems as well as future plans receive adequate attention.

5.   The supervisor's consideration for subordinates should be evident at all times. When workers recognize that their supervisor is genuinely concerned with their welfare as well as with job performance, they are more likely to trust his guidance.

6.   The supervisor should be judicious in selecting workers to fill particular jobs. He should do all he can to see that they are placed in situations designed to promote their functional effectiveness.

7.   The supervisor should be sure that outstanding service by subordinates is recognized.

8.   The supervisor should inaugurate a program for encouraging creativity and see to it that the working situation is conducive to free expression. There must be continuous experimentation with new ideas and activities, and attempts at innovation should never be dismissed out of hand. With supervisory assistance—but preferably without—each recreationist should be invited to submit any new suggestions for overall agency and program improvement. In such circumstances, program recreationists will gain self-confidence as well as the ability to evaluate their own proposals.

9.   The supervisor must be able to adapt to individual differences in education, experience, ability, and interest. He will have to give as much attention as necessary to those who require it, without making them overly dependent upon his assistance. To some employees he will act as a resource, to others he will give guidance, and to still others he will give instruction. He should allot his time in accordance with the needs of those who comprise his staff, and when he makes appointments he should always keep them.

In some instances, insensitivity to worker attitudes may produce inflammatory conditions completely at variance with acceptable practices.

I was the director of the X recreational center in a large East Coast city. One of the program workers employed at the center, a member of an ethnic minority group, came to me and accused me of being prejudiced because he had been assigned to one of the least desirable jobs in the center. Could it be that I was a covert bigot? My first impulse was to deny the allegation of racial bias and tell the fellow to get back to his job and get to work, but I stifled that intention. Instead, I found myself thinking back to the possibility that the charge might have some basis in fact. Could I have been guilty of racism? Was there a latent discriminatory attitude toward this person which had manifested itself in subtle or not-so-subtle ways?

I asked him to tell me about the ways in which he thought he had been treated unfairly during the time he had been employed at the center. He told me that he resented the fact that he had to work evening shifts every three weeks. Was there anything else that indicated bias against him? He did not like to work in the game room with high school age youth. His specialty was art and he did not feel that his talents were being utilized to their fullest extent when he was scheduled to supervise the game room. Additionally, he knew that some of the older teens often passed remarks about his accent and were sarcastic to him. He felt that people were frequently discussing him in a derogatory way. More specifically, he stated that some members of the center staff condescended to him or denigrated his character. He was sure that something was wrong because whenever he walked into a room whoever was there either stopped talking or left. He said that according to the affirmative action program under which he had been employed in the department, he felt that everybody should accept him as a peer and not attempt to make him feel out of place. He stated that the atmosphere in the center was poisonous as far as he was concerned. Either bigotry would have to be stopped or he was going to file a complaint with the municipal civil rights agency.

This litany of antipathy required some response. What could be done to determine the facts in this instance? According to the program worker, he was constantly being exploited, maltreated, and defamed. It certainly seemed as if his charges of racism were justified.

I checked the work sheets and found that he did have to work evening shifts every three weeks, but so did all of the other program level personnel. This was one of the ways that we could offer night activities to the community and spread the evening hours around to all personnel without any single individual having to be stuck with just evening hours. This did not mollify him; he stated that this was just rationalization and that prejudice was really the basis for his less-than-satisfactory working shift. Now this took another tack. It is one thing to level charges where there has been unjustified work assignments, it is another simply to be annoyed because the hours of work are not completely satisfactory. The nature of recreational service work is such that some people must be prepared to work when others have leisure. In order to provide recreational opportunities for people who constitute the group served by the center, it was necessary to rotate work hours. I did not see this as a consequence of racial bias, nor could I determine that any systematic effort had been made to assign less desirable work hours to this employee. One must be extremely careful in determining allegations of racial discrimination. Not only is there the possibility of litigation, but there is the question of professional ethics involved. No recreationist can ever stand accused of violating any person's civil rights by actions which are designed to denigrate him. The very nature of bigotry is to be avoided at all costs. Although we learn our attitudes towards others at a very early age, even when family rearing and peer pressure tend to influence one's outlook, the professional person should be able to overcome negative attitudes towards people through his learning experiences and exposure to concepts which can refute stereotyping, emotional affectations, and other defense mechanisms which give rise to prejudicial conduct.

Over the next few days I undertook scrupulous observation of the personnel who were employed in the center. I made discreet inquiries among the employees and requested personal interviews with all of them. During the interviews, ostensibly about developing programs, I interjected comments about discriminatory behavior which could be interpreted as being racially motivated. Some of the responses did indeed suggest that a few employees had negative attitudes toward minorities. What caused utmost concern was the fact that the employees who expressed an anti-minority attitude worked in an agency where members of minorities were clients. This was an intolerable situation.

The probability of getting anyone to modify attitudes and opinions where bias is concerned is extremely limited. Such emotionally produced feelings are often the product of learned responses assimilated over the years. It would take an inordinate amount of time and pressure to educate these employees. Nevertheless, I felt that it was part of my professional obligation to them, as well as to the clients of the center, to attempt the task. I instituted what we called a sensitivity-training session as a regular weekly in-service staff development program. Fortunately, I had developed rather good relations with most of the staff during my tenure as center director, and there were few who resisted the idea. Those who did were the same ones who had articulated their bias in personal conferences. I informed the workers that the sessions were being held to permit them to express things that bothered them without fear of any retaliation, no matter what was said. The only important guideline was that each person express himself, on any subject which bothered him, and reveal his actual feelings about subjects that could prevent him from offering completely objective services to potential clients of the center. The sessions were slow in starting and there was a great deal of hesitancy, withdrawing, or passivity on the part of some, but within three weeks of our first session, several of the workers began to open up. They complained about specific aspects of the program, voiced objections to a few of the directives that had originated from my office, and griped about superficial problems which almost everybody has experienced at one time or another. However, we did not come to grips with the central reason for establishing the sensitivity sessions, until one worker became more personal and tentatively identified some aspect of personality which he did not care for. This seemed to pave the way for others and soon the floodgates of inner personal fears, anxieties, and emotionality were released. A tide of invective and deep-seated hostility now came to the surface. This was something that I had not bargained for because I thought that such obvious hatred directed at one another and particularly at minorities would overwhelm any relationship that had been built up during the time these workers had come to know one another. For a while it looked as though my worst fears were to be realized. There was overt hostility freely expressed, shouting matches took place, and individuals hurled accusations, and displayed the classical signs of racism and other forms of bigotry which I always had associated with ignorance. This outpouring seemed to act as a catharsis. The latent hate and fear had, at last, been brought out into the open where people could look at it. For the first time, the workers began to realize what it was that they had been harboring unconsciously or covertly. Some were embarrassed, others troubled, and some were shocked. Nevertheless, we kept at it doggedly, and slowly but surely when the initial violence of saying the long-buried sentiments had passed, there was a new attempt made to begin to understand what had been discovered. Tentative and stumbling attempts were made toward reaching accord. There was an acknowledgement of fear and disgust against minorities together with a hesitant reaching out as recognition of long-standing attitudes was obtained.

There was no dramatic conversion or radical change overnight. Most of the attitudinal changes were slow in coming, but there were shifts. The sessions have become a part of personnel management now, and encounter groups are being utilized throughout the recreational service department of the city. The sessions for my center altered some behavior, but it hardened others. There was at least one individual who adamantly refused to depart from his long-held dislike of certain minorities. He often stated that he was only at the sessions because he was forced to attend, that his attitudes would never change. In this instance we did not succeed. He was a good worker and we did not want to lose him. We could not order him to change his biases, but we felt it would be in the best interests of the center to have him transferred to another installation where he would not come in contact with the minorities which he despised.

Insofar as the original worker's complaint dealing with bias, we found that much of what he said was true. There was latent bias which revealed itself in the behavior of some of the center workers toward him. However, the sessions also revealed a reverse bias on the part of the worker. He expressed just as many hostilities and emotionally based prejudices as anyone else. I did not permit this quid pro quo—your prejudice is balanced by mine—to remain. In going over specific complaints alleged by this worker, I determined that his job description called for his assignment to any and all activities within the center. He may have been a crafts specialist, but he was employed as a generalist and as such he would be assigned to those recreational activities which would best serve the interest of the clients. Since work records were kept, the center could show exactly how this worker had been employed and what responsibilities were his. While his original complaints had been investigated and were found to be valid, in most instances, there were some behavioral patterns of his that also needed correction. The sensitivity sessions had succeeded in uncovering biases in almost all of the workers, including him. One of the outcomes was to reduce a certain tension among the workers and offer an opportunity to develop better interpersonal relations among the entire staff. A great deal of resentment and not-so-hidden chips on the shoulder were disclosed and gotten rid of. To the extent possible, racial, ethnic, or religious prejudices were, if not exorcised, at least exposed and given a chance that recognition of the problem along with prolonged training sessions would be a way to alleviate them. We all learned a good deal about ourselves and about one another. The center employees experienced a sense of intimacy between them that had not existed before and which resulted in a more group-like feeling. It was a positive step in the right direction.

Unfortunately, there was little that we could do about client bias toward minorities. This was something that was beyond our capacity to change. We would have to behave in ways that would elicit anti-prejudicial responses from our clientele. It would be our responsibility to bring prejudicial conduct to the attention of perpetrators, and we would do whatever we could to modify attitudes towards minorities, but for the most part, minority discrimination is a blight that public recreational service agencies have little or no control over. We may educate our personnel in various ways and thereby obtain modified behavior and, it is hoped, attitude, but we continue to have negligible success with clients who frequent the centers and other facilities.

The Role of Communication in Supervision

Good communication is vital in obtaining the kind of cooperation necessary for optimum work performance. Although good communication is one of the fundamental aspects of leadership, it is also one of the techniques most often neglected by supervisors. The communicative process makes possible the transmission and execution of instructions and enables a supervisor to influence employees' attitudes and beliefs as well as their work. Thus, the supervisor's ability to gain cooperation and effective performance from his subordinate staff depends in large measure on the quality of his communication.[5]

Some guidelines to good communications are the following:

1. Recreationists must receive complete and honest supervisory appraisals on all matters which pertain to their work.

2. Recreationists must receive justification for policy statements issued by administrators.

3. Recreationists must receive clear explanations relating to any problems that affect the ability of the agency to conduct its operation.

4. Supervisors must develop a system for the free flow of communication throughout the agency.

5. Supervisors must elicit subordinate recreationists' ideas, suggestions, comments, and opinions in developing improvements in operations, policies, plans, programs, and general services.

6. Whenever possible, supervisors should be able to provide prompt answers to inquiries and render appropriate decisions on matters of immediate concern to employees in carrying out their functions within the agency.

---

5. "To Do Their Best Work, Everyone Must Communicate," *Industrial Research* (July 1970), p. 77.

7. Supervisors must strive for the greatest clarity before committing ideas to the communication channels.

8. Supervisors must examine the real objectives of each communication.

9. Supervisors must take into consideration the possible impact of a message upon its receiver.

10. Unless it is unfeasible or for some reason inappropriate, supervisors should consult with others concerned in a situation before preparing a communication regarding it.

11. Supervisors should always be aware that messages frequently carry overtones and meanings which may not be desirable, and therefore should be examined to eliminate unintentional nuances.

12. Supervisors should always make sure that communications sent are useful to those who receive them.

13. Supervisors must follow up communications to be sure that recipients have understood the message, even when the supervisor is sure that he has communicated clearly.

14. Supervisors must regard the communications process as vital to developing and maintaining good personal relations as well as to imparting information.

On occasion, even the clearest communication produces frustrating results because the recipient has an agenda of his own to promote. The following case represents such an incident:

I was employed as a supervisor charged with coordinating the professional in-service education in the recreational service department located in one of Gulf Coast States. I had been working in the department for two years and professional practices and staff development were well received. Now an opportunity arose for the development of a conference and it seemed propitious to work on material for a brochure which would describe the in-service program and potential opportunities in the field.

I had requested and had been allowed to make a career ladder speech to the staff. Now my section was flooded with requests for a workshop. A foundation grant provided the necessary funds. I contacted a local printer to have the brochure published for widespread distribution throughout the state.

I went to the departmental administrator, an individual named Milzam, and requested permission to have the brochure printed. He flatly refused saying, "Why, we've never done anything like this before. I don't know if the city would approve of it." I reminded him that it would cost neither the city nor the department any money, that the city had never refused financial aid from anybody regardless of the sum involved, and, in fact, was initiating a fund into which anyone could contribute. He maintained a steady negative answer despite my arguments. Everything was set to go. The printer had already been given some money as a retainer to hold his time open. I had not anticipated a refusal, but just the opposite—I had expected a pat on the back for diligence and enthusiasm. What was I to do?

My colleague, Jane Cupid, found the solution. "Put his picture on it," she suggested. I walked into Milzam's office the following morning with a new proposal. "Picture it, if you will sir. We will be the only department in the entire city with a brochure." I held up a dummy copy. "Look at these colors, the city's gold and blue, look at the text, and then on the last page where everyone will see it, your picture." He said, "I'm with you 1,000%."

The next day he gave me his picture which he wanted reproduced on the brochure. I staggered in surprise. The face staring at me from the frame was not the baggy-eyed, grey-fringed, bald-headed old man standing in front of me, but a blond haired stranger with an unlined face who could not have been more than thirty. In all fairness, I have to add that my picture was going on the brochure, too, but his picture looked like that of a younger man, and I was only 29. I commented to the effect, but Milzam only looked more pleased and preened himself. I then recognized the fact that I was dealing with an egomaniac. Nevertheless, I had what I wanted. The brochure was printed in due course.

The great lesson to be learned from this experience is to know your opposition. There are always obstructionists and know-nothings in every field of human endeavor. They infiltrate every agency and are tremendously difficult to dislodge. Their tenacity usually stems from political considerations in terms of who, rather than what, they know. When sheer ignorance, cupidity, or infantilism are combined to block a proposal which, on the whole, would be beneficial if instigated, then exploiting the frustrator's weaknesses is permissible. It may be the only course open to salvage what might otherwise be discarded through whim or stupidity. The progressive efforts of people to make positive contributions should never be left at the mercy of the puerile caprice of those in positions of power.

One of the more insidious aspects of leadership is manipulation. It connotes evil genius maneuvering people against their will to perform acts which are abhorrent to them but against which they have no power to counteract. It conjures up visions of some super being playing with the lives of hapless people. To some extent this is true. However, as the late W.C. Fields liked to say, "You can't cheat an honest man." No intelligent person can be manipulated. No person who acts ethically and honestly can be made to play the "flim-flam game."

Manipulation may, however, be a form of indirect leadership which can be used for purposes beneficial to an entire group. This depends upon the immediate situation and the people involved, particularly if specified objectives are being overlooked and advantageous positions are lost because of futile bickering. When people argue merely to hear themselves talk, instead of allowing logical discussion to run its course and taking constructive action, it may be permissible to employ manipulation as a *last resort* for the achievement of desirable goals. The ends never justify the means, if the means are ignoble. But there are situations where even manipulation becomes the means whereby unjustifiable use of authority is diverted and can act as a counterforce for the attainment of worthwhile goals.

In another instance, the manipulation was clearly a breach of ethics and should not have been enacted. In the case of the machiavellian connection there were other actions that could have been taken more advantageously:

The city of C had a legal recreational services commission operating its public recreational agency. The commissioners, all laymen, employed as their chief executive a recreationist who had had several years of experience as an administrator. During the first two years of his tenure, the superintendent was able to develop the physical facilities and program in a manner satisfactory to him. From the popularity of the program it seemed to appeal to the citizens of the community too. The superintendent was also able to gain some insight into the respective characters and personality of his commissioners. He became aware of a clique which had been formed from a combination of three of the younger men on the seven-man commission. There were also three other commissioners who would generally go along with whatever was proposed, and an isolet. This last individual had a reputation for being reactionary. He usually showed an intense negativism about the operation of the recreational agency. He had been appointed to the commission by the mayor because he carried one of the few remaining "old guard" family names. Reaction to this individual on the commission was almost uniform—contradiction wherever possible, tolerance, but no friendliness. Realizing the importance of the relative positions of each commission member gave the superintendent an advantage when he approached the commissioners with a recommendation for the acquisition of some property and its development into a recreational complex. The commissioners agreed that the superintendent's plan was feasible and that the agency had the financial wherewithal to support the project, but the commissioners could not agree as to the suitable location for the development. The superintendent had merely indicated that there was a need for the development of a recreational complex to offer adequate additional services to citizens of the community. The commissioners accepted his statements, but wrangled about site location instead of asking for the superintendent's recommendation. The superintendent knew that unless the land was acquired within a reasonable period of time, it would either go off the market or the price would rise. It was, therefore, necessary to obtain favorable action by the commission while the price was right.

The superintendent solved his problem by taking the isolet out to lunch and talking over the problem with him. He determined that he was in favor of a site selection which would have been literally valueless to the agency. The superintendent primed the commissioner to advance his idea at the next commission meeting. When the commissioner raised his point, he was immediately defeated by an overwhelming majority which recommended that a recreational site be developed on the opposite side of town from where the first commissioner had suggested. The superintendent was delighted with the reversal because, knowing the tenor of feeling toward the isolet, he had planted the idea of promoting the site selection in a place opposite from where he actually wanted it. He counted upon the other commissioners' resentment to counter-propose a site development where he really believed it could do the most good.

One could question the ethics involved in this transaction. The superintendent acted in bad faith through his manipulation of one of the commissioners. Perhaps a real leader would not have resorted to such an outrageous breach of conduct, although it was done so subtly that none of the commissioners ever realized they had been used. A leader might not have found it necessary to manipulate the actions of others to expedite some end. He would have felt more responsible for the basic rights and feelings of the isolet. Surely he would have attempted other ways to reach his goal.

Nevertheless, this manipulation of others to hasten processes and actions which are necessary for the probable benefit of the entire group, in this case a community, raises some important points to ponder. Should the leader sacrifice the individual for the cause of many, or are the rights and dignity of each person significant enough to warrant protection from abuse even when many others are concerned? Manipulations for specified objectives may conceivably be correct and morally untainted when the maneuvering is performed without ulterior motives which are damaging to the character and reputation of those needing stimulating for activity. On the other hand, it seems to be unethical to sacrifice overtly a man's dignity on the altar of personal aggrandizement.

Expediency can rarely be utilized as a proper motive for the reduction of the status of one person. Material benefits will seldom, if ever, justify the manipulation of human behavior for the lowering of anybody's self-respect, even when the recipient is unaware of his loss. It is all the more insidious when the individual undergoes such a loss without recognition of the deception. Positive benefits, however, may accrue to the group when a leader manipulates the actions of individuals toward supportable ends. Ethical gains, preservation of integrity, and residual values from the conservation of necessary spaces, vistas, or other physical property must be judged on individual merits and weighed before any principle of established practice can be obtained. In the last analysis, the method of manipulation is questionable, depending upon the situation for its utilization. The decision will be that of the leader.[6]

The Role of Incentives in Supervision

Incentives are rewards that motivate a worker toward achievement. A supervisor can stimulate workers to greater effort and productivity by offering them certain incentives which he has determined on the basis of his understanding of their needs and desires. Of all incentives, the ones with the greatest potential are the nonmaterial appeals to ego-satisfaction or self-actualization needs. Promotion, for example, is an effective incentive because it represents fulfillment of an ego need. A raise in salary is a material incentive, but often the concomitant increase in status and prestige is the stronger incentive. Public acknowledgement of outstanding work is another proven incentive based on appeal to the ego.

A key incentive at the supervisor's disposal is the delegation of authority. Fundamentally, delegation is a process of job enrichment. When the supervisor feels a subordinate is ready to take on greater responsibility, he can delegate to the worker some challenging task.

---

6.   R. K. Greenleaf, *Servant Leadership* (New York: Paulist Press, 1977), pp. 136–149.

Successful completion will leave the worker with a sense of achievement and increased self-confidence, and at the same time free the supervisor for other duties. Delegation constitutes a public display of confidence which provides a subordinate with the opportunity to earn a more significant place within the organizational hierarchy, permits him to express himself through his skills and knowledge, and offers valuable experience for future tasks. The subordinate realizes that he will be held accountable for the assigned task and that his contributions will be duly noted in terms of the authority which he handles.

In order to delegate appropriate assignments, the supervisor must know his subordinates well, understand their strengths and weaknesses, and be able to predict their attitude toward the work to be performed. Of great importance will be the subordinate's interest in advancement as well as his ability to act autonomously. When using delegation as an incentive, the supervisor must be quite certain that accomplishment of the task is within the capability of the worker.

QUESTIONS FOR DISCUSSION

1. What is the leadership concept of supervision?
2. What is supervision?
3. Who performs supervision?
4. Supervisors must overcome subordinate hostility to be effective; why is this valid?
5. How can the supervisor promote democratic relationships without destroying personal authority?
6. What defensive techniques do subordinates use to offset supervisor authoritarianism?
7. What types of supervisory practices are extant?
8. When should supervisors utilize counseling techniques?
9. How can supervisors promote effective communication?

BIBLIOGRAPHY

Burley-Allen, Madelyn, *Assertive Supervision* (New York: John Wiley & Sons, Inc., 1982).

Christenson, Christiana, and Thomas W. Johnson, *Supervising* (Reading, Mass.: Addison Wesley Publishing Co., Inc., 1982).

Doll, Ronald C., *Supervision by Staff Development Ideas and Application* (Boston: Allyn & Bacon, 1983).

Fallon, William, K., ed., *Leadership on the Job: Guides to Good Supervision* (New York: American Management Association, 1982).

George, Claude, *Supervision in Action* (Reston, Va.: Reston Publishing Company, 1982).

Keys, Bernard, and John Henshal, *Supervision* (New York: John Wiley & Sons, Inc., 1984).

Leatherman, Richard W., *The Supervisor's Complete Guide to Leadership Behavior*, rev. ed. (Richmond, Va.: Industrial Training Associates Consultants, Inc., 1981).

Reher, Ralph W., and Gloria Terry, *Behavioral Insights for Supervision* (Englewood Cliffs, N.J.: Prentice-Hall, 1982).

Roy, Charles M., and Charles L. Elson, *Supervision* (New York: Dryden Press, 1982).

Seryiovanni, Thomas J., and Robert J. Starrat, *Supervision: Human Perspectives* (New York: McGraw Hill, 1983).

Weiss, W. H., *The Supervisor's Problem Solver* (Saranac Lake, N.Y.: American Management Association, 1983).

CHAPTER THIRTEEN

Leadership at the Managerial Level

Administrators engage in the common procedures of decision making, planning, organizing, and directing the activities of personnel in the department. The primary task of the managerial leader is to select from various ideas, methods, and systems available those that will be effective in his particular situation. As conditions fluctuate, either internally or externally, the administrator must be capable of adapting himself to change and adjusting his techniques, concepts, and systems.

One of the essential skills of a manager is the ability to size up a situation. The leadership challenge is to assess factors like these: the resource mixture necessary to conduct operations; the complexity of responsibilities; the appeal that particular assignments have for worker-need satisfaction; the attitudes of subordinates; the social forces at work in the department; the power structure of the organization; and the expectation of policy makers as well as his own.[1] Founded upon his ability to appraise such primary factors, the administrator then selects alternatives for action, adopts planning and monitoring systems, and makes other important decisions that will produce success within the imposed situational limitations.

As a leader, the administrator must continually define and redefine the organization's function and goal. He does this through the efficient processing of information. The manager must be concerned about the adaptation of the department to environmental forces and must, therefore, promote changes. This is performed while the department's functions are maintained at the expected level. The executive stresses goal-setting and long-range planning. The organization is thus guided toward his anticipated vision. Nevertheless, he continues to handle daily functions in an expeditious manner. He promotes institutional integrity and defends his

---

1. R. H. Hall, *Organizations: Structure and Process* (Englewood Cliffs, N.J.: Prentice-Hall, Inc., 1982), pp. 167–169, 176–177.

department from external threats. The manager simultaneously engages in the coordination of agency tasks or activities. He is concerned about and encourages the welfare of the entire agency by deflecting or dissipating internal cliques and other vested interests. In this way he plays a major role in influencing organizational behavior and establishing the kind of institutional atmosphere that reflects his philosophy. A function as significant as any other is persuading his followers to contribute their ideas and efforts to the achievement of departmental objectives or mission. He generates action and gets things accomplished. He is the primary motivator of all those who work for the agency's success.[2]

ADMINISTERING AT THE MANAGERIAL LEVEL

Administrative positions are concerned with the management of some specific function and the personnel assigned to that activity. An administrator executes policy and is responsible for selecting the best methods to accomplish day-to-day assignments for which his department is responsible. To this end, administrators are concerned not only with personnel resources but also with all items of a material nature which are necessary to provide a worthwhile program of recreational services.

Administrative personnel may be called by many titles, among which are director, manager, general or area supervisor, and administrative assistant. Whatever the title, their function is basically the same. Some may be charged with staff responsibility as personnel or office managers; others may be responsible for providing technical assistance to line personnel so that the latter can perform more effectively.[3] Still others—for example, administrative assistants— shoulder some of the agency's more routine and time-consuming daily operations, including translating policy statements into action. In some instances, they may be called upon to act in the absence of the agency's chief executive, but in the main they assist him with technical and special aid.

Administrative personnel function under the direction of the agency's chief executive, as assistants to him or as administrators of one complete phase of the agency's operation. As such, they have

2. P. Hersey and K. Blanchard, *Management of Organizational Behavior: Utilizing Human Resources,* 4th ed. (Englewood Cliffs, N.J.: Prentice-Hall, Inc., 1982), p. 3.
3. A line employee is one who is directly responsible for the execution of recreational program functions; a staff employee is one who provides line personnel with technical advice and guidance.

broad latitude in making decisions and recommendations and in implementing policy, subject to review and approval of the chief executive. In addition, administrative personnel participate in the formulation of policies which govern the administration and operation of their particular department.

Some typical administrative duties are:

1. Establishing methods to govern the control, collection, and distribution of donations, gifts, bequests, grants, endowments, and awards for recreational purposes.

2. Assembling, studying, and analyzing statistics and other information in order to prepare comprehensive reports and draw up recommendations.

3. Assisting in the preparation of the annual report.

4. Helping in the negotiation, preparation, and administration of regular, periodic, and special forms of agreements the department makes with others.

5. Assisting in the management of complex and delicate public relations situations.

6. Preparing, after collection and examination of technical and advisory narrative data, numerous state, local, or regional requests.

7. Assisting the chief executive in whatever capacity he requires.

8. Fulfilling the chief executive's commitments when he is unavailable.

9. Participating in decisions with the chief executive on most matters in preparing the preliminary and full agenda of the local authority.

In addition to the duties listed above, an administrator may also be called upon for some of the following services, depending on his position within the organization:

1. Speaking before various community and professional groups.

2. Dealing with sensitive issues concerning employee relations within the agency.

3. Handling public relations, and especially answering queries or complaints about the area he administers.

4. Recommending types of recreational facilities, structures, spaces, and equipment to be provided for such public institutions as schools, parks, municipal buildings, and hospitals.

5. Representing his agency in the activities and programs of various local, regional, state, and national recreational organizations.

6. Directing the pre-service orientation of new staff members and the in-service educational program of others.

7. Managing the budget for a particular phase of agency operation.

In summary, administrative personnel see to it that all those activities are carried out which are necessary to maintain a high degree of efficiency and effectiveness in providing the service for which the agency was created.[4] It should be understood, however, that no one individual would be expected to have such an expanse of knowledge or technical skill that he could function in every capacity listed above. The various segments of agency operation, each headed by a separate administrator, include office management, personnel management, fiscal administration, maintenance, supervision of all phases of the recreational services within a particular geographic area, planning administration, or management throughout the system of specific personnel who are in charge of recreational facilities.

The relationship between chief executive and administrators must be characterized by close cooperation and coordination. More often than not, the executive selects his administrative subordinates. If the agency operates under a civil service or merit system, the executive chooses his administrators from a list of qualified persons, and he can decide whether to fill a position or leave it vacant. Where the agency operates at the behest of local governmental authority, the executive recommends the employment of individuals he feels will qualify for the position and who will be most likely to support him, his policies, and his practices without creating undue friction. Hence, a compatible relationship will usually exist between the administrative and the executive levels in the hierarchy of the organization.

The administrative worker is a specialist in some aspect of recreational service. He therefore has a professional obligation as well as a positional responsibility to assist in keeping the executive informed, not only of the problems and needs of his own division, but also of any developments and achievements in the entire field which have a bearing on the area of his technical expertise. If the administrator feels that he is doing his best to fulfill the demands of his position but that his efforts are being frustrated because of deficient equipment or facilities or incompetent personnel, it is his duty to bring these problems to the attention of the executive with definite recommendations for their solution.

---

4. R. G. Kraus and J. E. Curtis, *Creative Management in Recreation and Parks*, 3d ed. (St. Louis: C.V. Mosby Company, 1982), pp. 105–112.

In the case of the bowling buddies, the relationship between the levels may be observed, especially if there is some problem with rapport:

On Friday, as assistant superintendent of X recreational service department, I held a supervisory staff meeting with all of the district supervisors on several organizational changes I wanted to produce immediately. Only supervisor Jones objected to the changes, enumerating a number of reasons which I considered trivial. The modifications had been discussed with the superintendent of the department prior to the meeting and he had approved them in all respects.

On Monday morning the superintendent called me into his office and told me that he wanted the changes terminated. Perplexed, I left and stopped the changes. Later the same day I learned that Jones had gone bowling with the superintendent on Saturday night and had convinced him to abandon the changes. Many of the supervisors knew, and had commented at various times, that Jones and the superintendent were "bowling buddies" from way back, and that supervisor Jones had employed this relationship to obtain favored projects. This however, was the first time that he had done this to me. What can be done to alleviate this unsatisfactory relationship and the attendant problems it causes?

In this situation, apparently the relations between the superintendent and the assistant superintendent are not what they should be. It is common for any superintendent to choose his assistant. Initially, therefore, the superintendent must have had good rapport with his assistant. It is obvious that something has happened to degrade what must have been a formerly good relationship. The fact that the superintendent did not provide the assistant with any explanation for his revocation and the fact that the assistant did not feel he was in a position to ask for one are indicative of the situation. This is quite typical procedure for a superintendent and his immediate assistant. The superintendent almost always informs his assistant of everything because the latter has to execute all policy decisions.

At the same time, the superintendent would find it awkward to confess that he had rescinded the organizational modifications because supervisor Jones had asked him to do so. After all, the superintendent does not want to look ridiculous. This is significant when one deals with an individual who cannot justify his behavior on rational grounds. When an individual issues a public statement which is later proved erroneous, he either admits the error or attempts to save face. In the latter case, he may hedge about what was stated, deny the statement outright, claim that he was misunderstood, or defend his statement. Very few people will continue to defend a statement which they know to be false, but there are those whose egos are such they cannot bear to lose face. Under these circumstances, the individual who points out the error and forces the individual to admit he was wrong may gain a point and lose the game insofar as that person's opinion of him is concerned.

Intelligent people are able to admit mistakes honestly. Compassionate people are capable of enabling others to disentangle themselves from mistakes of their own making without making them appear foolish. Even if the individual does not appreciate the fact that someone has helped him out of an untenable position, it will be more advantageous not to remind that person of his embarrassment. Permit the other person to simmer down, particularly if he is a superior. In other words, do not continue to press the point, but give the individual enough time to evaluate the situation without being pushed.

Now, what about the relations between the superintendent and the assistant? We earlier observed that there is something wrong when the assistant cannot discuss a rapid shift of opinion with the superintendent. Doesn't the assistant have additional responsibilities? He had discussed all of the proposed organizational modifications with the superintendent and apparently the superintendent had felt that the changes were worthwhile. To the assistant's knowledge the conditions requiring change have not altered, therefore the changes are still necessary. Doesn't this facet deserve more consideration and discussion? Furthermore, the assistant superintendent realizes that when he informs the supervisors to halt the changes, they will demand an explanation. Should he indicate that word of the changes has probably been transmitted to other employees of the department, and that this revocation will confuse everyone?

When the assistant learned about supervisor Jones' interference, should he have gone back to the superintendent and informed him that bypassing the routine offices is not only bad for morale, but that it shows unmistakable signs of favoritism which can negatively affect all department personnel? These questions can only be answered if knowledge of the superintendent's reactions are predictable. Generally, an assistant superintendent should feel responsible for providing his superior with a complete assessment of the situation. However, he can argue only up to a point. Once the superintendent has been informed and is in possession of data which can keep him from making a mistake, it is unwise to carry the matter beyond that point.

Where the superintendent is known for his rigidity, there is little reason for his assistant to make recommendations to him, particularly when any suggestion is likely to be ignored. However, the assistant superintendent should not hesitate to respectfully disagree with the superintendent when he has information that indicates his superior is making a mistake.

It is perfectly natural that the superintendent might like one member of his staff more than others and might enjoy that person's presence socially. There are circumstances in which a superintendent may have good reason to confide in one subordinate more than another. Sometimes, the superintendent may find it much more beneficial to discuss matters with a trusted confidant than with others. This could be the case with the superintendent and supervisor Jones. But the superintendent is bound by the responsibilities of his position. To disregard the feelings or recommendations of all his subordinates solely on the basis of the objections of one person is inappropriate. Of course, the one person may be right and all of the others wrong. But even if this were the case, responsible conduct, common sense, and human relations require that the superintendent explain the situation to the others involved. Since it is uncommon for all but one of a group of professionals to be wrong, the superintendent should not behave in an arbitrary manner. More than one professional has decided to seek employment elsewhere because he felt that his suggestions were never listened to, while those of another were, merely because the latter was more socially acceptable to the superintendent. Many excellent people have been driven from the field by arbitrary or incompetent superiors.

The assistant superintendent has more to think about than the relations between the superintendent and supervisor Jones. He should examine his own relationship with the superintendent and the interpersonal relations among all supervisory personnel. It might be possible that neither he nor other supervisors have provided the superintendent with accurate information at the time it was needed and therefore the superintendent feels that he cannot depend upon them. It may be that a new understanding of supervisor Jones is in order. The assistant superintendent indicated that his proposed organizational modifications were acceptable to all of the supervisors except Jones, whose objections he had not bothered about. Can it be that the assistant is antipathetic toward Jones? Perhaps Jones' objections were given in the honest belief that the changes were wrong. At least they should have been given a respectable hearing. The assistant superintendent never concerned himself with Jones' friendship with the superintendent until the relationship served to thwart his own plans. The fact that other supervisors had been treated in this way apparently escaped his notice.

These circumstances require considerable reflection. It would probably be best for all concerned to accept the superintendent's reversal without additional bickering and turn attention to an honest appraisal of some of the relationships in question. To continue to object to the superintendent's seemingly arbitrary reversal might push him into a position where he feels it is necessary to save face before a subordinate. Permitting the matter to remain at status quo for the time being, taking it up at a later date when conditions are more favorable, will likely be the more successful solution.

POLICY-MAKING AT THE MANAGERIAL LEVEL

Responsibility for policy-making lies with the chief executive of the agency. Within the field of recreational service, this position usually carries the title "Superintendent" or "Commissioner." The term "executive" implies a greater range of responsibility than manager, director, supervisor, or coordinator. The executive is the individual solely responsible for the operational effectiveness and efficiency of agency employees. He directs and controls all aspects of agency projects, programs, and operations. He alone has the final responsibility for the quality of service provided by his agency.

Not only must the executive have the necessary education, technical proficiency, and prior experience in order to be effective in his position, he must also have considerable administrative skill and a great capacity for hard work. In order to keep all agency operations running smoothly, the executive must understand and be able to apply the basic principles of organization and direction. He must give close attention to fair employment practices and see that everything possible is done to establish an atmosphere in which good personal relationships among agency employees can flourish.[5] He must bring all the principles of leadership to his work, formulating his objectives clearly, planning with his subordinates the procedures to follow for the execution of these aims, and setting up a reporting system to

---

5.   Hersey and Blanchard, *Management of Organizational Behavior,* p. 5.

ensure that his directives are being followed. A primary attribute of a good executive is the ability to separate issues of major significance from those of minor significance and to delegate responsibility to subordinates for implementing all but the most important. It is this ability to view the entire scope of agency operations and focus the requisite amount of attention on the changing areas of crisis that marks the executive who is truly a leader.

Typical Duties of the Superintendent

Whether ultimate responsibility for the provision of recreational services to the community lies with a board, council, or commission or with a single official such as a mayor or city manager, the superintendent of a recreational services agency has certain powers and duties that do not vary with organizational structure.

As chief executive, he has direct and unshared responsibility for the effective and efficient functioning of his operation. He is responsible for the general organization, administration, management, and supervision of his agency and its employees and exercises all necessary powers incident to it. The superintendent is always associated with the management and control of personnel practices, fiscal administration, methodology, and the plans and operation of the overall recreational program in all the facilities, areas, and centers of the system.

When a board of directors oversees agency operation, the superintendent occupies a seat on the board and shares equally with other members in discussing and deciding on all matters before the board. He attends all meetings of the board and its committees. He compiles, collates, and prepares for board examination the minutes of all meetings, the annual report of the system, the annual budget message and financial statement, and all estimates for appropriations. He prepares annual, periodic, and special reports of recreational services provided throughout the community and distributes them to other agencies within and outside the community. He analyzes, collects, and assembles information that may be useful, required, or desired by the board and recommends any actions that promote recreational services to the community.

The superintendent is responsible for the progressive development of recreational service throughout the community, in accordance with approved principles, methods, and practices in the field. He keeps abreast of new developments and improvements and applies whatever is advantageous. The superintendent's duties may be divided into eight parts: 1) personnel management; 2) the service function; 3) space and facility management; 4) finance administration; 5) data keeping; 6) public interpretation and relations; 7) planning, research, development, and analysis; and 8) education and negotiation. While most of these duties are specifically delegated to subordinate specialists for execution, the ultimate responsibility resides with the superintendent. The following activities are normally associated with the executive of the recreational system.[6]

Personnel Management. The superintendent has the responsibility for the recruitment, in-service education, and supervision of all personnel (professional, ancillary, and volunteer); development of equitable personnel practices, standards, and levels of compensation; a position classification procedure; adoption of a merit as well as seniority system for workers; periodic appraisal and evaluation of workers; and maintenance of proper working conditions for personnel of the agency. He is authorized to:

1. Employ for a three-month period at established rates of compensation such part-time and special employees as may be needed in the recreational service function to fulfill the provisions of this responsibility.

2. Suspend for cause, pending investigation of the merits of the case, any employee for a period not to exceed thirty days.

3. Accept the resignation of any employees, grant leaves of absence, make all assignments or reassignments of personnel to various regions, districts, or areas within the community of his jurisdiction, sign or countersign payrolls, and perform other such managerial duties which may be required of him.

4. Provide administrative and technical supervision to the assistant superintendent and through him to all other employees of the system. He exercises this direction by generally planning the work of his subordinate, setting the objectives to be achieved, interpreting and applying the broadest policies, providing solutions to the most difficult problems, advice on in-service educational programs, and any needed information.

5. Accept general responsibility for the character and performance of all employees.

The superintendent also promotes morale and group spirit of lay and professional groups in the community by working on recreational problems which interest them and by stimulating cooperation among

---

6. George Hjelte and Jay S. Shivers, *Public Administration of Recreational Services,* 2d ed. (Philadelphia: Lea & Febiger, 1978), p. 385.

group members in the solution of common problems. He will assist individuals in developing the skills and attitudes that enable them to contribute to the group effort. He is interested in increasing group solidarity toward recreational objectives and in creating additional groups when needed to solve community recreational problems. He will attempt to discover the causes for the development or lack of group cohesiveness and morale. He will continue to seek out groups which have recreational interests or potential recreational problems.

Service Function. The rationale and justification for the local recreational agency is the provision of recreational services for the people of the community. The superintendent's objective is to facilitate effective recreational services through a program of activities which will actually satisfy the recreational needs of people. To this end, he exercises three spheres of authority in establishing this service.

1. *Program planning* is the interpretation of philosophy and policy into concrete experiences of a recreational nature. Such practice will be initiated from community interests and demands as well as selective criteria necessary for the provision of the program.

2. *Program direction* is the management of personnel and materials in a coordinated manner so that specific duties will be executed with a minimum of friction and a maximum of service. This phase of work is carried on through a system-wide utilization of records, periodic inspection and observation, reports of supervisors, staff conferences, and the analysis of studies relating to the departmental program.

3. *Program balance* is the maintenance of a well-rounded, full-range, year-round program offering a variety of activities in which all may participate if not restricted by physical or mental limitations. Thus, each age, sex, and racial, ethnic, social, and economic group is served without discrimination or inequality as to the types and variety of experiences.

Space and Facility Management. The superintendent is responsible for the planning, design, construction, and maintenance of all recreational spaces, places, areas, facilities, and structures which constitute the physical property or plant of the system.[7] At all times, he must bear in

7. These terms are differentiated as follows: *space* is a three-dimensional expanse, a non-specified area; *place* is a designated location or particular site; area is a level surface or piece of ground, i.e., playground; *facility* is a particular piece of equipment, building, or portion thereof designed for specific recreational activities, i.e., a gymnasium; *structure* is any construction.

mind the health, welfare, and safety of the users. A master recreational plan will permit him to acquire advantageous sites in optimum locations before they are priced beyond departmental means. In the construction of new facilities, the superintendent must be aware of and use the latest materials, designs, and methods; conform to local building codes; and ensure against inferior workmanship and materials. He is also charged with the responsibility for improving existing property and acquiring additional equipment and supplies for which a need has been expressed. He must always be alert for expanding the recreational system's holdings through gifts, donations, or bequests. His is also a custodial function delegated by him to subordinate personnel, for the upkeep and maintenance of spaces and facilities.

Finance Administration   The superintendent is responsible for all fiscal control and management. It is upon his estimate of services to be provided, and of activities and personnel required to operate the program that appropriations will be made. For this reason, he has recourse to past records and reports of the agency's operations. He must be prepared to study them in detail in order to arrive at a figure which will be utilized for operating the agency. He must look at past performance, expenditures, and accomplishments and relate these to the departmental program for the year ahead. He must:

1.   Prepare to explain and justify each item which he calls for in the budget.
2.   Countersign all checks issued to the department or board, if any, and allow no person to incur expenditures against departmental funds without prior approval of the superintendent.
3.   Establish methods to govern, collect, and distribute donations, gifts, bequests, and endowments presented to the agency.
4.   Supervise accounting and fiscal procedures in the department, which includes estimating adequate budget controls and developing accurate records, procedures, and reports of expenditures, investments, and collections.
5.   Accept responsibility for the preparation of periodic and annual financial reports, determine the cost of operating units within the system, and supervise the collections of fees, charges, and income from concessions or other services rendered.

Data Keeping.   All of the written information relating to the daily operation of the recreational system is submitted to the superintendent by program personnel. They include in their summaries an objective statistical accounting of the day-to-day activities carried on by the agency. Their subjective narrative records deal with behavior patterns of individuals participating in the program. The superintendent then:

1. Uses the written material collected in records and reports for making periodic studies and surveys for the continuous improvement and guidance of personnel.

2. Develops or designs and approves forms for records and reports in relation to the handling of departmental business, to ensure continuity by personnel and to facilitate the process whereby information may be readily obtained.

3. Sets up inventory procedures for control of office, program, maintenance, and administrative supplies, materials, and equipment.

4. Maintains records, central and field file controls, and adequate filing systems for the preservation of correspondence, studies, and legal papers of all kinds.

Public Interpretation and Public Relations. Public interpretation is the dissemination of information to the public on matters of interest to it. Where questions of policy statements, activity offerings, or agency priority schedules exist, these must be clarified for the public. Public relations is usually concerned with the reduction of conflict situations between the agency and its constituents. Since the executive is the chief public relations officer in the department, it is up to him to establish a procedure by which the agency is interpreted to the public. He is, in effect, the administrator of complex and delicate relations with all public and private agencies, the clientele served, and all of the citizens of the community involved with requests for improvements, leadership, facilities, program, land acquisition, and numerous correlated matters.

Planning, Research, Development, and Analysis. As the executive officer for the public recreational service agency, the superintendent must necessarily be involved in the study, survey, and analysis of the condition of recreational needs, both personal and physical, and must compile and report on such information. He will provide or prepare technical and advisory data and materials for numerous requests made by community, county, regional, or state departments offering recreational services. He is also required to furnish specific data on standard civil service prerequisites, efficiency or merit rating systems, retirement, budget, fiscal procedures, departmental organization, rules, regulations, plans, designs, and construction standards for indoor and outdoor recreational spaces, structures, and equipment.

Upon request, he will cooperate, guide, and advise in the development, organization, and structuring of local recreational agencies, departments, or systems for local legal subdivisions; give technical assistance in the design, layout, and development of recreational areas, facilities, and structures; and will offer competent aid in the planning, financing, and administration of public recreational services. Using his judgment and discretion, he will authorize the collection, analysis, and reporting of material facts and statistical studies on recreational services in specific areas. He searches source literature—publications, manuals, abstracts, periodicals, and other published materials—for the trends and developments in the field of recreational service, studies this material, and makes recommendations on its use and application.

He makes studies, in existing programs or agencies, of attendance, population, metropolitan and community trends and characteristics, and economic, physical, geopolitical, age and sex makeup of population for use in determining expansion and renewal of capital improvements. He prepares maps, charts, graphs, or exhibits in connection with these studies. He composes and sends questionnaires to other recreational service systems throughout the United States to discover the most widely accepted principles and practices for recreational service, specifically in public service administration and community organization. He correlates and analyzes data upon receipt of answered questionnaires and reports his findings. The superintendent is also responsible for the preparation of replies to queries which his agency receives. He studies, analyzes, and organizes the preparation of general and specific professional materials from which references or reproductions can be made for use by departmental staff or the departmental library.

Education and Negotiation. As chief executive the superintendent may be required to negotiate, prepare, and administer regular and periodic agreements between the agency and public, quasi-public, and private agencies or individuals for the purposes of enhancing the recreational services within the community. By virtue of his position, the superintendent attempts to educate the public to the need for recreational activity and the benefit that each individual will derive from participating in some phase of the agency's program. He further has the responsibility for providing activities of an educational nature—for example, adult classes—for the purpose of finding an interest suited to everyone in the community.

In the following case, the executive's function when dealing with an external agency executive points to the need for clear and purposeful communications.

The principal of a local high school was antagonistic to scheduling recreational activities in school facilities, because he claimed that the activities interrupted extra-curricular school plans and also presented additional custodial and maintenance problems. Furthermore, the principal stated that *his* building was not going to be opened to anybody just for fun. His building was well maintained and nobody was going to come in and disrupt his classrooms or utilize his supplies in carrying out a recreational program. As a result, he had given the program the least possible cooperation. As this matter was governed by the school board, the entire question had to be taken before it. When I, representing the municipal recreational agency, approached the board with this problem, considerable opposition had been stirred up by the principal, who had reiterated his objections, dwelling heavily on the expenses incurred by the operation of the recreational program. The board membership was a representative cross-section of the community. None of the board members had school-operated recreational program experience, but all were concerned over mounting costs in the school system.

After the basic argument had been presented, it was quickly indicated that some friendly persuasion together with documented statements had to be provided if the recreational program was to stay in the school.

I began by recounting the philosophy behind the recreational program, its beginning in the community, and the need for such a continuous service. I pointed out the educational preparation and experience it takes to be able to provide recreational services to the community. I called upon the principal as a professional person to try to understand that my program operating in his facility had the same purpose—the inculcation of educational, cultural, physical, and social experiences in a socially approved setting for the satisfaction of individuals in aiding their growth and development. I discussed the need for recreational activity by all the people in the community and I added that the program had been successful, despite hindrance, as indicated by the number of individuals participating in the variously programmed activities. To these points I also added the question of monetary support. I asked whether any of the board members as taxpayers knew how much it would cost to provide a recreational facility to take the place of the school, with its central location, accessibility, and varied physical facilities. I reminded them of safety features and supervisory factors that were now operating, but which might be lost if residents had to find another place to hold recreational activities. I spoke on the present costs of operating and indicated several alternatives which might be advantageously undertaken if the board wished to spend a little time studying the proposals.

I talked briefly about the several possibilities, and after I had finished, a member of the board took the floor and stated that he was convinced of the necessity of a continuing recreational service in the community, and of the need for the school to house a part of the recreational program, and asked that the board take time to study this problem further before rendering a decision. He moved that two board members, the principal of the school in question and I, be appointed to meet in committee and recommend to the board what further action be taken. In less than three weeks we had come to a unanimous decision and had scheduled a hearing before the board. The department of recreational service would enter into contractual agreement with the board of education to provide such recreational services as it considered necessary in serving the community and would bear all expenses incurred in the operation of the school on a pro rata basis. The school in turn would provide the facility. Program schedules were to be worked out so as to eliminate any conflict in the two areas.

It is always necessary to operate on the principle that school officials must be educated to the value of recreational activity for the constituent population of the community. No stereotyping of school principals can be made. There are those who are progressive, liberal, innovative, and constantly trying to learn how better to serve their respective communities. There are just as many principals who operate under the misguided idea that they are the final arbiters of any problems that arise, as they concern public school property. Each type of individual must be treated in a manner consonant with his own understanding and reasonableness. There are people with whom one cannot reason. They must be commanded to perform or they must be relieved of their position. The latter instance is always a traumatic experience for all involved. When an individual can profit by being educated, then every means should be taken to so educate that person. When, however, an individual remains intransigent in the face of logic and values contrary to his own opinion, then a plea to higher authority must be made. It is only by continually educating the public that the proposals and programs which are directed toward the satisfaction of human needs will be met.

As an educator and negotiator, the superintendent has the following duties:

1.   Although he delegates the actual work, the superintendent is responsible for the external information program carried on by the department. To this end, he collects, compiles, and prepares for regular dissemination all interpretive data to be used by the communications media and also collects for departmental use all material obtainable on cultural, aesthetic, creative, social, group, physical, educational, or other recreational experiences within the community.

2.   After having conducted a general information-gathering service on recreational functions both by phone and correspondence, the superintendent may act as consultant to other agencies on these matters.

3.   He is responsible for initiating the selection and purchase of professional books, other pertinent literature, and audio-visual material for use in the departmental library. He is responsible for all other details, by delegation of authority, of the establishment and maintenance of public good will.

From the above compilation of duties, functions, and responsibilities, it can be seen that demands upon the superintendent are manifold. If these were all his position required of him, the work would be more than sufficient to keep him busy. But beyond the required performance of executive assignments and the shaping or initiation of policy by which the agency operates, there is also the need to provide leadership. Many executives neglect this concept. They believe that once they have achieved the superintendency, they are automatically leaders. This, as we have discussed at length, is fallacious. A superintendent must first earn his leadership status and then maintain it with those in the community and with the staff of the agency in order to run the most effective operation and provide the highest quality recreational service.[8] The superintendent's concepts of human relations and interpersonal development will become the pervasive influence within his agency. If he is democratic in outlook and practices organizational democracy, this will be reflected at all levels of the hierarchy. And if, in addition, he has the flexibility and imagination to seek new approaches to the multitude of problems confronting his agency, he will be able to provide leadership in the best sense.[9]

---

8.   R. H. Hall, *Organizations*, p. 175.
9.   Kraus and Curtis, *Creative Management*, pp. 362–374.

Essentially, then, a recreationist at the managerial level—whether executive or administrator—is all of the following:

1.   He is a planner. As a conceptualizer of the organization, he is responsible for the philosophy which will permeate the agency and guide its personnel. He must project his plans and ideas in such a way that agency employees will be able to maximize their time, talent and knowledge. Managerial personnel anticipate the future, coming to grips with the potential problems posed by given sets of circumstances, selecting solutions and alternatives, and taking advantage of trends.

2.   He is an organizer. Personnel at the managerial level mobilize all of the resources of the agency—human, material, economic, or technical—and weld them into a smoothly integrated, cohesive unit so that primary objectives can be reached with optimum efficiency, maximum effectiveness, and a minimum of friction, duplication, and waste.

3.   He is a human relations specialist. He selects personnel not only with an eye to filling an agency need but also to the individual's potential for professional growth.

4.   He is an allocator. He determines what functions must be executed, assigns personnel the authority and responsibility for carrying out particular tasks, formulates standards by which performance may be measured, and holds workers accountable for meeting these standards.

5.   He is an evaluator. He directs the efforts of subordinates by maintaining a feedback system that provides him with sufficiently early warning that he can take corrective measures if necessary. This system also provides him material for initiating incentive plans and apprises him of outstanding performances on the part of subordinates. Through evaluation, he contributes to increasing worker proficiency.

6.   He is a leader. He sets up open lines of communication throughout the organization so that information about working conditions, job satisfaction, and organizational objectives can flow freely. He is concerned with the development of interpersonal relationships among those who work for the agency. He attempts to develop rapport with subordinates so that an atmosphere of democratic cooperation is created. Finally, his leadership style inspires members of his organization to undertake their respective functions willingly and in a way that reflects professional esteem, zeal, and technical competence. In all of his behavior, he exemplifies those characteristics which make others want to emulate him.

QUESTIONS FOR DISCUSSION

1. What are the primary functions of the administrative leader?
2. What relationship should the administrator have with his immediate supervisor?
3. The administrator's philosophy permeates the organization, affecting intrapersonal relations. How does this effect a climate for leadership?
4. Why should the chief executive have unshared authority in the process of hiring immediate subordinates?
5. How does the communications process influence the administrator's identification of organizational functions and goals?

BIBLIOGRAPHY

Bower, Joseph L., *The Two Faces of Management: An American Approach to Leadership* (Boston, Mass.: Houghton Mifflin Co., 1983).

Culligan, Mathew J., and Suzanne Derkins, *Back to Basics Management: The Lost Craft of Leadership* (New York: Facts on File, Inc., 1983).

Daniels, Madeline, *Realistic Leadership: How to Lead Others in Achieving Company and Personal Goals* (Englewood Cliffs, N.J.: Prentice-Hall, Inc., 1983).

Gribben, James J., *Leadership Strategies for Organizational Effectiveness* (New York: American Management Association, 1982).

Halloran J., *Supervision: The Art of Management* (Englewood Cliffs, N.J.: Prentice-Hall, Inc., 1981).

Hayes, Marion E., *Managing Performance: A Comprehensive Guide to Effecting Supervision* (Belmont, Cal.: Lifetime Learning Publications, 1983).

Hunt, James G., and others, *Leaders and Managers: International Perspectives on Managerial Behavior and Leadership Research* (Elmsford, N.Y.: Pergamon Press, Inc., 1984).

Klause, Rudi, and Bernard Bass, eds., *Interpersonal Communication in Organizations* (San Diego, Cal.: Academic Press, Inc., 1982).

Morgan, James E., *Administrative and Supervisory Management* (Englewood Cliffs, N.J.: Prentice-Hall, Inc., 1982).

IV

Leadership Effectiveness

CHAPTER FOURTEEN

Leadership Challenges

The great challenge of leadership lies in promoting human perfectability. The leader undertakes a most difficult task of attempting to meet the social needs of people by offering opportunities for them to attain desirable and beneficial achievements. His humanitarian understanding and motivation for providing the most valuable experiences possible to those who follow are indicative of his preoccupation with what the individual derives from activities, rather than with activities as ends in themselves. To the recreationist, what happens to people and why they are affected as they are is more significant than almost any other concept or technique at his disposal. How he meets this challenge reflects his deep concern for improving the status of people through recreational service.

Because the leader is unique, combining the talents, knowledge, and ability which give him influence with others, he is outstanding. The real leader has the strength of character and clarity of purpose to sustain him in moments of crisis. As such, he must realize the precariousness of his position. The very fact that he stands out from others puts him in tempting perspective to anybody.[1] The leader stands out and is, therefore, alone. Like a target silhouetted against the sky, he is an easy mark to all who want to destroy his ideas, goals, and personality. Nothing is more hazardous to individual security than the assumption of leadership status. This is true of leadership in every social field. Perhaps it is a life-and-death concept in the political field, where the probability of assassination is always very real. One need not look too far to judge the truth of this statement.

Western civilization has flourished as a result of what one might call the entrepreneurial spirit. All the advances in the various fields of human endeavor—economics, exploration, medicine, electronics, marketing, education, psychology—have been made by persons willing to take risks in order to achieve their ends. An entrepreneur by

---

1. M. W. McCall, Jr. and M. M. Lombardo, *Leadership: Where Else Can We Go?* (Durham, N.C.: Duke University Press, 1978), p. 29.

definition is a person who, with considerable initiative and risk, manages or organizes any enterprise, although common use most often relates the term to business.

Risk-takers are an intergral part of every group, subgroup, or culture in Western society. A true entrepreneur, recognizing the risks inherent in a given situation, first seeks to minimize these risks by careful preplanning. He collects all information concerning the object of his attention and carefully evaluates and analyzes these data. He brings his extensive knowledge and background of experience to bear. Unlike the gambler, the entrepreneur never relies on mere chance. His decision to act reflects risk, to be sure, but calculated risk. Overall is his need to better existing conditions, to challenge the status quo.

Recreationists who would be leaders must exhibit these entrepreneurial qualities. The recreationist is committed to providing individuals with the most valuable recreational experiences possible; the value is assessed by what the individuals derive from these activities, not by the activities in themselves. In order to achieve his purpose, the recreationist often must challenge the established order and risk jeopardizing his position in the community and in the agency. Within the agency, the recreationist's innovative efforts may be seen by fellow workers, as well as superiors, as the recreationist's attempts to better himself and his reputation at the expense of theirs. A well-rounded and creative new program is sure to emphasize any defects in existing programs. Ironically, the recreationist can probably expect the most opposition to innovation from those people who would most benefit by the program. He faces the large task of educating and influencing the public to cease relying on routine experiences that are rewarding only because they are familiar. He must also get voters to pay their money, in the form of taxes, to support these services. Those opposed to raising taxes usually form a highly articulate and vocal opposition.

The methods the recreationist uses to approach his agency colleagues, on the one hand, and the community his agency serves, on the other, will reflect the quality of his leadership ability. If the recreationist is to accomplish his purpose and give the service for which he is employed, he must, like the entrepreneur, be prepared to take calculated risks. The process may often be slow, and the recreationist must judge when the right moment arrives to risk setting his plan into action.

In order to weigh the balance of forces which may be opposed to his objective, and to promote the likelihood of success, the leader must develop conditions that tend to promote his purposes. This means creating conditions or waiting for situations that provide opportunities to get his message across.

THE CREATION OF A FAVORABLE CLIMATE

What is meant by the creation of a favorable climate? Answered simply, it means the process of putting men at their ease or reducing any friction or hostility which may be aroused because of an idea, a policy, or some action. It is the development of an atmosphere of mutual respect and trust whereby any person may speak his mind without fear of contradiction or ridicule. Under such conditions, each individual may make suggestions and know that they will be listened to, weighed, appraised, and then utilized or be discarded without prejudice.

A favorable climate is defined, for purposes here, as an environment in which opinions, questions, and statements may be given or taken without the insecurity or doubt that others may be laughing (at you). It is an atmosphere of conviviality, sociability, humor, and understanding where each person commands the degree of respect which human dignity requires. Perhaps freedom of thought is the best term to describe a favorable climate.

In order to present his ideas and get them accepted so that his influence will prevail, the leader must begin to build a climate which is favorable to his goals. He does this by determining the needs of those who are potential followers and playing upon those needs. He utilizes deliberate forms of persuasion to draw others to his point of view.

This climate may also be created in an atmosphere of mutual trust and satisfaction, where ideas are discussed with the certainty that all will be heard. The leader's cause may be advanced by patient waiting for the right psychological moment when people are looking for someone to show them the way or when they are relaxed and can give earnest attention to the leader's attempts at communication. A favorable climate may mean inciting to riot, so that the leader may be thrust into a powerful position and gain prominence. He seeks to further his cause through the weakness of others and stimulates their acceptance of him by plying them with the ideas which they want to hear. A climate favorable to gaining influence for the leader may be achieved by bigotry, demagoguery, playing one group off against another, or using arbitration where fair practices apply in a common arena for the settlement of arguments or friction-producing misunderstandings.

The recreationist, of course, must *never* utilize any technique which is destructive or unethical. His is the task of preserving high moral tone and equity in all of his dealings with people. Any of these techniques can be used to obtain influence with others, but the leader will feel his way cautiously among the unknown factors of human personality before committing himself to a single path of action. He will be aware of the contradictory behaviors of which men are capable, and he will proceed to inaugurate an accepting atmosphere most conducive to the effectiveness of his program.

Problem Solving versus Risk

The leader has an extensive knowledge and broad experience which he brings to problems confronting him in the field of his choice. Through an intimate knowledge of the workings of his specialty, he has gained the ability to appraise conditions and to select the most feasible avenue for resolving or satisfying them. It is only through direct and long experience that the leader obtains a view of the circumstances which are likely to cause conflict or produce problems.

The entrepreneur negates the apparent risk which appears to be inherent in the way he functions. By careful attention to details, which includes the collection of all information concerning the object of his attention, he assembles any and all data which might have a bearing upon the situation he wishes to act upon. His next step is to refine the material which has been collected and sort the specifically relevant data from those which are irrelevant to the problem at hand. Discriminating analysis of the information is the next step in his attempt to exclude any extraneous matter which might intrude upon and negatively affect a final decision. Once this process begins, it does not end until a select plan of action has been laid out for final development and testing. The validation of the material and analysis of its various stages comes about when the plan is put into action. If the idea succeeds, then what has been undertaken has been relevant and factual. If the plan is a failure, then the process must be repeated because a fact was missed or a wrong turn was taken somewhere along the line.

The act of leadership is not merely a mechanical problem-solving device. The questions of judgment and comparative value selection are probably the heart of the process. The entrepreneur possesses a feeling for the area in which he works. He has a sense of timing which he has developed during his association with similar problems. His previous experience and knowledge of other situations which required the same type of care give him an understanding and appreciation of the factors which confront him. He draws on this appreciation to help decide whether or not the time, circumstances, and conditions are right for action.[2] This process is called judgment. What seems to be a

---

2. M. F. R. Kets de Vries, *Organizational Paradoxes: Clinical Approaches to Management* (London: Tavistock Publications, 1980), pp. 122–132.

gamble to the novice or uninitiated is really a calculated risk involving the sifting of vast quantities of pertinent information and reliance upon a knowledge of the details of a specialization which have been obtained over a prolonged period of time.

The entrepreneur does not merely gamble. A gamble allows hit-and-miss or chance to decide how the play will go. The calculated risk, on the other hand, has to a large extent arranged the conditions of play beforehand; it has produced a plan in which all definable data have been calculated and analyzed. There is an unknown factor involved, but this unknown factor can be accounted for and thus negated by careful arrangement of all known information. Then, the solution to the problem can be found through use of the individual's judgment. His sense of timing and his basic knowledge of what is likely to be the behavior of others, given the prevailing conditions, are probably enough to tip the scales in his favor. While others feel trepidation at the apparent risk being undertaken, the entrepreneur awaits the final outcome with a confidence much like that a chess master has as his opposition falls neatly into the prepared trap built by seemingly random moves.

Entrepreneurial acts are those of the leader. The leader must take risks in order to develop his plans and to stimulate a following for himself. The risks, however, must be calculated to enhance his position; they must have purpose and direction. Risks cannot be assumed merely to bolster the ego or to convince others that the leader has daring. That is the difference between a leader and a gambler. The gambler shows his daring by risking everything he has on the chance that he might win. The leader indicates his good judgment, as well as daring, by calculating his chances for success and then laying out a plan which will place him in a position of greater strength than he had and will also add to his reputation as an individual of daring. What is apparent risk to others is in reality a careful analysis of the situation, evaluation of the existing hazards and unknown factors, and weighing of values by the judgment which the leader has.

The Hazards of the Status Quo

Every leader challenges existing conditions. He sees them as the routinized, conforming, channelized methods and pressures which continue to mold human beings and their thought processes in the usual or habitual way. Individuals continue to do the same things in the same ways because they are conditioned to do so. Unless innovators come along to change the methods which are habitually utilized, this world would continue to perform in the same ways. Many cultures have long since disappeared because they continued to utilize methods which grew stagnant and became outmoded, leaving them easy prey for other cultures.[3]

The entrepreneur seems to have a need to change things. By bringing about change, he profits and flourishes. It is only through change that the entrepreneurial process works. The leader also works for change. He cannot exist under conditions where everything is balanced. Status quo is an intolerable situation for the leader. He must bring about change in order to lead. Unless and until he can instigate dissatisfaction with "things as they are," he can obtain no popular following.

In addition to the need to change conditions, whether socially, politically, militarily, economically, industrially, or educationally, the leader must always question what has been taken for established fact. This questioning is coincidental with the need to modify, innovate, or institute change. If Democritus had not challenged Aristotle's statement concerning atoms, science could still be a primitive procedure. If Copernicus or Galileo had not challenged the then axiomatic statement that the universe was earth-centered, astronomy and other related sciences might still be suffering. If men like Pauling, Crick, Flemming, and others of their caliber had not challenged the accepted statements and practices of their day, how ignorant and disease-ridden this world would now be. There have been changemakers in every human era. These have been the leaders of their particular fields of endeavor. It is in the very nature of change that the leader displays his skill. The conditions he creates for his eventual assumption of power through influence with others are derived from his ability to invent ideas which cause people to desire that which they are denied or cannot have if present conditions remain as they are.

Recreationists must also take risks if they are to assume the status of leaders. Taking risks, of course, places the risk-taker in positions of jeopardy because of the disaffections which have to be incurred as challenges to the established order are made throughout the community. The recreationist assumes risks whenever he attempts to provide new and stimulating activities for individuals to enjoy. There are risks to reputation when the recreationist takes a position which may be unpopular with those who have seniority within agencies or when he makes plans that are antagonistic to the routine activities which run-of-the-mill operators prefer to schedule for their agency constituents. The recreationist invariably has to step on toes when unpleasant decisions must be made. Thus his opposition grows if he

---

3.   R. C. Tucker, *Politics as Leadership* (Columbia, Mo.: University of Missouri Press, 1981), pp. 130–139.

attempts innovation with the recreational program, because he emphasizes the discrepancies between a well-rounded and creative range of activities and the poorly planned program which may be heavily based on physical activities and nothing else.

Calculated risks also must be taken by the recreationist in educating the public to the countless ways in which recreational experiences can be enjoyed, since he invites excessive criticism from the very people who would benefit most by his program. Many people want to keep the same routine experiences which are comfortable and familiar to them. They resent all those who want to change a habitual existence. Others are so concerned about community tax rates that they oppose any and all attempts to add to or improve public recreational service. Perhaps this is one of the imponderables of human personality, but it is hazardous for the recreationist to try to educate people to new and stimulating activities. Regardless of the values of such experiences, unless the leader takes care to bring the group along slowly, but steadily, he faces some disappointment.

The leader is a real entrepreneur. The recreationist must be an entrepreneur if he is to give the service for which he is employed. He must be prepared to assume the burdens which accrue from working with the public. He must take the risks which are calculated to provide a broad and varied program of recreational experiences to all of the people all of the time. He must be aware of the pitfalls of public apathy and hostility. Simultaneously, with the collection of all information concerning the recreational needs of people within his community, he should have worked out a satisfactory plan of attack which can negate most of the hostility and indifference. This is the true meaning of the entrepreneurial process; it is one which the recreationist can utilize to his profit.

RISKS TO THE LEADER

The Leader as a Target

If a group is without specific ethnic, religious, or racial characteristics, individuals who wish to cast aspersions on the group will have a difficult job unless they find a target for their denunciations. The leader of any group provides the ideal target. He stands out and is easily identified. He is vulnerable because he can be separated from the mass of people whom he leads and singled out as a living symbol of the group and its ideas. The leader becomes a focal point of criticisms ranging from mild disagreement on issues of policy to rabid verbal attacks on his character and even, occasionally, attacks on his person.

Thus, by virtue of their position, leaders are constantly open to attack. This is one of the hazards of leadership. Leaders must be adept at handling the various forms of hostility directed against them. Those who cannot tolerate abuse run the risk of engaging in petty skirmishes and losing sight of their long-range goals. Leaders cannot afford to yield to the temptation of hurling accusations and verbal abuse at critics. They must rely on truth and good judgment to vindicate their policies, even when critics resort to subtle forms of slander or even outright character assassination. A true leader can only undermine his position by descending to the level of such antagonists.

Hidden Enemies

One great hazard to the leader is false friends: individuals who profess loyalty and support when in reality they are subverting the leader's aims and seeking to remove him from the leadership position. Leaders often risk their position by relying upon the loyalty of people who have in fact become disaffected.

Hidden enemies form a core of dissension and pockets of resistance, active and passive, to the leader's objectives. Such people usually occupy privileged positions within the organizational hierarchy and have the leader's confidence. From this vantage point, they exert tremendous influence upon the unsuspecting leader and thus represent a serious threat to his power and position. Often the treachery of such false friends in not uncovered until it is too late and the leader has lost the support of his loyal followers.

Recreationists are not immune from hidden enemies. Although recreationists can usually assume that their colleagues are generally supportive rather than antagonistic, inadequacies within the recreational program or the agency, or personality conflicts with those who operate it, may cause some persons to become disaffected. The disaffected individual can become the nucleus around whom others of the same opinion gather. These people may air their criticisms openly and solicit support for a change of leadership or even abolition of the agency.

Critics such as these are a serious threat to the recreationist, but the threat they pose is open. The greater threat comes from the disaffected individuals who work covertly, giving the leader no opportunity to confront his opposition. A person hostile to an agency, for example, is in an ideal position to discredit it or to limit its functions and scope if he or she can be appointed to the legal board or commission under which the agency operates. The following case illustrates subversion of this sort:

The teenage center in a southern town had been giving the local branch of a national youth-service agency considerable competition. The recreationist in charge of the teen program was extremely competent and continually originated highly attractive acitivities. Unable to accept the intense competition which the center afforded, the youth agency director gave as little cooperation to the center as possible. When he determined that lack of cooperation could not damage the center's program, he became a member of the community's inter-agency council and consistently attempted to hamper his rival's activities while seeming to offer assistance and material support. The recreationist did not realize that his program was being undermined until the director had actually persuaded seven of the council's ten members that *his* organization should be given complete control of all youth activities within the community, with the center to act only in a subordinate role. His sub rosa activities were quite successful; within a very short time, the teenage center was discontinued as a separate agency and its functions merged with the other. Naturally, there could not be two executives, and the former teenage director was discharged.

Here one can see what pettiness and envy can do. There is no community that cannot support recreational agencies if cooperation produces good coordination.

Polarized Factions

With decision-making comes the division between those who will follow the leader, supporting his aims and ideas, and those who will not. When a leader, confronted with two opposing paths which have equally vigorous support among his followers, decides to take one path rather than the other, he is certain to split the group into those who commend his decision and those who, to varying degrees, deplore it. The latter group may become completely antithetical to his objectives and methods.

Inherent within the decision-making process, then, is the potential for self-destruction. Every statement, direction, or procedure which the leader undertakes is likely to be distasteful to someone who may feel it a matter of principle to oppose him as effectively as possible. Unless the leader is extremely careful and discreet about his plans and operations, he may find that excessive hostility is beginning to develop in the form of opposing factions. This is one of the perils of leadership.

The recreationist also faces this peril, often from individuals who seek to gain advantages at the public's expense. For example, polarized factions may arise over the placement of parks or other recreational facilities which are likely to enhance the value of adjoining lands. There is always some pressure placed upon the recreationist by home or property owners when such plans are drawn up. Since the recreationist must consider population density, population movement, and many other factors in order to provide the best possible service to the community, he may have to override the wishes of some property owners so that the greatest membership of the community can benefit.

Another area in which the recreationist may incur organized opposition is in the employment of community members for work in the agency. Unless the recreationist protects himself from various forms of community pressure and establishes an impartial and defensible program for hiring help, he may find himself accused of unfair labor practices by some segment of the community.

Sometimes, just by establishing a particular activity, the recreationist can simultaneously establish a faction that opposes him. For example, there are still communities in the United States where dancing is considered immoral and taboo. In other communities, prevailing religious beliefs dictate that activities may not be carried out on specific days of the week. Whenever the recreationist chooses to disregard such local mores, he takes a risk. In seeking to enlighten the community and perhaps uproot prejudicial attitudes and outmoded beliefs, the recreationist is certain to arouse a determined opposition.

Negative Propaganda

Nothing is as harmful as the lie with a modicum of truth. And no statement is more difficult to combat, for the grain of truth gives the lie substance and makes it believable. A half-truth cannot be immediately disavowed on the basis of its patent absurdity. Across-the-board denial of a statement which is half-true will refute the truthful parts of the statement as well as the false. To issue no denial at all is tantamount to admission. Thus one is faced with making a denial fraught with explanations, which sounds equivocal and is less forceful than the original accusation.

The leader can answer a deliberate half-truth only with the whole truth, phrased with absolute clarity and precision. The only defense in the face of half-truths is complete and valid justification for the plans or action under attack and the rationale on which they are based. There is no better counterthrust to distortion than a well-delivered presentation of actual facts.

The recreationist must fight constantly against prejudice and distorted facts. His best preventive weapon is the maintenance of good public relations between the agency and the people of the community.

The basic objectives of public relations are aiding the agency in gaining and holding public friendship and respect, tailoring all agency practices and policies to coincide with the best possible interests of the community, and reaching every individual within the community with the complete and true story of the agency and its essential and professional functions in the life of the community. Through such measures the recreationist can reverse negative propaganda. Public relations help the recreationist to offer better service by: 1) discovering and listing all groups, or segments of the public, whose opinion is important to the agency; 2) ascertaining the attitude of each of these groups toward any or all phases of the agency's operations; 3) introducing such reasonable adjustments in the agency's policies and procedures as are necessary in order to make a more favorable impression on the public; and 4) explaining and interpreting for the public the policies and practices of the agency and any other feature of its activities which the public misunderstands or in which the public shows interest.

The recreationist employs public relations as part of the communications net by which information may be directed and channeled from the agency to the community and as the system by which the public's wishes are turned into recreational opportunities. The basic objectives of public relations are: 1) to help in every way to gain and hold public friendship and respect; 2) to have all practice and policies coincide with the best possible public interest; and 3) to reach every individual within the community with the complete and true story of the agency and its essential and professional functions in the life of the community. Such measures are necessary to countermand negative propaganda.

ERRORS MADE BY THE LEADER

The Compromise of Principles

The moment of decision is always the great test of a leader's character and ability. The temptation to choose the path of least resistance is often very strong, as is the lure of self-aggrandizement. The cost is compromise. The leader who is truly dedicated will remain true to his principles in the face of all odds.

Although a leader may find it expedient to make concessions to a stand he has taken, he must bear in mind that one concession may lead to further alterations of his plans, and may even undermine his integrity. Concessions cannot be made lightly; each must be examined in the light of principle. The recreationist is well warned against this danger. He must remain alert to avoid subordinating integrity and ethics to expediency. Subversion is best eliminated when open communication and truth (or at least the facts) are established and maintained.

Once the first step is taken against what is in the best public interest, it may become relatively easy to allow oneself to be talked into further concessions until there is nothing left for the public. A poignant reminder is offered by the concessions which have been made to park and wilderness areas. Spaces and lands now in use, or potentially useful, for recreational purposes are rapidly succumbing to developers, road builders, and shortsighted individuals who overlook the inherent value of such areas in favor of monetary rewards.[4]

One of the primary principles of the field of recreational service is conservation of recreational spaces and resources for perpetual use by the public. Recreationists have an obligation to protect wilderness areas, parks, and other open areas from encroachment by vested interests, or even those who seek to construct public edifices. In allowing any part of an open space or park area to be utilized for purposes other than recreational activity, the recreationist may be setting a precedent and, in effect, conceding that such areas may ultimately be used for construction. The first compromise in principle leads to further concessions in fact. After trees and grass have been uprooted and torn away, they can never be replaced. One need only look at urban sprawl to realize that where open and wilderness spaces have not been protected, the ever-widening spread of municipal development invades formerly beautiful places, replacing the flora and fauna with cement.[5] Although recreationists may have to concede some points to realtors and developers, they should never compromise on the basic principle of public-land maintenance.[6]

Arrogance

A leader may slip from the leadership role gradually, becoming a leader in name only or eventually losing his position entirely. The true leader is a person who believes in the dignity of all men; in this respect he may be termed "humble." But unless he is careful, he may allow himself to begin to feel superior to those he leads—this is the

4. J. F. Murphy, J. G. Williams, E. W. Niepoth, and P. D. Brown, *Leisure Service Delivery System: A Modern Perspective* (Philadelphia: Lea & Febiger, 1973), pp. 48–55.
5. J. N. Smith, ed., *Environmental Quality and Social Justice in America* (Washington, D.C.: The Conservation Foundation, 1974).
6. J. S. Shivers, "The Recreationist and the Environment," *World Leisure and Recreation Association Bulletin*, Vol. XIX, No. 2 (March-April 1976), p. 1.

beginning of arrogance. An arrogant person is disinclined to listen to advice, believing himself to be the arbiter of what is best. Arrogance gives the leader an exaggerated sense of his personal worth. When he loses sight of his responsibilities in relation to those who trusted him and gave him the leadership position, he upsets the critical balance between true leadership and dictatorship. He begins to see himself as indispensable, infallible, and omnipotent; his followers as dispensable, weak, and useful only in their capacity to perform his bidding. As the leader develops arrogance, the gap between his own goals and those of his followers widens and he gradually loses influence with them. When people finally realize that they are being used rather than led, they are quick to anger and to take steps to remove the offender.

Arrogance is not a trait the recreationist can afford. He is, in the best sense, a public servant who must keep an open relationship with those whom his agency serves. When his personal relations with his constituents weaken, he will find himself out of a job, as the following case illustrates:

Mr. B was superintendent of recreational service for a Midwestern state's capital city. He had been an appointed official and on the job for more than twenty years. Now that civil service had replaced the old patronage system, Mr. B was secure in his job through tenure. Over the years, Mr. B developed the attitude that he was an authority and in authority. His conduct was such that he considered his position sacrosanct. His relationship with the general public was very poor. He consistently kept people waiting in his outer office, whether he was occupied or not. This attitude gave him a feeling of importance. When anyone did get to see him, he never gave them his direct attention, but continued to sign his name or write during the discussion. He felt that his job was created for his own benefit, and he showed this feeling. He was heard to voice such statements as, "If you do not like what I am doing, have me fired." His "public-be-damned" attitude caused many people who visited his office or spoke to him over the telephone to form a low opinion of him and his department. When a new administration came into power, the recreational agency was taken out of civil service, the super-intendency was abolished as a job title, and B lost his position.

The moral to this story is that courtesy and willingness to serve are excellent traits for the recreationist to cultivate. Arrogance, on the other hand, precludes courtesy and fosters antisocial behavior. Discourtesy and condescension, two attributes of arrogance, can do more to imperil the recreationist's position and undermine his agency than almost any other weakness of character.

Changing Direction

Leaders gain their influence with others because of what they are trying to achieve. Usually it is not simply the person but rather what the person stands for that draws followers. The leader may offer totally new methods of pursuing an objective, but only so long as leader and followers share a common objective will the leader be able to retain the loyalty of his supporters.

The danger of an arbitrary change in goals on the part of the leader is, therefore, readily apparent. At best, followers will be alarmed, and usually they will also be infuriated. In any case, followers will not tolerate a reversal of direction. Even if the changed goal is beneficial to them, they will see the change as a betrayal of their trust. The leader may change his stated aims only as a result of consulting his followers and gaining their approval for the change.

It can be argued that emergency or crisis situations sometimes leave no time for consultation before making an important decision that necessitates retraction from some previously agreed upon stand. Each time the leader changes direction, he must either gain the consent of his followers or, if the situation warrants, convince them of the rightness of his modification after the crisis is past. No group will long tolerate mercurial shifts, either of goals or of temperament. Followers look to the leader for stability. Although the leader may be in a better position than his followers to judge the many factors that determine the advisability of altering goals, followers still want to be apprised of new developments and be assured that they have a voice in the plans and operations of the movement. Thus the leader must maintain close communication with followers on all matters of mutual importance.

Tempo

Going too far, too fast, too soon is also hazardous to those who would lead. Unless the leader takes his followers along with him, explaining and justifying his actions to those who continually need reassurance, and stimulating the understanding of those who fall behind, he will lose their interest and also his influence with them. Being an individual who talks, thinks, and acts faster than some of his followers can put the leader at a disadvantage if he allows himself to assume that everybody has his ability. When a leader is impatient to keep moving toward his objectives, he risks losing the support of the less well-informed members of his group.

The recreationist must be especially aware of the individual variations in intellect, ability, prior experiences in the group process, and any other factors which limit or restrict membership capability to perform. He must regulate the speed with which he pursues goals in order to assure that all group members comprehend his program. If the recreationist disregards the slower members of his group, he will inevitably lose their support. It may appear to them that he is neglecting them in favor of others or attempting to usurp their rights as partakers in the decision-making function. The following example illustrates what can happen when a leader tries to accomplish too much too quickly:

> Mr. R, superindendent of public recreational service in the city of Y, determined that his community needed several new recreational facilities and areas. Upon investigation, he found that several parcels of land would have to be acquired and that a new center and three playgrounds would have to be constructed and developed in order to serve the increased population. R assembled all of his facts and figures and went before the board of estimate with his proposals. He needed more than $2,750,000 to complete his projects. The board rejected his program. R decided to appeal directly to the people of this community. He simply requested that a bond issue be passed in the sum needed to provide additional recreational services to the people of the community. He indicated what the development was to be and left the problem up to the voters. R's program was defeated in the referendum. R could not understand why his proposals had not carried.

Basically, the trouble with R was that he had assumed everybody understood the need for the development aspects of his program. He had felt that this program was self-explanatory and so neglected to inform the voters of what their money was to be spent on and what benefits would accrue from additional land acquisition. He neglected one vital factor which all leaders must take into account if they are to rally support for their objectives, and that is to take the time and make the effort to determine whether or not support is a reality. Followers must be made to understand precisely what the needs are, why the needs must be met, and how they can best be satisfied. There is a definite requirement to interpret facts and figures in such a way that they will be clearly perceived by those whose aid is necessary in gaining an objective.

The following example concerns social movement and what can happen, even to an outstanding personality, when he moves too rapidly for those who follow him:

> G was brought into the growing city of P to reorganize the department of recreational services. He was considered one of the authorities in the field of public recreational service administration

and had been at the top of his professional career when summoned to P at quite a large salary. G's ideas were logical, attractive, and very progressive. Unfortunately, he did not bother to explain his program or the steps he was taking to his board or to the public. He just went ahead, cutting costs here, shifting personnel there, and generally stepping on toes as he did the job for which he had been hired. However, as G worked he began to create an intense antagonism toward his methods. He was too quick to criticize, too fast with his changes. He did his work without any preliminary interpretations, assuming that the public wanted him to perform in the manner to which he was accustomed. At the end of six months, the board called a public meeting in response to demands made by a vociferous and aroused citizenry. The outcome was predictable. Mr. G was discharged and his contract paid in full. The epilogue to this record is that every policy and program which G initiated or had expected to produce was unanimously adopted. G's successor provided the same type of progressive action which G had, but also initiated a public relations procedure coordinated with his activities.

Once again, it is plain that only when the public is informed as to what the leader expects to do and how he plans to do it will they lend their support. Keeping communications open between the group and leader is vital to the influence which the leader holds. He can go no faster than the slowest member of his group in order to achieve objectives satisfactory for all.

Strength and Consistency

A leader must seem strong and unwavering in the face of crisis. Regardless of the problems or the odds which confront him, he can show no outward signs of fear or disillusionment. If he loses his composure when threatened with reversals, he will lose the confidence and support of his followers. He must have the fortitude to assume the final responsibility for whatever results from his actions: victory or defeat. Excuses for failure and attempts to shift blame immediately expose him as weak and unfit to lead.

A leader must never give the impression of defeat. No matter how discouraged he feels or how hopeless he knows his cause to be, he must appear outwardly assured of success. Only if he remains calm, resolute, and completely in control of himself will he inspire his followers' loyalty and buttress their courage. It is a rare individual who can hold up under the hammer-like blows of despair, defeat, and demoralization. The greatest hazard to the leader is not the feelings themselves but their outward manifestations. If he seems to show signs of fatigue, disappointment, or strain, he places his influence with others in jeopardy. He must always maintain the detached look of one who is secure in the knowledge that his objectives will eventually be reached.

The recreationist also must play this confident role. He must often deal with antagonism and hostility directed at his agency, policy, or plans. Sometimes defeat seems certain as he confronts an apathetic public or a powerful branch of government that attempts to usurp his prerogatives or countermand his specialities. In order to maintain his position and fulfill his responsibility as a community leader, he cannot show fear of failure. The recreationist is often confronted with situations where he must prove himself. No matter how many times he has shown himself adequate to meet emergencies, the very nature of his job forces him continually to validate his ability. When working with small groups, for example, he must remain objective at all times. By soothing frustrations, helping members in overcoming deep-rooted fears, negating prejudices, and meeting problems in order to maintain group morale and group cohesiveness, he assures the group that they can count on him. He may condemn a particular action and praise another, but it is the consistency of his attitude toward group members which provides support for the group. He is solid, dependable, never panicky. This is the strength which helps group members to stabilize their own conduct and patterns of behavior.

The recreationist as a professional worker is no less a leader among his own peers, and while fellow workers may have a somewhat greater tolerance for debilitation as the results of undue strain or hardship, they nevertheless expect dependability, consistency, and optimistic pursuit of goals from their colleagues. Thus, manifestations of depression, defeat, or default by a leader, even among his own peer group, will undermine his position and result in loss of influence.

An example of this may be seen in the following record taken from the Y department of recreational service:

Mr. T, one of the more popular recreationists in the department, was approached by a group of teenage boys who wanted his help in building a supervised "drag-strip" where they could tune up, race, and work on their homemade cars. The boys were very enthusiastic about the possibility of having their own place for auto meets. Up to that time they had been using the main streets in the community as racing courses and had been warned by the police that further use would be met with swift punishment. Now they turned to the one person who they felt sure could aid them. Mr. T talked the situation over with the group and initiated a club which met every week to plan the drag-strip and the activities which were to be held on it.

Membership in the club grew, and there was much excitement concerning this activity. Mr. T began to check with his superiors about the possibility of organizing the type of activity which the boys wanted. He was told that the city council and the police department would probably have to be consulted for final authority. When a month had gone by without further action on the matter, Mr. T renewed his request. His supervisor indicated that the probability of constructing a drag-strip was practically nil. Mr. T continued his efforts, but soon realized the futility of the proposal. At the next meeting with the boys he bluntly told them that there was no hope of realizing their objective. He said that they would only be frustrated if they continued to plan for the drag-strip. There was never a next meeting.

Mr. T's failure may be attributed to lack of foresight on the part of both his superiors and the community, but much of it may be placed at his own door. By reacting to failure in such a negative way, he completely demolished any hope that the membership of his group may have had. Had he been more discreet, and perhaps a little more optimistic, he might very well have kept the club together. He was prone to accept the verdict of defeat without continuing the fight. He could have enlisted the aid of parents; perhaps he could have discussed the situation with others in the community in an endeavor to gain support for his project. Instead, he accepted a negative decision and dropped the entire matter. His feelings about the problem were very evident to the boys. They could see that he was disappointed and frustrated. They must also have realized that he was ready to give up. They could not depend upon him to carry on. Hence the entire membership broke apart, and T lost any semblance of the influence which he may have had with them. The principle is that no person who wants to retain a leadership position can afford to concede that all is lost. Once followers are made aware of the leader's pessimistic outlook, they will desert him. The leader may not win all of the time, but he must always appear to be sure of winning eventually.

Leadership may fail or become inoperative when it should have been efficient and gaining power. This lack of success may be explained by certain deficiencies within would-be leaders. For want of some humanity, confidence, or other necessity, the leader places himself at risk and thereby fails. Discontinuities within the leadership process, undue hazards which accrue because of the leader's ineptness, growing challenges to leadership, rejection on the part of the follower, and other factors must be examined to understand how compounded errors can imperil leadership.

The leader is a risk-taker, and must realize that he may fail. Still, he has to assume certain risks. There may be setbacks, but the leader may find it worthwhile if losses are not too severe and he can show some success in the end. Risks which succeed help to build confidence in the leader; those which fail tend to weaken the leader's influence. Followers will accord status to the leader only if he is right in his judgments most of the time.

The leader must be able to create an atmosphere which is conducive to his goals. Unless he can construct an environment in which his ideas are accepted he will inevitably fail and thus lose influence. Without the proper climate, leadership cannot occur. It is up to the leader to produce a situation which favors his goals, or he faces the hazard of ineffectiveness and subsequent loss of influence and followership.

QUESTIONS FOR DISCUSSION

1. Why is the leader a target?
2. How can a leader develop an environment favorable for his leadership?
3. Differentiate between the calculated risks of leadership and gambling.
4. How does the status quo stifle leadership attempts?
5. Why must leaders continually challenge ideas which have gained general acceptance?
6. The leader makes enemies while making friends. What is the meaning of this statement?
7. The leader can never act unethically to achieve objectives. Discuss the implications of this statement.
8. Why is "grass roots" opinion necessary to the maintenance of a leadership position?
9. The leader must move no faster than his followers in the direction of goals. Why?
10. What significance does self-confidence have when dealing with hostile forces?

BIBLIOGRAPHY

Adair, John, *The Skills of Leadership* (New York: Nichols Publishing Co., 1984).

Adams, Jerome, and Janice D. Yoder, *Effective Leadership for Women and Men* (Norwood, N.J.: Ablex Publishing Corp., 1984).

Betz, Donald, *Cultivating Leadership: An Approach* (Lanham, Md.: University Press of America, 1981).

Bothwell, Lin K., *The Art of Leadership: Skill-Building Techniques that Produce Results* (Englewood Cliffs, N.J.: Prentice-Hall, 1983).

Barker, Cyril J., and Gary H. Strauss, *Leadership: The Dynamics of Success* (Greenwood, S.C.: Attic Press, 1982).

Grieg, Donald, *Leadership in Crisis* (Ventura, Cal.: Regal Books, 1981).

Fiedler, Fred E., *Leader Attitudes and Group Effectiveness* (New York: John Wiley & Sons, 1981).

Fiedler, Fred E., and Martin M. Chemers, *Improving Leadership Effectiveness: The Leader Match Concept,* 2nd ed. (New York: John Wiley & Sons, 1984).

Goodwin, Bonnie E., *The Effective Leader* (Downers Grove, Ill.: Inter-Varsity Press, 1981).

Harrison, Buddy, *Understanding Authority for Effective Leadership* (Tulsa, Okla.: Harrison House, Inc., 1982).

Hunt, James G., *Leadership: Beyond Establishment Views* (Carbondale, Ill.: Southern Illinois University Press, 1981).

Kokopeli, Bruce, and George Lakey, *Leadership for Change* (Philadelphia: New Society Pubs., 1984).

CHAPTER FIFTEEN

Leadership Mythologies

People believe what they want to believe. Despite logical presentations, scientifically validated facts, and the evidence of their own senses, people tend to deny anything which does not square with either preconceived notions or the myths which they have come to depend upon. Some individuals would rather accept the distortions which their imagination and/or fears have created, rather than acknowledge the futility and speciousness of the stereotypes and basic misconceptions to which they cling.

The great man or hero concept of leadership theorizes that events of surpassing significance in national and world affairs are dominated by the men who possess leadership positions, "and that all factors in history, save great men, are inconsequential."[1] A spontaneous deed by a great leader could change the course of history or affect a nation's destiny.[2] According to this myth, leaders have personality characteristics that enable them to overcome what would be insurmountable obstacles to anyone else. Consistent with this concept, it is also suggested that if an individual has some of the traits necessary for successful leadership, he will undoubtedly have all of them. Although this fallacy is widely accepted, the idea of the existence of a single status ordering of people in regard to leadership has been empirically rejected.[3]

1. S. Hook, *The Hero in History* (Boston: Beacon Press, 1955), p. 14.
2. B. W. Tuckman, *The March of Folly From Troy to Viet Nam* (New York: Alfred A. Knopf, Inc., 1984), pp. 8–11.
3. B. E. Collins, *Social Psychology* (Reading, Mass.: Addison-Wesley, 1970).

ILLUSIONS OF LEADERSHIP

Leadership is composed of many ingredients and varied functions. In particular groups and missions, some functions will be more important than others. Since different functions can be emphasized in different groups, and because a certain personality may be in accord with one function and not another, it is quite spurious to predict that personality will always agree with leadership in practice.

Some areas of confusion in understanding leadership include the failure to define it as a process and different from the personality of the leader who tends to be the central figure in the process. Leadership is really an influence relationship between two or more persons who are interdependently associated for their mutual benefit in achieving certain goals within a group situation. The situation in question concerns a number of factors and includes group size, task, membership abilities, and structure, among other variables.

The relationship between leader and led is developed over time, and is concerned with events between leader and followers in which the leader provides some means whereby the group membership can satisfy its needs, and the group reciprocates by providing the leader with greater influence in the group.[4] The leader's status is enhanced and this affords added legitimacy to his appeal for influence and its acceptance. Naturally, there are various functions associated with being a leader. While the typical idea of the leader is one who organizes the group for subsequent action, the leader is also expected to perform as the intra-group problem solver, and as the extra-group spokesman. Very often it is the leader who establishes objectives, determines priorities, and decides upon the alternatives.

The personality characteristics appropriate for leadership are actually determined by the perceptions held by followers. How a potential follower looks upon a would-be leader is more important, in terms of specific role expectations and satisfactions, than the pattern of traits the individual displays under examination.[5]

Research on personality traits among leaders shows enormous diversity, probably predicated on the diversity of expectations of the leader's performance. There are contrasting leadership roles. It should be recognized that the leader in distinct situations may be concerned with task accomplishment, problem-solving, providing socio-

---

4.   H. H. Blumberg and others, *Small Groups and Social Interaction* (New York: John Wiley & Sons, 1983), pp. 216–220.

5.   J. McV. Hunt, "Traditional Personality Theory in the Light of Recent Evidence," *American Scientist,* Vol. 53 (1965), pp. 80–96.

economic support, making decisions, or acting as group spokesman. Personal characteristics of a leader, including intelligence, are more apparent and more relevant to group accomplishment under circumstances of engagement by the leader than in a rigidly institutionalized role structure.

Illusions about a leader's inherent goodness, incorruptibility, rightness of action and direction, strength and steadfastness give rise to the most frequent misconceptions of leadership. Often followers are in for a rude awakening once the leader attains the eminence he seeks. History is full of instances in which people have supported a leader, raising him to power on the basis of such illusions, only to be disappointed and shocked at the outcome. On the surface, the disillusionment is directed at the leader, but it is really the process of leadership that is misunderstood. By attributing impossible qualities to the leader, people escape from the need to think and act independently because it is so much easier to appoint someone to think and act for them. To refuse responsibility is to invite dictatorship. Dictatorship, as we have seen, is the antithesis of leadership.

LEADERSHIP EFFECTIVENESS

This entire interpersonal system is related to resolving questions about the leader's effectiveness. The leader is able to perform not only because he has influence with others, but because of the disparate processes in operation and the objectives to be gained. It is of greater significance to identify purposes, to structure a program specifically adapted to achieving the purpose, and to carry out operations for group satisfaction than it is to marshal personal support and maintain group stability through the customary process of solving routine problems. Any group operates with some resources at its disposal which it can use to produce particular results. Within this system, an exchange of resources for results takes place. These transactions are facilitated by leadership functions which, among other tasks, guide the operation. The leader's input and its consequences vary with system needs and his characteristic competencies. Isolated, the usual view of leadership as one person controlling others can be misconstrued. Although the leader provides a needed resource, the group's resources are not possessed only by the leader. It is the combined effort of leader and group which provides the basis for functions accomplished in the successful achievement of group aims.

The group must work within the constraints of its available resources and its effectiveness is measured in several ways. There is group performance, cohesion, and membership satisfaction with results of a leadership process employing the group's resources. Viewed in this way, the leader is seen as contributing his own resources so that other resources are able to operate. The leader functions so as to provide the program with his capabilities to the extent that his characteristics prove valuable under the conditions facing the group. In other words, there is a need for heightened recognition of the system portrayed by the group and its program. This recognition may be the way to offset the erroneous division of the leader and the situation which is still maintained. By utilizing a systems approach, the leader, the followers, and the situation identified generally, are envisioned as mutually dependent resources occupied in the production of satisfying consequences.

Some relaxation from the severely structured, positional view of leadership is required if its processes are to be clearly understood. Emphasis on leadership maintenance has been disproportionate and therefore has militated against a more exacting analysis of emerging leadership. Researchers will have to be made more cognizant of the possibilities and the varied meanings between emerging and continuing leadership. It is this concern—the importance of leadership legitimacy, its origins, and effects—which holds promise for anticipated studies.

In examining leader effectiveness, greater stress should be ordered on the consequences for the complete system, including the satisfaction of expectations by followers. The outdated and overweighted involvement with results, frequently expressed solely in terms of the leader's influence, must give way to a more enlightened understanding of relationships directed to reciprocal objectives. Related to this, the followers' perception of the leader, as well as their identification with him, requires investigation.[6] In this manner, several approaches may be made which comprehend the style factors involved which permit certain individuals to become effective leaders.

Among the many misconceptions of the leadership phenomenon, most are concerned with the leader, but others relate to the over-all process which is called leadership. The illusions seen in the leader, from his origin and rise to position until he stabilizes and consolidates his influence, are those of moral sanction, of inherent goodness, correctness, or rightness of action and direction, and of other aspects which have always been held to be true about the leader or leadership. The awakening arrives once the leader of a popular movement attains

---

6. R. C. Tucker, *Politics as Leadership* (Columbia, Mo.: University of Missouri Press, 1981), pp. 24–25.

the eminence which he seeks. With the delegation of responsibility comes the delegation of authority. Once authority has been delegated, there need be no thought at all, merely conformity, submission, and the abdication of all responsibility. If morally reprehensible actions are perpetrated, the followers can always blame the leader or hide behind the rationalizaation that "I was only following orders."

Perhaps the greatest myth involving leaders is one that assumes an individual is a leader because he holds a title. This fallacy has embraced figureheads, appearance, speech, skill, and position. Despite earnest attempts to disavow these erroneous ideas, they persist and refuse to die. In much the same way, another unfounded belief has been perpetuated. In our society it is said that sports build character. Although the idea is attractive and individuals never tire of repeating it, it has no justifiable basis. Investigation has finally proved the fallacy of this point of view.[7] Nevertheless, sports enthusiasts maintain this fiction.[8] Similarly, the fallacies of leadership are also long-lived.

Nomenclature

In all leadership contexts, misuse or misunderstanding of terminology is more common than not. Indiscriminate use of the word "leader" has caused confusion about both standards and concepts of leadership. The term is applied so generally that anybody, regardless of ability, can be called a leader.

For example, the term "leader" is often merely a bestowed title. Although this practice is common in many professional fields, it is particularly so in recreational service. All too many recreationists are hired to the *position* of leader, regardless of leadership ability, personal qualities, or understanding of human relations. They have been hired for some technical competency or program skill and for nothing else. It is even conceivable that if the employing agency had known beforehand that they were actually leaders, it would not have employed them. The common practice of giving titles to positions, rather than to the people occupying these positions, does much to maintain popular misconceptions about the process of leadership. The designation of leader should be reserved for those who have influence with others.

Leaders are an infectious breed with strong motivations and convictions and a propensity for testing axioms and upsetting status

---

7. B. C. Ogilvie and T. A. Tutko, "Sport: If You Want to Build Character, Try Something Else," *Psychology Today* (October, 1971), pp. 61-63.

8. C. E. Thomas, *Sport in a Philosophic Context* (Philadelphia: Lea & Febiger, 1983), pp. 191-197.

quo. Even when the hiring authority really needs applicants with leadership qualities and abilities, sometimes little thought is given to the applicant's character, personality, or preparation for a leader's position. Too often, skill in an activity, prior experience within a position, and perhaps specific preparation are the determinants. Leadership, and the techniques this term implies, is assumed to be a part of the individual's nature which the job will cause to flourish.

Instructional Skill

Many of the personnel within recreational service agencies are employed not on the basis of personality, professional preparation, or even knowledge of the field, but on the basis of their skills in various specializations. Thus, leadership has often been confused with program and instructional skills. Having specialized skills is an important part of the recreationist's background, but his preparation does not stop there. Above and beyond program skills are those attributes which are necessary for working and dealing with people.

Leaders approach any task and any group with the knowledge that all human beings are different and that these differences will show up in a variety of ways. On the basis of this realization, a leader will set about developing an influential relationship with the group. An instructor, on the other hand, will usually approach a group with the single idea of instructing them in achieving a particular short-range goal. It is fortunate to have an instructor who is also a leader, but it is not common.

Many who should know better are convinced that a recreationist can develop leadership only as a result of teaching an activity. For these people, it is inconceivable that there could be a leadership process beyond an instructional role. They believe that organizational hierarchy precludes any form of leadership that does not rely on headship.

Headship versus Leadership

We have previously discussed the difference between leadership and headship, but it may be worthwhile to reiterate some points in this context. Headship refers to the assignment of specific functions and responsibilities in an organizational hierarchy. In such a system, it is the position rather than the person holding the position that gains respect and therefore obedience. Leadership, on the other hand, is a process in which the leader gains respect and influence and thus attains the position.

Headship and leadership may appear to coincide in some instances, but although they may not be precisely dichotomous, some characteristics of each are at opposite extremes. Headship usually implies a position within an established system which is designed to maintain the system rather than to allow natural or indigenous changes to come about. The person in the headship position is not voluntarily placed in office by a following of those whom he has influenced, but by the organization itself. Conversely, the leader is accorded his position through influence with others who have chosen to follow his direction. Thus, the essential difference between leadership and headship lies in the origin of the central figure's power.

In the field of recreational service, the distinction between headship and leadership is especially important because so many agencies and organizations exhibit a hierarchical structure. When headship positions are allowed to be filled by people who are not truly leaders, the functioning of the leadership process goes awry. For example, an appointed leader concerned primarily with task accomplishment puts pressure on subordinates to conform to the existing system and to replace their own goals with those of the system. In view of the way most agencies are structured, recreationists must be on their guard to avoid submitting to such pressure.

Façade

Many people still believe that a person's appearance is an indication of how successful that person will be. Another of the myths of leadership is that a person must look the part if he is to be an effective leader. For example, the stereotypical leader is taller, heavier, and more intelligent than others; he also has a full head of hair, dresses well, looks distinguished, and generally presents the impression of immense power. In fact, leaders come in all sizes and shapes, have varying amounts of hair, dress as they see fit, and convey whatever impression their followers find worthy of adulation. An example of such a person from U.S. history is President Warren G. Harding. Elected because he looked like a man who should be president of the United States, Harding was in truth a man of mediocre abilities who was easily manipulated by self-seeking persons.

Reputation, closely allied to appearance, is often equated with leadership. An individual who has a good reputation as a problem solver, trouble-shooter, or mediator will be called upon frequently to exercise his skills. Each successful outcome enhances his reputation. The difficulty in relying on reputation as an accurate gauge of skill is that it is hard to determine on what basis the reputation has been built. Empty phrases and jargon falsely convince many followers. In such a manner an undeserved reputation for success will be reinforced. On occasion, the individual in a leadership position values his reputation so much that he indulges in unleaderlike behavior in an attempt to preserve it, shifting responsibility for his own failure to others with whom he works. Such face-saving is a time-honored response to failure, but it is not the response of a leader. Once again, appearances can be deceiving, and mere reputation does not necessarily denote a leader.[9]

Conformity

When an individual is confronted with a discomforting decision, conformity assures self-preservation and answers social pressure. In any organization's conference situation where a supervisor is present, unless rapport is established there can be a suspicion of the supervisor. This restrains worker spontaneity and retards progress. Rapport permits the loosening of tension so that professionals sincerely dedicated to the solution of problems affecting the agency and its personnel can make contributory efforts. Participating workers may be more afraid of losing their positions than in taking the risk of rejecting or objecting to supervisory statements. When workers sense that a supervisor is against a proposal or has an idea which he wants to push, they will often tend to turn away from the supervisor's disapproved course of action and favor those plans which are considered correct by the superior. Face-saving and job-saving pressures make for conformity. As each succeeding worker falls into line, other workers who may have wavered will also fall into line because they do not want to appear ridiculous in the eyes of their peers, nor do they want to be the person to go on record against the suggestions or orders of the supervisor. As individuals conform, tremendous pressure is built up for complete unanimity within the group.

There have been several experiments conducted to prove this conformity tendency in human behavior. Perhaps the best known is the experiment operated by Asch.[10] In this program, a series of conditions were set up in order to determine individual freedom from pressures for unanimity of thought. In a number of cases, it was shown that even when individuals had the evidence of their senses to indicate one set of facts, they could be pressured into changing their

9.   L. Lowenthal and N. Guterman, *Prophets of Deceit—A Study of the Techniques of the American Agitator* (Palo Alto, Cal.: Pacific Books, Pub., 1970).
10.   S. E. Asch, "Effects of Group Pressure upon the Modification and Distortion of Judgments," in H. Guetzkow, ed., *Groups, Leadership and Men* (Pittsburgh, Penn.: Carnegie Press, 1951), pp. 177–190.

statement of what they had seen or would simply go along with group opinion. Another current experiment confirms the outcome of group pressures for conformity.[11] How much easier could it be, then, to change ideas, opinions, or modes of behavior which are based upon mere ethereal judgments rather than on the concrete foundation of sensory perceptions?

When a figurehead is substituted for a leader, the individual wears the cloak of power and occupies a position of leadership but in reality he is nothing but a sham. Usually such an individual has come to his sinecure through the good offices of another person who is in a position to grant him this easement. To the world, the figurehead is the epitome of leadership; he even looks the part.

When the figurehead occupies a place in the field of recreational service, the effects are caustic, damaging, and cumulatively pitiful. Invariably, the figurehead represents some concentration of power within the agency because of *who* rather than *what* he knows. His professional preparation may be nil, but he holds his job by virtue of his affability and complete readiness to do the bidding of those who placed him in office.[12] The figurehead will never dare to question principles, policies, or actions. In recent years, some of the political placements in the executive offices of great American cities have produced mediocre programs, poor morals, and questionable recreational service practices. The figurehead cannot lead—not because he does not have the necessary experience to do so, but because he does not dare. A leader dares to test standards and axioms. A leader cannot be made to jump through hoops or follow blindly. The figurehead only looks the part of the leader; all else is empty jest.

Loss of Direction

Through the position of authority held by the individual, he is free to demand certain performances from subordinates, who must comply, even when such demands reach ridiculous proportions, if they want to retain their positions within the organization. The figurehead is neither qualified nor competent to carry out the responsibilities which rest with his position.

Perhaps the most malicious effect of the figurehead within a recreational agency stems from issuing directives which are unprincipled, unethical, or not appropriate for the situation or

---

11.   Diane Mackie and Joel Cooper, "Attitude Polarization: Effects of Group Membership," *Journal of Personality and Social Psychology*, Vol. 46, No. 3 (1984), pp. 575–585.
12.   Nigel Hamilton, *Master of the Battlefield* (New York: McGraw-Hill Book Company, 1983), pp. 468–474, 556–557, 608–609.

condition. More damaging are those directives, apparently of little significance and without any explanation, to those who are expected to administer activities under the aegis of these directives. Incongruities, duplication, lack of coordination, and tensions and frictions are thus produced within the agency. Policy-changing directives should be explained to those whom they will affect.

The unexplained directive leaves the recipient with a sense of loss. He has to carry out an assignment without proper guidance or direction. Perhaps it concerns the initiation of a new activity, the discontinuation of an old one, or the enactment of specific procedures which disrupt an organizational pattern. Whatever the outcome of such actions, there will surely be some disorder and perhaps a little more unwillingness on the part of program personnel to support the agency. The cancer of poor morale slowly eats into the personnel of the agency when they are in doubt about the plans of administrators. Lack of coordination and cooperation, along with the resigned worker who "just puts in a day's work," are the consequences of announcing directives without providing sufficient information about the whys and wherefores concerning their necessity. The figurehead is unable or unwilling to understand what must be done to prevent the loss of departmental morale and spirit.

The figurehead often practices in such a way as to present a front of sublime confidence in the face of almost total ignorance. The manner in which policy practices are modified indicates that a person who considers himself infallible guides the destiny of the agency. His dictates carry the weight of law and implied threat. He rejoices in the knowledge that he has undisputed sway over subordinates within the agency and fears no dismissal. He has tenure and/or an "in" with those who fill positions for the agency.

The Opinionated Personality

The figurehead in his complete unpreparedness for his job maintains that his is the only opinion which has any significance. He practices a "closed mind" form of staff meeting in which the only statements which count are his own. It is only a matter of time before his statements and opinions are the sole basis for staff meetings.[13] No one else offers any ideas, for they know that they will be rejected and perhaps criticized or held up to ridicule. What an unhappy circumstance for personnel who are employed in these situations! Why do

---

13.   M. F. R. Kets de Vries, *Organizational Paradoxes* (London: Tavistock Publications, 1980), pp. 88–110.

they remain in these positions? The answer is that those who want to achieve within their field usually withdraw from the agency and attempt to locate in situations where democratic tendencies are encouraged. This generally accounts for the high volume of personnel turnover in some agencies, whereas in others, longevity and cooperation are the norms rather than the rarities.

No one is so all-powerful or so well organized that he has every answer to all problems which arise in this field. No one is indispensable; all human beings exhibit some imperfections on occasion; no one individual is infallible. It is necessary to seek out many possibilities and alternatives before setting out on a particular course of action. Unless time is taken to study the many aspects of a problem, there is great likelihood that failure will ensue. Inflexible opinions develop from an overblown ego. Such a bias usually leads an individual to self-destruction, following a series of conspicuous failures which finally arouse even the dullest and most cynical administrator to the obvious ineptitude of the individual whom he sponsored.

Indecisiveness versus Leadership

An individual who lacks confidence in his ability to produce competent work is a liability when he holds a leadership position. Perhaps the lack of assurance manifests itself only when pressures of the job demand some urgent decision, but that is precisely the situation that most demands aggressive action on the part of the leader.

The following example shows how leadership is absent when the "leader" is insecure:

A Midwestern hospital employed a staff to operate the recreational program. The director of that program had been brought into the agency by the head of the special services division. Although the director had absolutely no professional preparation, the employing authority overlooked this fact because the special services chief specifically requested this individual.

The director had little or no understanding of the meaning of recreational activities and relied upon completely passive entertainments as a mainstay of his program. As a personality, the director was innocuous, although his practice was to be as negative as possible whenever staff physicians asked that he perform some of the services for which he was employed. However, he had occupied his position for the necessary length of time to secure tenure, and he was further protected by his immediate superior. He never wanted to appear wrong and he was inordinately afraid of committing some outlandish error through ignorance, so he did as little as humanly possible. His first concern was that his record should not have any marks against it.

His operating principle was, "If you do not do anything, you never get into trouble," or "I would rather take one step backward than stick my neck out and take two steps forward."

Such an attitude is antithetical to all the principles of leadership. To consider such individuals as recreationists, much less leaders, is not only an insult to professionals but a disgrace which the entire field must bear. Other professional fields have weathered the storms of quackery, malfeasance, and immorality. Other professions have protected themselves from incompetence by requiring licensing in order to practice. If licensing were required for recreational service, the illusion that a clean record is an indication of leadership would be dispelled.

Rationalization versus Leadership

An administrator who continually justifies his errors and poor judgment by making excuses, damning bad luck, or blaming adverse circumstances and inability of subordinates is rationalizing his own incompetence. The individual who knows that he is at fault, mistaken, or completely wrong in an action or idea admits the facts and tries to correct his errors, or else he rationalizes. Rationalization is a way of subordinating truth through self-deceit; the motivation is usually false pride. In order to preserve his image as a leader, such a person indulges in unleaderlike behavior. Take the example of Mr. W, administrator of a recreational service agency in one of the large municipalities in the Southeast:

As superintendent of public recreational service in the city of X, Mr. W had a reputation to maintain. He felt that a man in his position should command the respect of all. To his subordinates and also to community members, Mr. W appeared to be easygoing, chivalrous, courteous, and kind. He considered himself to be politic and diplomatic. In reality, he was weak, incompetent, vain, and ruthless in his insecurity. He was egotistical in the extreme. One might say that he was narcissistic. Mr. W had been interviewed on agency policy regarding the utilization of public facilities by private groups. The newspaper carried reports of the interview which stated that any private group could use any facility of the recreational agency at any time if proper payment was made to the department. The board of recreational service had laid down strict policy for facility use, and the statement contradicted the policy. Private funds could not be used to lease, rent, or otherwise provide space for other than departmental functions. Several telephone calls to the recreational agency apprised Mr. W of the situation, and he immediately called the newspaper in order to get retraction on the basis of a misquotation. The editor called in his reporter, and the latter indicated that his story was precisely what Mr. W had stated to him in the interview. The editor thereupon called Mr. W to inform him that the paper would stand behind the printed story unless Mr. W would admit his own mistake in giving out the statement. Mr. W refused because he said that he had not meant to be taken in such a literal manner and that he had been misunderstood. He also indicated that he would bring pressure to bear by going to the publisher of the newpaper, who was a personal friend. The result of Mr. W's error produced a very poor opinion of him in the press of the community. All this resulted in his eventual resignation from his post.

Because Mr. W was so concerned with maintaining his public image which, through his own error, he had endangered, he tried to cover up rather than own up to his poor judgment. In attempting to rationalize his behavior, he finally brought himself down.

A leader faces reality rather than escaping from it. No leader can ever afford the luxury of rationalization. People occupying leadership positions who rationalize their activities further the myths and misconceptions regarding leadership prowess.

The Superficial Harmonizer

It is from the office of the chief executive in any recreational agency that the psychological atmosphere issues. If the administrator wants a highly spirited, productive organization, he must set the tone which filters down through every level within the agency. The administrator has it within his power to build or destroy morale. Whatever attitude he adopts will be the one which permeates the entire system.

Ironically, the administrator who above all desires an agency which has the outward appearance of a happy family may merely be opening the way for serious discord. It is fallacious to equate agreement with leadership. To put peace foremost, the administrator may pay a high price. Conflicts which cannot be aired may create seething dissatisfaction and even passionate hatreds. Tolerance of incompetence, unethical or bigoted acts, concessions to vested interests, and entrenched mediocrity do not permit the organization to function in the best interests of those it serves.

The don't-rock-the-boat administrator who requires mere surface harmony will often find it all too easy to achieve. Unprincipled individuals or persons who are pursuing personal goals antithetical to those of the agency are quick to seize every opportunity to contribute to maintaining surface harmony because by doing so they can best further their own goals. An administrator who is interested only in the appearance of accord is incompetent; he is not a leader. Under his inadequate guidance, dedicated professionals will be frustrated and the productivity and effectiveness of the agency's programs will be decreased.

Harmony is not undesirable, of course, but there are valid ways to achieve it. With a little more foresight and a little less self-indulgence, the initiator of agency philosophy can do much for the morale of agency personnel and at the same time promote effective service. This is the harder road to follow. It is always easier to tolerate existing conditions, no matter how mediocre. Below is a description of an agency with such a problem:

A federally operated agency employed as recreational director an individual whose sole qualification for the job was his friendship with the employing authority. This individual was a busy-worker, a general term referring to an employee who looks busy but actually accomplishes nothing because he does not work. (Such creatures are found wherever administrators overlook unqualified performance and stagnant programs. They generally inhabit technical and specialized professional fields where the need for personnel greatly exceeds the supply.) During some six months of agency operation, this person did not perform his functions or engage in any of the tasks which were part of his routine assignment and responsibilities. It is true that he always looked busy. There were always papers on his desk; he periodically shuffled them, particularly when anybody happened to pass his office door. He invariably could be found in the snack bar or raising or lowering his venetian blind. But he did not work. All of this was known to the administrator, who did nothing about the situation. That individual still maintains his position as recreational director in the agency.

Which is better: to fight against intolerable personnel situations or to hide from the obvious decisions which must be made? It is easier to tolerate incompetence than to demand a high degree of competence from the incompetent. Typical of the administrator's rationalizations for adopting the easier position is the following: "I know his work is poor, but suppose I discharge him and obtain someone worse?" One person's substandard work is much the same as another's. Better than foisting off a completely substandard program on agency constituents would be leaving the position vacant. Not only would the agency, the field as a whole, and the public benefit, but greater harmony would surely result.

Below we have an example of how a don't-rock-the-boat administrator stifles leadership and betrays the principles for which recreational service stands. The example is taken from the records of a private hospital for cancer in one of the midwestern states:

> The recreational director had employed a new supervisor whose job assignment included the oncology (cancer) wards of the hospital. As is usual on wards where the patients are simply waiting to die of the disease which cannot be arrested, the morale was quite poor. Realizing this fact, the recreationist attempted several activities which could possibly improve morale as well as promote closer cooperation between the recreational section and medical staff. Within six months from the date of initial employment, the professional was discharged on trumped-up charges by the director who saw the worker as a threat to his job. The threat was real, because the worker possessed the professional education and experience which allowed him to perform competently and confidently. Any comparison which might have been drawn between the two would have detracted from the director.

Such self-indulgence on the part of an administrator discredits the entire field.

Infallibility

One popular misconception about an individual who is accorded leadership status is that he is infallible. People tend to assume that a leader makes only correct decisions, that his choice of methods for reaching goals reflects his good judgment, that he always knows what he wants, and that his objectives are beneficial and noble. No human is *always* right, good, accurate, and successful. Human fallibility invariably produces conflicts, questions, and unresolved situations which are detrimental to the individuals involved. Why, then, should the leader be thought to possess some mystical power which enables him to discern and achieve necessary ends? Leaders only appear to know what is right and to lead in the right direction because the group replaces those individuals who cannot successfully meet group needs. "Evaluation of leadership goes on without interruption over a time continuum; a leader is on permanent probation with his members."[14] If the leader were always right, or good, or true, such evaluation would be superfluous and leader retention would be automatic.

---

14.   E. T. Reeves, *The Dynamics of Group Behavior* (New York: American Management Association, Inc., 1970), p. 131.

Patronage Positions

Although there are patronage systems founded upon sound principles of public administration and personnel management which put so-called merit systems in the shade, we are concerned here with the more usual negative connotation of the term "patronage." The practice of assigning patronage positions—appointing close friends or relatives to posts for which they are not qualified or for which they lack specialized knowledge—has application to any study of leadership.

In the field of recreational service, political patronage often brings an unqualified person into a leadership position. Such an appointee quickly finds out that he must hire someone who can really operate the agency and conduct daily operations of the recreational program for which the appointee is nominally responsible. When the person in the patronage position is smart enough to realize that he is incompetent, the operation of the agency can be most efficient. By employing an individual who is qualified and competent, the appointee can ensure that the program is conducted properly. Only the taxpayer is cheated because he is supporting a drone. When the political appointee is unaware of his own shortcomings, everybody gets cheated.

The following case concerning Mr. G, former administrator of a large midwestern recreational agency, gives ample support to the above assertion:

Mr. G was superintendent of parks and recreational services in X municipality, a city of 100,000. He had been designated chief executive of the local recreational department as a result of long and faithful service to his political party. The mayor nominated him for turning out the vote on his behalf. Mr. G was a typical party hack. There was no mistaking his political affiliations. His every move was designed to win approval of those who had placed him in power. He considered it his primary responsibility to place his party's name before the public as underwriting the entire public recreational program. Perhaps this was his ultimate undoing.

Unfortunately for the people of X city, Mr. G knew little or nothing about the administrative procedures or techniques involved in the operation and management of a major recreational system. However, this lack of knowledge did not hinder his effort at all. He quickly filled key positions within the agency with local heroes who owed allegiance to him and knew as little as he about their functions. These individuals were former high school football players who had achieved nothing further, former college players who had not made the professional ranks, or would-be fight promoters. Mr. G's concept of recreational service was the promotion of team sport for youngsters. His favorite slogan was, "Sports will keep children off the streets and out of trouble." Leagues were organized, and football, baseball, and basketball contests were held frequently. This was the sum of the entire program.

After six months of constant team competition, even the participants were getting a little tired of the same old routine. The outstanding athletes of the community were having a fine time, but the rest of the population began to grow restive. Complaints started to come in to the city hall. Parents wanted activities in which they too could participate with their children. Parents asked where their daughters could find recreational experiences. There was some concern expressed by educators and physicians about the physical and mental anguish that competitors on league teams were experiencing. The ministerial association stepped into the picture when one team accused a second team of cheating, claiming the officials had not asked for penalties. It was later brought out that the officials were unfamiliar with the rules and regulations pertaining to the sport and had, in fact, been paid by one of the parents to look the other way when infractions were committed.

The PTA finally circulated a petition asking that the mayor discharge Mr. G and employ a qualified and competent person. So bad was the reputation of his department, and so often had he claimed that his political party was behind his program that, in the following election, the opposition candidate was swept into office on a reform ticket which promised that henceforth the recreational agency would be divorced from politics and placed under civil service protection.

A second instance, with a happier ending, also illustrates what happens when political considerations determine who fills leadership positions. Here, however, the appointee realized his technical deficiencies and employed as his second-in-command a professional to actually administer the recreational agency:

The mayor of an East Coast community employed, as the first superintendent of recreational service, a former Olympic athlete. The newly employed individual was soon found to have no real understanding of community recreational service and relied solely upon his athletic prowess and knowledge to develop competitions. Initially, there was much favorable comment about the ex-Olympian's expertise with sport and game activities, but shortly thereafter some dissident notes were heard from various sections of the community. There was increasing hostility toward the continued emphasis on athletics to the detriment of any other form of recreational activity. Finally, the mayor brought his appointee in and told him that a deputy would be employed to perform all of the programming operations while he would serve as the city's official greeter and "glad-hander." Subsequently, a recreationist was appointed to fill the deputy's slot and the operation and administration of the agency were reorganized to meet the recreational needs of those who had previously expressed dissatisfaction with and disaffection to the current political administrator. Although the ex-Olympic athlete remained on the city's payroll for many years, he was never really responsible for any of the programming enterprises. He joined all of the local civic and service organizations and was utilized as a front for the agency. In terms of professional capacity he proved to be a nonentity. Insofar as building goodwill for the department was concerned, he did provide a sound public relations image. Of course, this person should have been employed in a public relations capacity right from the start.

To the public, the political appointee, as the "leader" of his agency, symbolizes leadership in the field of recreational service. Although professional recreationists are not taken in by this false image of leadership, they are nevertheless powerless to combat its negative effect so long as recreational services are subject to political pressures. Only when the state recognizes recreational service as part of the obligation which it owes its citizenry and requires professional preparation, entrance examinations, licensing, and registration within the field, will true leaders emerge to provide faithful and dedicated service to all.

The illusions of leadership are many and of complex nature. They include a lack of understanding of the nature of leadership, a common misconception about the functions of leaders, and misnomers which confuse the role of leadership.

Basically, the phenomenon of leadership may be classified into six distinct segments: 1) ethics and behavior; 2) aims and objectives; 3) positions; 4) nomenclature; 5) practice; and 6) personality and character. Collectively, the facets appear as the types of leadership with which most people are familiar. Unfortunately, they also represent the most misunderstood quotient of the leadership phenomenon.

The term "leader" applies to few, but it is carried by many. The real leader is a rarity, although, with few exceptions, all persons have the innate ability to assume leadership status and perform as leaders. Individuals may act like leaders, and appear to be leaders but, upon close examination or even upon slight contact, they are revealed for what they are—actors playing a role for which they have been miscast. The heroic mold is for the courageous individual from whom leadership flows, not at his own bidding, but by some element quite beyond himself. It is that quality which people recognize and are drawn toward. It is understanding and communication and the dynamic interchange of ideas between individuals that produce influence with others for the individual and leadership for all.

The leader is a product of social need and has his own personal needs and abilities. This and the requirements from a particular group under specific conditions come together and interact simultaneously to provide the opportunity for leadership to occur. All else is illusory. Leadership does not depend upon position, economic control, personality, or bayonets. These are merely popular misconceptions relating to the phenomenon of leadership.

QUESTIONS FOR DISCUSSION

1. What are some leadership myths?
2. How do followers' perceptions of the leader influence their expectations?
3. Do leaders always lead in the right direction?
4. What is leadership legitimacy?
5. What are style factors in leadership?
6. Differentiate between headship and leadership.
7. Why may it be erroneous to use the term "leader" for one who holds an instructor's position?
8. Why is most organizational interpersonal influence of the leadership variety?
9. What outcomes may be expected from figurehead executives?
10. Explain the myth of leadership infallibility.
11. What is meant by this statement: The leader is a product of social need?

BIBLIOGRAPHY

Campbell, David P., *If I'm in Charge, Why is Everybody Laughing?* (Greensboro, N.C.: Center for Creative Leadership, 1984).

Knox, Alan B., ed., *Leadership Strategies for Meeting New Challenges* (San Francisco, Cal.: Jossey-Bass, Inc., Pubs., 1982).

Kottler, Jeffrey A., *Pragmatic Group Leadership* (Monterey, Cal.: Brooks-Cole, 1982).

Lassey, William R., and Marshall Sashkin, eds., *Leadership and Social Change*, rev. 3rd ed. (San Diego, Cal.: University Associates, 1983).

Reed, Harold W., *The Dynamics of Leadership* (Danville, Ill.: Interstate Printers and Publishers, Inc., 1982).

Robinson, Russell D., *An Introduction to Dynamics of Group Leadership* (Milwaukee: Bible Study Press, 1982).

Rosenbach, William E., and Robert L. Taylor, eds., *Contemporary Issues in Leadership* (Boulder, Col.: Westview Press, 1984).

Rothburg, David L., *Insecurity and Success in Organizational Life: Sources of Personal Motivation among Leaders & Managers* (New York: Praeger Pubs., 1981).

Stech, Ernest L., *Leadership Communication* (Chicago: Nelson-Hall, Inc., 1983).

Wilmer, Ann R., *The Spellbinders: Charismatic Political Leadership* (New Haven: Yale University Press, 1984).

CHAPTER SIXTEEN

Leadership Performance

The leadership process involves several general methods with which every leader must be familiar. None of these methods is, by itself, sufficient to cope with every circumstance. However, in the overall actions of the leader, each lends itself to the construction of a base of operations from which leadership can be effectively exercised:

The following actions are the underlying activities which every leader must undertake. In some part he utilizes all, many, or few of these methods to perform the tasks which are phases of leadership. Not one of these methods by itself, however, is sufficient to answer or to cope with every circumstance. Nevertheless, in the overall actions of the leader, each lends itself toward the construction of a base of operations upon which leadership will succeed.

1. *Challenging the accepted.* A leader must not automatically accept the status quo, but continually seek new and better ways of performing.
2. *Inquiring mind.* A leader constantly searches, questions, and is vigilant not only for his safety, but to keep progressive and current in his thinking.
3. *Common touch.* Sensitivity to others, the ability to perceive the general need of people and incorporate it into programming, is the basis of the common touch which a leader cultivates in order to estimate correctly the force and trend of social conduct.
4. *Unity.* By finding a common denominator which can appeal to all, a leader combines many diverse elements into an effective force.
5. *Promoting cohesiveness.* It is a leader's responsibility to create the atmosphere conducive to cohesiveness or solidarity through which group aims are best achieved.

Above all, the reader must recognize the fact that by the very nature of organizational structure, the recreationist is placed in a headship position. However, he must strive to convert headship to leadership. Thus, he has recourse to the methods which are indicated below.[1] But this material must not be taken to mean that leaders arise and perpetuate themselves because they have a knowledge of leadership techniques. Far from such an idea, this information is concerned with the recreationist who finds himself involved in an organizational hierarchy and seeks to have influence with others, rather than as an individual who attempts to retain, through various machinations, the position of leadership long after the need for a leader has been dissipated. Leaders will use leadership methods to retain their influence, but methods alone will not produce leadership. There must be a need before any methods can be applied.

Leadership methodology does not include Machiavellian intent. There is no manipulation of others simply for the sake of manipulation. Crises are not created so that the leader will be called upon to solve them. This is the technique of the political figure—not the recreationist. The recreationist must have long-range plans because his position calls for them, not because he has ulterior motives for self-aggrandizement or power.

Leaders have readily provided excellent materials on principle, goal, and frame of reference; but those who follow, the not-so-well informed, have been concerned primarily with specifics and procedures. Rank-and-filers are either not aware of the philosophy or are confused as to what the objectives and general principles of the field of recreational service are in relation to the social system and to the agency. It is to the methods of leadership, however, that this chapter is oriented.

General methods are concerned with ways of doing things, that is, how performance is achieved. Everything is done in a specific way. Usually, there are different ways of doing it. Many of the ways of doing things vary in terms of time of performance, efficiency, effectiveness, economy, and error. Trial and error, for example, may be one method utilized in the performance of recreationally oriented leadership. Dictatorial methods can be another approach. However, we will be concerned with the particular manner in which leadership is carried out. These methods have been observed at different times and in many places, and they can be described with precision. These methods should be used concertedly if the most effective leadership performance is to be achieved.

---

1. H. Butcher, *Group Participation: Techniques for Leaders and Members* (Beverly Hills, Cal.: Sage Publications, 1979).

THE DISCERNMENT OF OBJECTIVES

Unless the leader has a goal to which he directs all his efforts, he will fail. The leader cannot gain popular support without representing some concept which can elicit public attention. His well-defined aim assures that his actions are always purposeful. The leader also has to be able to evaluate goals. He must be able to select a project because its achievement will satisfy the greatest number of people. In the process of satisfying those who support him, he will also attain the leadership position which he seeks.

How can the leader establish a meaningful and stimulating environment? How can he keep his followers? How can he arouse interest in his plans and provide incentive to those who support him? All of these questions relate to the performance of the leader, and there are certain methods which the leader uses to establish and maintain his position. Leadership is considered effective when situations are arranged so that followers have an opportunity to act, want to act on a leader's idea, and when they achieve success.

The end which the leader visualizes is the direction or channeling of the energies of his group into constructive paths which will accomplish a common objective.[2] He needs to sustain the interest of those whose energies he taps and controls. Therefore, it is essential that the leader make his goals coincide with those of his potential followers and make them seem worth the effort which it takes to achieve them. Enthusiasm from the leader helps to transmit the desirability of the goals. When the leader can make every question and each effort seem exciting and when he can transfer some of his dynamic belief to his followers so that they will be stimulated to try and maintain their direction, he is using an effective leadership method.

It is the leader who discerns ends and utilizes them to make initial contact with a group. He holds out the tantalizing prospect of obtaining what everyone wants. He has analyzed the needs of people and has determined what will appeal to their appetites, their natures, and their character. With these ends known, the leader is in a position to make his situation more attractive, thereby gaining vital attention to his plans and influence with others. Leadership is a process wherein the members of the group are assisted, guided, and directed to discover the important and long-lived purposes which will bring them satisfaction.

---

2. N. D. Gardner, *Group Leadership* (Washington, D.C.: National Training and Development Service Press, 1974), p. 28.

Ends: Paths to Follow or Objectives To Reach?

One way to view goals is as directions for human growth and development, paths to follow rather than ends to reach. For instance, a leader may demand concerted action, and this is his aim. Some other leader may have group productivity as his aim. The major consideration in these cases is not what is acted upon or what is produced, but that the people concerned unite in their efforts, thereby achieving mutual satisfaction.

There are two critical aspects of goals as paths to follow: the situation in which each individual finds himself and from which he must develop; and the way or the step-by-step process by which he may continue to progress. Goals as directions are methods for movement, and guiding performance is furthered by providing plans on the ways to continue to the next stage of development.

Examine the illustration of a leader attempting to influence a group toward a specific objective. The leader's goal for the group is directive when two factors are satisfied. First, the leader must empathize and communicate with the individuals making up the group. He must be sensitive to individual emotions, concerns, and wants and know how well the individual understands what he is attempting to do. He has to determine the status of each person concerning his understanding of his plans and organize these items as the basis for leading. The second feature is founded upon particular activities which members of the group should do to achieve the commonly accepted aims. In harmony with the first point, the methods indicated by the leader will always be within the skill limits of his followers and not fall in areas beyond their abilities of comprehension or performance.

In obtaining the interest and attention of a group in order to gain influence with them, it is necessary to start from where they are and to go no faster toward the goal than each group member is capable of going. This does not preclude an attempt to educate individuals so that they can progress more rapidly toward a common goal.

Another view of goals is as objectives to be achieved or targets to be attained. Focus here is upon the destination rather than the path. Leadership aims conceived in this manner are not dependent upon the present environment of the follower nor upon the methods by which the end is to be attained. The ultimate goal is of primary importance; how it is arrived at is purely secondary.

In the philosophical and sociological literature of this century, so much argument has been put forth concerning "ends" and "means" that the two are often considered mutually exclusive. However, ends and means can be entirely compatible, the means supplying appropriate tools for attaining the ends, and the ends providing the frame of reference and the stimulus for discovering and utilizing the most effective means. Ends without methods for reaching them are dreams and are often obstacles to accomplishment. Methods without aims have no substance or appeal because they lack intent or design. All means may be viewed as immediate objectives; every objective, regardless of how remote from the immediate situation, does indicate some eventual path to follow from the original circumstance.

Ends and means are also inextricably associated by the process in which they are inherent; the dynamics of leadership situations require that any goal or end be viewed as a means to some additional end. Hence an end is not, in fact, a finish because it always carries with it the germ of a new beginning. Methods can be seen as relatively urgent or immediate ends, and ends can be regarded as relatively more remote methods. The distinction between means and ends is better thought of as the difference between immediate and remote ends.

Immediate, Intermediate, and Final Ends

Some leadership goals are immediate. They deal with what must be done at once to relieve some crisis and preserve the atmosphere necessary for furthering the leader's plans. Resumption of order is unlikely to be the final goal of leadership; it is only meant to serve other ends. If every successive aim is regarded as aiding the completion of some future objective, there is little doubt that objectives, no matter how small, contribute to some final goal. Where the succession terminates may be called the final end, and steps which are found between the immediate and the final end may be termed intermediate ends.

Few are willing to dispute the existence of immediate and intermediate objectives, but there is no such reticence concerning final goals. Vigorous advocates champion the idea that the unceasing movement of the life process and human thought makes it impossible for any transitory aim to encompass the satisfaction of all human needs. Thus, they maintain, theories that propose a final destination block progress and halt continuous exploration.

Others define a goal as any achievable aim on which one may concentrate regardless of its importance in leading to new goals. Some take the view, in partial accord with the idea that every aim leads successively to some final end, that an ultimate goal is vital to defining immediate and intermediate objectives. But the real goal is to discipline oneself in an effort to attain some ideal end to which all other ends are subordinate but which is, in the last analysis, unobtainable. An illustration of an unreachable final end is the satisfaction of all human needs. Each victory over deprivation can be regarded as a step toward this end, but although the goal can be approached infinitely, it can never be reached.

Achievable Ends

An example of an achievable end is the settling of differences between a group's mores and members' conformity to some social requirement. The aim of leadership in this instance would be to channel the conduct and behavior of followers into patterns acceptable by the community in order to maintain the cohesiveness of the group. Unless this adjustment was made, the possibility exists that the society would destroy the group. Group maintenance within a social context would be looked upon as an ultimate end, not necessarily to be approached by systematically achieving other aims.

Improving Conditions. One of the ends which the leader serves is achievement of better conditions for his followers. This end is also the means whereby the leader gains continued influence with others. Betterment of conditions embodies gaining political patronage, or raising the economic, housing, social, or cultural standards and status of those who are part of the group. A true leader never forgets those who assisted him in his rise to the position which he holds. He continually forages to determine how he can materially or spiritually aid those who have given him support during his formative years as an aspiring leader. He constantly seeks to raise his followers from their present level of existence to a higher level. Depending upon the background, experience, material goods, and services at the command of his group, the leader attempts to better his followers' environments and situations. If the group has economic, educational, and cultural security, the leader can bestow rewards in the form of additional prestige and recognition upon those who support him.

Here is an illustration of how a politically appointed administrator sought to better the conditions of his followers, unfortunately at the expense of all:

> Having served as the newly elected mayor's campaign manager, X was appointed superintendent of the public recreational service department in a large Eastern city. He finally had a chance to produce a record of assistance for the public's well-being. A national conference on aspects of aging was convened, and the several states were requested to select qualified individuals for participation. The governor's committee recommended that mayors should select

potential invitees. The mayor named the superintendent to a select committee organized to choose experts to attend the conference. The superintendent was given a list of experts from which to choose. He decided that the experts would only go to the conference to obtain information on this study and felt that they might not show enough appreciation for the honor that he was bestowing upon them by making them participants. He therefore nominated and selected unqualified individuals to attend the conference, solely on the basis of who supported the mayor's campaign for election. He was not concerned with the presentation which such individuals might make or of the uselessness of any information which they would bring back to the state because of a lack of understanding. He was mainly concerned with being able to hand out prestigious appointments to those who had followed his lead. Presumably, such selection could not benefit these people materially, but it would enhance their status and increase their recognition, which was probably their main object. Thus the superintendent used a valid method to continue to hold his appointment. As an individual concerned with guarding the public trust invested within his office, he was, of course, a failure.

From the above it can be observed that although the individual in the leadership position may utilize the right technique at the right time, his aims may be far from beneficial to all of the people and may, in fact, be irresponsible to many in order to curry favor from a few. Surely the method is correct, but the reasons for its use are beneath contempt.
The recreationist in the position of chief executive for a public recreational agency may also utilize this general method in order to maintain his influence with others, to enhance his status within his peer group agency, or to gain support for his plans and policies.

In the early 1960's, the superintendent of X recreational system in a medium-sized Southern community was faced with a social restriction concerning the provision of recreational services to the Blacks of that community. While the white community provided him with facilities for the recreational program for the entire community, that is, the Caucasian section of it, it neglected to appropriate a budget large enough to provide recreational facilities for the Black population of the town. Although the superintendent realized that social custom prevented integration, he was nevertheless determined to provide recreational facilities and services to the Blacks of the community, as it was his professional and ethical obligation to do. He was not obliged to attempt to integrate the two races of the community, but he had a professional responsibility to provide recreational service to all of the people. He therefore instituted a planned program which provided expenditures in his budget to construct facilities and acquire property upon which to build centers which would ultimately offer recreational opportunities to this racial minority. Although he followed the "separate, but equal doctrine," he actually bettered the condition of the Blacks in the community, because wherever a recreational facility was located in the Black section of town, land values increased and residents showed more pride in their neighborhood.

Shortly thereafter, the civil rights movement broke with full impact upon the town. Anti-discrimination laws were enforced and racial segregation was outlawed. The Southern traditionalists no longer used the public facilities, and many simply joined private "whites only" clubs. There was a good deal of bitterness expressed when Blacks entered formerly segregated swimming pools and parks for the first time. However, the youth of the community, especially elementary age children, were no longer segregated. The recreational service department together with the schools served as a modifying social force within the community and facilitated a change in overt public opinion and behavior. In consequence, the recreationist became one of the outspoken champions of the Black community and his position was enhanced within the greater community despite some diehard racism. His initial efforts were looked upon as enlightened progressivism and he was generally supported in the community.

In performing his function, this recreationist used the method of bettering conditions to affect certain physical modifications in the community to attempt to influence and promote social change. His aim was to provide recreational services to neglected citizens of his community and he succeeded in this aim. Others may have been content to allow the situation to remain at the status quo. However, without compromising his position, he persuaded his board to finance his proposals with a view toward making life a little more enjoyable and meaningful to a discriminated-against group. He did not lose status with his fellow townsmen, but he did gain additional influence with the Blacks in the community.

Perhaps his aim was twofold. He prevented or reduced what might have been a noisome situation, in that he initially provided separate but equal services to the minority group, thereby discounting any clamor which may have arisen over the lack of recreational opportunities for Blacks, and he adhered to the obligations which he has as a professional to serve all of the community.

Objective Overview

Objective oversight is the ability to view a situation or circumstance, and it may involve an individual's attempt to gain some impression of conditions in order to formulate a plan of action, impersonally and without bias, therefore eliminating pre-judgments. The method of objective overview is utilized by the leader in planning and controlling activities in which members of his group may participate.

The organization and structuring of experiences are modified from situation to situation because of goals to be reached or prevailing conditions either for or against the group, the leader, or both. Objectivity is the rejection of emotional aspects or the injection of self into a contingency. The leader may sometimes be called upon to guide, advise, or counsel others in distress. Unless he can withstand the temptation to become emotionally involved in the problem of the individual seeking his assistance, he cannot provide the solution nor will he be able to satisfy completely the person's needs. Wallowing in despair or sinking into a slough of emotionalism does not correct or alleviate the conditions which originally brought the situation into being.

By holding his emotions in check, the leader is able to view interpersonal and extrapersonal relationships and problems in a way that gives him a view of the entire affair, rather than merely one or two aspects of the problem. He must see the forest as a whole before he can indicate which trees must be treated, cut, uprooted, or destroyed. Concern with details at the onset of the problem is likely to hinder the organization of a plan which can reduce the emergency. It is through the method of generalized observation that the leader will be in the best position to act and carry out procedures designed to overcome friction or hostility.

Here is an illustration from the work record of Mr. S, supervisor of special activities in a medium-sized community in one of the midwestern states. Mr. S was employed as a line supervisor of newly employed workers in a municipal recreational agency within the community. The following is from the record:

> Miss R, for some reason, appeared to exhibit negative behavior toward the supervisor. She was sullen, suspicious of every word, and generally reflected a poor attitude for one who wanted a career in the field of recreational service. Mr. S arranged for agency visitation, observation of Miss R at work, a daily log of her activities and a supervisory conference each week. Through these Mr. S was finally able to determine the nature of her dissatisfaction. Miss R felt that she was not receiving the type of orientation which would

fit her for her job in the agency. She also felt that the supervisor was discriminating against her, although she readily agreed that she had selected the agency rather than having been recruited by it. She had been tardy to her appointments on several occasions. Nevertheless, she still insisted that she was being treated unfairly. In attempting to find out precisely what it was that seemed to be annoying her, S indicated that he might be able to help if he had a better understanding of her background, associates, and ambitions. R, who appeared to be waiting for this, immediately launched into her history. She stated that her parents had been divorced, that she had been sent to a succession of boarding schools, and that she had never been able to make any close or lasting friends. She felt that she was being "lost in the shuffle" within the department. She felt capable of performing well as a recreational worker, but did not seem to get along with others. She related several incidents concerning her inability to make social contacts and concluded with the statement that she was a failure and that nobody liked her. Mr. S listened to this testimony without comment. At the conclusion of the interview, he asked a few pertinent questions in order to determine why R felt the way she did. Placing the burden of proof upon R, Mr. S shifted all answers from himself and sought to stimulate R to answer her own questions. During the course of this session, R spoke about many of her personal problems whose roots were extremely emotional. By forcing R to answer her own questions and by attempting to understand without sympathizing, Mr. S was successful in drawing several factors from R which were contributing to her inadequacies. Instead of answering her questions directly, S parried them, turned them around, and indirectly forced R to verbalize her own problems and the reasons for those problems. In this way, he established excellent rapport with her without becoming involved with the personal dissatisfactions and emotions of this problematic worker.

In this instance, the supervisor used a counseling technique which provided him with an overview of the worker problem while maintaining his objective view and preventing undue involvement with the worker and her needs.[3]

In this second example, the recreational worker did not have the experience and background which might have enabled him to meet the situation as it evolved. In working with the conditions, he performed

---

3. G. Egan, *The Skilled Helper* (Monterey, Cal.: Brooks/Cole Publishing Company, 1975), pp. 116–124.

in ways which are questionable and might have had serious repercussions. The following incident occurred at a small quasi-public mental institution in one of the larger metropolitan areas on the east coast:

> The hospital had organized a full-range recreational program for patients. One of the activities was the publication of a weekly patient and hospital newspaper edited by patients with the supervision of one of the recreational staff. The paper appeared each Friday evening. One Friday one of the patients approached the worker with the statement that another patient was particularly upset because of an editorial which appeared in the paper that night. The worker went to the patient, heard his story, and then, without ever looking at the newspaper to verify the patient's story, went to the patient who was the editor and requested that the story be retracted. The editor, feeling persecuted, refused and stated that there was nothing in the paper concerning the patient in question. Upon investigation into the matter, the worker discovered that the editor was right, that the first patient's version was not confirmed, and that he had to apologize to the editor for his mistaken judgment.

The worker in this instance became emotionally concerned and identified himself with the patient, whose feelings had been apparently ruffled by a supposed derogatory editorial in the patient newspaper. If the worker had taken the time to view the situation with the objectivity and professionalism that he should have used, he would have discerned the obvious discrepancy between the patient's protests and the facts in the case. Because he let emotionalism blind him to the truth, he was not able to appraise the situation correctly and, as a result, acted rashly. No recreationist can ever allow himself to be stampeded into action before he knows precisely what is happening, who is participating, why such a condition exists, and how he may take steps to reduce or stop such activity. Unless the recreationist can see the entire picture in all of its ramifications, he will be acting blindly and not in the manner of a leader. The leader knows above all what he is doing, why he is doing it, where he is going, and how he is going to reach his objectives. Through objective overview the leader continues to gain influence with others.

Mutual Satisfactions.   Another leadership method is to discern what it is that others lack and adopt those needs as an aim. By championing the cause of potential followers and satisfying their needs, the would-be leader attains his own goal of recognition and influence with others while he fulfills his obligations to his supporters. Again, we can see the utilization of ends as means and means as ends. The leader's end is to gain influence with others. His proximate end is to satisfy the needs or desires of others. By carrying out one, he succeeds in the other, thus creating mutual satisfaction.

The method of promoting mutual satisfaction is derived from the leader's abilities to discover others' needs. Through tireless study of these needs, he is able to gain insight into the eccentricities of human personalities and human motives. With this as his anchor, he is in the best circumstance to make his aims coincidental with those whom he wishes as followers. The leader may truly adopt the aims of constituents, but he is more likely to use this as a device to capture their attention, assure their loyalty, and certify their support; if he follows their cause, they will return the favor by granting him the position and status which he desires.

MOVEMENT TOWARD OBJECTIVES

Once an aim has been identified, immediate movement in that direction is vital. The leader must utilize the method of forward motion to allay any fears which his followers may have concerning the possibility and the speed of goal achievement. The ability to move ahead is one of the more effective techniques the leader uses to preserve the loyalty of those who support him.

The leader realizes that the continuation of forward momentum is vital to the realization of any goals which he may have. The slackening of effort is rewarded by increasing attack against the leader and his program. One of the deadly consequences of reduced pace is the sharpening of hostile activity. With a curtailed production inevitably comes a slowing of enterprise, less spirit for the achievement of a sought-after objective, stagnation of ideas, obscurity of basic ideals and ideas for trivial matters, regression to mediocrity, and, finally, defeat. An essential leadership quality is the assertion of productive effort for the development of plans which lead to the ends which the influencer has programmed or originated. Without this plunging onward, the entire movement is jeopardized, and leadership fails in its task.

The leader cannot merely sit back and hope to whip up support on the spur of the moment. This is difficult to do without a schedule of procedures. A requirement in the leadership situation is an orientation toward the objective sought and a selected method of departure for gaining it. The leader will operate under tremendous odds when wandering in a maze of his own making, taking whatever develops as another rung up, using a hit-or-miss process in the hope of making the right choice for his situation. The leader needs a clearly defined path, with possibilities of mistakes taken into account, but with a reasonable course to follow as the result of selecting certain standards and weighing potentials and consequences. A carefully thought-out procedure, allowing for some error, considering the possibility of poor choice or judgment, will have a better chance of succeeding in a chosen area than no plan or a trial-and-error commitment.

Within the field of recreational service, the planned outcome is a necessity for leadership. The recreationist on any level must rely upon planned outcomes in working with participants in activities or with potential followers from the citizenry of the community in which he serves. This is particularly true as it concerns concepts of program planning.

Thought to Action

Basically, leadership begins with an idea. It is the thought which gives rise to the deed. The leader views his goals in terms of overcoming obstacles or resolving conflicts of interest. He visualizes a specific end as the object of his desire and plans accordingly. Unless there is some original concept which can be developed over time, there is no goal and therefore no method.

The method here begins with exploring possibilities, selecting standard procedures, and visualizing potential outcomes; the end product is practical action. The leader recognizes that the demands of the environment are modified as his group gains momentum. Some of his followers are partially aware of this modification. The leader has to explain the limitations which are imposed upon his group as each objective is reached and becomes a means for the attainment of a more remote goal. He clarifies and defines the criteria by which members will proceed.

The end in view is spawned by some thought which becomes the motivation for a particular program. All activity begins with an awareness of a need. The leader cannot rely upon hit-or-miss propositions to carry him along. He can never leave to fortuitous circumstance the probability that a set of conditions will evolve which will favor the situation. He must have a fundamental concept upon which to base subsequent activity. Hence, he must do as much preplanning for his campaign as possible. He must have an idea of the end which he seeks and the means to achievement, which is activity.

Without ideas as a starting point, there can be scheduled only whatever activities happen to occur spontaneously, without any thought as to whether they are appropriate, effective, necessary, or actually meeting the needs of the public. Perhaps this is why so many laymen-operated activities, such as "little league" and its ilk, have been spawned out of the lack of planned recreational programs in municipalities. One result of the lack of professional leadership and planning has been the over-emphasis upon prizes, commercialism of amateur sports, and the operation of activities by unqualified and non-professional people. With planning and leadership this could never happen. The product is instead well-directed, effective activities satisfying to all who participate. Thought before action is prerequisite to leadership.

Alternate Planning

Planning is the development of program material of both a physical and conceptual nature. It is the establishment of one distinct course of action after many possibilities have been evaluated. The plan, therefore, is a documentation of logical steps which must occur in the achievement of certain aims. But one plan is never enough when dealing with the vagaries of human personality. Alternate planning is essential if the various needs of individuals are to be met, and should not be construed as vacillation or willful change of direction.

While it is logical and consistent for the leader to have some preconceived idea as to the methods by which to achieve goals, it is poor practice to be inflexible. He must always be open-minded and astute enough to listen to and weigh the various possibilities contributed by others to his cause. The leader should never attempt to force the membership into accepting something which seems alien to it. Being in the leadership position, the leader may very well influence members to accept his proposal even though they have misgivings about it. However, when group members are unable to formulate or to verbalize their ideas, and it is necessary for the leader to fill that void with fruitful suggestions of his own, either of two positive results may follow: the group will utilize one of the suggestions, or their inarticulateness will disappear under the stimulation of the leader's suggestions. In either case the group will profit. The product of alternative planning is achievement of objectives.

Usually, group members have diverse interests and their own ideas about what should constitute the program of activities they want to undertake. If the leader has had experience with any of the types of activities which group members nominate, he will be able to evaluate these in the light of individual attitudes, abilities, and needs, as well as needs of the group as a whole. If he finds the suggested experiences potentially valuable or beneficial to both individuals and the entire group, he will reinforce the plan. If he feels that the results will be of doubtful benefit in the present situation or that their attempt is likely to end in failure, he will undoubtedly reject and seek to discourage any suggestions of that kind.

Continuous Progress

Vitally important in keeping the leader in a position of influence is continuous progress toward an objective. Through sheer force of forward momentum, the leader is perpetuated even as his ideas gain credence and acceptance. The most difficult thing to fight is an idea, and once an idea is carried into action, it is indeed a formidable task to halt the process and dampen the enthusiasm.

Leaders realize that they must press onward if they are to retain status and wield influence with others. A moving target is hard to hit, and concrete accomplishments are hard to refute. But a leader's policies and activities become easy marks when forward movement is obstructed. The leader who allows his projects to become bogged down through indifference, apathy, or antagonistic interference is vulnerable. As long as followers are aware that some advancement is taking place, they will be restimulated to work toward aims. Nothing causes flagging interest or hope more than immobility.

It is necessary for the leader to plan his movements with care, ensuring that possible interference with his activities is checked before it can take hold. By following up his plans with consistent action, he will leave no time for doubt and dissension to arise.

Resiliency to Frustration

The leader must be prepared for the thwarting of his most precious concepts. He may be subjected to conflicts of interest, with all of the tension and danger which such conflicts produce. His projects may be continually under attack by negative thinkers as well as by those who want to help but instead cause disorder and riot. He may constantly be the focus of demagoguery, slander, and sub rosa tactics designed to frustrate his ambition or curb his effort. His road may be threatened by those who would have him modify his aims, ideals, and the methods he utilizes in order to reach his stated goals.

One quality which the leader must perfect is his stability. This may be termed his protective device which guards him against the frustrating condition which may be imposed upon him as he attempts to lead. The ability to meet extreme disappointment, not once but many times, and keep moving toward an aim after having taken the necessary procedures to eliminate or override the impasse is mandatory. This resilience to active antagonism is one of the most important qualities that the leader can cultivate. Without it, he will soon be reduced to impotent rage, foolish statements, vengeful acts, and unfulfilled desires. Through the utilization of this resilience he may overcome most hindrances, maintain his momentum toward his goals, and retain the influence with others so necessary for leadership to prevail.

The following illustration keenly points up the value of the method and the validity of the foregoing statement:

An administrator of a recreational agency was fortunate to have on his staff an extremely competent recreational supervisor. The supervisor's skill was such that, although quite youthful, he had begun to attain regional and national recognition. In order to receive the full impact of this illustration, the character of the administrator as well as the supervisor must be indicated.

The administrator considered himself to be kind, efficient, impartial, and urbane. He was, in fact, almost the opposite of his self-concept. He is best characterized as incompetent, inadequate for his position, insecure by virtue of these faults, unfair, jealous, and reactionary.

The supervisor could be termed brilliant, rash, purposeful, needing and seeking status, unaware of people's feelings, and highly effective in his job.

Simply by knowing the make-up of these two personalities, one would automatically realize that conflict would erupt. The administrator was given the chairmanship of a committee on a special state project (for which he was unqualified). Realizing his inadequacy, he turned all of the work over to the supervisor, who took the necessary actions to complete the work. A technical report covering this specialization was needed, and this would ultimately be presented before a national professional body with suitable commentary. The administrator enjoined the supervisor to perform the work with the explicit promise of sending the supervisor to the national conference. However, when the list of delegates to the conference was prepared, the supervisor discovered that the administrator, and not he, was to go.

Because he had some insight into the character of the administrator, the supervisor had prepared for such an occurrence. Although his ambition had been frustrated at one point, he had made suitable contacts with national conference personnel and had finally obtained an invitation to all sessions of the conference as a special guest.

However, the administrator began to feel uneasy about the recognition which had started to accumulate for the supervisor. For one thing, he felt unsure in his position, perhaps thinking that the supervisor was after his job. For another thing, his envy at the supervisor's better qualifications and success rankled him. Instead of being happy at the thought of a stronger department and the prestige that would accrue to the department as well as to himself from the presentation, he could only think of the supervisor surpassing him. He resolved to place the supervisor in a position whereby his rash actions might justify his removal. In an interview between the two, the administrator forbade the supervisor to participate in the conference. He probably hoped that the supervisor would rebel against this mean act and go to the conference anyway. In this hope he was wrong. The supervisor clearly perceived the administrator's intent, and although deeply hurt at the unfair treatment, he did not attend, nor did he let this intolerable situation get out of hand by attacking the administrator. He simply continued to do the work for which he was employed. By keeping his head, he kept his job. In his position he was still able to command attention and gain the respect of those who came in contact with him. Within three months, the supervisor was hired away from the department to another agency, receiving higher rank and a substantial salary increment. One year after the supervisor left, the administrator was given the choice of stepping down as department head or resigning. He chose to step down.

More to the point, this report shows how frustrations make work difficult, and how the leader can rise above them so that he can continue with the task to which he is dedicated. What good would it have been to have struck blindly in the hope of raising some outcry against the administrator? Absolutely none. There could be no appeal to higher authority. The consequence of heedless action would simply have been a lost job and an end to any prospects of status, influence, or other rewards which went with the position. By holding onto his aim, the supervisor was able to maintain himself in spite of all frustration, and the quality of resilience enabled him to continue working.

CHALLENGING THE ACCEPTED

Whatever the leader is, he cannot accept the status quo simply because entrenched interests have always done things in certain ways. The leader continually seeks new and better ways of performing. He keeps trying to determine how more efficient and effective methods may be put to use in the production of materials, goods, and services which are necessary for the achievement of his goals. For the leader, the processes are grist for his mill, as he examines each for the attainment of additional value with the same or less effort. The leader does not believe in the phrase, "it cannot be accomplished."

The Inquiring Mind

The leader constantly searches for additional useful knowledge. He is always intent upon discovering faster, better, stronger, more adequate, more productive, and less expensive and time-consuming processes. The leader recognizes that there is and will be a need for improving the methods of working with people and producing the factors which contribute to success in achieving objectives.

The leader must be alert to many needs. He has to quickly identify and isolate issues which, if left unchecked, could conceivably grow to enormous proportions and create insurmountable difficulties. He cannot afford to wait until situations become critical before taking measures to correct them. Thus he inquires into the state of health, figuratively speaking, of his program. This vigilance is urgently required because it is often among the rank-and-file supporters, at the grass-roots level, that conflicts begin. These, in turn, build up tremendous pressure and finally burst all bounds and become insurrections, or at least withdrawals of support. Many of the problems which need the attention of the leader are first apparent to subordinates on the lowest working level. However, unless the leader has instilled a sense of intellectual freedom within his staff, they will not recognize critical items for what they are, and there will be rampant interference with the prompt and accurate transmission of these problems.

It is only when the leader sanctions independent investigation and with it the responsibility and authority necessary for its usage that communications will be free. As the leader is kept informed concerning performance of his group (or if his influence is wider, many groups or a nation) by his subordinates, identification of problems will be swift and sure.

The restless mind is one which is not satisfied with just getting an answer. It wants to know the reasons why. The inquiring mind is never content to wear blinders or follow the well-rutted path without determining if there are other paths to follow or if there is a wide world beyond the blinders. The leader has to develop the capacity to keep mentally alert, not only for his own safety, but in order to keep progressive and current in his thinking. Inquiry broadens horizons, stimulates interest, presents a challenge for each day, and enriches life. No one who is constantly impelled to learn more and more about other people, why they behave the way they do, what makes them follow, and what provides them with satisfaction, can ever be mesmerized into a stereotyped life and a conformist's routine. Inquiry frees the mind from stagnation. It allows for unlimited use of imagination as well as for the assimilation of factual representations. As long as a man is free to inquire, he may never be made a slave.

The recreationist is in the position of leader in the community. If he is to perform in a manner which will be of benefit to the entire community, it is necessary for him to augment his professional preparation with an open, inquisitive outlook concerning the variable manifestations of recreational experience, and the organization and operation of the program which provides those experiences. Unless the recreationist can inspire rapid and clear interpretations of what and how the citizens feel toward the recreational service agency or members of its staff, he can assure himself of a short-lived position as leader. It is just as mandatory that he maintain his own alertness and initiative to try new ideas and practices as it is for him to maintain a communications network which can provide him with prompt and accurate reporting on any trouble spots.

There is great pressure on the recreationist, at any level, to foresee minor frictions and prevent them from developing into major crises. With continual analysis of the performance of his followers, program participants or staff subordinates, there is good likelihood that disorder and disaffection will not occur. To obtain information concerning problem areas, recreationists should choose subordinates who are skilled in their performance while seeking new ways to better it, and should favor participants who take part in the program while experiencing the excitement of being a part of the planning organization. This acceptance of responsibility by layman and personnel who find satisfaction in the field but dissatisfaction with the way they perform, regardless of their skill, ensures that problems will be identified and thus resolved before they become critical. With early identification, there is time for a thorough analysis of the reasons for any friction. When some tender circumstance is uncovered, the recreationist will attempt to remedy the underlying causes and not merely the outward signs or the symptoms of the question. In this manner, the recreationist's influence will grow as it is seen that he has the ability to present a worthwhile program for the community without undue abrasion of individual, group, or community sensitivity.

DEVELOPING SECONDARY LEADERS

Empires have been built by men of iron constitution and unbending will only to fade or vanish after the demise of the builder because he failed to develop a new leader who could carry on after his death. History is replete with illustrations. Groups, like empires, have also come to ruin because a leader has not prepared subordinates to succeed him and to hold the group together.

In order to maintain and reinforce continuity of policy, objectives, standards, and aims after the departure of an original leader, it is necessary to have on hand individuals who believe in the ideas and methods of the former leader and who are prepared to assume leadership responsibilities. Preparing such individuals is one of the basic methods used by a leader for the preservation of his group and the ideals for which he stands. Secondary leaders, if they are properly prepared by the leader, are ready to assume full leadership responsibility and generally are well received by group members as the logical successors to their leader. Such a procedure is easily possible when the leader organizes and specifies the succession of leadership for the welfare of the group. In most cases, the leader prepares every follower for leadership; only certain ones will have the necessary combination of desire, drive, insight, attractiveness, and other attributes that can make them acceptable as leaders.

One method the leader uses to develop successors is delegation of responsibility and concomitant authority. Another is the teaching of skills, knowledge, and practices to group members so that they can participate in leadership situations and exercise their potential for group influence.

Delegation of Responsibility and Authority

As the leader attempts to initiate secondary leadership within the group, he must work to develop a proper sense of responsibility among those who are potentially capable of assuming the reins of leadership. One purpose of delegating authority for carrying out responsibility is to build confidence in the person to whom this trust is given. In order to live up to what is expected of him, the person is motivated to increase his productivity and competence. Proper use of the technique is vital to developing leadership potential within a group. No leader can ever hope to prepare future leaders to be anything except puppets unless authority and responsibility are delegated. Reluctance to do so is an indication of lack of confidence in the selectee and a sign of ineffective leadership.

In order to delegate the responsibility and the authority necessary for achieving any assignment, the leader must take the following steps

1. The hierarchy of the organization must be used; that is, communications must proceed from level to level so that no one's authority is bypassed.

2. The developing leaders must be clearly advised of the nature of their assignment, but must not be instructed in the method for fulfilling the obligation placed upon them. They alone should be held responsible for whatever results they achieve, and the leader should avoid intervening in the responsibilities which have been delegated.

3. Recognition should be given for displays of resourcefulness and competence. Such recognition should closely follow the activity.

4. Every effort should be made to allow potential leaders to perform the functions of the next higher level in the organizational hierarchy. Practical involvement in the problems encountered by superiors will develop an appreciation for the complexity of the position and the stability necessary to complete appointed assignments.

5. Provision must be made to ensure that a person is assigned to duties in keeping with his limitations and capacities.

6. Complete objectivity must be maintained in evaluating the performance of potential leaders. Alleged mistakes or failures must be investigated thoroughly and impartially, and support should always be tendered until conclusive and unbiased proof indicates that support should be withdrawn.

These methods are useful in the development of secondary leaders during the tenure of the leader. Without the leader's continual support and confidence, secondary leaders cannot be prepared. To prevent the negation or destruction of his work, the leader must take time to prepare those who will come after him.

Educating for Activity

One of the methods the leader can use to gain his ends is informing an individual of the benefits which will accrue to those who follow his ideas. The leader's efforts to enrich individual and group life are not confined to pronouncements only. He utilizes educative activities directly related to people's prior experiences. Educative methods require direct knowledge of stimulating circumstances, conditions, meetings, demonstrations, and a multitude of other motivations which impel men to understand.

Almost all of these experiences arouse response and awareness of what the leader is trying to do and, if properly cultivated, result in participation and following in the leader's program. It is extremely important that people be made aware of the world around them and the values and enrichments which await them with the experiences the recreationist may provide for them. Such recognition increases the probability of utilization and participation, intensifies the perceptive capability of the individual, and broadens his horizons in terms of general comprehension.

When the leader is a member, rather than the leader, of an organization's hierarchy, it may be that he will have to educate those in superior positions before his plans can be put into effect. When this is true, the leader must pursue a course of action designed to acquaint the superior with the benefits which the plan could have for the entire agency. He does this in the most innocuous but insistent way possible. For instance, the scheme can be effected by approaching the superior with the possibility of an idea which can be made acceptable by broadly suggesting that the superior thought up the entire proposal. Once the seed has been planted, it should be cultivated with subtle hints, compliments, and accolades to see the idea through. Probably the success of the plan will hinge largely upon the senior's actual belief that it is in fact "his." Of course, it is unfortunate that there are some individuals who must be treated in this manner because they are afraid to grant others recognition, but the leader is more concerned with the end result rather than the specifics of attaining it, as long as what he does is not unethical. When working for an individual who glories in self-aggrandizement, the only way to educate him in the values of a particular experience is to allow him to think that he conceived the plan and allow him to take the credit. Perhaps credit may finally devolve upon the original thinker, but the more important aspect is that the plan is accepted and allowed to proceed.

All superiors are not devoid of intelligence or ethics, and it may only be necessary to lay before one a well-conceived plan of action for his perusal before permission is given to continue. In this instance, the leader realizes whom he is dealing with and throws all subtlety aside in an effort to bring out every pertinent piece of information for final examination. Here, it is not so much a question of educating a superior as it is allowing the superior's good sense of values to be exposed to a stimulating concept.

Belief in Human Dignity

The leader has a basic respect for the rights and dignity of all people. He is therefore concerned with the maintenance of the individual rights, as well as the needs, of his own group members. He also believes that everyone must have his chance and that each deserves a place and a moment to shine. Thus, he feels that no one should bear a scapegoat's burden or that even one individual should be sacrificed needlessly. All are important to the life of the group, and each person contributes something to the maintenance and spirit of the group.

Because he holds this concept, the leader is aware that each man must be given a chance to select his own course of action. He knows that human personality is unpredictable, but that each person is valuable by the very reason of uniqueness and may have, among other attributes, something valuable to contribute to the group as a whole. Taking these facts into consideration, the leader utilizes every personal resource at his disposal to increase benefits to the group which he heads.

The leader carries out this conceptualization in a threefold manner: 1) guiding and directing human resources in problem-solving techniques; 2) creating and organizing acceptable social interactions in order to develop the support necessary for continued ethical practices; and 3) enabling individuals to formulate, apply, and evaluate the meanings of activities for themselves. In this way the strengths and weaknesses of individuals are exposed, treated, and corrected for the increased value to be derived from such an experience. Thus, the individual's concepts, opinions, and understanding may be modified to the extent that he will be able to maximize his skills and proclivities, while his knowledge of the social order and his environment become more susceptible to explanation. That person will have had a complete reorientation to the social situation; therefore, through the group process of individual recognition, an enrichment of life is possible.

Teaching

The significance of the teaching aspect of leadership must not be underestimated. The leader imparts knowledge, creates an atmosphere conducive to the transmission of ideas, and contributes to the learning process of followers as he encourages them to higher levels of aspiration and achievement. Regardless of community sanction or social acceptance or rejection, it is the leader who daily sets the assignments, helps individuals in his group develop at their own particular rates of speed, and shapes and molds their behavior patterns in conformity with his own concepts of what such patterns should be. It is the leader, in his teaching capacity, who stimulates, accepts, or rejects habits, attitudes, productivity, or personality traits. It is he who shapes group character and enables followers to approximate their potential in a social context. It is his philosophy of life, applied to the group situation, which is of the utmost importance. It is the leader's obligation to teach leadership behavior to his followers. No one else is in a position to do so.

QUESTIONS FOR DISCUSSION

1. How can leaders convert headship positions to effective leadership?
2. How are leadership objectives discerned?
3. Why is consideration for followers' condition a significant factor in leadership maintenance?
4. It is easier to achieve a position of leadership than to maintain it. Is this valid and, if so, why?
5. Why must the leader reject emotionalism in his interactions?
6. How does the satisfaction of follower needs enhance leadership?
7. What is the logical sequence of actions that eventuate in goal achievement?
8. Why must the leader be ready with alternative courses of action?
9. How can leadership overcome inertia?
10. Why is emotional stability necessary for leaders?
11. What is the essential ambiguity of leadership?

BIBLIOGRAPHY

Barker, Cyril J., *Leadership: The Dynamics of Success* (Greenwood, S.C.: Attic Press, 1982).

Bothwell, Link, *The Art of Leadership: Skill-Building Techniques that Produce Results* (Englewood-Cliffs, N.J.: Prentice-Hall, Inc., 1983).

Fiedler Fred E., and Martin M. Chemers, *Improving Leadership Effectiveness: The Leader Match Concept*, 2d ed. (New York: John Wiley & Sons, 1983).

Goodwin, Bonnie E., *The Effective Leader* (New York: Bantam Books, Inc., 1981).

Knox, Alan B., ed., *Leadership Strategies for Meeting New Challenges* (San Francisco: Jossey-Bass Inc., Publishers, 1982).

Kottler, Jeffrey A., *Pragmatic Group Leadership* (Monterey, Cal.: Brooks/Cole Publishing Co., 1982).

Selznick, Phillip, *Leadership in Administration: A Sociological Interpretation* (Berkeley, Cal.: University of California, 1983).

CHAPTER SEVENTEEN

Leadership Evaluation

The effects of leadership have been studied assiduously and numerous evaluative techniques have been attempted. Generally, it seems logical to state that leadership which relies upon consideration for followers while concomitantly pressing for group performance is more successful in achieving two highly prized objectives—group morale and task accomplishment. Together these results produce interactional qualities which are desired by members and organizations. The other variable that influences leadership capability is the situation in which the leader and his group find themselves at any particular time.

Situational variables may stimulate internal or external stresses which can reinforce or demolish the group. When the leader can maintain the group in the face of conflict or develop activities which group members perform, thereby nullifying any tendency toward disruption, then leadership has been accomplished. These are the bases on which effective leadership can be evaluated. There are a number of different procedures which may be helpful in any determination of leadership success or failure.

THE OUTCOME OF LEADERSHIP

The process of leadership evaluation concerns the outcome of leadership, the success of ongoing leadership, and the prediction of attempts at potential leadership. Leadership evaluation, then, is the process of formulating judgments that are to be utilized for subsequent action. It consists of establishing objectives, collecting evidence dealing with progressive movement toward objectives or, conversely, lack of progress, making appraisals of the evidence, and revising methods and objectives accordingly. It chiefly covers three things: 1) the subjective actions which occur as a result of leadership; 2) the quality of leadership, that is, its effectiveness; and 3) the personal contributions of the leaders insofar as influence and other attributes are perceived by followers.[1]

Leaders are forever testing and measuring the plans and operations they use to obtain their ends. They not only evaluate their own methods which in turn, are evaluated by others, but they evaluate specific conditions and circumstances to discover whether they are favorable to their needs. A characteristic of a leader is avoidance of status quo; he seeks solutions in action, and questions long-held or established ideas. In doing this, the leader performs his own evaluation process.

"But we have always done it this way." That is the anguished cry of a routinized job-holder who sees his pet method of work being discarded. Simply because a particular method found favor and was therefore utilized until it achieved the same status as the ritual of a religious order does not mean that it is practical, efficient, effective, or even worthwhile. Long usage does not imply productivity. It merely means that within the hierarchy of affairs there has been implemented a standard operating procedure, and the methods entrenched within that procedure have become almost sacrosanct.

Inevitably the established process or method comes within the purview and under scrutiny of the leader. He accepts it because the resulting product is excellent or finds that it cannot be improved upon, or he determines that there are more efficient and effective ways of performance in the production of a specific value and he formulates plans by which these newer techniques may be substituted for the habitual.

It is in the very nature of the leader to challenge the axiom, combat precedent, and overthrow tradition. Unless the leader is willing and able to analyze the various functions which are part of his organization, he will never discover how close his system comes to the attainment of the objectives which he has instituted. The entire method of evaluation and appraisal is inherent in the leadership process. The leader must be ready to determine not only the methods which must be evaluated, but also why and how that evaluation should occur in order to develop standards for action.

There are always more efficient methods for getting things done. It is the leader's responsibility to find those methods. Even when a method has succeeded over a period of years, this does not automatically indicate perfection. Recreationists, particularly those who assume the pragmatic view that anything which works is good,

1. Victor H. Vroom and Philip W. Yetton, *Leadershp and Decision-Making* (Pittsburgh, Penn.: University of Pittsburgh Press, 1973), pp. 123–154.

have tended to utilize certain activities and techniques within the program of operation on that basis. "It works; why change a good thing?" This is the usual statement or reply given to one who inquires about a specific item within the program or about certain functions within the administration.

Unfortunately, the lack of evaluation and appraisal precludes any stimulus for the improvement of these already tried-and-true factors. Times change, and so do the needs and interests of people. Only an individual blind to the facts of change will allow a routinized and stagnant program to be proclaimed adequate. Yet such activity was adequate at one time. Through the years, however, modifications in leisure, the mobility of people living in the community, the amount of money, education, and other facets of modern life have changed. With these new changes and increased pressures and tensions, the "old" ways have become passé, literally; the methods which were once valuable have long since lost their charm, practicality, and usefulness.

The individual who can visualize activities in only one way is handicapped and behind the times. While *all* standardized methods of work are not outmoded, a large number of them are. It therefore behooves the leader to critically analyze and evaluate the procedures which are in use to determine their effectiveness in relation to the original idea or reason for the creation of the agency or movement which the leader heads. When the leader has been able to set up principles for the establishment of criteria which can then be evaluated, he will be in a better position to retain or discard devices which are in use.

If the leader needs to justify the removal of procedures which have gained popularity through familiarity, he must show where these methods are inconsistent with the aims and objectives which have been devised for his group. Unless the leader is willing to undertake the responsibility for the constant testing and measuring of techniques and activities to monitor what is being produced, it is very likely that his aims will not be reached. While the leader may respect the traditions, mores, and methods of the group, groups, agency, or community which he leads, and although he may wish to conserve whatever is fruitful and effective, he never allows love of the past to be carried to the point of rejecting advantageous new ideas when their benefits have been ascertained. In fact, the leader is usually of a more liberal than conservative stripe, and he shows this trait in his attempt at establishing progressive and innovative concepts. He will adapt the old where possible. He will scrap the old without hesitancy when feasible. No one way exists for the attainment of immutable perfection. There is always room for improvement of the best techniques. The leader will continue toward his objectives as he examines established procedures against the validity of achievement.

What factors are defined as essential for the evaluation of leadership? What is it that the leader must be or do in order to be recognized as having influence with others? How is successful leadership determined? The answers to these questions will serve as guides for the development of criteria which can be used to evaluate leadership. Therefore, a preliminary analysis of existing values and objectives is of major concern; second, some interpretation of values and objectives into behavioral terms; and finally, development of an evaluation instrument by which evidence can be appraised.

WHAT SHOULD BE EVALUATED?

The following types of information are needed by evaluators of leadership: 1) attitudes toward group activities; 2) attitudes toward the agency of concern; 3) attitudes toward self; 4) attitudes toward existence; 5) interests; 6) identifications; 7) feelings toward other group members; 8) immediate objectives; 9) long-range goals; 10) anxieties; 11) preferences; 12) modifications in self-concept; 13) modifications in role perception in relation to significant groups within the social milieu; 14) needs and emotional patterns which have developed from influences derived from group membership and significant others; 15) emotional disturbances or problems which accrue in consequence of social impacts.

Evaluation should be a process that is essentially self-correcting. It should be designed to identify errors and modify procedures before negative effects are felt. The objective of examining the results of leadership is to determine whether goals have been accomplished; the objective of examining techniques is to determine whether certain methods are being followed. The reason for comparing outcome with technique is to determine whether the techniques should be changed in some way.

The evaluation of leadership is primarily pragmatic and subjective, although some objective criteria may be applied. Any basic understanding of leadership is concerned with the ability to measure it accurately. However, the relativity of evaluative attempts to measure leadership is well-known. In spite of all attempts to be objective, there are so many variables which may be factored into an evaluating instrument that its practical use may be relegated merely to the individual who uses it at any given time. Each person who evaluates leadership does it from a different point of view. Because it depends upon the source of individual orientation, leadership evaluation has never been developed to the point of applying a constant set of standards.

Perhaps the best indicator of leadership is the pragmatic approach—does it succeed? If leadership is adequate, it is successful. But this brings up the question of defining adequacy and success. What appears as success to an observer may be conceded as failure by the participant and vice versa. Previous studies attempted to evaluate leadership by using case histories, ratings, classifications, and other related methods. However, these have been highly subjective, imprecise at best, and heavily biased where opinions are the only criteria.

The evaluation of leadership may be made most effectively from several selected variables based upon distinct categories or points of view. Thus, leadership may be considered from four characterized orientations: participant membership, agency, leader, and evaluator.

Participant Membership

The group member or individual participating within a given activity views the leader's adequacy in terms which are dependent upon specific needs or desires. Presumably, if the participating individual can achieve his goals, he will classify the leadership as "good." Leadership adequacy can actually be based on whether or not, in the follower's judgment, the leader is functioning in a competent manner. Personal liking for the individual who performs the leadership role may have an effect on an appraisal of adequacy, but this is discounted in stress or problem situations, where the leader must be able to activate others. In less critical situations, personal friendship may influence judgment to favor the leader, but in emergency cases, competence becomes the criterion.

The participant's confidence in the leader's ability will be indicated by leadership emulation—imitation of dress, speech, mannerisms, walk, attitude, opinions, stance, method of problem-solving, etc.—and the intensity or quality of participation undertaken by the group at the instigation of the leader. This personalization continues to develop as long as the leader is able to maintain follower confidence. The same aspect is noted in individual participation. When the follower believes in the plans and objectives of the leader or in the leader's adequacy, he is more willing to engage in activities, suggestions, or projects which the leader devises. While intensity and quality of participation are not interchangeable, the presence of either indicates some sort of tacit leadership acceptance. Where both of these factors are present, the likelihood that the individual wholeheartedly accepts the leader is apparent. Intensity of participation refers to consistency or continued presence within the group. Quality of participation refers to actual involvement and absorption in any given enterprise or experience which the group undertakes.

Agency

The orientation from the agency's point of view is interesting to observe. Here, agency appraisal is based on examination of group processes and outcomes as they are effected by the leader. The object of this approach is to compare the experiences of group membership with proposed or desired agency policies, principles, or standards. To the extent that group members are influenced by the leader, the agency will be examining the following set of outcomes:

1.   Group membership involving formation, size, adhesion, hedonic tone, and group direction toward ethical and achievable goals.
2.   Group conformity to established agency standards of conduct, philosophy, or policy.
3.   Membership retention through personal interaction, degree of need satisfaction or frustration, decision-making, and desirable attitude change or development.
4.   Technical knowledge and skill assimilated as a result of leadership effectiveness.

From the agency's point of view, the most essential form of leadership evaluation is the direct measurement of what has been produced. The agency is concerned with how closely group members have approximated or conformed to specific objectives. Depending upon the agency, this achievement may be in terms of personal development, knowledge achieved, skill, health, profit, satisfaction, or some measurable goal. Ultimately, the test of leadership adequacy will be evaluated by individual followers' achievements.

Leader

From the leader's standpoint, his degree of influence with individuals, his ability to initiate and carry out concepts, and the ultimate success of his plans will be the best measure of his adequacy. The leader really has only one criterion—achievement. If he is successful in formulating ideas, organizing a followership, and ethically implementing his program until specific objectives are attained, then leadership has occurred, and he has performed in a manner consistent with his aims. If he has used methods which are socially acceptable, moral, and just, the product may be considered as the surest form of achievement.

The leader will be satisfied with his performance standards if he gains the confidence of those from whom he must obtain action in the pursuit of objectives. As the group moves in the direction suggested or emphasized by the leader, he will note improvement in his technique. Whether it is through rapport-building, increasing sensitivity to the needs of the group membership, or the ability to enhance the group's perception of him as highly concerned for their well-being, the leader's self-evaluation should be able to focus on gains or losses made as influence is achieved.

The leader will have certain expectations of objectives, agency directives, or group ambitions. The leader should understand how he is performing in relation to such expectations and develop strategies to attain the goals which incorporate group and agency desires. Because of the complexity in separating personal inability from superimposed intrusions, it is difficult to treat shortcomings as problems to be overcome rather than as personal failures. In the final analysis, only the leader can know if he has improved his effectiveness.

One of the chief functions of the leader is to create a situation in which individuals find group life so attractive, by virtue of its activities or its leader, that they resist other lures and remain steadfast to the group. The leader's own evaluation should detect the interactions and interpersonal responses which develop as coalescence and adherence to the group. It is on these bases that leadership may be pronounced most effective and real.

Evaluator

No matter who evaluates a leader, the interpretation will vary according to his perception. When leadership is evaluated from a superior, subordinate, or peer viewpoint the outcome depends upon what it is that is required of the leader. Thus, superiors in an organization may come to view the leader's behavior from the standpoint of group goal achievement or productivity. The emphasis will be upon task accomplishment. Subordinates will have other needs to be satisfied, with task accomplishment being only one factor in determining their appraisal. In all probability, subordinates or followers will perceive the most effective leader as one who shows the most consideration for them—consideration being a dimension of behavior that is characterized by impartiality, reliability, communicativeness, and a concern for the welfare of the membership. Superiors will rate the leader as being effective if he accepts the norms and values of the superior authority, thereby carrying out the role assigned to him by the organization. Simultaneously, the leader must win the voluntary followership of those who are subordinate to him. If he can do this, he will be able to exercise authority and influence which have been freely accorded to him. Under such circumstances, he will be rated highly by group members who utilize him as a buffer against the impersonality of the organization or of society at large, depending upon the situation of the group in question.

Evaluation is carried on by those who are directly affected by the leader, by the leader himself, by extra-group observers, or by those within an organization in which the leader is a subordinate. The outcomes of these evaluations will be considerably influenced by predisposed expectations or perceived behaviors and the consequences of such actions upon objectives gained, group members satisfied, problems solved, membership maintained, or other criteria used as measures.

Evaluation should not be confused with research.[2] Although it utilizes the devices and products of research and may develop leads for research, evaluation is neither technically capable nor sufficiently precise to perform as research. Evaluation is a dynamic process with intrinsic values that can be executed by anyone who wants to improve performance and has the determination to submit to the rigorous analysis, scrupulous observation, and those instruments which are available and applicable. For practical purposes, the fundamental measurement-appraisal factors in evaluation must be discreetly applied in a general pattern of leadership planning that involves an initial consideration of basic objectives and a subsequent use of remedial devices.

CRITERIA DEVELOPMENT

In evaluation, one criterion is the member's behavior, and its outcomes, achieved by a recreationist in practice. Since the recreational leader performs in a highly complex situation, where his efforts are influenced by the interaction of personality, personal skills, and various situational variables, criteria concerning leadership effectiveness will vary over time and change with the job situation. Among the personal variables comprising one aspect of interacting factors are intellectual and affective structures, perceptions, previous

---

2. M. Provus, "Evaluation or Research, Research or Evaluation," *The Educational Technology Review Series,* No. 11 (Jan. 1973), pp. 48–52.

experiences, and habits of decision-making. Situational variables will probably include personal characteristics of group members, needs as perceived by group members, the objectives of the recreational agency involved, the immediate objectives of the group and the leader, the physical setting, social pressures, and other external forces tending to influence the group and/or the leader.

The interaction of leader behavior and situational variables is dynamic and interrelated. It must be understood that the situational variables provide the basis for leadership performance. When there is dynamic interaction between leader and social milieu, there is a leveling effect on leadership performance. It is suggested, therefore, that criteria designed for evaluating leadership performance should recognize both the personality factors and characteristics which the leader brings to the working situation and the conditioning influences tending to delimit activity which his position in the agency places upon the individual.

Formulating Evaluative Criteria

Although often omitted, or given short shrift, an important step in evaluation is the selection of determining standards. These standards are objective statements of particular values to be sought and measured. Whatever the paramount objectives of recreationists, they should be included in the leadership evaluation process. A satisfactory set of valid objectives will probably be identified if an attempt is made to classify all of the possible contributions which a leader must make if he is to be successful and all of those personality factors which seem to be consistently reported as meeting the needs of the various groups in which recreationists serve. Once identified, they may then be translated into behaviors that can be observed or measured objectively.

The first step in recreational leadership evaluation at the departmental level is determining what is important in leadership. This procedure is essential to the evaluation process because it serves purposes: the foundation for identifying the particular leader behaviors and consequences of behavior that are desired (criteria); producing means to measure these behaviors and outcomes (measurement); and comparing measurement and desired results (evaluation). In attempting to define those factors which are considered important to leadership, several questions must be answered:

1. Who will determine the criteria and their relative significance?

2. What procedure will be utilized to gather the data necessary for making such decisions?
3. How will the data be analyzed?

Criteria decisions are effectively improved if they are developed from the pooled judgments of experts rather than the intuition of any single individual. The convention of authorities could be accomplished by involving, if it is relatively small, the entire known group of experts dealing with the subject matter of leadership, or by drawing from a random sample of known authorities in the field. The panel method may include any combination of individuals to make a group of experts who can develop criteria which are unbiased.

Procedures

Any number of procedures may be used to gather information, including free responses, statements, and impressions; responses to checklists; position description and analysis; description of critical incidents or detailed descriptions of actual occurrences and behavior that have been observed by experts; time studies or detailed samplings of leader behaviors based on systematic observation and recording over a period of time; psychosocial methods or the determination of factors and their importance by panel members, using such procedures as ranking and paired comparisons.

Analysis of Responses

After experts reflect on the aspects of criteria they feel are important, a final choice must be made of the criteria and their respective procedural requirements. A systematic and comprehensive approach needs to be instituted to choose pertinent criteria, which should involve descriptions of each criterion and statistical techniques to reveal the important operational behaviors associated with the attainment of the leadership objectives. Leadership evaluations will be effective only if criteria are founded on reliable information about the essential characteristics and behaviors required for leaders in the field of recreational service. Such information is obtained from close study and controlled investigation.

Particular Leadership Behaviors

Although behaviors for leadership effectiveness cannot be generalized because the behaviors and outcomes of such behaviors are peculiar to each situation, nevertheless, certain behaviors have been identified in the research literature dealing with leadership. They are stated here for those responsible for criteria selection and development:

1. The leader expresses ideas, objectives, and goals which closely approximate the unarticulated needs and preferences of those who make up the group membership.

2. The leader's style reflects the needs of those who follow and the social milieu in which he finds himself. The leader is capable of dealing differently with several kinds of followers in order to meet specific needs, and has the ability to adjust his tactics from one situation to the next. He is flexible.

3. The leader utilizes a complex conceptual frame of reference. This seems to be associated with the idea that analysis and diagnosis of any situation is required for leadership, or in other words, that judgments must be made in relation to goals and group needs, and that selection of correct alternatives for group success must be made.

4. The leader initiates structure. Group members appear to handle information more effectively when patterns for group operation are provided. Structure offers the security of knowing which member is responsible for what function, thereby permitting interpersonal reactions, group activities, and relations with other groups, individuals, or collectives.

5. The leader facilitates communication. Effective leadership is based upon the leader's ability to maintain a central position within the communications network of the group.

6. The leader initiates action. This behavior is viewed as suggesting prominence and persuasive ability on the part of the individual. The behavior associated with initiative appears to have an element of recognition-seeking and achieving by the leader through the group's acceptance of the projects and standards determined by the leader.

7. The leader promotes cohesion. The degree to which group members function as a cooperative body having little or no internal dissension may be one of the most significant elements of leadership effectiveness.

8. Hedonic tone is closely related to leadership effectiveness. If, through his behavior, the leader is enabled to promote hedonic tone, then the group is more likely to exhibit cohesion, goal achievement, intimacy, participation, potency, and stability.

Techniques for developing criteria for leadership evaluation seem to be moving toward a descriptive base and away from that which is by nature inferential. In fact, some of the newer procedures tend to emphasize description rather than evaluation and value judgments on the part of the observer.

DATA COLLECTION AND ANALYSIS

In practice, the activities of identifying leader performance criteria and identifying data collection and interpretation techniques run parallel. The dual functions are defined more by interaction than by a consecutive relationship. The criteria supply the central issue of the evaluation by signaling to the evaluator, and the individual who is being evaluated, what behavior, objects, or conditions relate to performance success; the techniques of data collection denote how information will be acquired and the measuring devices that will be used; and the methods of data analysis systematize the collected data so that explication may be made and a conclusion reached.

Planning for Data Collection

Planning for data collection is a vital step that is frequently overlooked or skimped in the evaluation process. Many evaluation efforts are found to be faulty because of a lack of planning. Plans for the acquisition of data should be accomplished concomitantly or immediately following criteria designation. The planning effort should supply answers to the following questions: What is the source of the data? In what form will they be assembled? What will be the sampling procedures used? Who will collect the data? What preparation will the collector require?

Sources of Data.   Initially, identification of data sources is required. Usually, sources are known at the time the criteria for evaluation are defined. However, it is necessary for the evaluator to investigate possible sources that may have been neglected during earlier stages. He needs comprehensive information about the kinds of data that may be collected and the types of measuring devices that may be applied. Typically, the sources of information include those persons who are likely to have observed the leader's behavior and its results. Because most of the data develop from some human experience, evaluators must recognize ethical standards concerned with their acquisition and application in evaluation. Access to data may be made easier if the evaluator first explains the objectives of the evaluation.

Kinds of Data. The form in which the data will be collected will have implications for any analysis that can be made. Whether data are gathered in "raw" or "refined" form will be a significant factor. Generally, the objective of the evaluation determines the form desired, and the form of the data materially changes the techniques used to collect and analyze them. However, if the data are not readily available in the form deemed most appropriate, adjustments in the collection and interpretation procedure will occur.

Sampling Procedures. The sampling procedures to be used in evaluating leaders must be planned for data acquisition. Sampling procedures are designed to gather only components of the entire sum of available data from previously determined sources. In leadership evaluation, sampling techniques are applied for two basic reasons: it is not possible to acquire and interpret all the available information; they permit the evaluator to allot the information needs over the available time and data sources in order not to impose unduly upon any one individual.

In applying observation techniques, sampling has its drawbacks. It has been found that when interaction analysis techniques are used, multiple observations need to be arrayed carefully over a given period to sample a leader's behavior adequately. Even when the extraneous presence of the sampler is discounted, data from observational techniques have to be interpreted with caution.

Choosing Measuring Devices

In the evaluation of leadership, measurement techniques are fundamental for the collection of data. They sometimes exert direct influence on the type of information to be gathered. They benefit collection by ordering the data, thereby reducing probable errors which can accompany informal human observation. Leadership evaluation is dependent upon measurement as a determinant of quality and quantity.

In making choices of measuring instruments, the evaluator should select the techniques and tactics that can provide the required data. The features that indicate the adequacy of any evaluative instrument should be considered before final selection is made. The adequacy of instruments will best be determined by the characteristics of validity, reliability, stability, pertinency, and facility.

1. *Validity* is concerned with whether the instrument actually measures the behavior, situation, or thing it is intended to measure.

2. *Reliability* is concerned with the accuracy of the instrument to measure from one application to the next.

3. *Stability* is concerned with the consistency of the instrument over time.

4. *Pertinency* is concerned with whether the instrument actually measures a factor that is considered important.

5. *Facility* is concerned with the practical application of the instrument in the evaluation process, that is, its ease of administration, cost, time, and resistance factors.

Who Will Collect the Data?   It is typical for the employing agency to determine who will evaluate its personnel. This may sometimes be performed by the immediate superior of the individual in question, or it may be assigned to some outside party (perhaps a consultant) who is brought in specifically to assess leadership accomplishment. Frequently, evaluation of personnel is performed by an administrator who has discretionary authority not only to make the evaluation, but to translate its outcome into substantive action: praise, promotion, or other emoluments; admonishment, criticism, or punishment. If the evaluation process is to serve its most important function—the improvement of performance—the evaluator must be an individual who is prepared to maintain complete objectivity regardless of information generated and to act purely on the basis of what is best for all concerned. Whoever the evaluator, he must be a professional in terms of education, experience, and disinterested performance.

Evaluator Preparation.   In order to collect pertinent information on which to carry out the evaluation process, the collector must understand why evaluation is necessary and what its major contributions may be to the agency and its personnel. Therefore, the evaluator must have some formalized education in the processes and techniques of evaluation. The evaluator must have developed skills which will permit the coordination of methods and capabilities to function most effectively in his technical role. If the evaluator is well prepared, he will have assimilated the concept which affects the agency's ability to operate. The evaluator must retain the idea that information collected in the course of the process will be readily available, valid, and useful within the decision-making milieu.

Whoever performs an evaluation will probably refer to the various standardized instruments which are currently available. However, it may be necessary to modify old or develop new measuring devices as the situation demands. It is vital that a variety of instruments be selected so that a more complete picture may be obtained. Among the variety of measuring devices useful in evaluation and which should be given careful attention are:

Ability tests	Anecdotal records
Performance tests	Leadership tests
Personality tests	Attitudinal modification
Rating scales	Group direction
Checklists	Skill and knowledge achievement
Achievement tests	Membership retention
Intelligence tests	Observation
Sociometric instruments	Interviews
	Questionnaires

Ability tests concern maximum performance. These tests have been utilized to predict performance in actual field situations. Tests are designed to determine the ability of the person being tested to respond instantly to various stimuli, to determine the degree of expertness in handling on-the-job demands, and the ease with which the potential leader permits himself to be distracted from pertinent objectives in a group dynamics circumstance.

Performance tests require the subject to demonstrate his skill in reaching some objective. Performance tests are also used to study general mental functioning, usually in conjunction with verbal tests. Verbal ability and the conveyance of ideas seem to correlate with leadership capacity as well as affording a well-differentiated opportunity for clinical observation. The great variety of tasks and the interest which they normally evoke are extremely helpful in determining interpersonal comparisons.

Personality tests place emphasis on scores which lay claim to empirical validity. Such tests seem to have the ability to discriminate against individuals who might not have the personal qualities necessary for leadership performance. In nearly every field, personality and mental health are critical. Workers with inadequate personal adjustment are unsatisfactory, particularly when their job depends on interpersonal relationships. Personality tests have varying uses, but they are most useful in eliciting information about home, health, social, and emotional adjustment.

Rating scales are used to summarize observations and to obtain descriptions of the subject from evaluators who are familiar with the subject's past behavior. Ratings are used as standards and as fundamental sources of information for many kinds of research. Furthermore, such scales have a practical application in selecting group workers and those who are to be placed in leadership situations.

Rating scales are typically employed to reduce perceptions to an easily processed form, and normally consist of a list of traits to be judged, the appraiser being requested to indicate the degree to which each behavior is characteristic of the subject. All rating scales are subject to rater bias. Thus, a halo effect is created when the observer forms a general impression of the individual being rated and the ratings which are given tend to reflect the general impression of favorableness or unfavorableness.

Checklists aid objectivity in scoring. Evaluation of performance is assisted when an objective record is made of what the subject does. Checklists are particularly helpful for showing how the individual performs, his style and work procedures, as well as errors made. Such a record focuses on weaknesses so that they may be reduced or eliminated by better educational methods. Checklists also systematize observation records; for example, an ability checklist typically lists the correct behaviors and the weaknesses to be acted upon. For such work it may provide a series of sections for categorizing activities. With this instrument, highly differentiated particular acts may be recorded quickly with extensive objectivity.

Achievement tests try to ascertain how much an individual has learned from an educational experience. Motivation can be improved by developing competitiveness based on equitable criteria. Showing a person the particular ways in which he needs further skill is a superior method for motivating study. Tests aid in standardizing the instruction provided for the assimilation of leadership skills. Thus, any deviation from standardized objectives would be noted in scores and thereby force instructors to offer the kinds of information necessary to effect positive leadership outcomes.

Intelligence tests, as now widely applied, are the most objective methods for determining the general mental capacity of an individual. Through successively difficult items an individual can display the tendency to select and sustain a particular direction, the capability to make personal adjustments in order to achieve a desired objective, and the ability to undergo self-examination. All of these tendencies display general intelligence, which appears to be a significant endowment in the makeup of a leader.

Sociometric instruments are designed to show how others view an individual. These techniques are neither observations nor self-reports although they closely approximate rating techniques, with the reports made by the subject's peers rather than his superiors. Sociometric instruments are tests which consist of descriptions of roles played by actual or potential leaders and other members of a group. Each group member responds to each description by indicating the individual he believes that description suits. Such instruments may be used for studying the social structure of groups and are also valuable for providing insight into developed cliques, leadership hierarchies, and other interpersonal dynamics.

Anecdotal records are an attempt to obtain a complete and realistic picture of the subject. The observer is permitted to note any behavior which appears important, rather than concentrating on the same characteristic for all subjects. Frequently, the anecdotes are reports of behaviors which are manifested by group members (if performed by the leader) or specific actions observed in daily contacts by the actual or perceived leader (if performed by an outside evaluator). The anecdotal record should be divorced from any interpretation and describe only and precisely what has been observed. The record is made immediately after the observation to avoid errors of recollection. Gathered over a period of time, the descriptions offer a much clearer picture of behavior than do other techniques of equivalent simplicity.

Leadership tests evaluate emotion and reactions to frustrating situations. Most such tests are very practical since they are generally employed for filling positions of responsibility. Before the candidate is appointed to an authoritative position, it is to the agency's benefit to determine as accurately as possible whether or how well he can cope with stress, criticism, and thwarting. If the agency, which desires individuals to fill leadership positions, had data about the intellectual processes, emotional reactions, and social responses of candidates, it would be in the enviable situation of being able to choose an elite staff. Leadership tests, though not able to provide the entire picture, do have the function of supplying information about the individual's penchant for cooperation, reaction to authority, interpersonal behavior, and so on. Such tests have become increasingly important in selecting leaders in all fields.

Attitudes may be subjected to study and measurement. Discriminatory practices, for example, of a racial, ethnic, religious, political, social, or economic orientation, may be quickly discerned. Attitudes toward self, agency, other group members, morals, health, and a large variety of personal beliefs are directly testable. Since one major objective of the agency may be to change individual attitudes on certain subjects, this may be an objective method to diagnose the influence of the leader. Since the leader ideally reflects the objectives of the agency toward particular values, the degree of modification of attitudes on the part of group members may well mirror actual leadership adequacy.

Group direction of several varieties can be measured. One of these deals with group movement toward desirable goals and the other with individual conduct or behavior. Observation of group members after the leader has made his presence felt should indicate whether or not his influence is real. Other techniques may be used to determine individual modifications of morals, integrity, esprit de corps, emotional stability, and social development. Sociometry can determine peer status in terms of acceptance, rejection, or isolation, which affects the degree of group participation, satisfaction, and security. Value changes concerning acceptance or rejection of agency standards and objectives or, in a broader sense, society's standards, illustrate group direction.

Behavior modifications in individual members may be validly tested by the use of standardized measuring devices which can, if properly administered, appraise the degree and kind of modification over a period of time. Behavior scales may reveal the nature of behavior which will probably undergo change determined by particular situations, and the variation in observed behavioral modifications in relation to the age of the individual, the adequacy of the leader, and other pertinent facts. Analysis of the written records of recreationists acting as group leaders will also provide a basis for leadership evaluation.

Skill and knowledge achievement are highly susceptible to testing devices and accurately reflect any individual changes. If the agency is interested in measuring leadership on the basis of skill or specific knowledge achievement, there are many evaluative instruments that have proven reliable in practice for such purposes. Where agency objectives coincide with the production of individuals skilled in motor activities or knowledgeable about manners, social conduct, morals, ethnic tolerances, and a wide variety of other assimilated facts, these may readily be discerned. Insofar as the recreationist responsible for the development of group members is able to instill the required knowledge or skill so that individuals in his charge are able to perform well, this may be taken as a measure of his adequacy as a leader.

Retention of membership over a period of time or for the life of the group will surely indicate leadership. The ability of the recreationist to hold a group of individuals together or to provide some ideas, projects, or goals which stimulate and interest members so that they remain within the group is a mark of effectiveness on his part. This is only true for the voluntary situation where there are no external pressures such as forced attendance, or assessment of fees which are not returned for drop-outs. When the recreationist can collect and stabilize a group, it is an outcome of his influence with them. Conversely, when a large number of individuals leave the group or when group cohesion is not attained, leadership adequacy is questionable.

Observation is probably the most common method of determining whether or not leadership performance is adequate. It is a fairly routine and recurrent procedure enacted to ensure that particular standards are met and maintained. By actually inspecting the performance of employees, nature of activities conducted, or behavior shown, some evaluation can be made as to the proximity of achieving the standard required by the employing agency. Observation is performed in order to ascertain if preconceived standards set forth by department policy are receiving compliance.

In the unlikely event that recreationists are negligent in their duties, specific measures are then undertaken to alleviate those conditions. Observation may reveal instances of incompetence, repeated tardiness, inefficiency, or substandard behavior or performance. Of course, it may also indicate highly effective leadership performance.

Observation, like bank audits, must be carried on without the foreknowledge of persons or employees who are to be observed. It is a method which allows the observer to appraise leadership performance at close range without injecting any artificial conditions of apprehension or falsity of action because the subject knows that he is being observed. The success of observation hinges upon relieving worker anxiety and allowing him to perform, for better or worse, as he does habitually and naturally. In this way, a factual representation of leadership adequacy may be partially gathered. Observation is merely one method which can be used. Other methods should supplement this technique to gather a composite picture of the worker in several situations and under varying conditions.

Interview, unlike observation, is conducted because there is a desire on the part of the superior to maintain personal relations with employees on the job. It is a procedure in which current information about leadership problems may be obtained for further study and use. Interviews are usually conducted in order to assist in the solution of a particularly pressing problem, to clear up personnel policy misunderstandings, or to explain new policies or procedures. The interview may be carried on informally, which is perhaps the best method, so that the interviewee is placed at ease and may more freely express his ideas.

Interviewing is an effective means of acquainting the recreationist with specific problems or of obtaining pertinent information concerning group or individual needs and then satisfying them. It is a ready tool for those who must learn about personal needs and practices. By personally interviewing a random sampling of people in any neighborhood and then checking whatever findings are elicited, compliance with standards of effective leadership performance may be ascertained. Questions concerning manners, appearance, personal enthusiasm, skill, and leadership adequacy are brought up by interview.

Questionnaires are desirable when information is needed from subordinate personnel concerning a superior or from a closely knit group concerning a member of that group. As a questionnaire allows the respondent to remain anonymous if he so desires, he is more likely to reply with what he conceives to be the truth. The questionnaire is also important as an instrument for measuring leadership in terms of prepared statements so that the respondent does not have to formulate preconceived notions about the topic, with the corresponding biases which might also be included. Of course, the questionnaire itself must be developed so as to omit leading questions, "loaded" sentences, and prejudicial concepts. Objectivity is of greatest benefit in the use of the questionnaire.

LEADERSHIP BEHAVIOR

Personality and Performance

Because leadership requires both personality inputs and a changing pattern of functional roles, the entire process of personality evaluation is one of enormous complexity and inconsistency. There is always the chance that relationships between personality and role performance may not be reflected in an investigation. As conditions change for a particular group, there may be specific personality traits which will be absolutely essential for achieving leadership of that group. Because situational demands vary from group to group, it becomes impossible to identify those personality traits which will always accompany an installation of leadership. Under such circumstances, it would be wise to adhere to Bavelas' advice: "Instead we must try to define the leadership functions that must be performed in these situations and regard as leadership those acts which perform them."[3]

A review of psychological literature shows a number of studies which have investigated leadership performance. Among these analyses have been suggestions that leaders exercise authority, make decisions, behave in ways that imply a sound knowledge of human nature, have empathy, and so on. Several studies have revealed

---

3. A. Bavelas, "Leadership: Man and Function," *Administration Science Quarterly,* Vol. 4 (1960), p. 494.

important distinctions between outstanding and poor leaders, while others have attempted to analyze the behavior of leaders and other group members by direct observation. Among exhibited behaviors by leaders, three were consistently revealed as being significantly different from those of followers. Leaders typically analyzed the situation in which they found themselves, interpreted possibilities, and then provided information as to how the group should proceed. Carter and others found that behaviors which characterized leadership in one situation did not necessarily carry over to another:

> There seem to be interesting differences in behavior depending on whether the group was working under emergent or appointed leader conditions. It appears that in the appointed situation the leader may perceive his role as that of a coordinator of activity or as an agent through which the group can accomplish its goal. In the emergent group, on the other hand, the person who becomes the leader may take over the leadership by energetic action and by trying to get the other members to accept his leadership.[4]

Perhaps the best method of evaluating leadership is to determine the major factors of personality and performance which characterize those who lead, and develop an evaluative instrument which can assess the presence or absence of these qualities. It is obvious that the kind of person the leader is relies heavily upon a number of factors. The behavior of any leader is closely associated with the needs of those who constitute his followers, the aims or purposes of the group at any given time, and the type of individuals who compose the group and their relations with one another.

Because of the variety of personality types which leaders exhibit and the different roles each leader must play, there are actually few generalizations which can be made about leadership behavior. It now seems apparent that leaders bring vastly different attributes to their diverse tasks, and changing tasks may require them to modify their behaviors or produce different qualities if they are to achieve success. It is very likely that all leaders have specific salient personal attributes. Currently, no measuring instrument is yet available that can appraise these attributes qualitatively. One can only surmise that such qualities exist and that they may be observable. To this extent, some investigation should be imposed to determine whether quantitative patterns are measurable. It is not possible at this time to indicate in what amounts or to what degree such attributes would have to exist in

---

4.   L. Carter, W. Haythorn, B. Shriver, and J. Lanzetta, "The Behavior of Leaders and Other Group Members," *Journal of Abnormal and Social Psychology*, Vol. 46 (1951), p. 591.

order to accomplish a given task or to solve a particular problem in a given situation. Moreover, it is not known in what combination such qualities would be needed as situations varied. It is also logical to state that, in the case of leadership, the sum of the parts does not always equal the whole. Even if the qualities of personality could be reproduced at will, it would still require something more to produce a leader. This "something" more is the force which characterizes the leader and is beyond the total of personality components.

Having provided precautionary guides, some of the factors which contemporary research distinguishes as being characteristic of leaders and leadership behaviors are offered here. Many of these factors have been reported in diverse studies for the past twenty years. For the most part, these reported behaviors are not discrete units, existing in isolation from all others. Rather, they are closely associated and, in fact, impinge on one another as demand requires. Currently, these qualities of personality reflect the best of what the leader is, and they may be quantified empirically:

1. *Sensitivity* or *empathy* is a personality trait that suggests the individual's ability to respond to emotional needs of others. Such social awareness as is implied by the term empathy permits the individual to perceive the needs of others, and fulfill them in such a way as to gain a reciprocal perception. More significantly, empathy permits insight and the ability to interact favorably with others who make up a potential following.

2. *Consideration* may actually grow out of empathy, but it also connotes a concern for those who constitute the followers. This really means practical assistance, explanation, willingness to communicate, and deference paid to the input of other members of the group. Additionally, it denotes a tendency to provide emotional support to those who require it in the advancement of tasks or the achievement of goals.

3. *Emotional stability* is a factor of vital importance to the individual's capacity to function calmly, objectively, and rationally despite the passions of those who surround him and the fluctuations of the prevailing circumstances. This behavior factor indicates an absence of suspicion, anxiety, and shows there is no lack of trust. It shows a well-integrated personality with ego-strength and the capacity to accept and deal with negative actions or behaviors directed against him or found within the group which he leads.

4. *Fairness* is an attribute marked by objectivity toward others and the weighing of facts before reaching conclusions. It implies consistency and reliability on the part of the leader. Of course, this may also be perceived as a characteristic of emotional stability.

Fairness assures group members that the leader deals justly with all individuals, does not show partiality, and can be depended on to follow an agreed-upon decision.

There may be many other behavioral dimensions which can be reported and evaluated, but these four personality qualities seem to be essential for the leader. Without these attributes, the leader's ability to lead becomes untenable. He will be looked upon with fear, hatred, suspicion, and uncertainty. The composite picture of a leader is much more complex than any mere cataloguing of personality characteristics. Those traits which seem absolutely vital if an individual is to be selected or emerge as a leader are nullified if the desire to lead is not present.

Evaluation can be based on those leadership behaviors which contribute to group cohesiveness, harmony, task definition, problem resolution, and secure adherence to group structure. Other factors are the facilitation of communication, or assistance to move the group along those vectors which will result in individual member satisfaction and final attainment of the ends for which they originally joined with others.

There has been a variety of studies which have employed a number of variables closely related to the leadership contributions. These studies may be utilized as the basis for an evaluative instrument capable of serving as a measurement of leadership actuality and effectiveness. For example, task-centered behaviors have been a primary focus of Likert and his collaborators,[5] who differentiated between job-centered and employee-centered supervision. Subsequently, other investigators have reinforced the idea that "consideration" and "initiating structure" could be viewed as having major significance for the behavior of leaders.[6] More recent studies have concluded that task orientation and social-emotional differentiations of leadership are the chief factors of leader behavior.[7] In fact, it may be shown that one of these factors operating to the exclusion of the other can be detrimental insofar as leadership effectiveness is concerned.[8] Leader effectiveness is supported on the

5. R. Likert, *New Patterns of Management* (New York: McGraw-Hill Book Company, 1961).

6 E. A. Fleishman and D. R. Peters, "Interpersonal Values and Leadership Attitudes and Managerial Success," *Personnel Psychology*, Vol. 15 (1962), pp. 127–143.

7. F. E. Fiedler, "A Contingency Model of Leadership Effectiveness," in L. Berkowitz, ed., *Advances in Experimental Social Psychology* (New York: Academic Press, 1964), pp. 149–190.

8. J. Misumi and T. A. Tasaki, "A Study on the Effectiveness of Supervisory Patterns in a Japanese Hierarchical Organization," *Japanese Psychological Research*, Vol. 7 (1965), pp. 151–162.

grounds of equity in social interaction, in which the leader obtains status and wields influence while assisting the group to accomplish desired mutual expectations as well as such individual social emoluments as recognition. Task accomplishment by itself is not a sufficient basis for effective leadership, however. Both high consideration and structure are most successful.[9]

Consideration is the leader's concern for followers, manifested in practical assistance, improved conditions, or personal welfare associated with group activity. High consideration will probably be readily perceived and appreciated by followers. Structure is the relationships and responsibilities which group members mutually share, as well as membership functions and performance. Follower perception of these relationships is clarified by leadership and the result is group structure.

Description

This device is based upon the previously stated premise that individuals who make up the group in association with a leader are in the best possible position to provide descriptions of the leader's behavior. Such a hypothesis implies that leadership is basically interaction between the leader and the led. In devising the descriptive instrument, a method has been provided which can effectively evaluate leadership in any group situation. It is also usable in many research designs where the problem of personal interaction between various leadership levels as well as within individual groups might be under investigation.

Based upon an operational definition of leadership, the description of leadership behavior is then classified in terms of specific functions or behaviors which the leader has consistently exhibited in expressing his influence with group members. A most important development of this technique came when John Hemphill and others created the *Leader Behavior Description Questionnaire*.[10] This method for obtaining descriptions of the leader's actual behavior and of what would be ideal leadership behavior for any given situation gave a precise measure to leader adequacy. Thus, leadership adequacy may be evaluated by computing the discrepancy between actual leader behavior and the behavior which is standardized as the criterion for ideal leadership.

---

9. E. A. Fleishman and J. Simmons, "Relationship between Leadership Patterns and Effectiveness Ratings among Israeli Foremen," *Personnel Psychology*, Vol. 23 (1970), pp. 169–172.
10. J. K. Hemphill, *Leader Behavior Description Questionnaire* (Columbus, Ohio: Personnel Research Board, The Ohio State University, 1949).

When the discrepancy score between actual and ideal leader behavior is small or negligible, the leader is adequate; as the discrepancy score increases, less adequate leader behavior is noted. This measure may be used as a self-reporting device by a subordinate reporting actual leader behavior, or by a subordinate recording his concept of ideal leader behavior. As an evaluative technique, the descriptive method has proved fairly reliable and practical.

Evaluation is a day-in, day-out process. Each person functioning in a leadership capacity must have some model concepts upon which to base his actions. Only by formulating standard leadership principles can the individual compare himself or be compared to an ideal. Objective ratings of leadership are completely dominated by so many variables and individual orientations as to be almost impossible. As Helen Jennings stated: "It is necessary to ask, leadership in what respect? For whom? In what sort of group"?[11] For this reason, evaluation scales can merely be theoretical. The theory must be validated in experimental programs. The aim here, then, is to produce understandable concepts so that anyone can devise his own scale in accordance with the established principles provided.

The basic problem, therefore, is to list and define the objectives of leadership which may vary with the leader, the situation, the group, or other pressures impinging upon the prevailing conditions. For example, objective measurement could be concerned with discrete items produced, field goals kicked, speed records broken, retention of pesonnel, bull's-eyes scored, art awards won, paperwork processed, bond issues passed, team captains chosen, dramatic leads cast, etc. Each goal depends upon the objective, and there are an infinite variety of goals. In spite of this, leadership may be operationally defined, its component parts listed and defined, and an instrument constructed to determine adequacy.

An example of one leadership objective which could be applicable to the practice of recreational service is presented in scale form with pertinent questions. This illustration may then be extrapolated for any leadership objectives in all their various forms. The scale deals with one leadership objective—the development of physical fitness, which is the degree of effectiveness and efficiency of organic processes, including strength, tone, physique, stamina, agility, etc. For simplication, the scale is divided into five equal points ranging from

---

11. H. H. Jennings, "Leadership and Sociometric Choice," in T. M. Newcomb and E. L. Hartley, eds., *Readings in Social Psychology* (New York: Holt, 1947), p. 408. Reprinted by permission of Harcourt, Brace & World, Inc.

one to five, with each number corresponding to a reply which can be measured or observed:

One equals *no*
Two equals *qualified no*
Three equals *undecided*
Four equals *qualified yes*
Five equals *yes*

1.   Does the individual recognize the need to become physically fit?

2.   Does the individual understand the methods and practices required for achieving physical fitness?

3.   Does the individual agree to perform and practice the routines necessary for achieving physical fitness?

4.   Does the individual actually perform the scheduled motor movement necessary for achieving physical fitness?

5.   Is the objective ethical and measurable by observation or standardized testing devices?

Evaluation

The preceding paragraphs have described aspects of leader behavior and vital characteristics without which the likelihood of leadership attainment would be unthinkable. Such descriptions have been useful in generalizing at least two behavioral products: consideration and structural establishment. The first obviously refers to task orientation and the latter to socio-emotional support, with all of the ramifications which these terms imply. It is probable that there are optimal degrees to be reached for both of these behaviors. Thus, after a certain point, consideration is no longer an effective behavior in obtaining group goals. The same is also true for initiation of structure. It would appear from previous investigations that a critical point is reached above or below which no advancement toward objectives is discernable. According to Fleishman and Harris, a study of foremen indicates that consideration is the more essential of the two behavioral modes. More particularly, the study suggests that low-consideration foremen are always ineffective, while high-consideration foremen can exercise high degrees of task orientation without endangering efficiency.[12]

An evaluation of leadership will be biased by the orientation of the evaluator. Evaluation can be carried on by those who are directly

---

12.   E. A. Fleishman and E. F. Harris, "Patterns of Leadership Behavior Related to Employee Grievances and Turnover," *Personnel Psychology*, Vol. 15 (1962), pp. 43–56.

affected by the leader, the leader himself, by extra-group observers, or by those within an organization in which the leader is a subordinate. The outcomes will be considerably influenced by predisposed expectations or perceived behaviors and the consequences of such actions upon objectives gained, group members satisfied, problems solved, membership maintained, or other criteria used as measures.

TYPES OF LEADERSHIP TO BE EVALUATED

Two kinds of attributes may be utilized to evaluate leadership: 1) those which describe the behavior of the leader; and 2) those which focus on the outcomes which occur to the group in consequence of leadership. In the former instance, evaluations can be made by utilizing instruments which measure frequency of selection of a leader as the most sought-after, most popular, most relied upon, most revered, most idealized, or the one to and through whom communications pass or are initiated. In the latter instance, such group-oriented factors as cohesiveness, hedonic tone, goal achievement, and membership satisfaction may be considered for effect along one, some, or all of these dimensional lines. In fact, as early as 1951, Cattell suggested that leadership could be evaluated by measuring group performance along lines of syntality change.[13] Syntality is to a group what personality is to the individual. To the degree that a leader can effect group syntality and produce positive changes, leadership can be measured.

If leadership is looked upon as a means to some end, rather than an end in itself, then leadership can only be evaluated in terms of its effects upon a given group in relation to norms, goals, and membership satisfaction. Since multiple goals occur in any group at any given time, there must be numerous ways for evaluating leadership. Almost any variable can be employed as a criterion on which to measure leadership technique or effectiveness. As previously indicated, the criterion used will undoubtedly reflect the bias of the evaluator. Whether evaluation is made from a democratic or authoritarian orientation will certainly color the results of any evaluation. The status of the evaluator will also impose some value judgments on an interpretation of measured outcomes.

---

13. R. B. Cattell, "New Concepts for Measuring Leadership in Terms of Group Syntality," *Human Relations*, Vol. 4 (1951), pp. 161-184.

INSTRUMENTS FOR EVALUATING LEADERSHIP

1. Leadership Opinion Questionnaire (Stogdill and Coons: 1957).
2. The SRA Supervisory Index (Schwartz: 1956).
3. Leadership Practices Inventory (Nelson: 1955).
4. How Supervise? (File and Remmers: 1948–1971).
5. Ideal Leader Behavior Description Questionnaire (Hemphill and others: 1957).
6. Superior-Subordinate Scale (Chapman and Campbell: 1957).
7. Leader Behavior Description Questionnaire (Hemphill and others: 1957).
8. Leader Behavior Description Questionnaire, Form 12 (Hemphill and others: 1971).
9. Leadership Evaluation and Development Scale (Mowry: 1964).
10. Leadership Opinion Questionnaire (Fleischman: 1960–1969).
11. Leadership Practices Inventory (Nelson: 1955–1967).
12. Leadership Q-Sort Test (Cassel: 1964).
13. Leadership Effectiveness and Adaptability Description (LEAD) (Hersey and Blanchard: 1974).
14. Tri-dimensional Leader Effectiveness Model (Hersey and Blanchard: 1974).
15. Leadership Contingency Model (Fiedler: 1967).

All of these devices may be found in J. P. Robinson, R. Athanasiou, and K. B. Head, *Measures of Occupational Attitudes and Occupational Characteristics,* (Ann Arbor, Mich.: Institute for Social Research, 1969) and O. K. Buros, ed., *Tests In Print* (Highland Park, N.J.: The Gryphon Press, 1974).

QUESTIONS FOR DISCUSSION

1. How can leadership effectiveness be measured?
2. Organizational changes typically create anxiety among workers. How may a leader promote change and reduce anxiety simultaneously?
3. Is there a difference between successful and effective leadership? If so, explain the difference.
4. How does the leader evaluate personal effectiveness?
5. What does the organization look for in terms of leader effectiveness?
6. How are evaluative criteria formulated?
7. What particular leadership behaviors lend themselves to evaluation?

8. What kinds of data provide the basis for leadership evaluation?
9. What measuring devices are available for leadership evaluation purposes?
10. On what basis should evaluative instruments be selected for determining leadership effectiveness?

BIBLIOGRAPHY

Chemers, M. M., and G. J. Skrzypek, "Experimental Test of the Contingency Model of Leadership Effectiveness," *Journal of Personality and Social Psychology*, Vol. 24 (1972).

Csoka, L. S., and F. E. Fiedler, "Leadership and Intelligence: A Contingency Model Analysis," *Proceedings of the Annual Convention of the American Psychological Association*, Vol. 7 (1972a), pp. 439–440.

Eagly, Alice H., "Leadership Style and Role Differentiation as Determinants of Group Effectiveness," Vol. 38 (1970), *Journal of Personality*, pp. 509–524.

Farris, G. F. and F. G. Lim, "Effects of Performance on Leadership, Cohesiveness, Influence, Satisfaction, and Subsequent Performance," *Journal of Applied Psychology*, Vol. 53 (1969), pp. 490–497.

Fiedler, F. E., "The Effects of Leadership Training and Experience: A Contingency Model Interpretation," *Administrative Science Quarterly*, Vol. 17 (1972b), pp. 453–470.

Graen, G., K. Alvares, J. B. Orris, and J. A. Martella, "Contingency Model of Leadership Effectiveness: Antecedent and Evidential Results," *Psychological Bulletin*, Vol. 74 (1970), pp. 285–296.

Graham, W. K., "Description of Leader Behavior and Evaluation of Leaders as a Function of LPC," *Personnel Psychology*, Vol. 21 (1968), pp. 457–464.

Lundegren, H. M., and P. Farrell, *Evaluation for Leisure Service Managers: A Dynamic Approach* (Philadelphia: Saunders College Publishing, 1985).

Ray, J. J., and F. H. Lovejoy, "The Behavioral Validity of Some Recent Measures of Authoritarianism," *Journal of Social Psychology*, Vol. 120 (June, 1983), pp. 91–99.

Index